Political Marketing in Canada

Political Marketing in Canada

...... Edited by Alex Marland, Thierry Giasson, and Jennifer Lees-Marshment

UBCPress·Vancouver·Toronto

21 20 19 18 17 16 15 14 13 12   5 4 3 2 1

Printed in Canada on FSC-certified ancient-forest-free paper
(100% post-consumer recycled) that is processed chlorine- and acid-free.

Library and Archives Canada Cataloguing in Publication

Political marketing in Canada / edited by Alex Marland, Thierry Giasson,
and Jennifer Lees-Marshment.

Includes bibliographical references and index.
Issued also in electronic formats.
ISBN 978-0-7748-2228-2

1. Marketing – Political aspects – Canada. 2. Political parties – Canada. I. Marland,
Alexander J., II. Giasson, Thierry III. Lees-Marshment, Jennifer

JA85.2.C3P64 2012   324.7′30971   C2011-907353-6

Canadä

UBC Press gratefully acknowledges the financial support for our publishing program
of the Government of Canada (through the Canada Book Fund), the Canada Council
for the Arts, and the British Columbia Arts Council.

This book has been published with the help of a grant from the Canadian Federation
for the Humanities and Social Sciences, through the Aid to Scholarly Publications
Program, using funds provided by the Social Sciences and Humanities Research
Council of Canada.

UBC Press
The University of British Columbia
2029 West Mall
Vancouver, BC V6T 1Z2
www.ubcpress.ca

Contents

List of Figures and Tables   vii

Abbreviations   ix

Preface   xi

PART 1: THE MARKETPLACE

1   Introducing Political Marketing   3
    THIERRY GIASSON, JENNIFER LEES-MARSHMENT, AND ALEX MARLAND

2   The Canadian Political Market and the Rules of the Game   22
    YANNICK DUFRESNE AND ALEX MARLAND

3   The Diversity of the Canadian Political Marketplace   39
    ELISABETH GIDENGIL

PART 2: POLITICAL PARTIES AND INSTITUTIONS

4   Amateurs versus Professionals: The 1993 and 2006
    Canadian Federal Elections   59
    ALEX MARLAND

5   Under New Management: Market Intelligence and
    the Conservative Party's Resurrection   76
    ANDRÉ TURCOTTE

6   The Impact of Market Research on Political Decisions
    and Leadership: Practitioners' Perspectives   91
    JENNIFER LEES-MARSHMENT

7   "Buyer" Beware: Pushing the Boundaries of Marketing
    Communications in Government   107
    KIRSTEN KOZOLANKA

8 Market Orientation in a Minority Government:
The Challenges of Product Delivery   123
ANNA ESSELMENT

9 Does Public Opinion Research Matter?
The Marketing of Health Policy   139
LISA BIRCH

10 Selling a Cause: Political Marketing and Interest Groups   156
ÉMILIE FOSTER AND PATRICK LEMIEUX

PART 3: THE MEDIA AND CITIZENS

11 As (Not) Seen on TV: News Coverage of Political
Marketing in Canadian Federal Elections   175
THIERRY GIASSON

12 Are We Friends Yet? Online Relationship Marketing
by Political Parties   193
TAMARA A. SMALL

13 Double-Double: Branding, Tim Hortons, and the Public
Sphere   209
PATRICIA CORMACK

14 Marketing and Efficacy: Does Political Marketing
Empower Canadians?   224
ROYCE KOOP

PART 4: CONCLUSION

15 Challenges for Democracy   241
THIERRY GIASSON, JENNIFER LEES-MARSHMENT, AND ALEX MARLAND

Glossary   257

References   264

Contributors   292

Index   295

Figures and Tables

FIGURES

1.1	The scope of political marketing	9
3.1	Disaffection with politics and politicians	41
3.2	Canadians' knowledge of politics	42
3.3	Knowledge of campaign promises	43
3.4	Implications for political marketing in Canada	54
5.1	The five types of public opinion polls frequently used in political campaigns	79
9.1	Evolution of POR contracts and expenditures from 1993-94 to 2009-10	141
9.2	Custom and syndicated government POR in Canada	142
11.1	Evolution of strategic framing in Canadian electoral news	184
11.2	Evolution of political marketing coverage in Canadian electoral news	185
11.3	Association with democracy in political marketing coverage	190
14.1	Canadians lacking internal and external efficacy, 1997-2008	234

TABLES

2.1	Types of market positioning in a competitive political market	27
2.2	Considerations for strategic and tactical marketing in Canada	35
3.1	Electoral volatility in Canada, 1965-2011	45
3.2	Views about the workings of electoral democracy	49
3.3	Affective engagement in politics	50
3.4	Orientations toward political parties	51
4.1	Types of political campaigns by early 2000s standards	60

4.2 Major parties' results in the 1993 and 2006 Canadian
     federal elections   62

6.1 Interviews with Canadian practitioners conducted by
     the author   93

8.1 Delivery and implementation units   124

8.2 "Stand Up for Canada" campaign platform, 2006   126

10.1 Ideal types of political marketing by interest groups   158

11.1 Summary of automated content analysis procedure   181

11.2 Horserace coverage in Canadian electoral news   183

12.1 Number of Facebook friends (June 1 to July 30, 2010)   198

12.2 Relationship marketing criteria for Facebook   199

12.3 Publishing of new Facebook content (June 1 to July 30, 2010) 200

12.4 Use of interactive features on Facebook pages   203

12.5 Use of Facebook as part of relationship marketing strategy   204

14.1 The impact of political marketing on citizen efficacy   225

Abbreviations

CES	Canadian Election Study
CIMS	constituent information management system
CPC	Conservative Party of Canada
FAA	Federal Accountability Act
GOTV	get out the vote
MOP	market-oriented party
NDP	New Democratic Party
PC	Progressive Conservative (Party)
PCO	Privy Council Office
PMO	Prime Minister's Office
POP	product-oriented party
POR	public opinion research
SOP	sales-oriented party

Preface

The sophistication and dissemination of communications and research technology, and the competitive pressures to reflect the needs and wants of the electoral market, are changing Canadian democracy.

Although the application of business marketing principles and techniques to politics is nothing new, the progressive complexity of those strategies and tactics is significantly changing how political actors behave. At one time, it was good enough to simply offer a commercial product or service, or to declare oneself a candidate for election, with little need to communicate because sufficient demand already existed in the marketplace. But competition brings pressures to edge out rivals, necessitating product differentiation, salesmanship, mass communication, and perhaps hyperbole. Some products and services find niche markets, as do political parties and politicians, and intentionally differentiate themselves from the demands of the mass market – think of high-end or community-oriented coffee shops or, in Canadian politics, the Bloc Québécois. Those seeking to attract the custom of the plurality or majority of the mass market, and hoping to remain or become market leaders, nowadays must rigorously research the marketplace, understand consumers' preferences, and attempt to appropriately shape the image and market positioning of themselves and their competitors – think of Tim Hortons and Starbucks, and of the Conservative and Liberal Parties. Some organizations, such as the myriad second-tier franchised coffee shops or the New Democratic Party, are market followers given that they successfully service a smaller but loyal customer base. In the consumer marketplace, there are, of course, always alternatives, such as brewing coffee at home or not drinking it at all, just as in politics there are alternatives, such as getting involved with interest groups or choosing not to follow politics and not voting. Moreover, just as consumers' preferences are subject to change, so are electors' – most recently with the 2011 election, when support for the Liberal Party continued to erode and many Quebeckers switched brands from the Bloc to the NDP. A diligent commitment to aspects of political marketing is one reason that the Conservative Party won a majority of seats and why New Democrats – for the first time – became the market challenger in federal politics.

Political marketing is narrower than brokerage politics and it is changing the way political actors operate in Canada, as it already has in other democracies. Yet, we must be mindful that public opinion research and mass communication are merely technological tools, for they alone cannot spur innovation or big ideas, are not enough to excite people and capture their imaginations, and are unable to reshape the marketplace or consumer landscape. Politics is, after all, about people and competing ideas, and even the cleverest sales tactics and marketing strategies cannot disguise a bad product for long. Fortunately, competitive pressures help foster the emergence of viable alternatives. In this way, political marketing is responsive to the electorates' preferences, making it a tool that strengthens democracy, though this assumes that it is used altruistically, that mistakes don't happen, and that the voter is always right. The increasing sophistication and availability of technology does mean that political elites have the opportunity to make more informed, more responsive, and more efficient decisions than they would otherwise.

Patrick Muttart, a Conservative strategist and former deputy chief of staff in the office of Prime Minister Stephen Harper, is often mentioned in this book and elsewhere as a pioneer of political marketing in Canadian politics. He observes that during an election, Canadian political parties battle a number of campaigns simultaneously:

- The earned media campaign (e.g., news coverage), which tends to be centred on the leader's tour;
- The paid media campaign (e.g., advertising), which has two distinct but important components: creative and media buy. A well-designed ad needs to target appropriate audiences, and there must be sufficient repetition within the limits of the campaign spending cap;
- The direct voter contact campaign (e.g., voter ID, voter-specific direct mail, voter-specific messaging for canvassers, get out the vote), which is one of the most unreported aspects of electioneering;
- The local campaign, which increasingly is a fused effort between national campaigns and the party's candidates in electoral districts; and,

- The social media campaign (e.g., web and mobile technologies), which is centred on peer-to-peer contact and engagement.

The views of such practitioners illustrate today's methodical, interrelated, and centralized approach to politicking but also a lingering penchant for market intelligence to foremost inform communication decisions and win votes, rather than for designing policy. In theory, political marketing is about developing and promoting political goods and services that the broader electorate wants (see Glossary for political marketing concepts); in practice, it is a competitive tool to win power by targeting segments of the electorate. "Close campaigns are decided by the least informed, least engaged voters," says Muttart (2011). "These voters do not go looking for political news and information. This necessitates brutally simple communication with clear choices that hits the voter whether they like it or not. Journalists and editorialists often complain about the simplicity of political communication, but marketers must respond to the reality that undecided voters are often not as informed or interested as the political and media class are." Given such businesslike pragmatism, readers of this book are advised to balance scholars' idealism of political marketing with its actual practice by party elites.

The idea for the book came about after the first Canadian political marketing workshop held at the Canadian Political Science Association conference in May 2009 at Carleton University. Dr. Jennifer Lees-Marshment, arguably the leading academic in the field globally, was an invited guest speaker and the genesis for urging the development of a Canadian book. Until that conference, political marketing was rarely a topic in Canadian academia and usually appeared under its various subcomponents, such as political advertising, opinion research, or electioneering. With the publication of this book we anticipate that will change as Canadian scholars become more acquainted with the nature of political marketing as an exciting, dynamic, and important genre.

All of the contributors to this volume share this excitement. Thierry Giasson and Jennifer Lees-Marshment have been fantastic co-editors who divided and completed tasks with remarkable enthusiasm, speed, and dependability. The chapter authors have impressively followed guidelines, met submission deadlines, and acted on changes requested by the editors and external peer reviewers. As with any production, there have been many others behind the scenes. The timeliness, efficiency, and professionalism exhibited by UBC Press senior editor Emily Andrew in particular, and by her colleagues at UBC Press generally, including editor Megan Brand and copy editor Judy Phillips, have been emblematic of customer service and product delivery. The editors would like to thank the two anonymous reviewers of the manuscript for their thoughtful remarks, which improved the quality of the book. Memorial University political science students Sean Fleming and Mark Coombs performed a meticulous proofread to ensure quality control and prepared a thorough index, respectively. Special thanks are extended to Elisabeth Gidengil (author of Chapter 3) for her recommendations about the democracy aspects of the introductory chapter.

The editors also wish to acknowledge a publishing subsidy award. This book has been published with the help of a grant from the Canadian Federation for the Humanities and Social Sciences, through the Aid to Scholarly Publications Program, using funds provided by the Social Sciences and Humanities Research Council of Canada.

The contents of this volume demonstrate that the old model of politicking in Canada has forever changed. For good or for bad, the nature of Canadian democracy is evolving. This book provides a basis for further inquiry into *Political Marketing in Canada*.

Alex Marland
Lead Editor

PART 1

The Marketplace

1

Introducing Political Marketing

Thierry Giasson, Jennifer Lees-Marshment, and Alex Marland

Worldwide and over time, technological advancements change the practice of politics, governance, and electioneering. Politicians no longer need to travel by horse to visit a community where they will stand on an overturned soapbox or a tree stump to give a speech to electors about their priorities. For some time now, office-seekers have been able to zip across the country, a province, or an electoral district by train, car, bus, or air, visiting multiple communities in a single day, and if their speeches attract media attention or are included in advertising, their messages can effortlessly reach millions. The most professional of these packaged politicians and their handlers use market intelligence, such as opinion research, to tailor their political offer to reflect constituent priorities.

The cost of opinion measurement and of communications technologies gradually declines even as the tools' sophistication grows, only to be replaced with newer, more expensive practices. As in commerce, the general diffusion of mass media and research technologies has increased their accessibility to those in the political game. The competition for political power is therefore often a battle for competitive advantages with respect to information collection, analysis, and dissemination, and for the funds to finance such operations. Professionals who embody the spirit and practice of information-based strategic and tactical political decisions are becoming known as "political marketers."

The application of commercial marketing techniques to politics has its origins in the United States, the global leader in such matters. The diffusion of American political strategies and tactics is constant, with the global media reporting on the latest innovations and political consultants selling their knowledge. Political actors throughout the world are inspired by the most recent US campaign, seek to employ successful tactics of American interest groups, and aim to duplicate American government action and hire American experts.

As an academic field, political marketing has grown in size, breadth, and depth with the establishment in 2002 of its own journal, *Journal of Political Marketing* (Haworth Press), and publication in 2009 of the first comprehensive textbook, *Political Marketing: Principles and Applications* (Routledge). Canada held its first workshop in political marketing at the 2009 Canadian Political Science Association (CPSA) conference at Carleton University, which led to the creation of a national network of scholars and practitioners and to the development of this book. Canadian interest became more prevalent when, after attending CPSA presentations, Susan Delacourt, the *Toronto Star*'s senior writer in Ottawa, initiated a "Shopping for Votes" blog during the 2011 federal election in which some of this book's contributors analyzed Canadian electioneering through a political marketing lens.

Political Marketing in Canada explores the nature of political marketing practices in Canada. Its chapters investigate a range of political marketing activities, including the use of market research, its impact on political decisions and leadership, communications in government, market orientation and delivery, marketing and interest groups, media coverage of political marketing, online relationship marketing, branding, and the impact on efficacy. Additional chapters set out the nature of the marketplace and institutional rules that affect how marketing can be used in Canadian politics. First, though, this introductory chapter explores what political marketing is, looks at how it differs from political advertising and from traditional conceptual ways of looking at Canadian politics, and sets up the debate on the potential implications of political marketing for Canadian democracy.

What Is Political Marketing?

Political marketing involves the application of business marketing concepts to the practice and study of politics and government. Marketing is not a synonym for advertising, public relations, or telemarketing; those are aspects of marketing communications. Rather, as the Canadian Marketing Association (2010) defines it, marketing is "a set of business practices designed to plan for and present an organization's products or services in ways that build effective customer relationships." In other words, when applied to politics, marketing entails a political organization using business techniques to inform and shape its strategic behaviours that are designed to satisfy citizens' needs and wants (see also this book's Glossary).

Political marketing focuses on understanding the managerial processes and activities associated with the use of market intelligence to design and implement political product offerings (Henneberg 2008; Henneberg, Scammell, and O'Shaughnessy 2009; Lees-Marshment 2001a, 2001b; O'Cass 1996; Ormrod 2005). There is a broad consensus that it has more in common with service marketing than with product marketing – that is, with the marketing of labour and skills rather than with the marketing of durable goods. This is because both service industries and politics entail inherently interactive processes that ideally link consumers/voters and providers/ political actors in a cooperative experience (Butler and Collins 1994; Henneberg and O'Shaughnessy 2007; Johansen 2005; Lloyd 2005; Scammell 1999). Moreover, the marketing of intangibles such as policy platforms, party and leader image, and organizational mindset is an integral part of overall management that involves all members of a party in the process of getting the product offering to the electoral market.

In both contexts, the processes of production and consumption are mutually constituted, as opposed to primarily entailing "managing a set of activities in order to persuade the customer to buy a product" (Johansen 2005, 87), and manifest themselves on three levels (Grönroos 1998; Lloyd 2005). First, in each instance, consumer/voter satisfaction is rooted in processes associated with the production of a particular outcome, as opposed to the outcome alone. In other words, there is a need for consumers and citizens alike to feel a sense of attachment to both process and outcome. Second, the notion of promise is central to marketing in both services and politics insofar as once promises have been made, the relationship between consumers/voters and the service provider/political actor can be greatly damaged if they do not materialize. Scammell (1999, 728) aptly summarizes the issues at stake by noting that in each context,

> the supplier must continue to nurse its reputation if it seeks to be a long-lasting player in the market. Reputation can be relatively easily destroyed if promises are not fulfilled and the coasts of re-building considerable.

Third, the practice of political parties establishing manifestos and/or policy statements, which can be acted on only once elected to power, parallels the practice within service industries of implementing a priori preparations for the eventual delivery of a service.

A MARKET ORIENTATION IN POLITICS

A prominent matter of interest within political marketing research is market orientation and, in particular, its influence on the performance of political parties. According to Kohli and Jaworski (1990, 6; emphasis in original) market orientation may be understood as

> the organization wide *generation* of market intelligence pertaining to current and future customer needs, *dissemination* of the intelligence across departments, and organization wide *responsiveness* to it.

This view suggests that market orientation is a continuous, rather than an either-or, construct. That is, the extent to which an organization is market-oriented is a matter of degree and exists on a continuum, as opposed to being either absent or present (Jaworski and Kohli 1996; Kohli and Jaworski 1990). Since most professional political parties collect public opinion survey data and other forms of market intelligence, their relative positioning on this continuum is linked in part to how much data they collect and, more importantly, the extent to which this information is diffused throughout the organization and used to influence organizational decision making.

It is important to note that being *market-oriented* is distinguishable from being customer-led or *marketing-oriented* (Gray et al. 1998; Lafferty and Hult 2001; Ormrod 2006; Slater and Narver 1998, 1999). The latter tends to concentrate on "marketing's functional role in coordinating and managing the 4Ps" (Gray et al. 1998, 886) of product, price, place, and promotion and, as such, emphasizes a reactive and/or short-term organizational focus on what consumers/voters want. Political parties with a marketing orientation tend to use market intelligence primarily to inform their advertising and message design strategies, as opposed to the actual design of their product offerings. Their organizational focus also tends to be centred on specific events (for example, the next election or even the next public opinion poll), as well as on specific segments of the electorate.

Equally salient is the need to avoid conflating being *market-oriented* with being *market-driven*. The latter entails a heavy reliance on consultation, as opposed to dialogue. To this end, market-driven political parties risk alienating their traditional supporters, are more likely to adopt policies that parallel those of their competitors, and may fail to clearly delineate what they stand for ideologically. The UK Labour Party under the leadership of Tony Blair was exemplary of a market-driven political party. In relying so heavily on polling data as a proxy for market demand, New Labour managed to design an initial, and ultimately popular, product offering that deviated significantly from the long-standing tenets of the party (Lilleker 2005a).

Being market-oriented, by contrast, entails a focus on internal and external stakeholder relationships and is rooted in an organization-wide commitment to understanding the expressed and latent wants and needs of consumers/ voters. This information, in turn, is used to generate organizational learning over the long term that is directed toward sustaining and enhancing consumer/ voter value. Market orientation, then, is a state of mind or general organizational will to incorporate the use of market intelligence into the generation of tangible and intangible product offerings that seek to lead consumer needs and wants, not simply to follow them.

Drawing on a similar conceptualization, Lees-Marshment (2001a; 2001b) and Lilleker and Lees-Marshment (2005) have adopted a view of political marketing management that posits that political parties may be divided into three ideal categories. The first, the product-oriented party (POP), is depicted as employing a marketing strategy that is guided by the assumption that voters will recognize the normative value of their ideas and, as such, will vote for it. Hence, little consideration is given to gathering and using market intelligence to design or communicate its product offering. The second, the sales-oriented party (SOP), relies on the use of market intelligence to design strategies for selling or push-marketing its product offerings to targeted segments of the voting population. Here, much emphasis is placed on research for advertising and message design, as opposed to the design of a party's actual product offering.

In contrast with the other two categorizations, the market-oriented party (MOP) is portrayed as actively engaging in efforts to identify voters' concerns and priorities and incorporate them into the design of its product offerings. MOPs are distinguishable from their sales-oriented counterparts by their use of "various tools to understand and then respond to voter demands, but in a way that integrates the need to attend to members' needs, ideas from politicians and experts, and the realities of governing, and to focus more on delivering and making a difference than employing sales techniques to persuade or manipulate opinion" (Lees-Marshment 2006, 122). Although market-oriented parties may also make use of polling data and other forms of market intelligence, they are prone to engage in an array of internal and external communication processes in their efforts to create a more comprehensive and cohesive product offering (Lees-Marshment 2001a, 2001b; Lilleker and Lees-Marshment 2005). It follows therefore that, in theory at least, MOPs engage in far more consultation and dialogue with the electorate than POPs or SOPs and, as such, are guided by and operate in partnership with the electorate (Lilleker 2005a).

Political marketing is also a modern interpretation of the classic questions, how and to what extent do elites understand, respond to, and communicate with the masses? As an area of practice, political marketing offers strategies and tools that political elites can use to help them navigate electoral politics, including polling, focus groups, listening exercises, segmentation, voter profiling, get out the vote (GOTV), opposition research ("oppo"), strategic product development, internal marketing, volunteer management, voter-driven communication, branding, e-marketing, delivery, voter expectation management, and public relations (see Lees-Marshment 2009c). It is a rapidly growing and controversial global phenomenon: political parties and governments around the world are using such tools when developing policies, creating communication, and making political decisions (Bowler and Farrell 1992; Lees-Marshment, Strömbäck, and Rudd 2010; Lilleker and Lees-Marshment 2005). The range of concepts once unique to business are now common in politics as political elites look at marketing to offer new ways of engaging with and responding to an increasingly demanding electorate.

THE PROCESS OF POLITICAL MARKETING

Political marketing explores how political elites – candidates, parties, governments, and interest groups – utilize marketing to achieve goals such as influencing election outcomes, as well as advancing policy change and ideology. It focuses on how they relate to their markets, which incorporate not just voters but all stakeholders (Hughes and Dann 2009), including party members, and how the political product they offer and deliver once in power responds to the demands of those markets. The product entails not just policy promises but everything a party or politician does, as well as broader aspects – for instance, how they accommodate, serve, and represent market needs and wants (Lloyd 2005).

As illustrated in Figure 1.1, political marketing studies and utilizes different concepts and activities. First, there are a range of tools to identify and understand the public and other markets, such as market research,

FIGURE 1.1

The scope of political marketing

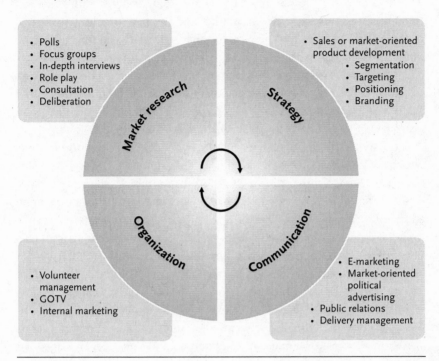

- Polls
- Focus groups
- In-depth interviews
- Role play
- Consultation
- Deliberation

Market research

Strategy

- Sales or market-oriented product development
  - Segmentation
  - Targeting
  - Positioning
  - Branding

Organization

Communication

- Volunteer management
- GOTV
- Internal marketing

- E-marketing
- Market-oriented political advertising
- Public relations
- Delivery management

segmentation, strategies, market positioning, branding, marketing communications, and organizing. Market research includes the usual quantitative and qualitative techniques such as polls and focus groups, but also consultation, role play, and deliberation. These tools are used by a political organization to gather information on the dominant needs and wants expressed in the electorate. What do electors consider to be the key political issues of the day? What are their conceptions of the ideal candidate, the ideal political party? What solutions does that candidate or party offer to contemporary societal problems?

Strategies include adopting a sales or market orientation toward electioneering, which involves either focusing on using research to create effective communication to sell the product to voters or utilizing the results of research to create a product that voters will want because it meets their needs and wants (Lees-Marshment 2001a, 2001b; Ormrod 2005). Segmentation and voter profiling help to identify, at an individual level, the different voter profiles composing the electoral market and the party's volunteer base in order to connect them into new groups that politicians can target (Bannon 2005a). Market positioning utilizes segmentation and analysis of the competition to suggest that parties and candidates occupy a distinctive and superior place in the political market from which they can attract support (Baines 1999; Butler and Collins 1999). Branding theory argues that politicians need to create a trusting relationship with voters that can sustain itself over the long term through crises and the ebb and flow of political fortune, while offering a differentiated brand from the competition (Cosgrove 2007; Needham 2005; Smith and French 2009). Communication tactics include e-marketing, market-oriented political advertising, delivery management, and public relations, all of which aim to engage in communication that suits both the producer and the receiver and to develop a positive long-term relationship between politicians and the public (Jackson 2005, 2006b, 2009; Jackson and Lilleker 2004; Lees-Marshment 2009c; C. Robinson 2010). It also offers concepts for how to organize effectively, such as GOTV campaigns that identify and motivate supporters to turn up at the polls (including ad campaigns, canvassing, phone or electronic reminders, daycare or voter transportation services), internal party marketing, and volunteer management (Bannon 2005a; Lebel 1999).

Political marketing is now a strong and active field of inquiry that attracts interest from a range of subfields in political science, both because it is an obvious area of practice and because it offers additional perspectives on age-old questions. Although political communication studies have tended to focus on the nature, content, and effectiveness of political messages, political marketing examines the processes and uses of market intelligence data that lead to the production of such discourses. And whereas public policy and party politics look at the nature of policy development and party organization, political marketing explores why elites choose to adopt certain policies or create certain structures to suit actual and prospective members. Furthermore, political marketing explores all factors that affect elite responsiveness, such as internal party culture, leadership ability, and the quality of mechanisms to identify and understand market demands. It also considers how effective political management strategies and tactics are at gaining and maintaining public support in elections.

Political Marketing in Canada: Conceptual Nuances and Distinctions

Political marketing is a dynamic area of study internationally. However, Canadian politics are rarely discussed in political marketing literature, and within Canada there is limited awareness of the nuances of this field. It is not a common expression among political practitioners nor in the mass media (see Chapter 11), Susan Delacourt being the exception. The field has not previously attracted much attention from Canadian academics, though its various components, ranging from opinion research to political communications, have. However, before engaging in the study of political marketing practices in Canada, it is important to establish some conceptual nuances. First, advertising and marketing are not synonyms; the former is a tool, whereas the latter is the framework – the overarching philosophy. Second, in the Canadian context, there is also a need to differentiate political marketing from the practice of brokerage politics.

POLITICAL MARKETING IS DIFFERENT FROM POLITICAL ADVERTISING

In Canada, as elsewhere, political advertising commands much attention, particularly during election campaigns. Advertising is clearly a strong feature of Canadian politics. For instance, among the first uses of political radio in Canada was the Conservative Party's advertising agency depicting a fictional "Mr. Sage" in 1935 political broadcasts, which made negative statements about Liberal leader Mackenzie King (Kinsella 2001; Ward 1999). The highest profile form of political advertising is the negative TV spot, which attacks opponents using unflattering images, sinister music, dark colour schemes, and accusations of unsuitability for office (Jamieson 1992; Romanow et al. 1999). The best-known Canadian example of an attack ad, the Progressive Conservative Party's Jean Chrétien face ads, occurred in the 1993 election (see Chapter 4) and, despite widespread condemnation, the very next federal campaign in 1997 featured more negative TV ads, in which the Reform Party decried Quebec politicians. Technological changes have also encouraged online forms of advertising (Small 2010) that reinforce mass media messaging, such as the Conservatives' negative advertising that weakened the brand values of Liberal opposition leaders while indirectly improving Stephen Harper's perceived leadership strengths. Throughout Stéphane Dion's tenure in 2007 and 2008, the Tories organized a media campaign proclaiming that he was "not a leader"; in 2009, soon after Michael Ignatieff replaced Dion, TV spots appeared stating that Ignatieff was "just visiting" – this pre-election campaigning continued until the dissolution of the fortieth Parliament and this theme was used by the Tories as a point of differentiation with their leader in the 2011 campaign. In addition to conventional media buys, some well-researched content was posted in a creative manner on websites such as notaleader.ca and Ignatieff.me, which provided a stable, 24-7 messaging mechanism to destabilize these politicians' public images and their own political communications. Audio and video ads and messaging were disseminated online via the Conservative Party's website, through friendly bloggers, by posting ads on social networking or file sharing sites such as Facebook and YouTube, and by communicating their availability via email and Twitter. Such inexpensive and unflattering websites about the competition often generate mainstream news media coverage and have an impressive reach. Political advertising is also used by advocacy groups (see Pross 1975 and Seidle 1991) and by governments to provide information about new regulations or government services, to promote civic events such as Canada Day and the Olympics, or to persuade the public about a policy such as free trade or taxes (Rose 2000).

The use of political advertising in Canada generates significant criticism. The emotional resonance leads to free news coverage as the advertising is scrutinized by pundits and, eventually, by academics. Supporters of negative ads maintain that they help shape the public agenda, that they weaken an opponent's values, and that they encourage political honesty and accountability. Critics counter that attack ads are unethical, that they are undesirable American imports, that democracy suffers as public attention is further diverted from scrutinizing policy proposals, that the debate is framed about imagery and the strategic game, and that "going neg" turns people off politics. For instance, negative advertising is often blamed for declining election turnout, though there is contradictory evidence of whether this is theory or fact (Ansolabehere and Iyengar 1995; Wattenberg and Brians 1999). In addition, in various referendums and after the 2008 economic crisis (see Chapter 7), Canadian government advertising has crossed into the realm of propaganda.

Nevertheless, this is not a book about political advertising. Political marketing is not just about advertising, though it is an exceedingly important communication tactic. Ads are one of several communication options available to political marketers – media relations, direct mail, and public appearances being others. When marketers do develop advertising campaigns, they use marketing concepts and tools (for instance, market research). Computer databases and online research allow parties to produce informative advertising that creates an evidence-based strategic messaging frame, one that can be quickly disseminated in response to emerging events. But studies also explore whether ads reflect voter preferences, how effectively they convey the political product, and if they support the overall brand (see, for example, C. Robinson 2010). Indeed, as with commercial marketing, the aim of political marketing strategy and research is to create a product that the market wants, so there should be less need for persuasive advertising, as opposed to informative advertising, that generates product awareness.

POLITICAL MARKETING IS DIFFERENT FROM BROKERAGE POLITICS
Since the 1970s, Canadian academia has looked at party politics through a lens of the electoral benefits of employing a brokerage model, whereby successful big tent parties embody a pluralistic catch-all approach to appeal to the median Canadian voter and to "broker" regional tensions (Bickerton, Gagnon, and Smith 1999; Brodie and Jenson 2007; Carty 2001; Carty, Cross, and Young 2000; Clarkson 2005). Forming government and maintaining that position necessitates adopting centrist policies and electoral coalitions to satisfy the short-term preferences of a majority of electors who are not located on the ideological fringe. Brodie and Jenson (2007, 40), for instance, state that since brokerage parties are foremost vote-seekers, there is "no basis for the systematic exclusion of any group" if numbers warrant. For some time, brokerage politicking has been widely considered essential in a country where regional differences and national unity tensions are so pronounced; Carty (2001, 25) refers to this as the "regional accommodation" function of brokerage politics. Regionalism is particularly acute given that the single member plurality (SMP) electoral system tends to exaggerate the seat counts of the market leader and of strong regional niche parties, which are often outlets for populist protests, at the expense of market followers and fringe parties. As national federalist parties, this has pressured the Liberals and Conservatives not only to broker left- and right-wing ideological tensions but foremost to manage various competing provincial interests, as represented by provincial premiers and regional party bosses who act as localized lobbyists for federal resources. In seeking to deal with the challenges this presents for garnering widespread electoral support, Canadian political parties have evolved so that local organizational autonomy, member participation, electoral segmentation, and voter mobilization work as separate yet united franchising activities (Carty 2002, 2004; Carty, Young, and Cross 2000).

Brokerage politics is in some ways comparable to a mass market approach to consumers. Major political parties are like department or grocery stores that offer many products that are needed and wanted by the masses, while simultaneously responding somewhat to local market preferences, but leaving specialized markets to be served by smaller competitors. The brokerage system is said to have foremost characterized Canadian parties between the 1920s and 1950s (Carty 2001; Carty, Cross, and Young 2000; Clarkson 2005), followed by a pan-Canadian system enabled by developments in mass media and polling, though others indicate that brokerage politics persisted until at least 2006, when Stephen Harper became prime minister (Brodie and Jenson 2007). One of the authors of this Canadian party system approach, R. Kenneth Carty, has, along with co-authors William Cross and Lisa Young, remarked on the representational linkages between Canadian political parties and the electorate. In *Rebuilding Canadian Party Politics* (Carty, Cross, and Young 2000), they suggest that a new party system emerged with the 1993 federal election that marked the end of the pan-Canadian era of broad national policies. It coincided with the increasing concentration of power in the party leader's office and a shift toward the brokering of the demands of special interest groups. A fragmented electorate resulted in parties offering policy positions "tailored to specific segments of the electorate" (9), and opinion polling becoming "more essential to the parties' electoral strategies than ever before" (189) as such data were used to inform the concentration of resources on swing voters in winnable ridings.

Along with technological advances, Canadian political parties have evolved into a modern form of brokerage parties. National central decision making coexists with some degree of local "franchise" organizational autonomy in riding associations to contribute to electoral segmentation and the simulation of member participation and voter mobilization. Although Carty and his colleagues do not explicitly refer to the notion of market orientation, this franchise model of Canadian political parties strongly echoes the importance that is placed on internal and external stakeholder relationships within political and service marketing literature. Of particular significance here is the recognition that local autonomy and national discipline must coexist, as parties must invest in local resources in order to build "an organization attuned to the needs and demands of the community they serve" (Carty 2002, 730), and national campaigns cannot succeed if "there is no local organization in the constituency to harvest voter support" (743). Equally important is the observation that modern brokerage parties are increasingly defined as targeting and aggregating various segments of the electorate rather than seeking "to catch all the interests" (726). This mobilization function is seen to be carried out by the franchised local party members and riding association personnel and must be in tune with the national promotional campaign aimed at undecided voters. These observations parallel a basic tenet of being market orientated insofar as every member of an organization, not just its leadership or the marketing department's staffers, is viewed as a potential part-time marketeer and a co-producer of the service to be provided to consumers/voters (Johansen 2005).

What Carty, Cross, and Young were describing about the post-1993 era was the onset of political marketing in Canadian politics. This was around the time of the rebranding of the Reform Party as the Canadian Alliance and, subsequently, as the Conservative Party, a political organization that has embraced business marketing techniques more fully than the other parties and yet at times has been constrained by the ideological underpinnings of its leadership, caucus, and membership. In Canada, the earliest adopters of political marketing techniques have been the Conservatives and the Liberals (Carty, Cross, and Young 2000; Marland 2005; Paltiel 1989). But in fact, the influence of inputs such as survey and focus group data on decisions related to outputs ranging from policy products to persuasion tactics has been growing since the Liberal Party first experimented with scientific polling in the 1940s. Often, such innovations have been used to structure targeted fundraising campaigns to finance the ability to collect data, to respond to it, and to sell the party's product(s). Marketing may be used by political parties and their local associations between and during election campaigns, as well as internally, such as during leadership contests and policy conventions and in local candidate nominations. Parliamentarians, governments, interest groups, and non-governmental organizations like charities may use marketing in response to emerging situations or as part of cyclical events such as throne and budget speeches, public awareness campaigns, or fundraising drives.

As this book shows, a new era of political marketing is therefore developing, marking a more sophisticated, if impersonal, model of party politics in Canada. Whitaker (2001) has described the presence of a vacuous "virtual political party" that is leader-driven, employs marketing specialists, and is replacing brokerage politics. He says that "as mass marketing gives way to niche or micro marketing, the 'public' becomes fragmented into many publics, each targeted for votes by parties that tailor and hone their appeals to particular niches" (19). Indeed, in the modern era of successive minority federal governments, we have seen how the practice of niche marketing, as used by the Bloc Québécois since the early 1990s, can create a seemingly impenetrable market share as long as the party remains in touch with its target market. But it is since the 2005-6 federal election campaign, when the Harper Conservatives used micro-marketing with reasonable success, that we have seen the fragmentation of publics forecast by Whitaker. With that election campaign, so meticulously described by Tom Flanagan in *Harper's Team* (2007a; 2009), the Conservatives put the other parties on notice that technological advances in database management, market segmentation, and media targeting have reduced the viability of the old brokerage model of party politics in an era of the virtual political party that is preoccupied with elector segments as targeted through research intelligence. This has increased the competitive pressure on other Canadian political parties and on interest groups to employ a political marketing approach.

Political Marketing and Democracy

Previous research on political marketing has raised a number of concerns about its potential impact on democracy, which this book also considers within the Canadian context. Newman (1999a, ix, xi) warned that American democracy is "on shaky ground" and is "bent on self-destruction" because political leaders rely so much on opinion polls and mass marketing. Thus, the adoption of US-style political marketing in Canada could produce significant democratic implications, such as giving elites the tools to both reflect and manipulate citizens' viewpoints. To practitioners such as Steinberg (1976), political marketing is foremost a management tool used to win elections, whereas to academics such as O'Cass (2009, 204), it raises philosophical discussions about the repercussions for democracy as political parties "develop policies which seek to solve the social, economic and political problems" faced by some electors. There are several areas of potential concern, which this book seeks to broadly identify if they are also relevant in Canadian politics. Concerns about political marketing raised in previous research include:

1   The concentration of political marketing practices in the hands of party outsiders such as political consultants and pollster-led researchers, which

can encourage consultants to have more impact on policy design and in the daily affairs of new governments;

2   The pandering of politicians said to be governing by polls and the consequences of poll-driven leadership;

3   The passage of the political debate from substance (issues) toward image preoccupations;

4   The merchandizing of the political and the consideration of citizens as consumers, and thus the transformation of governance into permanent campaigns;

5   The thinning influence of party members and staffs in campaign organization and governance because of centralizing marketing strategies;

6   The explosion in campaign costs;

7   The implications that segmentation and targeting of voters might have on interest representation; and,

8   The negative impact on levels of political trust and participation in the electorate.

These themes are discussed throughout the book, but it is worth expanding on three areas here: unelected advisers, market segmentation, and treating voters like consumers. For example, Newman (1999a) notes how political marketing has exacerbated the potential influence of unelected advisers, as they provide advice on the decisions made by elected officials, senior bureaucrats, and non-governmental organizations in relation to their potential impact on public opinion. Knowledge, after all, is power, and the ability to respond well to strategic information can make the difference in determining who governs, which public policies exist, and the overall quality of life of a polity's citizenry. This produces debate over the democratic implications of public servants and their political masters employing advertising agencies and opinion research specialists to develop communications programs. In Canada, for instance, there is much vexation about whether the government advertising and polling that result have an educational informative value or whether they are of a persuasive agenda-setting nature (Roberts and Rose 1995; Rose 2000).

Market segmentation encourages political parties, including the governing party, to use opinion research and other intelligence to target groups whose support they need, and thus exclude others, rather than represent the public as a whole. This marginalizes those who are not targeted; Lilleker (2005b) argues that segmentation creates a division between the public whose interests are already represented and those whose interests have been abandoned, and it risks demobilizing non-target groups. Market segmentation also may enable extremist parties to increase their support (McGough 2009). The use of market research to isolate target groups limits the broad appeal of a pan-Canadian big tent party because other parties can narrowcast messages that resonate with target groups. For instance, when the Conservative Party of Canada won a minority of seats in the 2006 and 2008 general elections, its strategists targeted the conservative middle class and dismissed electors who prioritized progressive social values (Flanagan 2009; Paré and Berger 2008).

A broader concern is the notion of citizen-as-consumer (Blumler 1997; Farrell 1996; B. Franklin 2004; Kraus 2000; Newman 1999a). Satisfying needs and wants is much less straightforward in the political realm than in the marketplace. Giving people what they want is not necessarily giving them what they need, individually or collectively. Lilleker and Scullion (2008, 4) explain how politics involves consideration of self and society, whereas consumerism encourages people "to be selfish, vain and individualistic." Needham (2003, 7) argues that political marketing has "turned democracy into a marketplace" and downgraded citizenship; Savigny (2008b) argues that it encourages self-interest in politics (see also Slocum 2004; Walsh 1994). For example, the Harper Conservatives' reduction of the maligned goods and services tax (GST) was a popular political decision. Opinion research indicating that cutting the GST would be a vote-winner trumped the educated opinions of many economists that cutting income taxes would be better public policy.

Yet, the literature also asserts potential positives about political marketing which this book considers, including:

1   Getting politicians to listen and understand the electorate more effectively;
2   Enabling effective targeting, not just of majorities but also of minorities;
3   Making government focus more on actual delivery than rhetorical promises;
4   Elevating citizens' position in the political process;
5   Developing a more mature relationship with the electorate, where political consumers are active players in the political system, understand the complexities of government, and move away from demanding to helping create government;

6   Reducing elite domination of the political process; and,
7   Keeping politicians responsive and accountable.

Political Marketing in Canada considers both sides of the debate. Without exploring what makes a political system democratic – which is a question for other books – we can say that liberal democratic theory is pretty straightforward regarding the centrality of the role that citizens play in its workings: government of the people, for the people, by the people, as Abraham Lincoln famously said in his 1863 Gettysburg Address. As Verba and Nie (1972, 1, cited in Burt 2002, 234) have stated, this means that the nature of a democracy is measured by the participation of the public in political decision making. Political participation of the citizenry is essential because that is what anchors a democratic political system. Citizens' input is needed – and expected – to ensure a healthy democratic life. Yet, political science has been suggesting that post-industrial democracies are experiencing a crisis in representation and participation. Citizens are said to be expressing a malaise toward their political elites and institutions, as measured by indicators such as declines in electoral turnouts, weak levels of political trust, lower levels of party membership, higher public cynicism toward political life, and declines in forms of civic engagement (Cappella and Jamieson 1996, 1997; de Vreese 2005; Patterson 1994; Putnam 2000).

Canada's political system is likewise said to suffer from democratic uneasiness (Gidengil et al. 2004; Nadeau 2002). The last two decades of Canadian electoral studies point to the same democratic decline, as indicated by lower voter turnout figures and fluctuations in levels of public confidence in political actors and institutions (Gidengil et al. 2004, 104-7; Nevitte 1996, 54-58). In addition, public opinion surveys consistently show that a majority of Canadians share a negative opinion of their political class that is expressed by an abysmal trust level of politicians (Angus Reid 2010; Léger Marketing 2006, 2007). Canadian citizens, the primary actors of representative liberal democracy, are voting in lower numbers and have less faith in their electoral system (Gidengil et al. 2004, vii). Simultaneously, and perhaps not coincidentally, political marketers and consultants have become increasingly and actively involved in the Canadian political process, and thus we need to consider whether this has played a part in the democratic malaise noted by non-political marketing studies, while also allowing for the possibility that political marketing may facilitate the electoral transaction by engaging electors in the definition of the political offer and enhance democracy. All the chapters in this book reflect on the possible democratic implications that might be generated by the increasing use of political marketing activities by parties, governments, and groups in Canada.

The Structure of *Political Marketing in Canada*

This is the first book on political marketing in Canada and, as will be seen in subsequent chapters, the practice is both emerging and thriving with divergent democratic implications. Political advisers continually monitor international developments to identify new approaches that can be utilized in Canadian politics, the Government of Canada uses public opinion research data when developing policy, and political marketing is even used in the private sector. This book explores how political marketing is being implemented in Canada, whether its use is similar in countries such as the United Kingdom and the United States, and if Canada is developing its own unique version. It also discusses whether political marketing, by guiding elites to listen to public opinion, is improving the quality of representation and democracy and whether it is changing the nature of Canadian politics itself.

The material covers a range of topical and Canadian perspectives about political marketing. Its chapters consider the potential and constraints for political marketing in terms of the nature of voters and the rules of the electoral market; the utilization of market research and its influence on politicians' decision making and the strategic approaches that Canada's federal political parties take; branding in terms of parties but also the utilization of popular public locations such as Tim Hortons; the role of e-marketing and the impact of the Canadian media on political marketing communication; the way that Canadian interest groups utilize political marketing; the commissioning and influence of public opinion research by government departments; the scope and effectiveness of delivery management in a minority government; and the impact of political marketing activities on citizens' political efficacy levels.

Political Marketing in Canada therefore provides an informed insight into the way that political marketing is used in Canada. It addresses a knowledge gap in Canadian academia where the rarely mentioned term "political marketing" has tended to be used synonymously with political communication, advertising, media, and persuasion. It demonstrates that Canadian parties tend to be slow adopters of innovations in campaign management and that techniques employed by the Conservative Party of Canada have put pressure on their competitors to modernize. Moreover, it identifies differences as well as similarities with the rest of the world, providing a rich perspective on the way political marketing is developing in the early twenty-first century, which will be of interest to all those concerned about the democratic impact of political marketing around the globe.

ACKNOWLEDGMENTS
The authors would like to acknowledge the contribution of Daniel Paré (Université d'Ottawa) and Elisabeth Gidengil (McGill University) to certain sections of this chapter.

2

The Canadian Political Market and the Rules of the Game

Yannick Dufresne and Alex Marland

Strategic marketing refers to the use of market research in the development of the political product or service; tactical marketing, to that product or service's promotion. The popular conception of political marketing, unfortunately, is often confined to the tactical process (i.e., political communications). Nevertheless, the strategic side, particularly the role of market intelligence in informing decisions, is at the core of the marketing concept. By highlighting the particularities of the Canadian political marketplace, in this chapter we show that the political marketing framework is a complement to current approaches and methods for understanding Canadian electoral behaviour.

The Canadian Political Marketplace

In Western societies, there has been a shift in how democratic politics works. Some political marketing scholars identify technical advancements such as television and polling as the cause of the entrance into an era of manufactured images (Newman 1999a). Others contend that a more profound social transformation is taking place. The former contend that the "rise of the political consumer" follows the weakening of partisan ties, the fading of traditional cleavages, and the growing importance of political issues (Lees-Marshment 2001b; Lilleker and Scullion 2008). The increase in electoral volatility, in turn, results in greater party competition and encourages parties to develop more sophisticated and efficient marketing strategies. For this reason, the Canadian context may be considered fertile political marketing ground: the conventional wisdom holds that the Canadian electorate is and has historically been highly volatile and susceptible to short-term campaign effects. Nevertheless, some particularities about the Canadian electorate deserve mention (some of which are expanded on in Elisabeth Gidengil's subsequent chapter in this book).

TRADITIONAL CLEAVAGES

According to Dalton (1996, 345), "Social positions no longer determine political positions as they did when social alignments were solidly frozen." This alleged fading of traditional cleavages is said to increase the viability of political marketing because of the need and opportunity to persuade citizens. In fact, the stability of these cleavages represents the main theoretical foundation for the claim that electoral campaigns do not matter (Campbell et al. 1960).

In Canada, there has been a decline in traditional cleavages (Clarke and Stewart 1992), but their nature differs from those in other countries. For instance, although the decline in class voting represented an important change in Britain (M. Franklin 1985), most scholars agree that class voting has never been prominent in Canada.[1] However, on the other hand, the persistence of religion as a political cleavage has remained a puzzle to Canadian scholars (Blais et al. 2002; Gidengil 1992). In any event, it is regional divisions that tend to predominate: Canadian provinces have been described as "small worlds" (Elkins and Simeon 1980), and more recently it has been suggested that a geographical division of nine areas, not defined by provincial boundaries, might account for more variation in political attitudes than provinces (Henderson 2004). More importantly for political marketing, however, is that despite the persistence of social cleavages, these cleavages cannot be considered to constitute a fixed political environment. As Blais and colleagues (2002, 96) write, "Social groups need to be treated as live social forces, not static categories."

The Canadian marketplace is evolving, and political marketers need to be mindful of demographic considerations. Strategists can no longer split the population simply along an English and French linguistic line, especially not in cities and suburbs where immigrant populations are concentrated. Market intelligence is increasingly used to evaluate allophones' attitudes, behaviour, beliefs, and group norms and values. The Conservatives have been actively targeting ethnic groups that have long been courted by the Liberal Party (Flanagan 2009), and all parties are reaching out to allophones in their policy development, candidate recruitment, and communications.

PARTISAN IDENTIFICATION

The suggestion of a recent shift in political behaviour is supported by work showing a partisan dealignment in advanced industrial democracies (Dalton

and Wattenberg 2000). This detachment from political parties is the consequence of a growing mistrust of parties and the erosion of traditional cleavage
lines. In Canada, trust of the government and of politicians has decreased in
the past few decades (Nevitte 2002), and some evidence shows that party
identification has followed a similar pattern (Clarke and Kornberg 1993).

The conventional wisdom suggests, in fact, that partisan identification
has never really been relevant in Canada. In fact, some early Canadian electoral studies claim that the concept of party identification "may be almost
inapplicable in Canada" (Meisel 1975, 67). High individual-level volatility
is thought to create a context of "stable dealignment" that is propitious to
wide electoral swings (Leduc 1984). However, this so-called textbook theory
(Sniderman, Forbes, and Melzer 1974), which indicates that there is a higher
degree of volatility and weaker partisan ties in Canada, has since been contested. Challengers to this textbook theory contend that partisan identification
is no less relevant in Canada than in the United States or United Kingdom.
The middle-ground position is to draw a distinction between durable and
flexible partisans, with the majority of Canadian electors falling into the latter
category (Clarke et al. 1984).[2]

In any case, the conventional wisdom may overstate the elasticity of
Canadians' partisan ties. For example, party identification has been shown
to be essential for making sense of recent electoral outcomes in Canada (Blais
et al. 2002; Gidengil et al. 2006). Questions concerning the relevance of
partisan ties and higher electoral volatility do not seem to be wholly the result
of a new social transformation but might be a particularity of the Canadian
electoral landscape.

Political Issues

The Canadian electorate has often been portrayed as less influenced by issues
than it is by other short-term forces such as party image and leader personality
(Meisel 1975). The minor importance given to political issues in Canadian
politics is thought to have less to do with voters' lack of interest in issues than
with the consequence of the choice by the major parties to engage in brokerage politics (Clarke et al. 1984). This situation results from a fragmentation
of the Canadian electorate, which encourages parties to elaborate a strategy
based on leadership and managerial competence. As Clarke, Kornberg, and
Scotto (2009) have pointed out, the so-called presidentialization of Canadian
politics reflects the increasing focus on parties' leaders rather than their teams,
policy ideas, or local candidates. Even if this is the case, the fact that issues

may be less important in Canadian politics does not undermine the applicability of political marketing. Political marketing is not solely centred on issues, even if voters often drive parties toward issue-centred marketing strategies. The more general claim is that parties select strategies based on voters' needs and wants, irrespective of whether these strategies focus on political issues or leadership. It may be, for example, that voters are more concerned with party or leader image. Whether about the issues or about party and leader image, political marketing will apply. Indeed, brokerage politics can be considered in particular contexts as an optimal strategy, focused primarily on the image component of the political product rather than the substantive offer.

However, many scholars show that the importance of issues is greater in Canadian politics than is often suggested. For instance, free trade was a critical issue in the 1988 federal election; health care (to a lesser extent) in 2000; and corruption and accountability in 2004 and 2006. Issues matter, and those that become salient are not necessarily the same ones from one election to the next. The fact that electors' choices are not static necessarily encourages further competition between political parties. Parties must be cognizant of voters' needs and wants, but also of their own strategic positioning in the partisan competitive environment.

The central idea of political marketing is that political parties can seek advantage by integrating the electorate's needs and wants into the development of their political product. This is thought to be the key to electoral success (Newman 1999b). But why, then, do parties not all follow this simple prescription? The institutional rules governing their behaviour certainly act as constraints that are largely out of a party's control. But there are other reasons why Canadian political parties choose not to simply follow the ebbs and flows of the electorate, most notably positioning and ideology. Before turning to a discussion about the institutional rules of the game, we first discuss these two considerations.

Positioning

Focusing on the needs and wants of the electorate as a whole is not always the most efficient strategy, and targeting specific population segments is often more useful. Political parties might also need to develop a position within the competitive environment that is attractive to the electorate and that differentiates them from the positioning of opponents. If the median of voters' needs and wants is represented by a point in multi-dimensional space, a party's optimal strategy to maximize vote share might be to position its political product precisely on that point, as rational choice theorists would advocate. However, parties must also be attentive to the competitive context by detecting market opportunities and seeking to differentiate themselves from other parties. To illustrate this idea, Butler and Collins (1996) adapted a well-established framework in business marketing to the study of political parties. According to this framework, the strategic behaviour of a party can be analyzed based on its current position in the competitive market, as determined by its vote share in the last election. A party can either be the leader of the market, a challenger, a follower, or a nicher. A party's market position is thought to be useful in providing some indication of its resource endowments and opportunity for growth. The composition of the Canadian party system seems to fit easily in this framework (see Table 2.1).

In addition to market research about the electorate, Canadian political parties also must therefore be attentive to the competitive environment. They must be able to seize the opportunities that occur from their opponents' mistakes or changes in strategy. A challenger, for instance, may decide to focus on issues that are supported by segments of the electorate that cease to be satisfied by another party leader. Similarly, parties may concentrate their efforts on undecided voters within strategically targeted regions and ridings. Even more sophisticated targeting techniques now exist. For example, Conservative strategists used cluster analysis in 2006 to segment the electorate into voter types, which could then allow for more precise targeting (Flanagan 2009). This strategy is reminiscent of the psychographic segmentation methods developed in the business world, such as the values and lifestyle (VALS) and list of values (LOV) techniques. Micro-targeting is also performed by Canadian political parties with the use of voter database management software. For example, the Conservative Party developed its constituent information management system (CIMS), and the Liberal Party's "Liberalist" system was partially developed by the same company that created the VoteBuilder application used during Barack Obama's presidential campaign. The implementation of these systems then allows for more efficiency in tactical marketing techniques such as telemarketing and direct mailing, and increasingly online marketing, which aim to precisely join targeted voter population segments.

More generally, some scholars also mention the necessity of party differentiation and the maintenance of a political brand (White and de Chernatony 2002). The image of a party or candidate might be affected for

TABLE 2.1

Types of market positioning in a competitive political market

Competitive positioning	Characteristics	Strategic directions	The market repositioning of the Conservative Party of Canada	Canadian party system (2011)
Market leader	The market leader got the largest share of the vote/seats in the last election Constantly under attack	Defend its market share Invade new market segments Enlarge the market	Progressive Conservative Party of Canada (1988, 1993) Conservative Party of Canada (2008)	Conservative Party of Canada
Market challenger	The challenger has the opportunity to become the market leader The official opposition or the parties that are positioned in the electorate as an alternative to the current government	Imitate the market leader's strengths Attack the market leader's weaknesses Invade new market segments	Conservative Party of Canada (2004, 2006) Canadian Alliance (2000)	New Democratic Party
Market follower	The follower concentrates on precise market segments	Imitate or adapt competitors' strengths	Reform Party (1997) Progressive Conservative Party of Canada (1997, 2000)	Liberal Party of Canada
Market nicher	The nicher is the market leader in a specific niche or submarket	Create, enlarge, or defend the niche	Reform Party (1993) Bloc Québécois (1993-2008)	Bloc Québécois Green Party of Canada

NOTE: Adaptation of Butler and Collins (1996).

various reasons, including weaknesses highlighted by opposing parties or past mistakes. Under these circumstances, parties might accord disproportionate attention to some issues as a way to counter negative perceptions. Bill Clinton's Democratic Party and Tony Blair's New Labour Party are often cited as examples of this repositioning. This also happens to various degrees in Canada, with the creation of the new Conservative Party being one example.

Ideology

The consistency and credibility of a party's positioning is also important. Some scholars stress the merits of a party's political product being based on an ideology that is linked to its history and traditions (Bernier 1991). Ideology, however, is not always used for such instrumental reasons as maintaining the consistency or credibility of a political product. Parties often prefer to advocate ideologically driven positions that are detrimental to their electoral performance. But to be relevant they must balance the necessity of appealing to the electorate as a whole and, at the same time, appealing to the core of their constituency that provides campaign contributions and can be internally and externally vocal in its opposition to ideological moderation. This can be thought of as a two-level political marketing game between an internal and external market. Political marketing neither denies nor opposes the importance of ideology. It aims only to differentiate between less and more optimal political strategies and tactics. A market-oriented party is not necessarily better in a normative sense than other parties, but it may be considered more efficient at winning elections. For instance, in the 2008 federal election, the Liberals proposed a new "green shift" policy that the Conservatives derisively branded a "carbon tax" (Brooke 2009). Few would question the good intentions behind then Liberal leader Stéphane Dion's belief that taxing polluters as a means of reducing carbon emissions was good public policy. But this proposition to address climate change, as a political product, was an easy target for opponents, especially in a political environment demanding responses to an emerging economic crisis. The green shift is perhaps a classic case of weak external, and eventually internal, political marketing.

Political marketing is often associated with negative advertising, unethical fundraising, and dirty tricks. The choice to engage in such tactics is the responsibility of political parties, but such behaviour can also be restrained by the electorate and analyzed through the political marketing approach. The Conservative Party's repositioning was facilitated, for example, by the sponsorship scandal, which was linked to the Liberal brand in Canada, particularly in Quebec. Thus, while political marketing may create opportunities for dirty tricks, it can also create those that favour the marketing of ethical behaviour, which may potentially spill over to promote more ethical practices. Such behaviour, as the next section highlights, is facilitated and constrained by the rules of the game.

The Rules of the Political Game in Canada

Understanding the rules of the game in Canada is essential to recognizing the types of political marketing behaviour and related opportunities. In Canada, political parties and their candidates, just like businesses, unions, interest groups, and media organizations, are subject to regulations that constrain their political marketing strategies and tactics. These rules fall into two broad categories: the inter-election period and the official election campaign period, both of which are publicly subsidized for federal political parties. Indeed, one of the most important considerations in studying political marketing in Canada is political financing. Federal parties are significantly subsidized from the public purse, and their electioneering is heavily restricted during official campaign periods. The idea behind these rules is to limit political competitors' undue advantages and shadowy influences. After a federal election, parties qualify for a partial rebate of their expenses if they obtained a small vote threshold nationally or a small share of the vote in the electoral districts where they fielded candidates. Candidates likewise qualify for partial rebates of their expenses if they meet a slightly higher vote threshold and if, like the parties, they submit an audited expense statement.[3] Consequently, a party's strategic and tactical emphasis may be related to achieving various minimum vote thresholds.

INTER-ELECTION PERIOD

Except during party leadership and candidate nomination contests, the inter-election period is not regulated by extraordinary limitations on fundraising activities, spending, or political communications. Elected officials receive general advice on conflict of interest rules and other matters of political morality from an ethics commissioner in their legislature. Apart from this, however, they are generally free to engage in standard politicking. The most institutionalized laws concern lobbying. The Office of the Commissioner of Lobbying of Canada oversees a code of conduct, administers the registration of political lobbyists, and maintains a searchable database.

Non-lobbying activities during this period are largely governed by codes of ethics maintained by industry associations (such as the Canadian Code of Advertising Standards administered by Advertising Standards Canada), by umbrella membership organizations (such as the Canadian Association of Broadcasters), and by individual organizations (such as the Canadian Broadcasting Corporation). For example, the code of conduct of the Marketing Research and Intelligence Association advocates obtaining consent from respondents, reporting data accurately, and generally behaving in an ethical, competent, and professional manner (MRIA 2007).

The federal government's activities are also regulated. Its public opinion research (POR) is subject to government policies, industry standards, and external accountability. Such research, however, tends to be used primarily to test the persuasiveness of policy messaging rather than to inform policy development. As Page (2006, 190) states, in the bureaucracy, "the strongest suit of opinion research is its ability to help with communications" (see also Chapter 9, by Lisa Birch). Since 2006, the final versions of most POR reports are required to be deposited with Library and Archives Canada, and an independent adviser reports on the government's POR practices.[4] Public Works and Government Services Canada also maintains a POR directorate that houses annual reports of government-sponsored opinion research.[5] Spending on such data collection is reviewed by the auditor general. Opinion research is subject to access to information legislation; one can thus assume that such regulation may lead to sensitive questions not being asked and prompt the oral delivery of some recommendations.

OFFICIAL ELECTION CAMPAIGN PERIOD
A well-known institutional consideration in Canadian politics is the single member plurality (SMP) electoral system in which the candidate with the plurality of votes in an electoral district is the winner. This makes it possible for parties without the majority of votes to win a majority of the seats. This has strategic and tactical implications for political parties. For example, campaigning efforts may vary among ridings depending on the closeness of the race. In Canada, concentrating one's resources on winnable ridings rather than on country-wide vote share can lead parties to focus strongly on regional campaigns, for the SMP system creates a bias that favours parties with concentrated regional support (Cairns 1968). This results in minor pan-Canadian parties receiving a lower proportion of total seats than their vote share would suggest. In this regard, Carty, Cross, and Young (2000, 189)

state that, in Canada, "geography is the first concern in developing an electoral strategy."

In addition to the institutional constraints imposed by the electoral system, extensive limitations are placed on registered parties and candidates during the official election campaign period. Plasser and Plasser (2002, 152) has classified Canadian electoral rules as a western Europe–United States "hybrid." The enactment of these rules is the consequence of a series of historical events.[6] These can be traced back to the public demand for campaign finance reform after the Pacific scandal of 1873, wherein the governing party accepted donations from an entrepreneur involved in railroad development (Canada 1966, 1991; Stanbury 1991). The resulting Dominion Elections Act (1874), which was modelled after Britain's Corrupt Practices Act (1854), included restrictions such as the requirement for agents to authorize expenses and the need to submit a campaign expense statement so that expenditures could be subject to public scrutiny. However, the sources of funds were not legislated, and there was a general absence of enforcement. Amendments made to the Elections Act in 1908 to restrict corporate donations were influenced by the United States' first federal campaign regulations, the Tillman Act (1907), but a lack of enforcement led to the Canadian restrictions being repealed in 1930.

It was not until the age of television advertising that public pressure led to the formation of the Committee on Election Expenses (the Barbeau Committee) to investigate political finance regulations. At the time, rules were regularly ignored, broken, and unenforced (Canada 1966). The committee's recommendations were implemented through the Election Expenses Act (1974), which intended to encourage fairness, facilitate democratic access, and limit excesses such as image advertising in competitive campaigns (Canada 1991). Since then, amendments have been passed on an almost annual basis, including to the current laws prescribed in the Canada Elections Act (2000).[7] Consequently, the Elections Act is a long, detailed piece of legislation and embodies many of the political reforms advocated by Newman (1999a): there are limits on campaign contributions and spending, electioneering is publicly financed, parties are provided with cheap broadcast airtime, donations are required to be publicly disclosed, soft money spending by advocacy groups is restricted, and official campaign periods are limited to thirty-six days. Not surprisingly, there are long-standing suspicions that more communications spending occurs immediately prior to the campaign proper than during the official campaign itself (Laschinger and Stevens 1992).

Furthermore when no party has a majority of seats, as during the period of federal minority governments from January 2006 to May 2011, political marketing and permanent campaigning feature prominently in the daily political landscape.

Other than electoral boundaries and the administration of voting processes, the areas of the Elections Act that influence political marketing foremost involve the management of the list of electors, the rules surrounding communications, and financing and spending. Technically, sanctions for failing to comply with the act include fines and jail terms, and can include the suspension of a Member of Parliament (MP) from sitting in the House of Commons. But in practice, Elections Canada often experiences difficulty in applying penalties. This has been the case, for instance, when it failed to impose significant sanctions against the Bloc Québécois in 2000, and the Conservatives in 2006, for using a loophole in the electoral laws to increase their campaign refunds (for example, Cheadle 2010). However, the Liberal Party's role in the sponsorship scandal is an example of how subverting the spirit of the electoral rules and the resulting public embarrassment can exceed short-term monetary gains.

One of the more significant aspects of the Elections Act is the provision that Elections Canada maintain a list of eligible voters. This Register of Electors includes an elector's name, sex, date of birth, and address. Once a year, this information in each electoral district is transmitted to the MP and to political parties that fielded a candidate in that district during the previous election. Furthermore, at the start of each election and during the campaign, names and addresses are provided to all current candidates. Section 110 of the act explicitly states that the list of electors may be used for communications purposes such as recruiting party members and soliciting donations. Not surprisingly, this is valuable information for targeting one's marketing resources and has enabled the development and maintenance of the previously mentioned CIMS and Liberalist systems.

Media outlets are also subject to the Elections Act. Radio and television broadcasters are required to make a block of prime time hours available for sale for political advertising. A broadcasting arbitrator allocates these hours to parties based on various statistics from the previous elections: the number of seats won, the vote share obtained, and the number of candidates they fielded. Parties are also awarded a minimum of two minutes of free broadcasting time per network. There is a ban on reporting new opinion polls one day before the election, as well as an advertising blackout on election day itself.

When opinion research data are first publicly reported, media outlets and polling organizations are required to publicly identify the methodology used.

Parties are not restricted in their solicitation of individuals for tax-deductible donations, and only individuals are allowed to donate to parties, candidates, or parties' electoral district associations (EDAs). This means that donations from businesses and unions are prohibited. Such contributions, including the value of goods and services or donations, are significantly limited: as of 2011, individual contributions were limited to $1,100. This rule encourages parties to put effort into fundraising from as many individuals as possible. The parties are allowed to spend a set amount per elector based on the number of ridings that they contest. Candidates' spending limits are based on the number of registered electors in the district, with an increase for districts with less than ten electors per square kilometre. For example, in 2011, the Conservative, Green, Liberal, and New Democratic Parties were permitted to spend a maximum of approximately $21 million nationally, whereas the Bloc Québécois, which ran candidates only in Quebec, was allowed to spend less than $5.4 million. Expenses include promotional activities, meeting spaces, labour, and research, as well as candidates' personal expenditures. EDAs may accept donations and transfer funds to – and receive funds from – a candidate or a political party. They may also receive a candidate's surplus funds as long as the EDA is registered with Elections Canada. But EDAs are not allowed to advertise during an election campaign, and registration requires that they report details of their finance activities annually.

Election spending limits would be meaningless without restrictions on other political organizations (i.e., special interest groups, businesses, unions) because, otherwise, parallel campaigns could be organized. "Third" parties are allowed to receive donations and, like political parties and their candidates, must file fundraising and advertising expense reports, but they are ineligible for refunds. These chiefly environmental, religious, and corporate bodies are required to register with Elections Canada upon incurring a moderate level of expenses, and their spending is significantly limited.[8] They are prohibited from breaking up into separate organizations for the purposes of circumventing these restrictions, and electoral candidates are not allowed to sign written pledges to such groups that could result in preventing "freedom of action" in Parliament (section 550 of the Canada Elections Act). Constitutional challenges arguing that spending restrictions placed on interest groups violate the freedom of expression guaranteed in the Charter of Rights and Freedoms have been unsuccessful on the grounds that expenditure equality is for the greater good of democracy (F.J. Fletcher 1994; Smith and Bakvis 2000).

Implications for the Quality of Democracy

The characteristics of the Canadian political marketplace and the rules of the game have strategic and tactical implications for political marketers (see Table 2.2). For instance, Canada may seem to be closer to the institutional ideal with respect to campaign finance laws than other countries, where party financing is often closely linked to big business and special interest groups, because the power and influence of money rests mostly with individual Canadians, even if regulations are constantly scrutinized for competitive loopholes. This results in parties focusing primarily on engaging with the citizenry to attract small donations and to secure a stable base of support. The idea of forcing political parties to be financially dependent on a mix of popular and public funding was directed at creating a system that was less elitist than elsewhere, particularly the United States. But the unintended consequence of such regulations is heightened party competition. Indeed, the political financing system tends to favour minor parties (Flanagan 2009). Moreover, Canadian financing rules, along with the SMP system, make it more difficult for major parties to gather pan-Canadian support.

The heightened party competition, the period of minority government, and a 24/7 media environment have pushed political parties to adopt a style of permanent campaigning. This has led to stricter, more centralized communication management (for more on this issue, see Kirsten Kozolanka's Chapter 7). Efforts are also made to sustain popular financing between elections by continuously using the list of electors to raise more money and finance market intelligence. But market research in the Canadian context is more often used to inform decisions surrounding image positioning rather than for policy development (Bernier 1991). In other words, Canadian political parties make extensive use of tactical marketing techniques, but they seem more hesitant to implement strategic ones.

This hesitation may be the residual of a traditional style of Canadian politics more focused on party image and leadership than on issues. Conversely, Canadian parties could be just too ideological to modify their policy goals. It is perhaps also merely an illustration of the risk adversity sometimes attributed to Canadian political culture (Adams 2003, 115) and concerns about the "Americanization" of politics, which are common worldwide. It is easy to see how political marketing may be associated with the

TABLE 2.2

Considerations for strategic and tactical marketing in Canada

	Strategic implications	Tactical implications
CHARACTERISTICS OF THE CANADIAN POLITICAL MARKETPLACE		
Decline of traditional cleavages	Viability of political marketing Need for local market intelligence Need for targeted policy development	Persuasion tactics Multilingual communications Use of communications technology
Partisan dealignment	Opportunity to attract opponents' supporters Risk of losing own supporters Advantage of establishing public trust	Communication of group norms and values Internal communications Emphasis on party leader in communications
Softness of political issues	Market intelligence about self and opponents Exploitation of opponents' ideological inflexibility	Emphasis on brand image, leadership competence, and personalities Negativity (e.g., regarding opponents' positioning)
Positioning	Targeting of specific elector segments that are unsatisfied and/or located in targeted ridings Micro-differentiation from opponents Willingness to shift away from median voter when faced with market opportunity Maintenance of a political brand	Conscious communication as a market leader, a challenger, a follower, or a nicher Use of database management Direct marketing and online marketing Permanent campaigning
Ideology	Balancing of ideology between internal and external markets	Internal party communication
RULES OF THE GAME		
Codes of behaviour	Emphasis by party centre on adherence to ethics Caution to avoid detection when "bending the rules" in election campaigns Exploitation of opponents' unethical tactics	Communication of more ethical practices Internal party communication Negativity (e.g., claims of opponents' improper behaviour)

▶

◀ TABLE 2.2

	Strategic implications	Tactical implications
Fundraising limits and public financing	Outreach to electors to solicit donations	Direct marketing
	Use of electoral district associations	Communication with party members
	Triage of electoral districts and emphasis on marginal ridings	Grassroots presence
		Permanent campaigning
	Market research	Get-out-the-vote (GOTV) activities
	Presence of interest groups during elections	Negativity (e.g., by interest groups)
Spending limits and declarations	Use of new techniques	Effort to avoid detection of new techniques
	Pre-campaigning	Permanent campaigning

Americanization of politicking, where political pragmatism often seems to be favoured over political conviction. One of the repeated rationales for many of the rules related to campaigning in Canada was precisely to guard against such American-style politics. This objective is, of course, not always perfectly met. For instance, campaign spending limits are thought to only increase the lag time between the development and use of marketing innovations in the United States and their implementation in Canada (Axworthy 1991).

It may be justified to argue that the actual focus on short-term political strategies may result in fewer institutionalized rewards for meaningful citizen engagement or for the development of viable policy alternatives. Indeed, it is difficult to see how an increased control over political communications or some political marketing tactics, such as negative advertisements, enhance the quality of the Canadian democracy. There might seem to be nothing to temper the perception that political actors in Canada are focused on one-upmanship and seek foremost to further their own narrow interests. Political marketing does not seem in this context to assist political parties in finding a way to address citizens' waning trust in elected officials and government that has been observed in Canada (see Nevitte 2002).

However, it needs to be stressed that political marketing techniques are not necessarily in contradiction with democratic principles. Page (2006) might be right when he notes that the minimal role of opinion research in policy development may itself be rational given the limited sophistication of mass public opinion. But, as other chapters in this book show, nuance is required when evaluating the impact of political marketing techniques as a whole on the quality of Canadian democracy. The negative or positive impact that political marketing has on democracy depends largely on the ways and intentions with which these techniques are used. Basing political decisions on market research is not wrong in itself. In fact, depending on one's conception of citizens' competence, what is perceived as a lack of political leadership and pandering to public opinion by some may be considered as greater democratic responsiveness by others. Opinion research can assist political parties and presumably other political entities to develop offers that better suit the electorate's needs and wants. If this is not always done, the reason could be because of ideological inflexibility or a lack of awareness of professional methods. Nevertheless, the complexity of the Canadian political marketplace itself should be associated with more opportunities for political marketing.

NOTES

1 For an opposing view, see Stevenson (1987).

2 This typology has been criticized both on its measurement and its conceptualization (Blake 1982).

3 In 2011, the election refunds were 50 percent of party spending and 60 percent of candidate spending. Eligible parties must have received 2 percent of the vote nationally or 5 percent of votes in their candidates' districts; eligible candidates must have received 10 percent of the vote and have spent at least 15 percent of the expenditure limit. Beginning in 2004, the same thresholds were used to calculate quarterly allowance payments from the federal government based on the number of votes that parties obtained in the previous election. Each party's annual allowance was about $2 per vote when in 2011 the federal budget stated that this subsidy would be gradually reduced until it is eliminated by 2015-16.

4 The POR reports are accessible online at http://www.porr-rrop.gc.ca.

5 This information is accessible online at http://www.tpsgc-pwgsc.gc.ca/rop-por/.

6 Provincial elections are regulated by a province's own electoral legislation and supervising organ.

7 For this reason, and because calculation formulas and dollar amounts frequently change, we are concerned only with explaining the broad parameters of election limitations. For current formulas and amounts in effect, consult the Canada Elections Act or Elections Canada.

8   In 2011, registration was required after spending $500. The third-party spending
     limit was $3,765 per electoral district or candidate and no more than $188,250
     in total.

3
The Diversity of the Canadian Political Marketplace

Elisabeth Gidengil

Canada's electoral arena spans a vast territory and is characterized by deep regional and linguistic cleavages. Indeed, a referendum on Quebec sovereignty in 1995 brought the country to the brink of breakup. Canada has experienced dramatic changes since the late 1960s. The population has grown and become much more diverse, and more of it is concentrated in Canada's largest metropolitan areas. Employment in the service sector has grown tremendously in the wake of economic restructuring and globalization, and women have moved into the paid workforce in unprecedented numbers. In few other countries have the transformations been so extensive. At the same time, Canada's party system has undergone significant transformations. One of Canada's two traditional major political parties has disappeared and new parties have come and gone, yet others have emerged and survived. And although Canadians' commitment to democratic principles remains sturdy, confidence in governments has eroded and political parties and politicians are held in low esteem.

As Yannick Dufresne and Alex Marland point out in Chapter 2, all of this makes for a challenging context for party strategists, especially for parties that aspire to govern. Multiple cross-cutting cleavages complicate the task of building a winning electoral coalition, and parties that fail to satisfy voters' wants can find themselves suffering humiliating defeats. This was the lesson of Canada's electoral earthquake in 1993, when the governing party was reduced to two seats and lost official party status. That lesson was reinforced in 2011 when the Liberal Party found itself, for the first time ever, as the third party in Parliament. At the same time, though, there are aspects of Canada's electoral arena that are conducive to the successful implementation of a market orientation. Moreover, electoral volatility provides strong incentives for parties to become more market-oriented. The 1993 election ushered in a period of Liberal dominance marked by easy Liberal victories. However, with the merger of the parties on the right to form the new Conservative Party, elections have become more competitive, with no party able to achieve a majority in the 2004, 2006, or 2008 elections. As this chapter shows, the changing dynamics of the Canadian electoral marketplace have implications for political marketers.

Case Study: The Nature of Canada's Electoral Arena

Since 1988, turnout in federal elections has dropped a massive sixteen points, reaching a historic low of 58.8 percent of registered voters in 2008. Much of the decline reflects generational replacement: young Canadians are much less likely to vote than their parents or grandparents were at the same age (Blais et al. 2002). In 2008, the estimated voter turnout rate among eighteen- to twenty-four-year-olds was only 37 percent (Elections Canada 2010). However, declining turnout may be spreading to other age groups: in 2008, the estimated drop-off in voting was even greater for older Canadians.

This steep decline in voter turnout might seem to be evidence of growing disaffection with politics and politicians, but this turns out to be only part of the story. When non-voters are asked why they did not vote, the single most important reason is typically lack of interest (Pammett and LeDuc 2003, 18). And although there are certainly expressions of negativity, loss of confidence in politics and politicians cannot explain why turnout to vote has fallen to such low levels (Blais et al. 2002). This is especially true of young Canadians, who tend to be *less* politically disaffected than older Canadians.

That said, Canadians are often cynical about politics and politicians (see Figure 3.1; also Royce Koop's discussion about political efficacy in Chapter 14). Many believe that politicians will say anything to get elected and, once elected, quickly lose touch with the people. According to the 2008 Canadian Election Study (CES), fully a quarter believe that parties hardly ever keep their election promises. Well over half doubt that the government cares much what people like them think, and there is a fairly widespread perception that the government wastes taxpayers' money. A substantial minority also believes that there are quite a few crooked people in government. Similar numbers say that there is little to choose among the political parties and that they lack a say about what the government does. Only 16 percent are very satisfied with the way democracy works in Canada; fully a quarter are either not very satisfied or not satisfied at all.

There has, however, been a decline in political disaffection since its peak in the mid-1990s. In 2008, for example, 56 percent of Canadians believed

FIGURE 3.1

Disaffection with politics and politicians

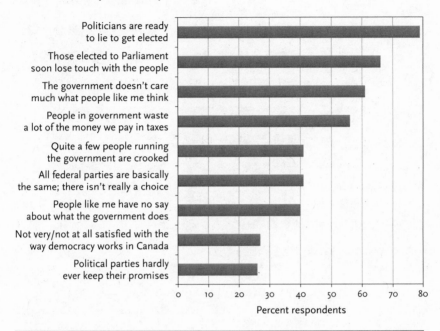

SOURCE: 2008 Canadian Election Study.

that people in government waste a lot of taxpayers' money, but that is significantly lower than the 80 percent recorded at the time of the 1993 federal election. Similarly, the perception that the government "doesn't care much what people like me think" decreased from 74 percent in 1993 to 61 percent in 2008. There is a similar pattern for the belief that those elected to Parliament soon lose touch with the people. This reinforces the point that declining turnout cannot be explained in terms of growing disaffection with politics and politicians. Indeed, satisfaction with the way democracy works in Canada as measured by the percentage of Canadians who are fairly or very satisfied has actually increased by twelve points since the question was first asked in the 1997 CES. We have to look elsewhere for an explanation of the dramatic decline in turnout.

Many Canadians are not so much turned off politics as tuned out. When the 2008 CES asked people how interested they were in politics, their average rating on a scale from zero to 10 was 6.2 for interest in the election and 5.8

FIGURE 3.2

Canadians' knowledge of politics

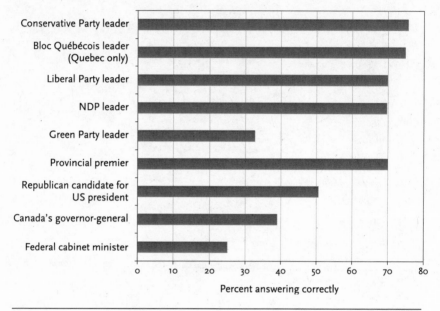

SOURCE: 2008 Canadian Election Study.

for interest in politics generally. However, one in five people rated their interest in the election at 4 or less, and this figure rose to more than one in four for politics in general. The main source of information about the election for most Canadians was television (58 percent), followed at some distance by newspapers (20 percent), radio (8 percent), and the Internet (8 percent). The average amount of attention paid to news about the election in each medium ranged, again on a zero-to-ten scale, from a mere 1.8 for news on the Internet to 5.4 for news on television.

Self-reports are subject to possible social desirability bias, and the meaning of a given rating is not necessarily the same for all respondents. Perhaps the best indicator of people's political awareness is how much they know about politics.[1] In the closing days of the 2008 campaign, fully a quarter of CES respondents were unable to name the leader of the Conservative Party, even though he was Canada's incumbent prime minister and had led the party in two previous elections (see Figure 3.2). This was the fifth election for the Bloc Québécois leader, but fully a quarter of the Quebeckers surveyed

FIGURE 3.3

Knowledge of campaign promises

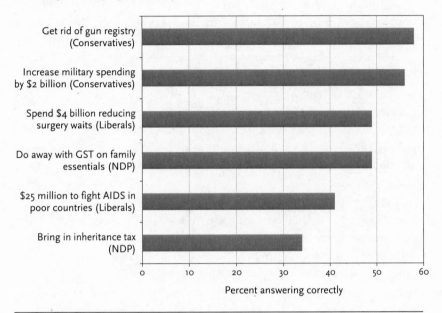

Percent answering correctly

SOURCE: 2008 Canadian Election Study.

were unable to come up with his name. The knowledge deficits are not confined to knowing party leaders' names. Almost a third of those surveyed were unable to name their provincial premier, and fully three-quarters were unable to come up with the name of a single federal cabinet minister. Only 7 percent named the federal finance minister, the person charged with charting the country's fiscal and monetary course.

This lack of political awareness is not simply a function of election fatigue as Canadians went to the polls for the third time federally in four years. Earlier studies reveal similar knowledge deficits (Fournier 2002; Gidengil et al. 2004). They also reveal that these deficits extend to party promises. At the time of the 2004 federal election, for example, there were only two campaign promises that more than half of those surveyed could associate with the correct political party, and only bare majorities got those answers right (see Figure 3.3). Moreover, many Canadians are not simply *un*informed about politics; they are *mis*informed about basic policy-relevant facts like the gap between the rich and the poor, the crime rate, and the condition of Aboriginal peoples, and this misinformation skews their policy attitudes in predictable fashion (Gidengil et al. 2004).

Declining voter turnout is often linked to declining partisanship. It is difficult to track party ties across time in Canada. Prior to the 1988 CES, the party identification question lacked an explicit option for non-identifiers, which may have inflated the proportion of identifiers. When the option "none of these" was added in 1988, the number of non-identifiers increased from 18 percent in 1984 to 35 percent. What is clear is that this figure has not increased since 1988.[2] Indeed, in 2008, only 28 percent of those surveyed answered "none." What has increased is the number of very strong identifiers, up from 13 percent in 1988 to 21 percent in 2008. These numbers suggest that the drop in voter turnout since 1988 is not attributable to partisan dealignment.

The larger point about party identification in Canada relates to the flexibility of partisan ties. Some scholars have even questioned whether party identification is meaningful in Canada. Indeed, John Meisel (1975, 67) concluded that the concept of party identification was not applicable, since it appeared to be "as volatile in Canada as the vote itself." However, the omission of an explicit "none" option in the early election studies may have induced some people who lacked meaningful ties to name the party they were voting for, making it seem as if their party identification travelled with their vote. Analyses based on the revised question wording suggest that it is difficult to make sense of vote choice in Canada without taking account of party identification (Blais et al. 2002; Gidengil et al. 2006). That said, the willingness of many Canadians to vote for another party speaks to the flexibility of their partisan ties. In the 2008 election, for example, close to a third of Liberal identifiers voted for a different party. Still, the fact that they nonetheless continued to identify themselves as Liberal confirms that party identification is not as volatile as the vote itself. Canadians have psychological attachments to parties, but their party loyalty cannot be taken for granted.

This is reflected in the volatility of elections (see Table 3.1).[3] The period from 1965 to 1980 was marked by relative stability, or what Lawrence Leduc (1984) has termed "stable dealignment." As LeDuc emphasized, however, the aggregate stability masked a good deal of individual-level volatility, and the potential was there for considerable volatility in vote shares if forces emerged to push significant numbers of voters in the same partisan direction. This potential was realized in the 1984 election and in spectacular fashion in the 1993 election, when the incumbent Progressive Conservatives saw

TABLE 3.1

Electoral volatility in Canada, 1965-2011

Election	Volatility	Election	Volatility	Election	Volatility
1965	7.80	1980	6.20	2000	8.75
1968	4.00	1984	17.35	2004	12.70
1972	7.20	1988	7.40	2006	8.55
1974	4.95	1993	39.90	2008	4.40
1979	3.30	1997	6.60	2011	14.40

NOTE: Volatility is measured using the Pedersen index (1979).

their vote share plummet from 42.9 percent to 16 percent. No less dramatic was the increase in NDP (New Democratic Party) support in Quebec in the 2011 federal election, which saw the party's share of the vote more than triple from 12.1 percent to 42.9 percent as the Bloc fell out of favour.

Another indicator of the potential for electoral volatility is the number of Canadian voters who decide how they are going to vote only once the campaign is under way. Since 1980, when the question was first asked, the figure has typically hovered around 50 percent. The 2008 election was no exception: 48 percent of voters reported that they had waited until the campaign began to make up their minds. Fully 15 percent waited until the very day of the election to decide on their vote. This figure has been steadily rising over the past three decades. According to Peter Donolo, a political strategist with Strategic Counsel and one-time chief of staff to former Liberal leader Michael Ignatieff, "The electorate has never been this volatile ... That's the real story" (quoted in *Globe and Mail*, October 6, 2009).

Voting in Canada is highly regionalized. In the 2011 election, the Conservative vote ranged from a high of 54.7 percent in the west to a low of 16.5 percent in Quebec. The NDP, meanwhile, fared best in Quebec, with 42.9 percent of the vote. The Liberal vote was regionalized as well, with more than twice as many Atlantic Canadians (29.3 percent) and Ontarians (25.3 percent) as westerners (11.9 percent) voting for the party. These regional figures mask even greater interprovincial variation, especially for the Conservatives, whose share of the vote ranged from only 16.5 percent in Quebec all the way up to 66.8 percent in Alberta.

These differences are not simply an artifact of variations in regional demographics: voters sharing the *same* social background characteristics vote differently from one region of the country to another (Gidengil et al. 1999). Regionalism reflects a variety of factors, including the tensions between the country's centre and peripheries, distinctive patterns of immigration and settlement, structural differences in regional economies, and distinctive political cultures.

The west is typically portrayed as being more conservative than other regions, both socially and economically. Quebeckers, meanwhile, are often seen as being more statist and socially progressive on issues like gender and sexual orientation. Atlantic Canadians, for their part, tend to be portrayed as socially conservative but supportive of the welfare state and government intervention in the economy given the region's heavy reliance on federal transfers. It would not do to overstate these differences, however. When it comes to explaining regional variation in vote choice, differences in the political agenda from one region to another are more important than differences in issue attitudes (Gidengil et al. 1999). Different issues tend to matter in different parts of the country. For example, when the 2008 CES asked people to rate the importance of various issues, creating jobs proved to be much more important to residents of Ontario (77 percent) and Atlantic Canada (77 percent) than to western Canadians (60 percent). Fighting crime, meanwhile, was much more important to westerners (70 percent) than to Quebeckers (53 percent), while improving social welfare programs was more of a concern for Atlantic Canadians (55 percent) than their western counterparts (40 percent).

Region trumps social class as a factor differentiating vote choice in Canada. Almost half a century ago, Robert Alford (1963, x-xi) characterized Canada as a case of "pure non-class voting": even the United States ranked higher than Canada on his class voting index. Subsequent studies have failed to refute Alford's conclusion (see Gidengil 2002). No matter how social class is measured, how political parties are classified along a left-right scale, or how class voting is measured, there is little evidence of a class cleavage.

The low level of class voting has often been attributed to a lack of ideological differentiation among the major parties. Certainly, many Canadians lack a firm grasp of basic left-right terminology. When Ronald Lambert and his colleagues (1986) set out to discover what the terms "left" and "right" meant to Canadians, they found that only 40 percent could – or would – define the terms, and many of those definitions revealed a fuzzy grasp. Despite the media attention to the fight for the right in the decade following the Progressive Conservatives' near-collapse in the 1993 election, there is little to suggest that Canadians' understanding of left-right terminology has become any clearer (Gidengil et al. 2004).

Canadians may have difficulty with the terminology, but this does not mean that ideological considerations are irrelevant to their choice of party. On the contrary, many Canadians have ideologically coherent beliefs, and these beliefs can have a substantial impact on their vote. It would be difficult to make sense of Canadians' vote choices without taking account of their beliefs about free enterprise and the appropriate balance between the state and the market or their views about gender roles and questions of morality (Blais et al. 2002; Gidengil et al. 2006; Nevitte et al. 2000). Like elections elsewhere, "Canadian elections do not take place in an ideological vacuum[;] they engage voters' competing world views" (Blais et al. 2002, 191).

These beliefs also play an important role in explaining gender differences in vote choice. Since 1997, Canada has exemplified the "modern gender gap" (Inglehart and Norris 2003): women are more likely than men to vote for the party of the left, whereas men are more likely than women to vote for the party of the right. Underpinning these gendered patterns of voting are differences in political values and beliefs: women tend to be more skeptical than men of market-based arguments, less ready to embrace closer ties with the United States, and more liberal when it comes to social mores and alternative lifestyles (Gidengil et al. 2005). However, it would not do to overstate these differences. Women may be less likely than men to vote for the party of the right, but they are still more likely to vote for the party of the right than the party of the left.

The fact that women tend to be more religious helps to explain why many remain attracted to the right. Indeed, religion has been an important factor in how Canadians vote. Traditionally, Catholics were more likely than Protestants to vote Liberal, but the Catholic-Protestant cleavage has been weakening. Canada may well be witnessing the emergence of a new religious cleavage based on Christian fundamentalism. Christians who believe that the bible is the literal word of God preferred the Alliance to the Liberals by a margin of fifteen points in 2000. By 2008, they preferred the Conservatives by a margin of almost fifty points.

This partly reflects the politicization of issues like same-sex marriage. According to conventional wisdom, issues do not play much of a role in Canadian elections, but more recent studies indicate that issue attitudes have a significant effect on vote choice and matter more than perceptions of the economy (Blais et al. 2004). There are at least two reasons why economic perceptions typically do not have much impact. First, Canada's highly decentralized federal system makes it harder for voters to attribute credit or blame to the government, and, second, perceptions of the economy are influenced by voters' partisan attachments.

Evaluations of party leaders clearly influence how people vote, but this does not necessarily translate into a strong impact on party fortunes. If one party leader is not markedly more – or less – popular than another, and if the impact of leader evaluations is similar across parties, the net effect will be small (see Blais et al. 2002). Interestingly, despite the importance of party attachments and leader evaluations, there is evidence of a personal vote in Canada: evaluations of the local candidate factor into Canadians' choice of party, especially in rural ridings (Blais et al. 2003).

HOW DOES CANADA'S ELECTORAL ARENA COMPARE WITH OTHER COUNTRIES'?
Canada is hardly alone in experiencing declining voter turnout. However, few other established Western democracies have experienced as large and consistent a decline over the past two decades. Moreover, Canada's turnout was already low, reflecting the combined effects of a single member plurality electoral system and a vast, thinly populated territory. Canada's turnout is about twenty points below the median for this group of countries (even excluding Australia and Belgium, which both have compulsory voting), and only Switzerland ranks lower.

This raises the question of whether Canadians are more politically disaffected than their counterparts in other established Western democracies. Based on data from the Comparative Study of Electoral Systems (CSES) project, Canada ranks near the bottom on three key indicators. When respondents were asked to place themselves on a five-point scale where one meant that it makes a difference who is in power and five meant that it does not make a difference, only 16 percent of Canadians placed themselves at one (see Table 3.2), compared with three times as many Swedes and Icelanders. Only Britain ranked lower than Canada. Canada also placed near the bottom on the question of whether who people vote for can make a difference to what happens. At 22 percent, Canada ranked well below the median (40 percent) and trailed far behind Portugal, Iceland, and the United States. The final indicator relates to people's perceptions of how well elections in each country do in ensuring that the views of voters are represented by majority parties. Only 40 percent of Canadians responded that elections performed quite well or very well in this regard. This put Canada just ahead of Portugal and far behind Denmark and the United States.

TABLE 3.2

Views about the workings of electoral democracy

	Who is in power makes a difference (%)	Who people vote for makes a difference (%)	Voters' views are represented (%)	Satisfaction with democracy (%)	Democracy is best form of government (%)
Australia	36	33	56	82	48
Belgium	18	15	63	70	36
Britain	14	21	49	73	35
Canada	16	22	40	71	48
Denmark	27	41	79	93	74
Finland	27	28	48	70	43
France	20	41	61	56	52
Germany	17	27	38	55	57
Iceland	52	54	55	69	68
Ireland	32	41	63	80	33
Italy	36	40	45	38	33
Netherlands	n/a	n/a	60	51	46
New Zealand	25	36	56	69	44
Norway	20	34	n/a	78	66
Portugal	46	58	39	45	26
Spain	44	40	64	78	33
Sweden	48	43	58	78	56
Switzerland	27	40	58	76	53
United States	40	45	72	78	62

SOURCE: Module Two of the Comparative Study of Electoral Systems project, http://www.cses.org/download/module2/module2.htm.

Compared with the citizens of other established Western democracies, then, Canadians appear to be disaffected with politics, but their disaffection does not run deep. This is apparent when we turn to more general views about the workings of democracy. Canada is at the median in terms of overall satisfaction with democracy: 71 percent of Canadians were fairly satisfied or very satisfied with the way democracy works in Canada, well behind Denmark and Australia but well ahead of Portugal and Italy. Canada is also at the median when it comes to agreeing with the statement that "democracy may

Table 3.3

Affective engagement in politics

	Politics is very/ somewhat important (%)	Somewhat/very interested in politics (%)
Australia	49	58
Britain	40	44
Canada	49	53
Finland	28	38
France	48	37
Germany	42	62
Italy	38	37
Netherlands	46	51
New Zealand	41	56
Norway	58	77
Spain	29	32
Sweden	63	60
Switzerland	57	72
United States	51	59

SOURCE: World Values Survey, 2005-6 wave, www.worldvaluessurvey.org.

have problems, but it's better than any other form of government," though barely half of Canadians expressed strong agreement (compared to three-quarters of Danes).

As we saw above, it is not so much political disaffection as a lack of interest in politics that is keeping many Canadians from voting. However, Canadians are not distinctive when it comes to how much they care about politics. Data from the 2005-6 wave of the World Values Survey (WVS) indicate that Canada ranks close to the median for established Western democracies (see Table 3.3). This is the case whether we look at the perceived salience of politics in people's lives or at their level of political interest. One Canadian in two considers politics to be at least somewhat important in his or her life, and a similar proportion have at least some interest in politics. Still, this leaves Canada trailing countries like Norway, Sweden, and Switzerland.

Political parties often serve as a lightning rod for political disaffection. Certainly, there is a pervasive lack of confidence in political parties, with barely a quarter of Canadians professing much confidence (see Table 3.4).

TABLE 3.4

Orientations toward political parties

	Great deal/ quite a lot of confidence (%)	Close to a political party (%)	Party representing views (%)
Australia	14	84	83
Belgium	n/a	34	n/a
Britain	18	35	73
Canada	23	38	69
Denmark	n/a	50	84
Finland	28	47	64
France	16	57	59
Germany	13	37	58
Iceland	n/a	54	64
Ireland	n/a	28	77
Italy	16	41	41
Netherlands	23	38	72
New Zealand	15	56	74
Norway	29	41	82
Portugal	n/a	42	45
Spain	28	61	74
Sweden	33	49	78
Switzerland	26	42	86
United States	15	56	74

SOURCE: World Values Survey, 2005-6 wave, www.worldvaluessurvey.org, and Module Two of the Comparative Study of Electoral Systems project, http://www.cses.org/download/module2/module2.htm.

This figure is not atypically low, though. Indeed, Canada ranks a little above the median in this regard. However, Canada's ranking drops when we look at the prevalence of party attachments: only 38 percent of Canadians feel close to any political party. And although a solid majority of Canadians indicate that there is a party that represents their views, Canada's parties are falling short compared with some of their counterparts.

Flexible party ties create the potential for electoral volatility and, relative to other established Western democracies, Canadian elections have been characterized by a fairly high degree of volatility in party vote shares. According to Susan Scarrow's calculations (2010), only France, New Zealand, and Italy rank higher than Canada in terms of average volatility for the period from 1978 to 2003.[4]

Mark Franklin (1992) has characterized Canada as a "historical decline" country, where social cleavages have effectively ceased to structure vote choice. He suggests that Canada, like the United States, was "at the forefront of a development that appears to be ubiquitous" (390). This certainly applies to the class cleavage. Russell Dalton (2010) has looked at the relationship between left-right self-placements and various social background characteristics. Canada ranks near the bottom of the list of established Western democracies. With the exception of Sweden and Finland, social class is only weakly related to left-right orientations in most of these countries; in Canada, the relationship is non-existent.[5] However, the structuring role of religious denomination and region are equally apparent from these data. Indeed, Canada ranks second only to the United States when it comes to the salience of religious cleavages. And regional tensions smashed Canada's traditional two-plus-one party system in the early 1990s.

As noted above, perceptions of economic conditions do not typically have a strong impact on Canadians' choice of party. Canada is not exceptional in this respect. Timothy Hellwig's analysis (2010) of economic voting indicates that the impact of economic perceptions in Canada is only slightly below the average for a number of established Western democracies.[6] Variations in the issue agenda across countries make it difficult to compare the impact of issues on vote choice. However, a study of eleven Canadian, British, and American elections between 1987 and 2001 indicates that issues typically mattered more than the economy for vote choice and party fortunes alike in all three countries (Blais et al. 2004).

The State of Political Marketing in Canada

The Canadian electoral market offers both opportunities and challenges for a political party that attempts to adopt a political market orientation. With as many as half of voters making up their minds during the campaign, there are strong incentives to adopt a market orientation. These so-called late deciders are the voters who are going to be most susceptible to persuasion. They are typically fairly interested in the campaign, and they pay at least a modicum of attention to media coverage. At the same time, they are less likely than early deciders to have strong partisan attachments. As such, they are likely to be both reachable and persuadable. And there is certainly evidence that the vote intentions of campaign deciders are affected by campaign events and media coverage (Fournier et al. 2004). Using market intelligence to understand the needs and wants of late deciders – and modifying their product offering accordingly – could have a significant electoral payoff.

The flexibility of Canadians' party ties offers further inducements to pursue a market orientation. As Jesper Strömbäck (2010) notes, the fewer strong partisans there are, the stronger the incentives for political parties to become market-oriented. When party attachments are flexible, parties have a realistic prospect of inducing defections, provided that they can design a product offering that addresses the needs and wants of those most likely to consider voting for another party. The prospects for successful implementation of a market-oriented strategy are further enhanced by the fact that about 40 percent of Canadians either have weak party attachments or no attachments.

Canadian parties also have more scope to reposition themselves than their counterparts in countries where the level of class voting is higher and the left-right placement of parties is more salient (Lees-Marshment, Strömbäck, and Rudd 2010; Strömbäck 2010). Moreover, their ability to reposition – or even rebrand – themselves without losing credibility with the voters is helped by low levels of political awareness. Substantial numbers of Canadians do not know such simple facts as the names of the party leaders; even fewer are aware of where the political parties have been standing on the issues of the day.

Conditions in the Canadian electoral market are certainly conducive to a market orientation, but any party aspiring to be market-oriented also faces some important constraints. One such constraint relates to partisanship. The emphasis on the flexibility of Canadians' partisan ties should not lead us to overlook the fact that each party has a core of strong partisans. Parties cannot afford to take the loyalty of these partisans for granted. A party that goes too far in its efforts to reposition itself risks losing the votes of its core constituency. Whereas strong partisans typically show their displeasure with their party by simply not voting at all (Blais et al. 2001), those with more flexible ties are apt to vote for another party. Either way, a party that seeks to steal votes from another party risks losing some of its own voters if it moves too far from its accustomed position.

A second constraint relates to the low level of political awareness. True, this reduces the risk of losing credibility as a result of repositioning, but it also means that a party must work harder to reach the voters who are the

Figure 3.4

Implications for political marketing in Canada

- Targeting late deciders will pay off – these voters are both reachable and persuadable.

- Flexible partisan ties create opportunities for successful implementation of a political market orientation.

- Communication strategies have to take account of low levels of political awareness and high levels of political cynicism.

- The heterogeneous nature of the electorate means that sophisticated market segmentation techniques are required in order to maximize a party's vote share.

---

target of this repositioning. This task is made more difficult by pervasive cynicism about politics and politicians (see Mortimore 2003). Voters who believe that political parties rarely keep their promises, that politicians lie to get elected, and that, once elected, MPs soon lose touch with the people are not going to be very receptive to what the parties have to say, despite their efforts to maximize voter satisfaction by paying attention to what voters actually need and want.

Finally, the heterogeneity of the Canadian electorate complicates the task of political marketing. As noted above, the vote is highly regionalized, and political priorities differ from one part of the country to another. That people who are otherwise similar may vote differently depending on where they live points to the importance of market segmentation. At the same time, other cleavages are dealigning or realigning. Catholics, immigrants, and members of visible minorities were until the 2004 election the bedrock of Liberal support, but their loyalty to the party has been eroding steadily. As Lees-Marshment and her colleagues (2010) observe, the weakening of traditional voting blocs puts a premium on the use of sophisticated market segmentation techniques to target particular subgroups. See Figure 3.4.

Implications for the Quality of Democracy

The impact of political marketing on Canadian democracy will depend very much on how marketing techniques are used. If the parties simply use these techniques to hard-sell their "product," the relationship between voters and parties is unlikely to improve. If, on the other hand, parties put voters' needs and wants at the centre of their activities, the prognosis may be more positive.

Take voter turnout. When non-voters are queried about their reasons for not voting, lack of attraction to any of the parties or candidates and not caring about the issues both emerge as important, along with a general lack of interest in the election or in politics more generally (Pammett and LeDuc 2003, 65). This suggests that there is considerable potential for a market orientation to combat political apathy.

A market orientation could also help to counter the pervasive disaffection with politics and politicians (see Mortimore 2003). Canadians' frustration with political parties has its roots in failed interest intermediation (Gidengil et al. 2001). This partly reflects a perceived lack of differentiation on the issues. The less difference voters see among the parties, the more negative their attitudes are toward political parties in general. A more important factor, though, is a perceived lack of issue representation. If no party is perceived to be close to the voter, parties in general tend to be viewed more negatively. But by far the most important factor is whether the incumbent party is perceived to be close or not on the issues that matter.

This necessarily qualifies any optimistic assessment of the potential for a market orientation to re-engage voters who are apathetic about politics and/or disaffected with the political process. The regionalization of the vote, combined with the dynamics of multi-partyism in a first-past-the-post winner-take-all electoral system, means that many Canadians lack representation in the caucus of the governing party. If the governing party pays lip service only to the market orientation as a way of outpolling its rivals, voters may end up feeling even more cynical about politics and politicians. And even if the party is sincere in adopting this orientation, the constraints of governing may make it difficult to deliver on its promises, and voters will end up being disillusioned.

Indeed, it is far from clear whether adopting a market orientation would strengthen or weaken Canadian democracy. In principle, by placing citizens first, political marketing should engage citizens more actively in the political process, reduce elite domination, and enhance responsiveness. In practice, the benefits may be much harder to realize. For example, as Canada becomes ever more a community of minorities, the potential importance of practices such as market segmentation can hardly be overstated. At the same time, though, market segmentation carries the risk of leading to "a division in society: those to whom politics belongs and those whom politics has abandoned" (Lilleker 2005a, 23). If so, non-target groups are likely to become disengaged, if not alienated, from the political process. Heather Savigny

(2008b, 41) makes the point well: "If political wants are not satisfied through the formal political process, then there is no reason to assume the public will take part in that process." And in a context of low voter turnout, political marketing may enable a minority of voters to achieve a degree of influence out of all proportion to their numbers.

The use of political marketing can also create unrealistic expectations. A true market orientation requires that parties focus on citizens' needs as well as their wants, but what citizens need may not necessarily be what they want. If parties are too market-driven, needs may be sacrificed to wants, but driving the market in citizens' best long-term interests requires very careful use of market intelligence and effective communication strategies. This is especially true of a country like Canada that is characterized by deep regional and linguistic cleavages. The price of failure could be high.

NOTES

1 We cannot track knowledge levels across time because of differences in both question wording and election context.

2 The figures cited here are based on the campaign surveys.

3 Volatility is measured using the Pedersen index (1979), which is equal to the net percentage of voters who changed their votes between elections. It is computed by summing the absolute values of all gains and all losses and dividing the total by two. For 2004, the calculation for the Conservative Party is based on the combined Progressive Conservative and Alliance vote shares in 2000. The threshold for inclusion in the index is a minimum vote share of 2 percent. Pedersen reports an average score of 8.1 for thirteen European countries for the period from 1948 to 1977.

4 Spain and the Netherlands ranked only slightly below Canada. The other countries in the ranking are Australia, Belgium, Britain, Finland, Germany, Italy, Norway, Portugal, Sweden, Switzerland, and the United States.

5 Dalton's data are taken from Module Two of the CSES. Although the limited understanding of left-right terminology in Canada warrants caution in interpreting these results, the pattern of findings mirrors the weakness of the class cleavage in voting and the strength of religious and regional cleavages.

6 His data come from CSES Module One. The comparison countries are Australia, Belgium, Britain, Denmark, Germany, Iceland, New Zealand, Norway, Portugal, Spain, Sweden, Switzerland, and the United States.

PART 2

Political Parties and Institutions

4
Amateurs versus Professionals: The 1993 and 2006 Canadian Federal Elections

Alex Marland

This chapter explores political marketing in the new party system that emerged in the 1993 Canadian federal election vis-à-vis the next change of party government in 2006.[1] It treats political marketing as an organization's consideration of market intelligence to inform its political strategy and tactics, particularly for advocacy or electioneering purposes. As this comparison of cases will indicate, the competitive need in Canadian politics for informed decisions has increased with the affordability of ever more sophisticated research and communications technology.

There are a number of indicators that we might look for to establish political parties' use of marketing research in the design of election strategy and its tactical implementation. Gibson and Römmele (2001), Plasser (2009), and Strömbäck (2007) have identified a range of characteristics that roughly fall in line with the product, sales, and market(ing) orientations described by Lees-Marshment (2001b). When these typologies are customized into a political management format (see Table 4.1), the distinctive nature of the various inputs, processes, and outputs of political marketing become clearer.[2] They illustrate that, in the past, competitive parties relied on strong local organizations and personal contact until the emergence of the mass media increased the authority of the party hierarchy. Today's professional campaigns utilize technologies that enable the maintenance and analysis of sophisticated datasets, including detailed election results; ongoing interactions with targeted segments of the electorate via direct mail, telephone banks, and online media; and national decision making where control is centralized in the party leadership and political consultants but which is still responsive to local outfits. In labelling campaign organizations as amateur, semi-professional, and professional, we must bear in mind that the descriptors of each category are constantly evolving (Negrine and Lilleker 2002). For instance, some activities that were innovative in the 1993 campaign, such as a war room or quick response messaging, were standard practice by the 2006 election. The same

Table 4.1

Types of political campaigns by early 2000s standards[1]

	Amateur	Semi-professional	Professional
Ideology	Strong	Mainstream	Right of centre
Preparations	Short term, ad hoc	Long term	Permanent campaign
Decision making	Local-centric, party leader and staff	National-centric, party campaign managers and external communications experts	Local-/national-centric, bifurcation, special party units, specialized political consultants
Resources	Volunteer labour, low budget	Capital-intensive, increasing spending	Spiralling spending
Market intelligence	Meetings	*Polls, focus groups*	*Computer databases, opposition research*
Targeting	Loyal partisans, cleavage- and group-based, stable voting behaviour	Loyal and floating partisans, rising volatility	*Consumers, issue-based, highly volatile voting behaviour*
Positioning	Ideological, party messages	Persuasion, spin, sound bites, image management	*Product adjustment, issue-specific, micro messages*
Strategy	Interpersonal, unprofessional, mobilization	Mediated, indirect, converting and mobilizing	*Marketed, targeted, continuous, interactive*
Tactics[2]	Print media, posters, rallies, door knocking, leafleting, radio	National TV spots, broadcast TV news coverage and spots, colour print adverts, mass direct mailings	*TV narrowcasting, targeted direct mail, telemarketing, continuous campaigning*
Execution	Error-prone	Bureaucratic	*Military-like efficiency*

NOTES:

1 Indicators of market orientation in italics.

2 Internet tactics have been omitted due to the evolving nature and rapid diffusion of technology; see Chapter 12 by Tamara Small for examples.

SOURCE: Modified from Table 1 in Gibson and Römmele (2001, 34); Table 3.1 in Plasser (2009, 26); Figure 1 in Strömbäck (2007, 52); and Figure 1 in Lees-Marshment (2001a, 697).

evolution of standards will occur in subsequent campaigns, especially with respect to technological change. The components of Table 4.1 therefore provide an illustrative point of reference and a conceptual framework for differentiating between types of political campaigns.

Case Study: Political Marketing in the 1993 and 2006 Canadian General Elections

One overarching truth about Canadian politics is that although amateur parties are unlikely to form government, they may, in a public atmosphere of regional tensions, achieve better results than a more professional party. The NDP breakthrough in 2011, when it grew from a single seat in Quebec to fifty-nine seats despite some of their candidates not campaigning in their ridings, is the latest example.

The 1993 election has become a classic case of the significance of the single member plurality (SMP) electoral system in Canada (see Table 4.2). It marked a breakthrough for niche products that specialized in serving the needs of a defined market: the two regional parties that had previously only elected Members of Parliament in by-elections. In 1993, the Reform Party, which did not run candidates in Quebec, executed a model amateur campaign and won forty-eight of the sixty seats it contested in Alberta and British Columbia. The Bloc Québécois, which fielded candidates only in Quebec, also operated an amateur campaign and won fifty-four of Quebec's seventy-five seats. Because of its geographic niche specialization, the Bloc has been a rare case of a Canadian party being mentioned in political marketing literature (Collins and Butler 2002; Marland 2005; O'Shaughnessy 2002). Like Reform, its origins and initial success can be found in the anger associated with the failure of Brian Mulroney's constitutional accords, but after the 1995 Quebec sovereignty referendum the Bloc's product began to evolve with its market's preferences. Its durability, sometimes linked to generous state financing (Young, Sayers, and Jansen 2007), has displaced parties challenging to form a majority government; however, its gradual failure to stay in tune with the needs and wants of the Quebec electoral marketplace eventually led to a dramatic collapse in 2011.

By comparison, in 1993 the market-leading Progressive Conservative (PC) Party and the traditional market follower, the New Democratic Party, were established national organizations with access to customized opinion research, but they failed to elect enough members (twelve) to even achieve official party status in the House of Commons. Whereas these parties were

TABLE 4.2

Major parties' results in the 1993 and 2006 Canadian federal elections

Party	1993 Leader	Seats	Vote (%)	2006 Leader	Seats	Vote (%)
Reform	Preston Manning	52	19	–	–	–
Progressive Conservative	Kim Campbell	2	16	–	–	–
Conservative	–	–	–	Stephen Harper	124	36
Liberal	Jean Chrétien	177	41	Paul Martin	103	30
NDP	Audrey McLaughlin	9	7	Jack Layton	29	17
Bloc Québécois	Lucien Bouchard	54	14*	Gilles Duceppe	51	10**

NOTES: Vote data are rounded; * 49.3% in Quebec; ** 42% in Quebec

unable to defend their market share, the Liberal Party, as the main market challenger, operated a semi-professional campaign that resulted in leader Jean Chrétien forming a majority government. The party system evolved a decade later when the PC Party merged with Reform's successor to become the Conservative Party of Canada.[3] After this brand repositioning, the Conservatives operated a textbook professional campaign in 2006 and became Canada's governing party after nearly thirteen years of Liberal rule (see André Turcotte's explanation in Chapter 5).

When the indicators presented in Table 4.1 are loosely applied to these cases, it seems that only new or fringe protest parties engage in amateur campaigns, though the grassroots charm of regional outfits can upstage more institutionalized competitors. But the failings of governing parties, such as the 1993 Tories and the 2006 Liberals, which have extensive access to state-sponsored market intelligence, is a reminder that market data matters little if the party cannot or does not respond to it, for as O'Shaughnessy (2002, 210) has observed, political marketing is merely a tool that is "seldom alone a panacea." As this chapter illustrates, a market challenger that is ready to form the government exhibits professionalism in its use of market intelligence and targeting; an outgoing market leader is likely to be semi-professional in the areas of ideology, preparations, positioning, and execution; and market followers and nichers can exemplify a wide variety of marketing characteristics.

MARKET INTELLIGENCE

A Canadian political party's use of market intelligence reflects its ideological flexibility and the priority it places on using such data for informing communications decisions. In 1993, within the Reform Party, the Bloc, and the NDP, there were suspicions of polling-driven policy development. Reform's most active supporters wanted "a grassroots party in which the members would control organization, policy, even strategy" (Flanagan 2001, 629). It purchased basic survey data from a Toronto research company and marginally supplemented this with customized surveys that could be administered inexpensively by local volunteers (Ellis 2005; Ellis and Archer 1994). Literature about the Bloc Québécois rarely mentions the party's use of market intelligence, possibly because its core product is so well known (i.e., to work toward Quebec sovereignty). We do know that it has often shared resources with its provincial counterpart, the Parti Québécois (PQ), which endorsed future leader Gilles Duceppe as a Bloc candidate in a federal by-election only after it had considered its pollster's findings (Bernard 1994; Carty, Cross, and Young 2000).

The NDP has gradually professionalized its operations. The party's experiment with decision-making inclusiveness failed in 1993 because, by integrating party executives, it was difficult to break away from ideological priorities. Its American pollster, whose understanding of Canadian politics was criticized internally despite contributing to the party's best-ever result in 1988, was replaced with a Canadian pollster, who became a member of a pan-Canadian steering committee of fifteen to twenty inner strategists, which included representatives of the Canadian Labour Congress. Polling was administered throughout the campaign, particularly in targeted ridings, and was used to search for salient messaging, while focus groups were conducted to test advertising and messages. But by opting to emphasize free trade in 1993 in order to appeal to its labour supporters, the NDP ignored intelligence indicating that this issue was passé, and this contributed to serious internal disputes over personnel, positioning, and strategy (Gosselin and Soderlund 1999; Whitehorn 1994). By 2006, the NDP's election planning committee had grown to forty people, including a representative of the Canadian Labour Congress, but a smaller sixteen-person group, which included a media and a polling consultant, met daily during the campaign and was in regular contact with the party's media headquarters. In the pre-campaign period, a survey was administered in forty targeted ridings, including almost all incumbent seats. During the campaign, in addition to administering limited polls, the party's pollster tested slogans, messaging, and advertising in focus groups (Whitehorn 2006).

The most successful campaign war room in Canadian history was arguably the Liberals' in 1993. To defend the party and destabilize its opponents, a "task force" of eight staffers, modelled after Bill Clinton's rapid response team, collected and disseminated intelligence about their opponents (Kinsella 2001; Kippen 2000). Select information from this database of statistics, voting records, and public statements was provided to candidates and reporters, sometimes anonymously. The communications function of "oppo" (opposition research) nicely complemented the party's market research. Its decision-making structure leaned on advertising professionals and a party pollster who met regularly with Chrétien. Polling data were used to supplement existing market insights that had been collected via internal discussions and through a "thinkers' conference," which would later be emulated by leader Michael Ignatieff in 2010. Liberal incumbents were provided with demographic analyses of polling data to assist in local voter contact operations.

As these examples suggest, usually not even all members of the inner circle of a Canadian political party have access to proprietary market insights. This nucleus tends to comprise less than a dozen people, including strategists, a fundraiser, an organizer, media personnel, a personal assistant, a pollster, and an advertising director (Noel 2007). Kim Campbell's PCs commissioned considerable polling and focus group research, but the results tended to be guarded by a handful of strategists. One of the Harper Conservatives' strategists, Patrick Muttart, was a political marketer who was the link between the party centre and its virtual advertising agency, and who made informed decisions by "segmenting the electoral marketplace, strategic positioning, intensive research of voters through surveys and focus groups, use of television to frame issues, and micro-messaging to target voter groups" (Ellis and Woolstencroft 2006, 71; see also Chapters 5 to 7). By comparison, Paul Martin's Liberal campaign director held the dual role of the campaign's pollster, which surely encumbered analytical objectivity.

TARGETING, POSITIONING, AND STRATEGY

Canadian political parties tend to use opinion research to achieve their objectives rather than to foremost deliver what electors want (Marland 2005; Paré and Berger 2008). They discuss diverting tactical resources away from partisans and safe seats and toward winnable ridings and persuadable elector segments, a seats triage approach that is simply pragmatism forced by competitive necessity, especially in periods of minority governance (Flanagan

2010a). Campaigns that are preoccupied with partisans are more sales-oriented than are those of parties that see electors as consumers, which focus on issues, and which operate within a highly volatile electoral market. A party that is ideological and which seeks to persuade voters of its positions is less market-oriented than a party that is willing to adjust its product, that is issue-specific, and that engages in micro-messaging. Likewise, a party whose strategy is centred on mobilizing at the grassroots level and/or that prioritizes converting opponents into supporters is less modern than is a market-oriented campaign that is targeted, continuous, and interactive. However, during an election campaign, all Canadian political parties engage in short-term sales, with an emphasis on assessing competitors' current strengths and weaknesses and selecting what to attack and what to avoid.

A handful of partisans write a Canadian political party's election platform. The authors are members of, or report to, the leader's inner circle and emphasize the party membership's ideological preferences but temper these with domestic market intelligence about the electorate and cost estimates of the pledges. The crafting of this important campaign product involves reflecting on ideas generated in policy conventions, much like a publicly traded business considers the concerns expressed at a shareholders' meeting, and its own perceptions of the consumer marketplace. These might be tested using public opinion research. For instance, the Reform Party's socially and fiscally conservative policies, such as opposition to bilingualism, support for plebiscites, and a commitment to deficit reduction, were initiated and ratified by delegates at assemblies. The Chrétien Liberals likewise had detailed policy proposals, but theirs were carefully designed to appeal to the median voter while balancing competing left-right ideologies within the party. These were publicly presented in a red book that was inspired by British Conservative Party manifestos. The document became a media prop symbolizing the party's competence on economic issues, and it conveyed a credible product that helped to attract displaced PC supporters concerned about national unity (Gosselin and Soderlund 1999; Kippen 2000; McLaughlin 1994). The red book set the standard for future domestic campaigns; previously, such documents had rarely been instrumentalized so openly in Canadian politics.

This product development contrasted sharply with Campbell's PC Party, which prioritized speechwriting over policy development despite a need to distance itself from some aspects of Mulroney's record (Woolstencroft 1994). Likewise, in 2006, the governing party was out of ideas, whereas the official opposition had well-developed policies. The Martin Liberals made pre-campaign announcements of massive spending commitments and tax cuts, as governing parties tend to do. Yet, their manifesto was underwhelming. During the leaders' debates, Martin attempted to create a policy wedge with the Conservatives by announcing that his party would remove the federal government's eligibility to use the notwithstanding clause of the Charter of Rights and Freedoms, but this merely substantiated suspicions that policy was being invented on the fly.

By comparison, the Harper Conservatives' core policies were a mainstream form of conservatism that had been endorsed at a 2005 convention where party delegates had been "in a mood to vote for electoral success, not doctrinal purity" (Flanagan 2007a, 205). As also mentioned in other chapters in this volume, Muttart, the Conservatives' political marketer, proceeded to analyze primary research to develop strategies drawn from secondary research that had identified international cases of conservatives appealing to the middle class: the 1968 Richard Nixon Republicans, the 1979 Margaret Thatcher Conservatives, the 1994 Newt Gingrich Republicans, and the 1996 John Howard Liberals. It was this Australian case that inspired the Conservatives to develop policies that would appeal to working people, families, married women, and Roman Catholics while cultivating support among ethnic and visible minority groups (Flanagan 2007a, 2010a; Wells 2006). This involved stereotyping and giving names – such as Dougie, Eunice, and Zoë – to fictional voters whose socio- and geo-demographic profiles indicated their propensity for voting Conservative. Policies were designed to appeal to residents in middle-class suburbs who had conservative leanings, particularly those in the 905 area code region around Toronto. This produced a sharp contrast between the Liberals' macro policies and the Tories' micro-targeting: whereas the Liberals advocated a national daycare program, the Conservatives pledged monthly $100 cheques to parents of young children; and whereas the Liberals had reduced income tax rates, the Conservatives pledged to reduce the maligned point-of-sale goods and services tax (GST). Toward the end of the campaign, the Conservatives' policies were packaged into conservative themes (accountability, tax relief, tough on crime) and progressive themes (child care, health care) under the general umbrella of the five priorities of a future Conservative government.

That year, the NDP also targeted soft Liberal supporters, but from the left flank, as it had in past election campaigns: those who were most likely to be attracted to the NDP label, to leader Jack Layton, and to policies supporting strong social programs – especially health care. As with Reform in 1993 and the Conservatives in 2006, the NDP has likewise positioned itself with a tinge of populism as advocates of ordinary Canadians' concerns. In

2006, its manifesto was designed by the aforementioned sixteen-person election planning subcommittee, which consulted resolutions at party conventions and which circulated a draft version to the full committee and to caucus immediately before the campaign. Although the NDP platform contained the expected calls to strengthen public health care and education, it sought credibility with pledges of no new taxes or deficit financing that are uncharacteristic of a party espousing democratic socialism. This hinted at its evolution into an unexpected market challenger in the 2011 campaign.

In 1993, the Bloc Québécois promoted an anti-establishment position that included demands for devolution of Ottawa's authority. But rather than narrowcasting to francophone Quebeckers, the Bloc brokered conventional policies of traditional parties, such as advocacy for deficit reduction while seeking to protect the welfare state, so that soft nationalists and disenchanted federalists were not frightened off by ideological dogma (Bernard 1994). By 2006, the party's regionally concentrated brokerage development could be seen in its strategy to appeal to recent immigrants and to attack the Liberals. The Bloc released a recycled symbolic centre-left platform that foremost called for more money for Quebec (Bélanger and Nadeau 2006, 127), and its slogan of *"Ici, c'est le Bloc"* (Here, it's the Bloc) conveyed a political uniqueness in Quebec and a classic in-group/out-group social conformity. This lack of brand renewal reoccurred in the 2008 and 2011 campaigns and cultivated a market demand for Quebeckers to experiment with representation by the Layton New Democrats.

TACTICS AND EXECUTION

All parties employ elements of the promotion mix, such as advertising, direct marketing, media relations, and e-marketing, but only a market-oriented party executes a strategy of precision by continuously employing TV narrowcasting, targeted direct mail, and telemarketing. Amateurs are likely to be prone to mistakes, and semi-professional campaigns may be encumbered by bureaucratic structures. Conversely, a professional political marketing organization operates with military-like efficiency.

In political advertising literature, Canada is known for a single notorious blunder: the PCs' TV spots that profiled Jean Chrétien's facial paralysis (Gosselin and Soderlund 1999; Kinsella 2001; McLaughlin 1994; O'Shaughnessy 2002; Woolstencroft 1994). Focus group research had failed to predict public outrage over what have since become known as the Chrétien face ads. Anger filled talk radio airwaves, and callers decried the attack ads as a nefarious American tactic; even some of the PCs' own candidates issued apologies. The controversy led to stress between the PCs' political consultants, who believed the ads were weakening support for the Liberals, and its leadership circle, which publicly apologized and discontinued the ads. What is less commonly known is that the Liberal Party had earlier addressed Chrétien's facial paralysis in a pre-emptive defence-positioning manoeuvre by using self-deprecating humour in advertisements in Quebec and that the Liberal Party coordinated much of the negative response by urging partisans to express public outrage. But this type of hubris displayed by a governing party and egged on by an opponent seeking to exploit an opponent's gaffe worked against the Liberals in 2006 when their own negative advertising backfired. An ad claiming that a Conservative policy would put armed soldiers in cities was posted online, and the resulting news coverage, bloggers' commentary, and talk radio banter portrayed the Liberals as "confused, unorganized, and inept" (Clarkson 2006, 50; also Wells 2006).

A significant and continuing change in Canadian political advertising is that targeting ethnic groups means communicating in their mother tongue. Given the nature of their targeted seats in 2006, some of the NDP's broadcast advertising was in French, Chinese, Korean, and Punjabi. The party circulated multilingual issue pamphlets, as did the Canadian Labour Congress, and postcards that were customized to reflect regional priorities, which were distributed by its sales force during door-to-door voter identification. The NDP also targeted strategic voters by distributing colour-coded "smart cards" to houses that displayed signage supporting NDP opponents; for instance, a house with a Conservative sign received a blue flyer advising that only the NDP could prevent a Liberal victory in that riding (Whitehorn 2006, 105).

Regional advertising is also a reality of Canadian politics. Like Reform in 1993, the Bloc Québécois benefited from the free national TV time provided under the Canada Elections Act. Its media campaign was restricted to Quebec, including television advertisements positioning the Bloc as a team of people with new ideas (Cunningham 1999), whereas Reform purchased regional ads outside Quebec. In 2006, the Bloc avoided the sovereignty issue in its broadcast ads by featuring feel-good testimonials from Quebec citizens or reminding electors of the Liberal sponsorship scandal. Pamphlets highlighting its immigration policies were circulated in targeted Montreal seats, and newspaper advertising with the headline *"On ne laissera pas Calgary décider pour le Québec"* (We won't let Calgary make decisions for Quebec) warned Quebeckers that Harper would prioritize western Canada's interests (Bélanger and Nadeau 2006). The realities of regionalism were also reflected in Martin's Liberal campaign, which had relatively independent organizational units in

Quebec, Ontario, and British Columbia to coordinate localized messaging of national policies (Clarkson 2006; Wells 2006).

Direct marketing has evolved considerably in the business world, and its political application is no exception. The 1993 campaign marked "the single most important technological innovation in Canadian politics" in a century, for this was the first time that Elections Canada provided political parties with an electronic dataset of the list of electors (Kippen 2000, 10; see also Chapter 2). This would come to revolutionize the ability of campaigns to organize, encourage the redirection of resources into the development of campaign management software, and reduce the need for constituency staffing. Within one electoral cycle, the Liberal Party would develop electoral list manager software to integrate Statistics Canada socio-demographic data, as well as voter canvass information inputted by a constituency campaign, so that customized direct mail could be generated (Carty, Cross, and Young 2000, 202). The use of such electronic data would later be mastered by the Harper Conservatives, whose constituent information management system (CIMS) database was used for direct voter contact and fundraising (Flanagan 2007a; also Young, Sayers, and Jansen 2007). The CIMS was an evolution of the Republican direct-mail fundraising techniques imported by the PC Party in the 1980s and an adaptation of Reform's fundraising letters, membership sales, and telemarketing in the 1990s. It was also emblematic of national parties' efforts to coordinate their candidates' use of automated telephone surveys and voter identification telemarketing, often on a regional basis (Marland 2008).

The contrast in campaign technology is significant. In 1993, to obtain a copy of the red book, electors needed to visit a Liberal candidate's headquarters or else view it in text form on Freenet. An innovative response at the time was to copy a Clinton campaign tactic of inserting a toll-free phone number within advertising so that the document could be mailed to the thousands of callers (Kippen 2000). In the Liberal war room, investments were made in dedicated lines for fax machines; broadcast faxing was used to issue customized information to targeted media outlets and messaging to candidates; voicemail was introduced on telephones; email was used between central offices and the leader's tour; and basic text such as candidate biographies was posted online. The party opted against predictive dialling because it was too expensive and, in electoral districts, computers and technical skills were sporadic. The difficulty that a left-of-centre party has with adopting technology and professional techniques is further illustrated by the 1993 NDP. Although it was labour representatives who introduced that party to computer-assisted telephone interviewing software, an internal furor emerged over a Clinton-inspired town hall video being edited in the United States, which resulted in a communication staffer's resignation (Whitehorn 1994).

By 2006, all parties had reasonably sophisticated websites. They included leader and candidate information; platforms and opposition research; donation requests; news releases; and podcasting, blogs, and Really Simple Syndication (RSS). The Liberal site was deemed to be the best due to its content, design, and transparency, but like all of the Canadian parties' sites, its interactivity was poor, and the overall quality lagged behind those in Britain and the United States (*Hillwatch* 2006). Controversy over a Liberal official's blog and the online leak of the party platform are examples of the online integration of offline politics; Tamara Small describes others in Chapter 12.

The art of political media relations is as much an exercise in rigidity as it is in creativity. As might be expected of an amateur campaign with momentum, in 1993, Reform earned news media coverage of the leader's tour, and its volunteers coordinated lawn sign delivery, mass waving at intersections, neighbourhood coffee parties, and the distribution of millions of pieces of photocopied literature (Ellis 2005; Ellis and Archer 1994; Gosselin and Soderlund 1999). But occasionally the party was thrown off message by an unscripted comment, such as a candidate making a racist remark, which heightened the need for candidate screening and controlled media management. Given the destabilizing nature of ad hoc remarks in 2006, the Harper Conservatives executed a strict centralized message control that has become emblematic of their communications. The party's highly disciplined media management was highlighted by Harper making a policy announcement each morning that established the Conservative Party's credibility and often set the media agenda. The daily micro-messaging of policies such as narrow tax credits was designed to gradually resonate with issue-based segments of the electorate, who were reached through creative ad designs and narrowcasting by media buyers, including middle-class suburban imagery of Harper, his wife, and his two young children. A particularly successful instance of targeted earned media occurred when the policy announcement of a GST cut was supported by a photo-op of Harper slapping sale stickers in an electronics store to illustrate the tax markdown (see Chapter 8).

These two elections also reveal a contrast between the organizational prowess of a tired governing party and an enthusiastic government-in-waiting party, reminding us that marketing alone is unable to salvage damaged brands, political management crises, and the resulting disarray. In 1993, the PC campaign succumbed to "inexperience and sloppy organization"

(McLaughlin 1994, 203). Members of the leader's tour had little input into daily campaign events, and discussions with Campbell about logistics superseded communications and policy discussions. A separate unit organized its Quebec operations, where there were unclear lines of authority and bickering over strategy. By comparison, in the Harper campaign organization, decisions were informed by multiple conference calls each day between strategists in the war room, the leader's tour, and communications personnel, who would also strategize with the leader. Four people had to unanimously approve of its war room outputs, which included intelligence and messaging for targeted ridings (Flanagan 2007a). The same sort of organizational contrast occurred for the incoming Liberals in 1993 and the exiting Liberals in 2006.

The State of Political Marketing in Canada

These case studies can lead us to at least a half dozen important Canadian considerations for the implementation of the political marketing indicators identified in Table 4.1.

GOOD ORGANIZATION IS ESSENTIAL FOR SUCCESSFUL POLITICAL MARKETING

When campaign units operate with military-like meticulousness, regularly interact, and stick to a plan with a developed product offering, they are more likely to experience marketing success than when they are disjointed, isolated, and impulsive. Of course, the former is easier in theory than in practice. Implementing a campaign plan occurs amid a hectic pace and unpredictable circumstances demanding intuition and quick decisions, but it is especially important for parties informed by research, who must temper others' compulsive reactions to events. As well, the organizational logistics of coordinating the leader's tour across one of the world's largest political territories is a reoccurring subject in Canadian politicos' reflections, hence the inclusion of an "execution" indicator for distinguishing between amateur, semi-professional, and professional campaigns.

THE ELECTORAL SYSTEM PLACES SIGNIFICANT CONSTRAINTS ON POLITICAL MARKETING

Political marketing decisions in Canada are complicated by the oddities of the electoral system. The profiled cases seem to substantiate Gibson and Römmele's position (2001) that well-funded, mainstream right-wing parties with a centralized power structure that recently lost an election are more likely to adopt professional marketing techniques, whereas left-wing mass parties are more suspicious of adopting such business practices. Given that the Reform Party, and indeed the entire 1993 election, is such an outlier, perhaps their claim applies only to established parties in normal circumstances. The amateurism of the Green Party in 2006, when they did not win any seats despite receiving 4.5 percent of ballots cast, is another example of the method of seat distribution failing to reflect market demand. Parties cannot, therefore, avoid the geographic clustering of the Canadian electorate, and thus in the SMP system are motivated to target winnable seats instead of adopting mass market and segmentation strategies that would be viable in a proportional representation system. Moreover, strategists must be mindful that grassroots regionalism can trump sophisticated political marketing.

Canadian Party Strategists Selectively Import Political Marketing

Leading Canadian political parties introduce marketing techniques that have been successful in other jurisdictions, and other Canadian parties adopt these practices after they have been assured of their success in the Canadian market. In other words, Canadian political marketing involves copying and customization, rather than innovation. Marketing in Canada is inspired by successes in Australia, Britain, and especially the United States; popular American tactics are eventually used by even left-of-centre parties. Just as the Chrétien Liberals' red book and war room, both imported ideas, have had a long-standing influence among other Canadian parties, we might expect the same of the Harper Conservatives' disciplined marketing campaign and CIMS database. The political marketing by "blue" Tories (i.e., US Republican sympathizers) in 2006 may have changed the political game in Canada, for though regional clusters remain, the battleground has been altered to Tim Hortons coffee drinkers, Canadian Tire shoppers, and the hockey moms of suburbia. Policy issues that appeal foremost to suburbanites, and increasingly to allophones, are prioritized by the Conservative marketing team, rather than, say, those of the Quebec region in its entirety, a market niche once dominated by the Bloc Québécois that in 2011 opted instead for a product trial with the NDP. By comparison, other than the global lessons of the Chrétien face ads (which are a constant reminder in Canadian politics of the risks of "going neg") and the Bloc's niche marketing, there is no comparable exporting of Canadian political marketing knowledge.

Anti-Elitism Positioning Transcends Time and Ideology

The "throw the bums out" positioning of opposition parties is a common mantra against a governing party that is branded as arrogant and corrupt and which must defend its past decisions. Those parties that exceeded expectations in the profiled elections all presented themselves as fresh alternatives to a tired government. Their leaders embodied policies with mass appeal that can transcend left-right ideologies, be it Jean Chrétien as the "little guy from Shawinigan" (national unity and clean government), Lucien Bouchard and Gilles Duceppe as trustworthy nationalists (Quebec regionalism), Preston Manning as the anti-politician (political reform), Stephen Harper as the outsider (libertarian conservatism and clean government), or Jack Layton as the social crusader (populist democratic socialism). This societal marketing exploited the vulnerability of parties that were seen to embody an Ottawa establishment that was popularly perceived to be self-interested and failing to satisfy its customers.

PERMANENT CAMPAIGNING IS MORE LIKELY IF AN ELECTION IS LOOMING

The proximity of an election is related to the intensity of campaigning and has implications for political marketing. Throughout the 1980s and 1990s, successive majority governments reduced the urgency of inter-election campaigning, though reoccurring Liberal majorities did spur the rebranding of parties on the right. When successive minority governments were formed beginning in 2004, all major parties remained on campaign footing after each election. This era featured unprecedented (in Canada) relationship marketing, fundraising, and negative communications, as well as more active ground organizing, such as early candidate nomination contests. For instance, after Martin was replaced as Liberal leader, beginning in 2007, the Conservatives financed a "not a leader" strategic communications campaign against Stéphane Dion and, beginning in 2009, a "just visiting" theme against Michael Ignatieff. Conversely, after Prime Minister Harper prorogued Parliament in late 2008 and again in early 2010, the opposition parties and outraged citizens used social networking technology to coordinate mass demonstrations in a crisis-like atmosphere that suggested a change of government may be imminent. In response to these public rebukes, the Conservative Party issued urgent e-fundraising appeals to its supporters to finance further political marketing communications.

POLITICAL MARKETING REQUIRES ACCESS TO TECHNOLOGICAL INNOVATIONS IN RESEARCH AND COMMUNICATIONS

Political marketers need a competitive advantage in information technology. Political parties must adopt technologies because election campaigns involve the strategic allocation of finite resources in a competitive marketplace. Governing parties' preoccupation with the daily business of running the government increases their reliance on technology, which, unless it is used to cultivate relationships with supporters and invigorate the political product, can be similarly used by opponents to expose a serious vulnerability. Specialized skills and knowledge of data-gathering tools and communications mediums allow a party, especially a government-in-waiting, to develop and communicate a more desirable product.

Implications for the Quality of Democracy

The institutionalization of political parties' scientific analysis of public opinion is contributing to an evolution in the study of political behaviour where intelligence-based strategy is becoming the unit of analysis. Pammett and Dornan (2006, 18) have remarked on concerns that Canadian political parties and the media are preoccupied with strategy and tactics rather than with issues and policies, and that style triumphs over substance to such a degree that an election becomes "a referendum on electoral machines and tactics rather than a contest between political philosophies." They maintain that such attention to the quality of party machinery is warranted because it signals the preparedness of a party to run the government. The parties' emphasis on winning, rather than on representing electors, is what concerns others. Marketing is not being used to encourage "a constructive dialogue for both specific and broader societal development and fulfilment of social and economic goals" (O'Cass 2009, 198). Rather than encourage customer satisfaction, political marketing in the SMP electoral system enables a party like Harper's Conservatives to achieve the organization's needs whether or not these accurately reflect the electorate's (Paré and Berger 2008).

Governing parties that seek re-election for the sake of preserving their status are more likely to have underdeveloped agendas to advance when they resume governing. Although technology provides an excellent mechanism to gauge what the public wants and to communicate responsively – notwithstanding the potential of web interactivity – in practice, it displaces grassroots engagement, for it has become an efficient but lazy way for party personnel to design and promote their political products. The party centre's competitive drive to use technology to fundraise and a ferocious appetite for mass communications supersedes any interest in meaningful engagement in civil society.

Competitive political organizations in liberal democracies have been evolving from mass parties that foremost address the needs of partisans to catch-all parties that seek to appeal to flexible partisans. As ideological underpinnings, principles, and party bosses make way for issues-based management, malleability, and political consultants, we are seeing technology-enabled permanent campaigning that prioritizes marketing activities over a market orientation. There appears to be a gloomy outlook for the quality of democracy not only in Canada but in other Western societies as well. A more optimistic view is that, should a market-oriented and voters-first party achieve success over self-interested and marketing-oriented parties, it is likely that the spirit of engagement and representation upheld by democratic theorists will be rejuvenated, given the tendency of political organizations to copy winning strategies and tactics.

NOTES

1   An earlier version of this chapter was presented at the Political Studies Association political marketing workshop, March 30-April 1, 2010, Edinburgh.

2   These are not rigid categorizations, and an assigned characteristic does not necessarily imply exclusivity to a type of campaign.

3   In 1998, Reform leader Preston Manning advocated a proposal that would result, in 2000, in the rebranding of the Reform Party into the Canadian Alliance party. The goal was to "unite the right," thereby positioning the Alliance as an alternative to the governing Liberals. Eventually, former Reformer Stephen Harper would become leader of the Alliance, and his inner circle would continue professionalizing their political marketing techniques after Harper agreed in late 2003 to merge the Canadian Alliance with the PC Party. For more on the evolution of these parties, see Chapter 5.

5
Under New Management: Market Intelligence and the Conservative Party's Resurrection

André Turcotte

Over eighty public opinion polls measuring the voting intentions of Canadians were released in the media in 2009. Although this pales in comparison to the 174 such polls released a year earlier (Election Almanac 2010), it is remarkable to realize that, on average, the media monitor the hypothetical vote choice of the Canadian electorate more than once a week. One can certainly ponder about the necessity and usefulness of this abundance of public opinion research (POR), but, as Lisa Birch illustrates in Chapter 9, no one can deny that measuring public opinion has become a central component of the workings of democracy. The modern research instruments designed to gauge public opinion have moved from an incidental or secondary position in politics to "star billing" treatment (Sherman and Schiffman 2002, 232). More importantly, it is also an essential governing instrument.

Politicians have always had an uneasy relationship with market intelligence in general and POR in particular. Some of them believe polling results, especially when they corroborate their personal views on issues. In this sense, to paraphrase the late Brooklyn Dodgers sportscaster Vin Scully, many politicians use polls like a drunk uses a lamppost: more for support than illumination. In public, they decry the influence of polls and other market intelligence tools and deny any reliance they may have on these strategic instruments. Most would not go as far as John Diefenbaker, who famously declared that polls were for dogs (D. Smith 1997), but politicians are constantly worried that the voting public will equate listening to polls or conducting focus groups with a lack of leadership and vision. Despite such public denials, it is generally accepted that an in-depth comprehension of public opinion is fundamental to the modern practice of democracy. As Carballo and Hjelmar (2008, v) suggest, "[Public opinion polling] shapes public policies; it helps politicians to connect with their audiences; it reveals underlying issues that are of utmost importance for decision-makers." Some even suggest that public opinion research and television are the two developments that have had the most significant impact on modern political systems (Donsbach and Traugott 2008, 5). And although public opinion polls are not perfect instruments, the conversation they generate between government and the public can potentially help bridge the gap between them.

Politicians rely on market intelligence to decide on issue priorities, develop communications strategies, and help present themselves as the most competent to address those issues. Market intelligence interacts with the overall campaign strategy in different ways. As Rademacher and Turchfarber (1999, 202) suggest,

> [Market intelligence] is gathered in different ways, depending on the stage of the campaign: in the early stages it identifies what messages to send to whom, and later it measures the effectiveness of different messages to inform any necessary changes. Intelligence can be used to inform the presentation of the leader or to inform the development of political advertising.

The collection and interpretation of market intelligence data is a multifaceted process. It is at times ad hoc and unscientific, but most often this process is a technical and sophisticated practice. Political parties garner intelligence informally in various ways; they poll their members via mailed party correspondence and use straw polls during party conventions and general assemblies. Members of Parliament have the resources to mail letters to their constituents and request their feedback. Many now rely on email and social marketing tools like Facebook and Twitter to interact with voters. Moreover, door-to-door and telephone canvassing by volunteers remain key campaign activities at the local level. The focus of this chapter is on the more scientific dimension of market intelligence. It looks at analyses of past voting results and demographic trends based on census data, as well as opposition research. More specifically, it focuses on understanding how modern parties use scientific quantitative and qualitative research instruments as part of POR. But before going any further, let's first look quickly at some key terms associated with scientific market intelligence.

A central tenet of marketing is the principle that in-depth research must be conducted "to determine the needs and wants of the marketplace before a product or service is developed" (Newman 1999a, 39). Applied to politics, research is designed to ascertain the prevailing values, beliefs, and opinions in the political marketplace. Both quantitative and qualitative instruments are available to accomplish this objective. Quantitative research is based on statistical comparison of information gathered in the form of numbers (Manheim et al., 2008, 429; Neuman and Robson 2009, 396). This type of research provides surface-level data and identifies not only the opinions and beliefs of the group under study but also the strength of those opinions. It is generally costly and yields precise findings. Surveys, in one form or another, are used in quantitative research. A survey can be defined as "a detailed investigation of the behaviour, attitudes, values, opinions, beliefs, and/or personal characteristics of individuals" (Leslie 2010, 66). Although telephone interviewing remains the prevailing mode to collect quantitative data, Internet-based surveys are increasingly popular despite their methodological shortcomings (see Turcotte 2009, 213-14, for a fuller discussion).

In contrast, qualitative research is based on the researcher's informed understanding of the events and people under study and relies on information gathered in the form of words, pictures, or images (Manheim et al. 2008, 429; Neuman and Robson 2009, 396). It is used to explore attitudes, feelings, and motivations. Focus groups are the prevailing approach used to garner qualitative data. This methodology has been used for decades by market research firms to test out new products, corporate communication strategies, and advertisements, and such applications have invaded the political marketplace. This technique is used in politics to identify issues important to a segment of voters, to evaluate leaders' image and party advertisements, and to test the campaign platform and other aspects of the overall communications strategy. The literature on market intelligence illustrates the prevalence of surveys and focus groups but also demonstrates how other techniques are part of the market intelligence arsenal. Specifically, politicians can draw on research tools such as census data, election records, and, as is discussed later, telemarketing, to refine their understandings of the public opinion environment. Such tools are important, though they tend to play a supporting role to surveys and focus groups to the extent that the information they yield helps make the conduct of surveys and focus groups more targeted and efficient.

Ever since Theodore H. White (1961) documented the role of pollster Lou Harris in the 1960 US presidential election, polling has played a major role in election campaigns. Although some have expressed doubts about the extent to which Harris was instrumental in JFK's victory (see Wheeler 1976), today's campaigns unquestionably rely on the information collected by the tools of market intelligence. Various types of campaign polling (see Figure 5.1) are used in most political systems, and the scope of the voter research

FIGURE 5.1

The five types of public opinion polls frequently used in political campaigns

1   *Benchmark poll:* Typically the most in-depth poll (in terms of sample size and number of questions) conducted prior to the official beginning of the election campaign and designed to gather information on every relevant aspect of the campaign (issues, leaders' images, voting intentions, key segments, etc.).

2   *Strategic poll:* Poll conducted after the benchmark poll and designed to delve into the key findings gleaned in the benchmark poll. A strategic poll is often timed in conjunction with focus group research.

3   *Tracking poll:* Small poll (both in terms of sample size and number of questions) typically conducted on a daily basis throughout the campaign and designed to look at the dynamics of vote choice, allowing for immediate strategic changes or readjustment in tactics.

4   *Brushfire poll:* Small poll (especially in terms of number of questions) designed to focus on an emerging issue or problem during the campaign.

5   *Post-election poll:* Large poll (in terms of sample size and number of questions) designed to ascertain the nature of the electoral mandate and evaluate the reasons for success or failure.

programs is largely contingent on available funds (Steeper 2008, 594). As described above, focus groups too play a key role in modern elections campaigns. Campaigns also conduct "dial tests" to mix discussion with quantitative results (596). In this instance, focus group participants are given a handheld device to register reactions to advertising, messages, or images. Steeper (596-97) suggests that campaigns have also begun using online advertising tests. Another important development is the increasing use of voter tracking programs, which combine polling technology with direct marketing strategies. More on that development as we turn our attention to the Conservative resurrection and the changing role of market intelligence in Canadian federal elections.

Case Study: The Resurrection of the Conservative Party

Electoral earthquake ... political cataclysm ... conservative meltdown ... these are only a few of the metaphors used to describe the 1993 Canadian federal election. Indeed, the scope of the Progressive Conservative (PC) defeat was unprecedented; the party lost a total of 167 seats (out of 169) and saw its vote share plunge from 43 percent to 16 percent (see LeDuc et al. 2010; also Table 4.2). For about a decade or so, three national political parties tried to capitalize on the PC demise. Alongside the remnants of the PC Party, the Reform Party of Canada, the Canadian Alliance, and eventually the Conservative Party of Canada vied for political supremacy to emerge as the alternative to the Liberals. This period also witnessed one short-lived parliamentary coalition, the PC-DRC, and another short-lived political movement, the United Alternative. During that time, Conservatives were more likely to fight among each other than to direct their attacks toward their real political adversary. Divisions were so deep that most observers predicted years of Liberal rule (see Blais et al. 2002; Clarkson 2005; Simpson 2001).

Many factors can explain the improbable Conservative resurrection and others have provided such explanations (LeDuc et al. 2010; Plamondon 2009). The objective here is to examine the different ways market intelligence was used by the Reform–Canadian Alliance–Conservative Parties between 1993 and 2008, the election before the rebranded party finally formed a majority government in 2011. Using Lees-Marshment's model (2001b), it will be suggested that the Conservative resurrection parallels a change in the use of market intelligence. In many ways, only when the Conservative Party decided to use market intelligence from a more market-oriented approach did its message become more coherent. Although not the sole reason for its electoral success, this change has certainly contributed to it.

The 1993 Federal Election
In 1993, the emergence of the Reform Party of Canada was as surprising as the collapse of the PCs. The party had been unable to elect a single Member of Parliament in the 1988 election and had only one sitting MP – Deborah Grey – who had won her seat in a by-election in 1989. Four years later, fifty-two Reformers were elected to the House of Commons.

It has been generally accepted that electoral success in Canada depends on adapting to the realities of brokerage politics (see Clarke et al. 1991; also Chapters 1 and 15). Accordingly, parties rely on market intelligence to present a platform that will appeal to the largest number of voters. Reform's electoral success in 1993 appeared to challenge this assumption, since this political formation was as close to a product-oriented party as we have seen in modern Canadian politics. As Lees-Marshment (2009c, 46) explains, "A product-oriented party (POP) ... argues for what it stands for, believing its product is of such value that people will vote for it because it is right. It doesn't use marketing to change its product or even its communication, even if it fails to gain support."

In accordance with the model, Reform Party strategists had little use for market intelligence. They did not have a pollster of record, did not commission their own internal polls, and did not conduct focus groups or any other proprietary research. They consulted publicly available market intelligence – especially the daily POR tracking published by Environics Research Group – and enlisted the services of Republican strategist Frank Luntz for strategic advice. As Alex Marland describes in Chapter 4 of this book, Reform relied on volunteer phone banks and developed a rudimentary direct marketing program designed to identify potential supporters and raise money. Preston Manning (2010) explained in an interview with me that the product they presented to the electorate, the party platform, "was the result of a process of interaction between the party's brain trust – under the leadership of Tom Flanagan and Stephen Harper – and numerous grassroots consultations, including annual policy conferences, designed to change and ratify the content of the platform." Acknowledging that the lack of financial resources was a factor contributing to scant market intelligence, Manning recalled that "pollsters and pundits were all telling us there was no public appetite for deficit reduction as described in our 'zero-in-three' proposal and for most of our policies. We went ahead because we believed these were the right policies for Canada."

THE TRANSITION ELECTIONS: 1997 TO 2004
Once the euphoria of sending fifty-two MPs to Ottawa subsided, Preston Manning and his advisers recognized the shortcomings of their limited use of market intelligence. Manning acknowledged that in the 1993 campaign, had they realized the scope and strength of their surge in Ontario, they would have reallocated resources to try to win more than one seat in that province. Market intelligence may have also persuaded them to make an extra campaign stop or run a few extra TV ads in Edmonton to defeat Liberal Anne McLellan, who won in Edmonton Northwest by only twelve votes. As a result of those reflections, the Reform Party embarked on a process toward a more market-oriented approach to the use of market intelligence, which culminated in the Harper victory in 2006.

In 1995, Preston Manning hired me as the party's first pollster of record. The transition away from a product-oriented party was difficult. As a populist party, the rank and file viewed market intelligence with suspicion. Moreover, the fifty-two MPs had been elected without relying on polls, and most failed to see their usefulness beyond diluting their message. But Manning was determined to make Reform more than another western protest movement.

As a first step, Reform morphed into a sales-oriented party (SOP) (Marland 2005, 62; see also Table 10.2). A SOP is reluctant to change its product but relies on market intelligence to inform persuasion communications. Reform policies still originated from grassroots consultation and annual party conventions, but market intelligence was designed to identify the policies that should be given prominence and to evaluate the best way to communicate the party's message. For the next five years, the party conducted quarterly tracking surveys and regular focus groups across the country. Because of the regionalized nature of Reform support and its polarizing effect on voters, market intelligence was focused on segmenting the electorate into different groups of voters, ranging from core supporters to hardened opponents. The strategy was designed to retain core voters and appeal to the "*NEXTVoters,*" defined as voters who supported key Reform policies and had a favourable impression of the leader but were not yet ready to vote Reform.

Market intelligence activities ramped up in the lead-up to the 1997 election. A large benchmark survey was conducted before the campaign, followed by a strategic poll combined with nationwide focus groups. The Fresh Start platform was tested to identify its most popular policies, and a series of potential campaign ads were also evaluated. A general sense of uneasiness toward market intelligence continued to plague Reform, and the campaign team decided to forgo tracking surveys during the campaign. The logic behind that decision was that once the strategy had been agreed on, the campaign should focus on delivering the message rather than tinkering with it. In his memoirs, Manning (2002, 81) retrospectively expressed some doubt about the wisdom of that decision.

The transition to a more market-oriented approach to market intelligence continued after the 1997 election. Polls and focus groups were conducted to evaluate support and to sell the concept of the United Alternative. Once Stockwell Day became leader of the Canadian Alliance, the new team of strategists fully embraced the modern tools of market intelligence. Key strategist Rod Love had been an adviser to Ralph Klein and the Alberta PCs and insisted that the Canadian Alliance use the basic tools of market intelligence, such as nationwide campaign tracking polls and focus group testing. An interesting development occurred in the 2000 election with the introduction of a voter tracking program. Such a program borrowed heavily from direct marketing techniques. It aimed to build a database of potential voters – typically in key ridings – and to remain in contact with those voters through direct mail and recorded voice messages. Special attention was to be given to those voters on election day to ensure that they actually went to the polls. This was a clear step toward a market-oriented approach; however, internal fighting within the Canadian Alliance meant that the data from the voter tracking data program were never used (Brodie 2010).

The election of Stephen Harper as leader of the Conservative Party brought new discipline to the use of market intelligence. By the 2004 election, the transition away from a POP was complete, but the party was still stumbling its way out of being a SOP. In that election, the Conservatives retained the services of Dimitri Pantazopoulos of Praxicus Public Strategies to conduct a benchmark poll and nightly nationwide tracking polls throughout the election period. It also contracted the Toronto-based firm Responsive Marketing Group to conduct voter tracking and the get-out-the-vote (GOTV) activities (Ellis and Woolstencroft 2004, 86). The Conservatives were successful in reducing Paul Martin's Liberals to a minority, but there was some dissatisfaction with the campaign strategy in general and the use of market intelligence in particular. In *Harper's Team*, Tom Flanagan (2007a) – who managed the Conservative national campaign in 2004 and who had been Harper's chief of staff when he became leader of the Canadian Alliance – described how the post-2004 election consensus pointed to the need for a more integrated "command-and-control structure" (197) to better execute the campaign strategy. Similarly, Ian Brodie, who was a senior member of the Conservative team and later became chief of staff for Prime Minister Harper, suggested that one of the main lessons of 2004 was that it is necessary to develop a market intelligence structure to ensure that the campaign could be "more responsive" and "more nimble" (Brodie 2010).

THE CONSERVATIVE VICTORIES OF 2006 AND 2008

The most important change that Conservative strategists made after the 2004 election was to bring all market intelligence in-house. They broke away from the usual practice of relying on a pollster-of-record and took internal control of the market intelligence process. One has to go back to the early days of political marketing in Canada to find a comparable situation. During the Second World War, the Mackenzie King government developed an internal public opinion program within the Wartime Information Board and relied on the Gallup Organization for technical expertise (see D. Robinson 1999; Chapter 4). Such a program was severely criticized and eventually dismantled by King because it gave an unfair partisan advantage to the ruling Liberals. Prime Minister Harper did not have similar qualms.

The Conservatives hired Patrick Muttart, whose professional background was as marketing director for a hotel chain (Flanagan 2007a, 219; Paré and Berger 2008, 47). Conventional wisdom dictated that the pollster should operate at arm's-length from the core group of advisers in order to remain an objective judge of the effectiveness of the campaign strategy. In fact, it has been suggested that one of the reasons behind the disastrous 1993 PC campaign was that Allan Gregg had become both party pollster and strategist and, in so doing, lost the capacity to make the campaign team in general and the leader in particular listen to the critical perspective he was providing (McLaughlin 1994, chaps. 7 and 8). But as Brodie (2010) indicated in an interview with me, the decision was taken "to combine marketing and strategy into one unit to improve our response time and keep everyone focused on the campaign objectives." The way Tom Flanagan (2007a, 220) described Muttart is indicative of the changing role of market intelligence within the Conservative strategy:

> We had never had someone like Patrick on the campaign team – a high-level strategist with an ability to think in visual terms and dramatize policy ... Patrick has an eye for colour schemes, photo ops, sound bites and all the other things that bring political communications to life.

Muttart's role was not that of a conventional political pollster but more akin to that of a vice-president of marketing in the private sector (for more on this, see Jennifer Lees-Marshment's Chapter 6 in this volume, about practitioners). He used POR not solely to evaluate the mood of the electorate and test policies but also to identify ways to communicate the Conservative product to appeal to a sufficiently large number of voters to form government. He wrote the campaign narrative that combined polling data, policy, photo ops, and advertising into a coherent message (Ellis and Woolstencroft 2006, 71). This new approach to market intelligence led to a second important development.

Traditionally, Liberal and Progressive Conservative campaigns have adopted a mass marketing approach to winning elections. Although they looked at different subsegments of the electorate to evaluate the best ways to garner the most votes, the outlook was toward appealing to the median voter (see Downs 1957). In contrast, Reform campaigns in the 1990s and the Canadian Alliance campaign in 2000 relied on segment marketing

(Marland 2005, 68-69), with a view to transform a coalition of subsegments of the electorate – social and fiscal conservatives, disillusioned Quebec federalists, western populists – into a governing plurality. As described by Marland earlier in this book, the Conservatives took important steps in 2004 to develop a more in-depth understanding of their potential electorate. Their relative success opened the door to an even more sophisticated approach in 2006.

The approach adopted by the Harper Conservatives can be described as hypersegmentation. The party's polling program was designed to first understand the composition of the political marketplace and then to identify the values and policy positions of certain segments of the electorate that would maximize their electoral market share. In this sense, the Conservative Party evolved into a market-oriented party, using market intelligence to identify voter demand. The benchmark poll yielded findings that allowed isolating very specific groups of voters and ways to specifically appeal to them. The groups were not large entities such as "western populists" or "disillusioned Quebec federalists." Rather, the profiling of voters was very specific and creative. As Flanagan (2007a, 223-24) explained,

> To make [strategic segmentation] understandable ... [Patrick] created fictional people to epitomize our core and swing voters ... Dougie – single, in his late twenties, working at Canadian Tire – represented one type of swing voter. He agreed with us on issues such as crime and welfare abuse, but was more interested in hunting and fishing than politics, and often didn't bother to vote ... Rick and Brenda, a common-law couple with working-class jobs, represented another set of swing voters, as did the better off Mike and Theresa who probably would be Conservative core supporters except for their Catholic background.

The result was that out of a sea of about 23 million eligible voters, the Conservative strategy was able to focus on a pool of about 500,000 voters, which made the difference between victory and defeat. The other elements of the polling program were directed toward those voters. Strategic polls were conducted to craft the platform to appeal to those key voters. Moreover, focus group testing was conducted with participants representing those subsegments, and nationwide nightly campaign tracking was replaced by nightly tracking in winnable ridings and among key groups only.

This hypersegmentation was to some extent inspired by the electoral success of John Howard in Australia. Muttart was intrigued by Howard's ability to end thirteen years of Labour rule in 1996 and to win three more consecutive elections thereafter. Of particular interest was the market segmentation and positioning used by the Australian Liberal-National Coalition and its focus on what party leader Howard had called "the battlers," or families struggling to raise their kids on a small income (Flanagan 2007a, 223). Strategic focus on this group had contributed greatly to Howard's victory, and Muttart was determined to find equivalent groups for the Canadian Conservatives. Starting in 2005, Muttart, Brodie, and others would establish ties with Howard and his strategists. This led to visits by Conservative campaign staff to Australia and visits by Howard's strategists to Ottawa (Brodie 2010), as well as meetings between Harper and Howard (Flanagan 2007a, 223).

Hypersegmentation could not have been successful without another development introduced after the 2004 election. As noted above, the Canadian Alliance had attempted to design a voter tracking program in the 2000 election, but it was the Harper Conservatives who made such a program work. A "war room within the war room" (Flanagan 2010b) was set up to execute the direct voter contact program. The objective was to use techniques associated with direct marketing to locate key voters one at a time. Using a telemarketing firm in Toronto, the direct voter contact program was conducted in ridings identified by the campaign team as winnable – mostly located in Ontario and British Columbia. Voter contact was effective because it guided the GOTV efforts, but it also guided general local door-knocking efforts and provided constituency campaigns with highly targeted "walk routes," where volunteers as well as the candidates could visit as many of those electors as possible. It also had a benefit extending beyond the election campaign itself, since the names of those supporters were included in the party's fundraising efforts. It increased the party's ability to raise millions of dollars from small individual donations. Tom Flanagan (2010b) commented that this type of "slice and dice politics" played a large part in the Conservative victories. For him, in the current context of voter apathy and low voter turnout, direct marketing efforts may be more important than the mass marketing associated with polling and focus group testing.

The State of Political Marketing in Canada

Electoral success cannot be narrowed down to one or two factors. The way voters come to decide who to vote for is a complex and multifaceted process.

However, it remains that thirteen years after being reduced to only two seats in the House of Commons, the party of John A. Macdonald returned to power. The ways in which Conservative strategists used market intelligence played a major part in this improbable resurrection. They learned from the experience of the Reform Party and the Canadian Alliance to design a market intelligence program that retained the Conservatives' core supporters and expanded beyond that to form government. The changes made by the Conservatives after the 2004 election appears to have contributed to the party winning the next three elections. If we look at the Conservative practices in a broad context it is very likely that the state of market intelligence in Canada is about to undergo fundamental changes. Three specific reasons support this assertion.

First, although the internal structuring of market intelligence activities, with its focus on hypersegmentation and integration with direct marketing and GOTV efforts, may be the latest innovation in Canadian federal politics, variations of this can be found in other contexts. The similarities with Australia are discussed in the previous section. The Tony Blair victories in the United Kingdom also relied on specific segmentation of the electorate (Lees-Marshment 2001b). Newman (1999a, 263) suggested that Bill Clinton's presidential re-election campaign successfully tailored its message toward four specific subsegments of the electorate. However, the Blair and Clinton efforts were unsophisticated compared with more recent elections. US Republican strategist and mastermind of George W. Bush's two presidential elections Karl Rove was greatly influential in introducing the type of micro-segments that guide most modern elections (Moore and Slater 2004; Rove 2010). Davidson (2005) and Seawright (2005) have discussed the role of micro-segments in the 2005 British election. It would appear that this practice has found its way to France (Teinturier 2008) and the Philippines (Abad and Ramirez 2008). As the discussion of the Canadian case suggests, using market intelligence to identify key subsegments of the electorate is most efficient if combined with direct marketing and GOTV. On this front, it appears that most countries are playing catch-up with the level of sophistication in the US campaigns. Accordingly, what the Canadian case is demonstrating is that the Conservatives have adapted market intelligence in Canada along lines that have proven quite successful in other countries, and other Canadian parties have incentives to do the same thing.

Second, the proliferation of media polls is allowing political parties to focus their market intelligence resources on specific geographic areas or segments of the electorate. It was noted above that a new media poll showcasing national party standings is released on average more than once a week. During an election campaign, the frequency increases to one poll every three days or so. Ian Brodie (2010) explained that the Conservative war room relied on the media polls to stay informed about national trends. He believed that, with all the polls released in the media, resources were better directed toward monitoring the battlegrounds. Parties are better off concentrating their market intelligence efforts and resources on those voters who may lead them to victory, while keeping an eye on the national picture through the work done by the media's polling firms.

Finally, using market intelligence resources more efficiently has become a major concern for national political parties in Canada with the adoption of Bill C-24, which was introduced by the Liberals and came into effect in 2004. Of special interest to political parties is section 9 of Bill C-24 (emphasis added):

> Election expenses include amounts paid, liabilities incurred and non-monetary contributions used to promote or oppose a particular candidate, a registered party or its leader during an election campaign, and *also include the conduct of election surveys or other surveys or research during an election period.*

Until 2004, the amount of money spent by political parties on election surveys and other research was not specifically identified in the spending limits regulating electoral expenses. With Bill C-24, political parties have to decide how much of their electoral expenses they will allocate to market intelligence in comparison to other resources, such as advertising, campaign events, and so on (see Dufresne and Marland's review of the rules of the game in Chapter 2). This legislation is likely to have two specific consequences. First, more emphasis will be given to market intelligence activities conducted prior to the election campaign itself. Benchmark and strategic polls, as well as focus group testing conducted before the writ is dropped, will gain more prominence as parties try to garner as much strategic information as possible before polling becomes restricted by electoral law. Second, once the campaign is underway, market intelligence is likely to focus on key subsegments of the electorate – as the Conservatives did in 2006, 2008, and again in 2011 – simply because it may not be financially possible to continue to monitor the electorate as a whole. This may be an unforeseen consequence of Bill C-24 that will impact the quality of democracy in Canada.

Implications for the Quality of Democracy

Much has been written about the impact of political marketing in general and market intelligence in particular on democracy.[1] For instance, Marland's comment (2005, 74) that an "MOP is responsive to electors because, in many cases, responsiveness wins seats and this type of party should better satisfy electors" represents the positive side of the argument. In this vein, the tools of market intelligence are used to understand the needs and aspirations of voters, and the development of party platforms aims to address those needs. Accordingly, market intelligence has the potential to give a voice to the electorate. A more pessimistic view was put forth by Savigny (2007) in the context of recent UK elections. She argued that when New Labour crafted its platform as a response to focus groups with certain segments of the population – specifically "Tory switchers" – it explicitly listened to voters who were not representative of the electorate at large. From that perspective, market intelligence can silence some voters.

What is of particular interest in the Canadian context is that Bill C-24, designed to improve the workings of Canadian democracy, may have the unintended impact of institutionalizing an approach to market intelligence that makes the voices of a few voters much more important than that of the electorate as a whole. As discussed in this chapter, focusing on a small number of key voters has proven to yield positive electoral benefits. When political parties have to decide how to incorporate POR and other research expenses within their allocated electoral budgets, hypersegmentation may make sense not only strategically but financially as well. To increase their chances of winning an election, parties may choose to turn their attention on only those voters they need to form government. It means segmentation based on key ridings and finely defined groups of voters. Such market intelligence is less expensive and more efficient than the traditional nationwide and untargeted polling. However, it systematically ignores the views and attitudes of most voters who are already committed to a specific party. More worrisome, a political discourse designed to resonate with only a select few may potentially alienate the majority. This sense of discourse alienation has been suggested as an explanation for low turnout among young voters (Turcotte 2005, 2007) and may extend to other groups. Moreover, strategists will be reluctant to go beyond their known segments and will lose incentives to expand the franchise. This will create the culture of contentment described by Galbraith (1992). When asked about the potential negative impact of the Conservative approach to market intelligence, the key architects were largely dismissive of gloomy scenarios. Flanagan and Brodie agreed that their innovative approaches to market intelligence resulted in a strategic focus on a few voters to the detriment of the larger electorate. In the end, Brodie insisted that an election campaign is only one part of the overall task of governing. However, as Christopher Page described (2006) and as Lisa Birch explains in Chapter 9, the prominence of opinion research has spilled beyond campaigning and is entrenched in the activities of governing. Market intelligence may allow parties to focus on key subsegments of the electorate, but it also allows a government to interact with specific voters throughout their mandate.

Once in power, governing parties dismiss the majority of voters at their own electoral risks. The art of being re-elected rests on the ability to reconcile the will of the stable majority and the needs of the fickle few. Canadian voters have a proven record of punishing leaders who take them for granted. Their propensity to "throw the rascals out" may be our best safeguard against the potential abuse of market intelligence.

NOTE

1   For a full discussion of the pros and cons of political marketing, see Lees-Marshment 2009c, chap. 10.

6

The Impact of Market Research on Political Decisions and Leadership: Practitioners' Perspectives

Jennifer Lees-Marshment

This chapter explores the impact of market research on the decision-making process by political leaders by utilizing the perspectives of practitioners who advised recent Canadian leaders, including prime ministers and premiers. Previous research has predominantly argued that for politicians to get elected, they should use market research in the form of polls and focus groups to develop a political product that aligns with voter demands and thus be market-oriented (see Lees-Marshment 2001b; Ormrod 2005), like Bill Clinton's New Democrats in the United States and Tony Blair's New Labour in the United Kingdom, as well as other parties around the world (Bowler and Farrell 1992; Lees-Marshment, Strömbäck, and Rudd 2010; Lilleker and Lees-Marshment 2005). However, the few studies of orientation in Canada have found that party behaviour does not always fit into the market-oriented concept (Marland 2005) and thus that the way market research is used may be more varied. Furthermore, there are democratic issues raised by research-driven policy making. Paré and Berger's conclusion (2008, 58) from studying how the Canadian Conservative Party was elected in 2006 was that it revised its product offering with short-term and personal gain proposals in areas such as national unity, social policy, and economic policy that were aimed at appealing directly to the demands of voters, but then strategically chose to avoid "engagement with contentious policy considerations that appeal directly to contending social values" (see also Chapters 4, 5, and 8 in this book). Comparative studies have also raised concerns that market analysis threatens leadership and could undermine creativity and new ideas (Newman 1999a, 41). Market research elevates voters' input in political decision making through focus groups rather than formal elections, and because marketing offers the tools of voter profiling and segmentation, politicians end up focusing their research on select target groups only and thus "hear" some voters more than others, which undermines the democratic ideal of equality of influence (Lilleker

2005a; Savigny 2008a, 57; Temple 2010, 271). Another criticism is that market research cannot ascertain voter opinion accurately because moderator bias creeps into data collection. Savigny (2007, 130) argued that in the case of New Labour, strategist "[Philip] Gould also used focus groups as a site to test his own ideas. Rather than listening and collecting the opinions of the selected public, this was significant in communicating to participants what was important" (see also Wring 2007, 87). However, such concerns are based on outside critiques of single case studies; there have been no studies considering the perspective of the political practitioners who actually do the marketing.

This chapter utilizes the Canadian data collected as part of a comparative study using one hundred in-depth qualitative interviews with practitioners in Canada, the United Kingdom, the United States, Australia, and New Zealand (Lees-Marshment 2011). The starting ontology for this research was first to better understand the empirical reality of political marketing by listening to practitioners – that their perspectives were valuable, and that their activities were potentially positive, not just negative. The methods were inductive, so research was organic, open-ended, and exploratory, allowing rules and conclusions to evolve from the data. It sought to identify a collective wisdom from practitioner understanding of political marketing rather than prove a particular theory or model. The aim was to take a maximum-variation approach by including as broad a range of participants as possible (Kuper, Lingard, and Levinson 2008, 688). The Canadian data considered in this chapter are drawn from interviews conducted in 2009, including with general market researchers and consultants, as well as with advisers to Canadian prime ministers and premiers; see Table 6.1. Interviewees were not selected; rather, all leads were followed, but this resulted in a bias toward the two major parties at the federal level at the time, which suited the focus of this chapter on leaders' decision making. Interviews were qualitative, unstructured, soft, and intensive, with content led by the participant. Rather than having specific issues or questions about events or parties to ask, the generic question "What works and what doesn't work in your role?" was asked, and thus the interviewee directed the detailed content of the conversation depending on his or her perspective and experience. There was therefore what Sarantakos (2005, 270) terms as "absence of standardisation" whereby there was "freedom to respondents to express their views without external limitations." It is important to retain the integrity of the inductive approach but also to acknowledge openly that the data are not presented as a truth, but merely as they are: the perspective of practitioners that provides their insight into Canadian politics.

TABLE 6.1

Interviews with Canadian practitioners conducted by the author

Name	Date	Location	Position at time of interview and relevant experience
Ian Brodie	May 29, 2009	Ottawa	Consultant at Hill and Knowlton; former chief of staff in Stephen Harper's prime minister's office
John Duffy	May 20, 2009	Toronto	Consultant at Strategy Corp; former advisor to Prime Minister Paul Martin
Martha Durdin	May 19, 2009	Toronto	Consultant at Navigator; former staffer in Prime Minister Pierre Trudeau's office, as well as ministerial advisor
Alexandra Evershed	May 29, 2009	Ottawa	Consultant at Ipsos Reid Canada
Goldy Hyder	May 28, 2009	Ottawa	Consultant at Hill and Knowlton
Brad Lavigne	May 28, 2009	Ottawa	National director of the NDP; former advisor to party leader Jack Layton
Ben Levin	January 7, 2008	Auckland	Former deputy minister of education, Ontario; former deputy minister of advanced education and deputy minister of education, Manitoba
Patrick Muttart	June 25, 2009	Telephone	Communications consultant; former deputy chief of staff in Prime Minister Stephen Harper's office
Nik Nanos	May 28, 2009	Ottawa	CEO of Nanos Research
Leslie Noble	May 20, 2009	Toronto	Consultant at Strategy Corp; former strategic advisor to the Ontario Progressive Conservatives and campaign manager for former Ontario premier Mike Harris
Scott Reid	May 19, 2009	Toronto	Consultant at Feschuk.Reid; former senior advisor and director of communications to Prime Minister Paul Martin; director of communications for the 2004/2006 Liberal Party campaign
Chad Rogers	May 19, 2009	Toronto	Consultant at Navigator; former senior advisor to Nova Scotia premier John Hamm
John Wright	May 20, 2009	Toronto	Senior vice-president public affairs with Ipsos Reid Canada

Case Study: Canadian Practitioners' Perspectives about Political Marketing

This section presents the main themes that arose from the data, which fall into two main areas: why market research is valuable in politics, and how market research informs decisions and helps politicians achieve change. As André Turcotte states in Chapter 5, market research is valuable in politics because it provides accurate information that politicians can use when making decisions. For example, as Duffy observed,

> The great thing about polling is that it settles arguments among professionals. There's a wonderful line I quoted in a book I wrote from one of Canada's pre-eminent pollsters ... Allan Gregg ... [who] said, "Before polling, you could get into an argument about what was the most important thing to say, and old Fred, or old Bob would tell you, 'Oh, I know the people in the state of Alberta don't want to hear that.' Well with a poll, you can say that Fred's [wrong]." (2009)

Research also ensures that politicians talk about what the public – not the political or media elite – are concerned with. Brodie noted how "a lot of the nonsense that got thrown around here, and got thrown around question period about what [Stephen Harper] was or wasn't, turned out to not be supported by the data" (2009). The data need to be rigorous and of high quality, otherwise such benefit is lost, and when using ideas from other countries, Muttart explained, practitioners need their "local-reality lenses" (2009). The use of social networking, which was so successful in the 2008 Obama presidential campaign, may not be always "directly exportable"; the United States has distinctive factors that enabled that to be successful, as Muttart noted: "There's more civic engagement to begin with in the United States, the electorate as a whole is more web 2.0 oriented, [and] the campaign season is longer." Thus, Canadian practitioners look for tools from a range of countries, not just the United States, and pick out different elements to suit the Canadian market. The literature's concerns that market research is of low quality and is being abused seem unfounded: practitioners are aware of the need for it to be accurate and appropriate.

In terms of how such research is used and influences decisions, the data suggested that market intelligence is used in a range of ways. It does inform politicians of public demands. It helps identify regional differences. Brodie noted how "the uniqueness of the Quebec political situation compared to the rest of the country is an issue that you have to keep in mind continuously" (2009). It affected public perception of the party leader and party, encouraged different demands, and thus necessitated different responses but without being contradictory because "people will call you, to your detriment, on saying different things on different sides of the Ottawa River." It also identifies the underlying emotions of the electorate. Muttart explained how the Conservative Party's research found that right-of-centre voters responded to three key drivers: aspiration for "something better for their families and their children" from their hard work; family, including those who get legally married; and the need for cohesion, "this belief that we're all in it together, and that there should be broad-based societal norms." Thus, when you "craft a marketing program, what we do is try to tap into these broader themes of aspiration, of family, and of cohesion" and then "develop specific policies, specific marketing styles, types of pictures, types of articles, that tap into these underlying themes" (2009).

Research is also used to identify differences between social classes and the self-images that citizens project. The public wants a government to look and feel like them in some way. As democracy and Canadian society evolve, this is reflected in the composition of the legislature, which increasingly reflects a broader range of occupations, ethnicities, and social classes. Whereas in some countries, notably the United States, it may be acceptable for politicians to project an image of wealth and success, in Canada, a degree of modesty, humility, and self-deprecation is thought to resonate better with the electorate and media. Citizens want their government and elected officials to have an image similar to that of the median voter and not that of the political class. In Canada, therefore, people want a Tim Hortons, not a Starbucks, government (for more on this see Chapter 13, by Patricia Cormack). As Rogers explained,

> We want to elect people who are very close to who we are without very many exceptions ... Where the political class is in effect a Starbucks class, they very much have to present themselves as a Tim Hortons class – if you're familiar with the two coffee brands in Canada. Tim Hortons is the omnipresent national brand of coffee that costs about $1 a cup. It's about a third of the price of Starbucks and it's got about 10 times as many outlets across the country. It's named after a former hockey player. I'd encourage you to go across

the street to Tim Hortons and see what average Canadians look like, because average Canadians don't go to Starbucks. You'll find that the political class of staff, and campaign organizers, and advisers are a Starbucks class; the class that get elected and run local campaigns to get candidates elected are a Tim Hortons class. (2009)

However, market research is also used to help politicians change public demands or views. Rogers describes how the Nova Scotia Tories used research to find out how best to communicate that they had delivered on reducing provincial taxes and would reduce taxes again:

"Cutting taxes" as language never engendered the public support we thought it would ... it sounded too much like things people had heard or seen previously, but couldn't identify a benefit with. We tested about 50 variations in language of describing reducing taxes ... until we could actually find the five words that could do the heavy lifting that the public immediately agreed with, which were ... "lower taxes help working families." (2009)

Research can help politicians achieve change, not change themselves. Duffy claimed that "the best use of market research, in my experience, is – and this is true in government and politics, but also true in the private sector – it can show you a pathway through what appears to be an insurmountable barrier" (2009). He noted the example of potential reform of publicly owned utilities, and how if you do polling that directly asks, "We want to privatize this, we as a government are thinking of privatizing this, what do you think?" the response will be, "That's a terrible plan." Duffy said that public opinion on privatization had "inhibited successive governments for about twenty years from doing this privatization, which everybody in public policy knows ought to happen, is inevitable, will produce enormous benefit, very few dis-benefits." Research could, however, find a way to link the agenda and policy to conservation in aid of environmental best practices, which would be more positively received. Nanos remarked, "If they're going in saying 'I have an objective,' then they are on the right track. Can it be achieved? Is it the right objective? What are the resources that are going to be needed to achieve that objective? How relevant is it?" (2009). Analysis can be used to understand why people hold a position and also how strongly it is held; it can therefore assess the risk of moving against it. As Evershed said, "It's about understand-ing where the minefields are, so that you can negotiate the minefield, and you can bring your important policy to fruition, if indeed it is an important policy" (2009).

Research can, of course, identify where leaders can't make something work, and then they end up having to give up on that issue. Although this might raise democratic concerns for working against creativity, against what is "right," and against leadership, it can also be seen positively. Duffy explained how former Ontario NDP premier Bob Rae would say, "Democracy's important, inclusion is important. So too is understanding when the conversation is over, and you have had your say, and sometimes you carry the argument, and sometimes you don't. You've got to accept it when you don't carry the argument and move on" (2009).

Furthermore, even when market research shows opposition that proves insurmountable, this does not mean politicians will always give up on their positions. This is partly because of a leader's personal beliefs, regardless of their impact on electoral support. Duffy noted how former Liberal prime minister Paul Martin cared passionately about reconciling European and Aboriginal descendents within Canada, and when his staff advised him against it by saying, "Look, there are no votes in this stuff. Will you stop carrying the torch for it?" he replied,

No, I don't care. This is the right thing to do. This is coming. We can't escape it. This is so overwhelmingly important. If you scratch any social problem in Canada and look at the statistics, you'll usually find that it's really concentrated enormously in one of the Aboriginal populations. Then, there is the question of right and wrong. There is no getting around this from a moral or public policy standpoint. (2009)

Martin did not get political support for such a stand; moreover, subsequent governments undid the policy change.

Interviewees also have a pragmatic understanding of how changing too much can lead to failure. Noble (2009) explained how in one provincial election, 1999, the Ontario Progressive Conservative campaign team conducted opposition research against the Liberals' new leader, Dalton McGuinty, and identified four or five issues where he had flip-flopped, which they then used in an advert to label him as someone who didn't really stand for anything and thus was not up to the job. Similarly, Reid suggested that Stephen Harper faced difficulties in managing the global economic crisis immediately after the 2008 federal election because he ended up overseeing policies that expanded the public state, a position at odds with his original conservative standing. Thus,

> When [Harper] goes out and he markets the budget that he brought forward, he'd tick the boxes, in my view, of saying, "We're doing this because people need help and we have to work through it." Okay, good, this guy gets it. My focus is on jobs and making certain that people are able to do well. Okay, well, he's well motivated, all right, fine. Is he credible? No, he wasn't credible in any of those things ... you've got to be authentic. (2009)

In addition, sometimes leaders can succeed by being prepared to stick it out long enough to give change a chance, even if they aren't media-friendly. Rogers (2009) tells an important story about a necessary decision that Nova Scotia premier John Hamm took in 1999. One main promise that Hamm's government had been elected on was that of dramatically reducing government spending by shutting down a coal/steel plant in Cape Breton. Its previous owner had tried to close it in 1968, but the premier of the day said the province would take temporary custodianship. In 1999, temporary had become permanent, with the custodianship making up about 35 percent of the province's net debt. But the plant still had about twenty-five hundred employees, crucial to the island's economy, so the premier made the commitment that he would always advise the workers of any policy development first. However, residents picketed the airport when Hamm tried to fly in so that it would make the news. Rogers recalled how there were threats of physical violence, and staff were even under constant police protection at one point. The premier stuck by his decision, even though it would hurt him and the party electorally in the area for some time – and even had the coal/steel plant blown up to stop it being reopened. As Nanos explains,

> Politicians commonly use public opinion research as a substitute for making decisions, and they even lose themselves in the process because they think that's what people want. What they don't realize is that people have an innate sense of whether someone is genuine or not. Sometimes politicians can cover it up in the short term, but in the long term, when you're the leader of a democratic country and you're in the news, things either ring true or they don't. Many politicians weren't successful because they're not true to themselves,

and voters will say, "There's something I can't put my finger on that's not right there." (2009)

However, Muttart argued that, in practice, market research does not dictate the decision or remove judgment or leadership. Speaking from his experience advising Prime Minister Stephen Harper, he noted how "at some point ... you just have to make a judgment call on these things ... you use research the best you can to inform the decision, but it's a lot more art than science" (2009). There is a process of interpretation and deliberation that political elites undergo, which makes the market research-leadership relationship more nuanced. Research is part of the conversation between government and the people, and politicians can use it to achieve progress, which Nanos also alluded to:

Think of it as a learning process. Compare [it] to the dating process. You don't meet someone and say, "I love you. I want to marry you. We're going to have four kids. We're going to live here." Instead, you're going to shake hands and learn about each other. It's going to be a gradual learning process. If someone started a relationship and said, "If I can't get everything I want, then I'm not doing anything," the relationship is not going to be successful. Politics is no different. The politicians that understand that concept and have more of an incremental and gradual approach are more successful. They are hedging on their personal abilities to communicate, educate, and to slowly nurture and get the country moving in a particular direction, even if the majority is not there at that particular point of time. (2009)

The State of Political Marketing in Canada

From these interview data, we can conclude that there is greater thought and reflectivity around the extent to which market research influences leaders and decision making. Political leaders and advisers in Canada use market analysis more proactively, both to identify current public concerns and to explore ways to change opinion and achieve change. Market analysis results are not just taken and followed; they are interpreted and considered in relation to policy, leadership, and party goals. Those who advise Canadian leaders see the potential for their leaders to use marketing to inform a range of decision-making and leadership positions.

This more nuanced understanding of market research fits with the results of comparative research (Lees-Marshment 2011), which similarly found that even though there are undoubtedly problems with the way market research can be used in politics, there are also ways to overcome weaknesses and to make it a valuable process. Politicians need to use multi-methods and sources to analyze all stakeholders rather than just voters, and to consider different options from results. Market analysis can be used in a range of ways, such as to find new groups to represent, find who to talk to and how, put resources in the best place, confirm existing decisions, make adjustments, change parts of the product, change for segments, and identify where you can't change opinion. Politicians should try not to abandon vision in response to the first voices of criticism, and they can try to change opinion in some cases, because changes in position need to have a good reason to be seen as credible. Market analysis can be used to find or restore balance between leading and follow-ing. Getting political marketing to work is not about black and white or lead and follow categorizations that fit neatly into academic models, but is more nuanced, being about balance, options, degrees, and multiple uses of the same tool.

Nevertheless, this does not mean that Canadian practitioners simply follow the rest of the world blindly. On the contrary, both Brodie and Muttart spoke of the need to adapt tools from other countries to suit the Canadian market; Brodie noted how regional differences affected the nature of the advertising used. In Quebec, this is because the culture is different and the market demands more subtle use of humour. He recalled that the Conserva-tive team had a television advertisement in the 2006 campaign that he did not fully understand himself; it featured a guy on a bike sweating and strug-gling while peddling, and as the camera pulls out it becomes clear that the bike is propped up on two sets of concrete blocks and that it's not going anywhere (see also Ellis and Woolstencroft 2006). This was done to suggest that the bike was the Bloc Québécois – the bike was decorated in the Bloc's colours. Internally, the ad was considered a success because it conveyed the message that the Bloc was not getting Quebec voters anywhere, but had to be devised to suit the market and nature of communications in the province. It also meant that the Conservatives' support developed differently in Quebec compared with the rest of the country, as Brodie explains:

In Quebec, Stephen Harper is seen differently than he is in the rest of the country. In the rest of the country it doesn't really matter region to region – the regional disputes in the country are vastly overstated. The Conservative Party is seen differently. The Liberal Party is seen differently. Different political leaders are speaking in a different language. It goes on differently in Quebec. It's very peculiar. (2009)

This also made strategy more complex: "In Quebec there's two sequential games that go on with completely different characters," Brodie remarked. Of course, as discussed elsewhere in this book, political marketing offers segmentation strategies that can help identify and understand different markets within one country. Although we might expect segments to be regional in Canada, segmentation could in fact be applied more deeply. Brodie argued that "you have to have your eyes open to how local the issue appears to be, in Saskatchewan, or Ontario, or British Columbia, or for that matter Montreal" (2009). Segmentation can be used more broadly and deeply to create micro-targets not just on geographical lines but also on the basis of lifestyle, family cycle, income, and occupation. As the *Globe and Mail* reported during the 2011 election campaign, Canadian political parties are moving away from brokerage politics toward micro-targeting to identify, respond to, and communicate with new segments of the electorate that cut across regions, such as visible minorities (Friesen 2011).

In addition, Muttart emphasized the importance of being aware of the difference between Canada and other countries. As a Canadian, he learned a "tactical and a technological" lesson from the United States, but it was harder to get "big-picture branding and position lessons" because "every candidate runs on their own personal brand, not on a wholly defined party ticket. With Britain, the constituencies are roughly the same size, the voting system is identical, the party names, in some respects, are similar, and Britain has regional ethnically based parties with Scottish nationalists, Welsh nationalists – we have our Quebec separatists in Parliament" (2009). A lot of the dynamics of the British election campaign are applicable to Canada, but there are two crucial differences, namely the ban on television political advertising and the relative smallness of the country: "British campaigns don't have to plan 40-day campaigns that extend over five or six time zones, and they don't have to plan TV campaigns," noted Brodie (2009). However, for this, Canada can look to Australia, where they do have to plan leaders' tours across a large geography. As well, television advertising is part of Australian election campaigning. But Australia also has differences, such as its proportional electoral system. Canadians, therefore, need to ascertain the relevancy to Canada of lessons and tools from a range of countries. Muttart cited one striking example of difference between Australia and Canada, which is that in Australia everything goes quiet in the last few days of the campaign when there is a television advertising ban, in sharp contrast to Canada, where significant effort is put into media in the final days of the campaign. In addition, Muttart explained that

> because [Australia has] mandatory voting, there's no in-house, highly detailed focus get-out-and-vote operation ... [Whereas in] the last seventy-two hours of the campaign in Canada and in the United States, the campaign office is a mess-house. Everyone is going full-throttle. They're right at the wall, because we're blowing our brains out on TV in terms of the budgetary expenditure; everyone's pushing the vote, whereas in Australia, this is the time they take to clean up the office, to wind down. It was fascinating to sit there in the office and nothing was happening, and to compare it to our experience. (2009)

Thus, although it is clear that market research and political marketing strategy is being used by Canadian practitioners, it is not without significant thought and reflection, suggesting that our interpretation of political marketing behaviour, but also the democratic implications, needs to become open to more nuanced conclusions.

Implications for the Quality of Democracy

As noted at the start of the chapter, previous research (such as Savigny 2008a) raised a range of democratic concerns with the use of market research in politics and in Canada in particular (Paré and Berger 2008). However, the perspective of Canadian practitioners analyzed here suggests that, in practice, marketing is being used in a more nuanced and potentially positive way. That is not to try to claim that political marketing practice in Canada is universally positive, but simply to suggest that there remains the potential for positive behaviour. Those in key advisory positions to Canadian leaders are self-reflective about the impact of their work. Practitioners were universally of the view that, despite the problems that can occur with public opinion formation and expression, people should be consulted, but within constraints. As Evershed explained, "Should [voters] get to have a say? Yes. Should they get to have all the say? No" (2009). They concede that polling can be used in a way that compromises principles and conviction, but it depends how elites choose to use it. Research needs to be used wisely, and politicians can make sure the research identifies more detailed views rather than just for and against to find unifying courses of action. Nanos noted that it was particularly important to avoid oversimplifying complex and controversial issues, such as abortion, to create "sensational divisive research":

> A good example is the war in Afghanistan [which] has been very controversial in Canada ... When we do polling on the war in Afghanistan, however, we're asking Canadians: "What do you think of the objectives of the war? Do you support or oppose the objectives? Do you think we're providing the necessary resources to achieve those objectives? Do you think we can succeed?" More nuanced research is more helpful to decision makers, and importantly, it shows the potential for unifying courses of action, so parties can fulfill the traditional role of bringing different interests together. Then, what emerge are commonalities of opinion. It might sound obvious, but there are actually more commonalities of opinion related to a controversial mission than division because people want to have the fewest number of casualties, they want Afghanistan to be stable, they don't want resources wasted, etcetera. Thus, the issue becomes determining how to improve a particular situation. (2009)

This reflects academic research carried out by Fletcher, Bastedo, and Hove (2009, 916) that found that "Canadians are struggling at both cognitive and emotive levels to reconcile their understanding of themselves as a peace-keeping nation with the evolving demands placed on Canada and its military in Afghanistan." When war involves not just fighting the enemy, as in the great World Wars of the twentieth century, but also reconstruction of peace and democracy, more complex responses are likely to be made by the public in response to government policy, and market research needs to take this into account. Research could enhance public policy formation and government's ability to tackle issues in which its position may be in the minority. Public opinion research on controversial public policy issues needs to be used to identify common goals across differences of opinion and find a way forward. It then gives government more choices, "as opposed to saying, 'Abortion? Not going to deal with it because we're a minority view on it. We're not going to get what we want, so we're going to ignore this'" (Nanos

2009). Thus, *the manner* in which different methods of research, whether polling, focus groups, or otherwise, are used, rather than just *which* is used, has influence on the value of market analysis to government, politicians, and, indeed, society. Political marketing and polling could be used to achieve long-term change. As Muttart said,

> We're all driven by the next electoral contest. I was joking with a colleague of mine here in the States, I said, "Can you imagine if energy exploration companies were as short-term focused as political parties?" We would never, ever locate new sources of energy around the world, because they recognize that on the one hand you have to meet quarterly revenue targets and earning targets for your share-holders, but that you also have to work on ensuring a reliable long-term supply of energy, and they tend to be very focused on where they're going to be in ten years, fifteen years, twenty-five years. (2009)

Politics and the media encourage a day-to-day focus, but it is possible to choose to consider longer-term needs. However, this involves a change in attitude and viewing not just political marketing but politics itself as an exercise that does not have to be tied to election cycles. As Nanos observed, "Politicians should invest in research the same way they invest in personal savings, ultimately to say: 'This is the long-term policy objective. I might not necessarily be personally realizing it, but my party or my country will be realizing the gains.' If they had a longer-term policy horizon, it would really change the use of public opinion research" (2009). More qualitative and solution-oriented research may be more useful than quantitative methods for politicians, particularly once in power, to identify new solutions and choices. Market research can therefore guide politicians in how to introduce new ideas to the public and help reconcile the leadership/following dilemma. Analysis can explore the consequences of several courses of action the leader may take in advance of the decision. The practitioners interviewed were searching for and sometimes finding a more balanced use of market analysis and leadership. As Rogers said,

> Polling is a democratic act ... We get a very limited licence to govern, and we must make sure that we execute that in the spirit of the people who gave us the licence to do it. That being said, we can't be popu-lists, or we'd never get a tax to pay for public service, or we'd never

make a difficult decision, or we'd never shut the school that has to
be shut down, or blow up the steel plant that's killing the province's
finances. (2009)

Hyder added, "You need to listen to lead: monitor that dialogue, engage
in that dialogue, and take into account what people are looking for and what's
being said. Ultimately, lead. If the people are wrong, and you think they're
wrong, then run on that. People are not stupid. They're willing to be convinced
otherwise" (2009).

The conclusion that can be drawn from these data is that the elevation of
market research and strategy into political decision making offers politicians
tools to inform their decisions; but it does not lead politicians to pander to
public opinion. This reflects the conclusions from more quantitative non-
marketing studies of polling and policy making. Jacobs and Shapiro (2000,
13) argue that "presidents can use polls to determine how to explain and
present already determined proposals and policies to the public." Goot (1999,
237) studied how the Australian Liberal leader John Howard used market
analysis to make the proposal to sell the publicly owned telecommunications
company Telstra more attractive and thus concludes that it is not true "that
on every issue, or even on all the important ones, polling necessarily commits
politicians to the position of the median voter." Murray's study (2006, 495)
of the Reagan presidency concluded that although some party-driven issues
were sidelined and changes were made if too much opposition was encoun-
tered, survey data were also used to find potential overlap between the leadership goals and public opinion, "to thereby identify political opportunities
where it could accomplish some of its ideological goals and satisfy some of
its partisan constituents, while staying within broad constraints established
by majority opinion." In Canada, Wlezien and Soroka (2007, 813) found
that there was similar variance in the relationship between public opinion
and elite policy making, concluding in answer to the question "Does democracy work?" that "in some cases, it appears as though it may work better
than many of us anticipated." Such studies have utilized external data; this
chapter provides internal perspectives from those who actually carry out the
research and strategizing. It will always be problematic to collect fully systematic and transferable data on a process that is essentially about the private
conversation and thought process of researcher and political leader, but what
the data gathered here show is that politicians do research the market and
use the research to inform their decisions, and thus that they do listen, but

that they do not just follow public opinion, therefore offering a new voice to the generic question of how political elites respond to the public. Political marketing informs political decisions, but it still allows room for leadership. Thus, political marketing can be used both to win elections and to enhance democracy.

ACKNOWLEDGMENTS

Acknowledgments are due to the Centre for the Study of Democratic Citizenship led by Professor Elisabeth Gidengil, which provided a visiting professorship that part-paid for my visit to Canada to conduct these interviews in May-June 2009; to Auckland University for grants to fund travel and research assistant work in the form of transcription, literature searches, and manuscript formatting; and to the practitioners who were interviewed and without whom this research would not have been possible.

7
"Buyer" Beware: Pushing the Boundaries of Marketing Communications in Government

Kirsten Kozolanka

Although there is a growing body of literature on political marketing, relatively little attention or analysis has been paid to a key aspect of this recent development: What happens after a political party uses political marketing to win an election and then finds itself negotiating the very different terrain and constraints of a government bureaucracy? In short, what happens the morning after the election? In Canada, earlier transformations in communications practices in government, the rise of new practices of governance concurrent with the development of political marketing, and the case of the Stephen Harper government's use of political marketing to promote its Economic Action Plan in 2009 collectively demonstrate the increasing centralization of power that crosses between the political and the administrative arms of government. This raises ethical questions about the use of political marketing in government and its impact on democracy.

This chapter uses a critical communications perspective (Mosco 2009) to examine political marketing by a governing political party. This approach enables a holistic examination of the shifting material and symbolic relations that over time have transformed governance in Canada (Brodie and Trimble 2003), as well as of the specific contexts within which the communications imperatives of recent governing parties have influenced public policy and the associated commodification of the citizen as a consumer. The chapter emphasizes power relations by identifying the early manifestations of centralized communication (Savoie 1999) under the Liberal government from 1993 to 2006 and the ensuing hypercentralization of control and management of information and communication when the Conservatives formed the government in 2006.

From the 1980s on, as the New Right market ideology of minimizing the state permeated federal politics, and by extension the public service in Canada, the traditional and informal understandings between the politicians in power and the career administrators in parliamentary democracies began to change.[1] However, it was the Chrétien Liberal government in the 1990s that completed the task of structurally downsizing the public service and introducing a New Right-led management ethos called "new public management" (NPM) into the leaner public service (Tupper 2003). NPM was a set of results-based, private-sector techniques with a service and client orientation that "focused on government as a service provider, not a policy initiator" (Whitaker 2008, 64). By reorganizing and reorienting the public service toward replacing the "hegemony of the market [rather than the state] as an organizing structure and dynamic" (Havemann 1998, 141), traditionally held conceptions of the public interest's "universal benefit to society" (Cohn 2003, 63) gave way to "a new politico-bureaucratic class of 'spin-doctors' shouldering aside public servants with more traditional analytic skills" (Hood and Lodge 2006, viii), laying the groundwork for political marketing as the eventual communications manifestation of NPM. As Savigny (2008b, 44) has written about the extension of market behaviour into aspects of public life in the United Kingdom,

> acceptance of the dominance of markets as the means through which public goods should be organized and resources allocated has been brought about, in part by changing ideological, social, political and economic climate and by responses of political actors to that climate, [thus,] it would seem somewhat logical that political actors would come to use these methods and mechanisms to inform their own electioneering behaviours.

By 2004 in Canada, parliamentary experts testified to the standing committee on public accounts that the independence of the public service was eroding. Moreover, the bureaucracy had been drawn into market behaviours by selling and being responsible for electoral success, and political staff was influencing the operations of government.

The shift in the Canadian public service, which is administered by the Privy Council Office (PCO), from policy advice to a service delivery model and its creeping politicization by successive governments had unexpected repercussions for communications in the public service. Once confined to disseminating information on policy, communications took on new importance. Growth in the size, functions, and prestige of communications began in the late 1990s after the massive cutbacks to the public service as it became clear that it was needed in order to sell controversial policies that shifted away from the Keynesian postwar social welfare policies toward a market-driven ethos. As communication began to be seen as a strategic function for government, other shifts took place, including what I have elsewhere referred to as institutionalization and centralization (Kozolanka 2006).

Between 2001 and 2003, the communications community within the public service grew by 28 percent, with one-quarter of its staff engaging in strategic communications, corporate communications, or marketing. The federal government's communication policy was revised, adding many new promotional practices to the communications function. Two benchmarking surveys in 2001 and 2003 assessed how it could be used more strategically. Budgets for public opinion research grew steadily, peaking at $31.4 million in 2007, as did advertising at $111 million in 2003 (Kozolanka 2006, 350). At one point, the government created its own national public opinion survey, which even polled views on party preferences; in Chapter 9 of this book Lisa Birch describes some of the public opinion research (POR) undertaken by Health Canada. Further promotional activities included a fairs and exhibits program to brand Canada and mass-mailed "householder" newsletters sent to targeted constituencies, which were also branding exercises to demonstrate the government's service delivery to Canadians. Later, householders were also produced under the Conservative government. The communications function within the Privy Council Office (the administrative counterpart in the public service to the partisan Prime Minister's Office, or PMO) expanded as well. For several years, a cabinet committee on communications existed to coordinate communications efforts across government, supported by a self-standing government department, Communication Canada, whose main activity was to be the "primary planning, production and delivery agent for the Government of Canada's corporate communication activities" (Canada, Communication Canada, n.d., 3).

The institutionalization and centralization of government communications within a gathering New Right political project, in which the downsizing of government put stress on the lines of accountability, also fostered an environment in which the lines became blurred between administration, which falls under the aegis of the PCO, and politics, led by the PMO. The sponsorship scandal is the most public manifestation of what can happen within such an environment when a long-term majority government, secure in its hegemonic dominance, oversteps.

The sponsorship program became an example of overuse of promotional vehicles and misuse of government funds for partisan purposes and, ultimately, a warning for subsequent governments. The program grew out of the national unity debates of the late 1980s and early 1990s, as well as the second referendum on Quebec sovereignty in 1995. Seeded by funds left over from the federal government's promotion of a united Canada and with considerable additional funding around 1995, the purpose of the program was simply to "inform Canadians" and to "heighten federal awareness," mostly in Quebec – at the time a vote-rich province for the Liberals (Canada, Communication Canada, n.d., 1). This exercise in brand recognition had another, more dubious goal: its stated intention was also to "build a strong and united Canada" (ibid.). As became clear after an eventual public inquiry in 2005, that latter goal led the ruling Liberals to spend nearly $145 million in inflated commissions and production costs to Liberal-friendly businesses. Some companies that received sponsorship contracts also gave more than $100 million of public money in donations and kickbacks to the Quebec branch of the Liberal Party (Canada 2005). Importantly for our understanding of how political marketing can work in government, part of the blame for the scandal fell on the lack of checks and balances in public service decision making that created openings in which political staff in the PMO and a key minister had unprecedented influence over decisions and actions, resulting in the self-promotion of the political party in power while using public resources (Kozolanka 2006).

In the wake of the scandal, many of the more visible aspects of promotional communications were dismantled. One alarming aspect of this was that much of the decision-making apparatus for public opinion research relocated to the Privy Council Office, placing responsibility for core political marketing tools in the hands of a centralized agency; over time, this has raised concerns about the Privy Council Office's politicization, from providing policy advice to now undertaking work formerly carried out by the PMO and the governing political party. The scandal also had an impact on the 2006 general election, in which the Conservatives came to power with an election platform that stressed accountability in government as the opposition parties sought to exploit Canadians' frustrations with the Liberal Party (Paré and Berger 2008, 51; also see Chapter 8). Subsequently, the new government passed the Federal Accountability Act (FAA), and the ensuing Paillé Report on government POR in 2007 recommended that the government clarify "the currently fuzzy concept of political neutrality" (Paillé 2007, 13).

Case Study: Communications in the Harper Government
Despite the negative publicity from the sponsorship scandal, political marketing practices in government continued and were strengthened under the

subsequent Conservative government. In the key areas of POR and advertising, the expenditure levels initially increased in 2006. However, in 2008, $10 million was removed from the polling budget, among other cost-cutting and accountability measures (Canada, Treasury Board, 2003a). Whereas governments are required to produce annual reports on such activities, political parties are conducting unknown amounts of their own party-paid research, which is invisible to the public.

Such reductions in public spending on polling and advertising, however, do not mean that political marketing efforts within government are waning. Instead, the tactical approach of the Conservatives to media, the public, and information management, from requests for media interviews to access to information requests, has only obscured their activities. Elsewhere, I have summarized the approach of Prime Minister Stephen Harper's government as "communication by stealth," which describes how the Conservatives "decentralized their media management strategies, closed down channels of communication flow and tightly controlled their communications strategies centrally" (Kozolanka 2009, 223).

Media Management

Much of the government's initial communications efforts bypassed the Ottawa-based parliamentary press gallery and instead focused on regional or local media and online media, where the government felt its messages would be better received and less likely to be subjected to editorial filtering. This strategic decentralization and dispersal of what could be termed "anti-media" tactics is in keeping with early political campaign analysis, which suggests the importance of free or earned media coverage – stories that do not appear to have a partisan political origin, as stories emanating from a press gallery might be perceived to have (B. Franklin 1994; Harris 2001). Over time, instances of tight control over the information flow to the media have mounted, along with criticism of the government's tactics, as the example of the message event proposal (MEP) tactic so aptly demonstrates.

One way that the Harper government has attempted to control the media, and thus public information, "stealthily" has been through a process in which, since 2007, public employees have filled out a detailed MEP form for every media request for information, interviews, or planned public events (Blanchfield and Bronskill 2010). A completed MEP form is approved by a minister's office, then goes to the Privy Council Office, after which it is sent to the Prime Minister's Office. A typical MEP is returned to the PCO with changes to be made and then sent back to the PMO, sometimes more than once, in a lengthy process that can mean missing media deadlines (Davis 2010b, 2) or at least resulting in "logjams, delays and ... [the] cancellation of planned events" (L. Martin 2010, 58). Critics see the MEP process as an example of role-blurring between the administrative and political offices, as public employees take on the role of media strategizing on behalf of the political party in power (Blanchfield and Bronskill 2010). The sponsorship scandal under the previous government was supposed to be the impetus for putting an end to practices such as this. However, here the same mistake was being made, demonstrating again that what is good for the party isn't necessarily good for the public as well.

Many see the governing party's lack of cooperation with the press gallery and its attempts to control the flow of information as more widespread and ominous than the media-obsessed MEPs themselves. In a June 2010 open letter, various organizations representing Canadian political journalists said that the government's "information control has reached new heights" and that "genuine transparency is replaced by slick propaganda and spin designed to manipulate public opinion" (Canadian Association of Journalists 2010, 1). The letter cited developments that had seen the PMO – via the public service – restrict media access to public events and replace media photographers with the PMO's own photos and footage (ibid.). The letter noted as well the decline in quality of the information that is available from the government, since public employees with expertise in different fields are no longer allowed to speak freely to the media. Instead, subject experts and interviews have been replaced by "an armada of press officers" (2). Taking into account the prime minister's aforementioned fight to bypass the parliamentary press gallery when he first came to power in 2006, this is part of a continued effort by the PMO to control the prime ministerial and Conservative Party brands.

INFORMATION CONTROL

The Conservatives have also made the work of all-party parliamentary committees more highly charged as they have attempted to control information flow. Legislative committees are an important hub of media activity and thus public awareness during times of key legislation, scandals, and other contentious issues. Early in their mandate, the Harper Conservatives prepared a two-hundred-page manual for their Members of Parliament on what opposition MPs said were directions on how to "obstruct" and "disrupt" parliamentary committee meetings when debate becomes hostile to the government

(Canada, House of Commons 2007, 27-30). In 2010, the government refused to supply secret reports on Afghan detainees to the parliamentary committee on access to information, privacy, and ethics, until eventually the Speaker of the House of Commons had to rule on a process that released twenty-six hundred pages of redacted material (deleted for reasons of national security) to a special all-party committee to vet. According to access-to-information specialist Ken Rubin (2010, 2), "The unaccountable redaction process renders the ... [Access to Information] Act an even less effective and credible tool" and prevents meaningful understanding of the material. In addition, access to information offices in government departments remain underfunded, creating delays in responses, with the information commissioner ranking the PCO as having one of the worst records (Canada, Office of the Information Commissioner 2010). The commissioner noted that the most important determinant of compliance with the act is departmental leadership (ibid.). Since the PCO plays a key role in leading the public service, its lack of leadership regarding public information is of concern, especially since, as Anna Esselment confirms in Chapter 8, the PCO has worked closely with the PMO in assisting the government to fulfill its electoral commitments. This has the potential to put the PCO in conflict with the public interest by withholding information at odds with its own and the government's interests.

Such tactics by the Prime Minister's Office to control information flow turn attempts to gain democratic access – either by the media, the political opposition, or the public – into a long and tedious process with a watered-down outcome that is more acceptable (or less unacceptable) to the PMO. This goes beyond controlling the release of information to include silencing or muzzling of critics (Stanbury 2010, 18). Whereas the first set of tactics blocks access and forestalls disclosure of information, the latter attacks critics or denies the validity of information that does get into the public realm. Considered in the context of the limited financial or time resources of those who request the information, this can be an effective way to discourage requests.

Instances of the government's information control over the public service extend to communications activities. One example is the requirement, as of 2008, that ministers – not deputy ministers who are members of the public service – approve all public opinion research contracted in their departments (Canada, Public Works and Government Services 2009a, 2). This action, taken "to provide greater oversight and rigour" (6), may result in more politicized decision making. Similarly, in the 2008-9 report on public opinion research, the role of the PCO is specified for the first time as having "a central role in the leadership, challenge, strategic directions and coordination of departmental and horizontal [across-government] public opinion research activities" (2). It is logical that the highest office in the public service would play a role in a promotional activity that has been controversial in the past. Yet, this also suggests how easily such control can be misappropriated, as it was when the sponsorship program was centrally controlled.

COMMUNICATIONS CONTROL

The ability of the Conservative Party to manage communications operations has been made easier by more communications personnel in the public service. The 2008 benchmarking survey reported that the number of such employees increased by a further 23.4 percent in the four years between 2003-4 and 2006-7 (Canada, Communications Community Office, 2008, 22).[2] Yet, the survey also indicated that communications in government had less of a strategic role and more of a service delivery role, with "major trans-formations" and "major structural change" taking place in communications, as well as more formalized connections with ministers' and deputy ministers' offices to examine MEPs, announcements, question period, and media rela-tions (140). In addition, communications branch heads or directors reported that the PCO has become "less an enabler and advisor and more the director" and that it "is more hands-on in managing files" (141). Whereas the 2001 report emphasized the need for the management of the communications function to be made up of "strategic thinkers" (158), in the 2008 report, by contrast, the heads indicated that this competency was "not as much in de-mand today. With the centralization of communication conceptualization, planning and approval activities, the role falling to both NHQ [National Headquarters] and regional communications branches is *less strategic and more tactical implementation*" (159; emphasis added).

Together, these changes indicate the strengthening of central control over communications specifically and the shift from an advisory to a service role. A large number of communications officers in government now support and deliver centrally conceived strategic political marketing activities. Further confirmation of the intensified and central strategic communications role of the Prime Minister's Office can be found in the communications strength of its own employees. In 2007, over a third (37 of 106) of the PMO's staff members were engaged in communications activities. In contrast, only 8 (7.5 percent) were working on policy (Canada, Public Works and Government Services 2009b) in a PMO that has continued to grow.[3]

In sum, the Conservative government has more invasive control of the Privy Council Office and the communications and information apparatus of the public service. It has reduced the role of the administrative arm of government to service delivery while building its own strategic communications apparatus, both within its own political office (the PMO) and in its use of the PCO as an adjunct office where the political marketing tools of advertising and public opinion research are funded and controlled. Although they rationalize this in the name of accountability, in so doing the Conservatives call into question their commitment to their own election platform priority of accountability and transparency. This also fosters the conditions for an enhanced promotional culture within the administrative arm of government and can be a formidable incumbency advantage for the governing party.

POLITICAL MARKETING AND THE ECONOMIC ACTION PLAN

This brings us to a key political marketing campaign undertaken by the Conservative government soon after its re-election in 2008 and in response to the international economic recession that began in late 2008. The tightly controlled information and communication environment carefully built by the governing party was tested in its response to the recession. It was the right issue for the Conservatives to use to consolidate their brand, as right-of-centre parties often promote themselves as better at handling economic issues. Since the New Right political project focuses on economic policy and well-being, discourses used over the years to condition citizens to conservative fiscal policy were also at the ready. Although the Conservatives made the decision to stimulate the economy through government spending, they had to be careful to do so without alerting their core supporters that they were fighting the recession by spending taxpayers' money. At the same time, they assuaged the majority Opposition's advocacy for stimulus spending, which Conservatives have long derided Liberals for doing. Thus, a substantial political marketing campaign on its stimulus plan – instead, called an "action" plan – was inevitable.

On January 27, 2009, Finance Minister Jim Flaherty tabled a budget "to stimulate economic growth, restore confidence and support Canadian families and business during a synchronized recession" (Canada, Department of Finance, 2009a, 1). The news release listed the specific themes of the plan in phrases that emphasized the word "action" in each of its six themes. Strategically, the other political parties had little choice but to be seen as fighting the recession rather than rejecting the budget and subjecting Canadians to another election just months after Canadians had already gone to the polls. On March 11, another news release unveiled a website to "allow Canadians to hold governments and public officials accountable for action on the economy" (Canada, Department of Finance, 2009b).

The website became the focus of considerable negative attention from the political opposition, the media, and the public. With its Tory blue colour scheme and forty photographs of the prime minister, the website was immediately subjected to criticism that the plan was promoting the Conservative Party by conflating it with the economic action plan. This criticism was strengthened when it was noted that the phrase "Harper Government," instead of the traditional "Government of Canada" phrase, recurred throughout the references to the plan, which further branded the prime minister with the action plan (Macleod 2009, 1). This way of referring to a government initiative ran counter to existing Treasury Board guidelines for websites (Canada, Treasury Board 1990). As the plan was being implemented, the action plan website was still up and running, with new photos of the prime minister, ministers, and Conservative Members of Parliament "supporting," "investing," and "celebrating" at sod turnings and other photo opportunities (see www. actionplan.gc.ca). Rather than providing accountability, as suggested by the news release, the website created a sense of partisan opportunism.

Further issues were raised about how the economic plan was being promoted when a saturation advertising campaign started on September 21, 2009. The campaign included six ads for each of radio and television, as well as print and Internet ads in both English and French. In all, advertising eventually totalled $89 million (Davis 2010a). A main point of contention was their timing. When the advertising started, much of the stimulus money had already been allocated, which made the ad campaign less informational and more clearly promotional of the Conservative Party. The timing also pointed to the possibility of a fall election in which the Conservatives would have already primed the electorate through the extensive public-paid advertising. An investigative media report confirmed allegations by the media and political opposition that action plan funds were allocated in higher amounts to Conservative ridings (McGregor 2009). In addition, some Conservative MPs conducted photo opportunities in their ridings with giant novelty cheques imprinted with the Conservative Party logo instead of the regulation Government of Canada logo. The ethics commissioner said the cheques "went too far" and "had the potential to diminish public confidence in the integrity of elected public officials and the governing institutions they represent," but ruled not to pursue the matter on a technicality (Canada, Office of the Conflict of Interest and Ethics Commissioner 2010, 2).

Political marketing for the Economic Action Plan made visible the blurring between the partisan work of the PMO and the administrative role of the PCO. The marketing was managed centrally by the PCO "as determined by the Prime Minister and the Cabinet" (Canada, Privy Council Office 2010, 22). The PCO added twenty new staff and received an additional allocation of $3.6 million for the project in 2009-10, with a further $3.6 million to come in 2010-11 (14, 22). Although oversight was centralized in the PCO, the actual funding and activity related to the plan was spread out across four departments. This may have technically complied with accountability rules, but it also obscured the breadth and cost of the campaign.

The Privy Council Office normally does and should play an enhanced role on the government's most complex projects, but the embedding of staff and resources on a project that required strategic positioning to maintain the internal cohesion of the governing party takes on an aura of partisan politics. This raises concerns about the relationship between the Prime Minister's Office and the Privy Council Office, the blurring of boundaries between the two offices, and the impact on democratic governance.

The State of Political Marketing in Canada

A burgeoning literature on political marketing has yet to fully analyze how governments use promotion after an election.[4] Clearly, however, political marketing has long been present to some degree in federal government communications in Canada. The groundwork can be traced back to the ongoing retrenchment of the state in the 1980s and 1990s as part of the New Right project that saw a market management ethos enter into the public service. Enhanced government communication was needed to play a more strategic role in selling controversial shifts in the structure and role of the state. Political marketing has the same service relationship with citizens as new public management has with public employees and can be seen as the communication arm of NPM.

In the case of the sponsorship scandal, the Liberals reorganized and reconstructed the promotional practices of communications to encompass a strategic role. It was under the subsequent Conservative government, however, that we see the full spectrum of political marketing, with the tactical knowledge gained from significant party investment in public opinion and other research prior to the 2006 campaign that brought the Conservative Party to power (see Chapters 4 to 6).

One reason for the Conservative government's all-encompassing focus on media, communication, and information management arose from the reality of electoral politics in Canada, in which the Conservatives have not had the hegemonic success of the Liberals, until 2011 Canada's other major party federally. To be successful electorally, the Conservative Party took on the challenge of building a "broad centrist conservative coalition" and positioning the party to win "not just this election, but *many others to come*" (Plamondon 2008, A15; emphasis in original). Tom Flanagan, former campaign chair for the party, publicly shed light on its controversial media strategy when he wrote that "the media are unforgiving of conservative errors, so we have to exercise strict discipline" (Flanagan 2009, 283). He also revealed the party's incremental strategy toward achieving hegemony, saying that "small conservative reforms are less likely to scare voters than grand conservative schemes, particularly in Canada, where conservatism is not yet the dominant philosophy" (Flanagan 2007b, A1).

While in opposition, the hegemonic strategies of the Conservatives may be appropriate; however, how do they stand up the morning after the election? For Westminster-style governments, the key liberal democratic assumption is the inviolability between the administrative side of government (the bureaucracy) and the political side (the elected party in power), which in Canada has been supported since the Civil Service Act of 1918. The apolitical side of this relationship is laid out in the public service code of ethics and values, which states that public employees must "maintain the tradition of the political neutrality of the Public Service" and perform their duties "so that public confidence and trust in the integrity, objectivity and impartiality of government are conserved and enhanced" (Canada, Treasury Board 2003b, 8).

Yet, it is also clear that elected political parties "come to power with principles, policies and proposals" of their own (Negrine 2008, 117), and it is a truism to say at times – especially during regime changes – that this might be in conflict with the existing bureaucracy and its rules and ethics. Flanagan says successive minority governments in Canada over three elections meant that a permanent campaign was underway in federal politics, which "caused the Conservative Party to merge with the campaign team, producing a garrison party. The party is today, for all intents and purposes, a campaign organization" (MacCharles 2010, A13). This confirms a continuing role for political marketing in Canadian federal politics, particularly in minority governments, which pose many challenges, as Anna Esselment delineates in Chapter 8.

Canada's political history since at least 1983 shows us that the assumed inviolable barriers between the political and administrative arms of government have weakened (Savoie 2003). If the current government is in permanent campaign mode, the blurred lines between the PMO and PCO could weaken further. A contributing factor is the waning influence of political parties across Western democracies as power has shifted to professional political advisers outside of government (Savoie 2010). In effect, as the lines between politics and government blur, political parties are being recreated *within* government.

The Federal Accountability Act, the legislative tool meant to both enforce and instill public service neutrality while forestalling partisan politics, is a double-edged sword. A report from the Public Policy Forum concluded that the FAA "is killing morale and stifling innovation, creativity and effective leadership" (May 2007, A1), a gap that the PMO is likely to fill. The Conservatives' message event proposal process surely contributes to that culture by reducing the competencies of public employees to endlessly revise a form that impedes the media's role as a watchdog for transparent and accountable government. Instead of public employees providing their expert information directly to the media, Conservative political staffers in ministers' offices or in the PMO deliver their own carefully crafted messages. However, the Conservative government also drew on the act strategically as a rationale for centralizing activities such as the implementation and communication of the Economic Action Plan within the PCO. As this chapter shows, this can facilitate a more politicized approach to government activities with the PCO's complicity. Such centralization can play a positive coordinating role, but only if it is not reduced to the top-down command and control that we have seen under the Conservative government (Doyle 2007). In effect, the Conservatives have no need of a self-standing government department like Communication Canada. Given the Harper government's hypercentralization of communications within the PMO, that department's ideological management functions are no longer required (Rubin and Kozolanka 2010).

The Conservatives have hypercentralized and maintained strict control on communication and information in what can only be considered as permanent campaigning mode. These tactics risk becoming operationalized into government and, if political history holds true, we can expect that they will be emulated, if not surpassed, under governments to come.

Implications for the Quality of Democracy

In liberal democracies such as Canada, certain assumptions are made about the nature of our political processes and how citizens interact with their government. It is assumed that every citizen is important, particularly in terms of his or her ability to make rational choices alongside other citizens who are his or her equals. Further, political science literature "positions political engagement, participation and thus the act of voting, as a unique behaviour, a civic duty, grounded within citizenship" (Lilleker and Scullion 2008, 3).

The permanent campaigning implied by political marketing and that is evident in the political behaviour of the Conservatives presents risks to rational choice and interaction by citizens. Its reliance on promotion fosters a societal environment in which citizens do not necessarily deliberate on how they want society to be so much as they satisfy their personal wants and needs at any given moment. In other words, such voter-consumers have little loyalty to a stable, long-term, overall vision of society (Kesteloot, De Vries, and De Landtsheer 2008) and instead depend on their "personal" relationship with an individual party candidate (Harris, Lock, and Rees 2000). For Savigny (2008b, 41), this situates the voter-consumer in a responsive mode within a political marketplace that has already defined the parameters of debate and charted the direction to be taken (Stanyer 2007, 75), not as citizens actively and deliberatively engaging in shaping society (Savigny 2008b, 40-41).

As Lees-Marshment (2009b, 221) has written, today's citizens already seem to want "a more tangible rather than a rhetorical product, want more evident and instant delivery, and prefer achievement over inspiration; they may seek pragmatic effectiveness over moral principle." The implication of permanent campaigning for government in a market-driven society is that it needs to constantly renew itself and exhibit tangible evidence of service delivery to voter-consumers, using the various promotional tools of political marketing.

Scammell (2008, 97) sees branding, the latest "hallmark" of political marketing, as "indicative of a truly consumerized paradigm of political communication," in which "the prime relationship (with voters) is shaped by the approach, methods and conception of voters as citizen-consumers." The obvious implication for citizens is that they are passively consuming politics rather than actively engaging with it, though some argue that consumption has its active qualities (Lilleker and Scullion 2008). Where government information is concerned, if citizens are treated as research outcomes and consumers of highly managed information, coming to rational judgments may be beyond their reach. Political marketing's claim of being responsive to the needs of the voter is hollow if one considers that the outcome of this relationship is not in the latter's best interest, but in that of those who steer the process. It is also reasonable to suggest that increasingly interested rather than neutral information from government cannot be considered democratic communication, as the outcome is that the party in power gets what it wants, rather than fulfilling the democratic needs of voting citizens (Paré and Berger 2008, 58-59).

The trajectory over the short history of political marketing in Canada suggests that its intensifying use has short-term successes, but also pitfalls. Although there can be little objection to governments amassing the means to inform citizens of relevant information in persuasive ways, pushing the boundaries of political marketing while in government and using the public service to aid and abet the process enters into ethical areas yet to be explored fully. O'Shaughnessy (2004, 181) suggests that the discipline and managerial skill exhibited in political marketing in a winning election campaign beg to be carried through into governing. He puts forward the claim that "the management of the state's communication may even rival in importance the management of the state itself, at least according to its rulers" (173).

In the context of governing, Paré and Berger and O'Shaughnessy draw attention to an important gap in our understanding about political marketing by a political party in power: we know little about how successful a mandate through marketing can be over the long haul. Even when party governments engage in considerable promotional efforts over long periods of time – the Blair-Brown governments in the United Kingdom, the Liberal dynasty in Canada – in democratic systems they eventually falter:

> Governments are always seeking new ways to respond to the challenges they face, finding novel means to control negative publicity and connect with citizens ... Over time, they still become unpopular, and increasingly the very effort of "handling the media" and managing public opinion itself becomes the news story, creating an image of governments as deceitful, calculating and obsessed with their own popularity. (Stanyer 2007, 42-43)

Ultimately, parties need to consider that their brand – at the very least – can be damaged over time by this political behaviour. Moreover, O'Shaughnessy (2004) cautions that such a government – which he refers to as "symbolic government," in which "the creation of symbolic images, symbolic actions and celebratory rhetoric have become a principal concern" and "a central organizing principle" (172-73) – may also fall prey to authoritarianism, cynicism, manipulation, and deceit (185-86).

The Harper government has demonstrated that political parties can maintain a political marketing orientation after an election, despite its battles with the ethics commissioner and the information commissioner, among others. New governments taking up the challenge of market orientation should also keep in mind the fate of the previous government, however, and be concerned that some aspects of the sponsorship scandal, the product of the last government's politicized promotion gone awry, can be compared to the Economic Action Plan in that it blurs the boundaries of state and party, as well as the political and administrative arms of government. With this in mind, as with the concerns expressed by O'Shaughnessy (2004), Stanyer (2007), Savigny (2008b), and Scammell (2008), among others, it would be prudent to consider the level to which endless promotion can control and prolong an inevitable outcome and damage democracy along the way. A different route would be to rethink the concept of a market-oriented government and to consider allowing democracy to take its course instead of indulging in ever more sophisticated ways to contain it.

NOTES

1   The New Right is a melding of economic libertarianism and moral conservatism and is the conservative response to the postwar Keynesian consensus. When this market ideology became evident in the Thatcher and Reagan governments (1979-90), it was referred to variously as "neo-liberalism" and "neo-conservatism," but the term "New Right" is inclusive of both these philosophical strands.

2   The numbers used here refer to those supplied in the 2008 report. The totals for 2001 and 2003 are slightly different in the original reports.

3   This includes a communications unit, a strategic communications unit, an issues management unit, a market researcher, events coordinators, media advance assistants, and photographers.

4   Notable exceptions are Lees-Marshment (2009b) laying the groundwork and Paré and Berger (2008) in the Canadian context. See also Chapter 8 by Anna Esselment.

8
Market Orientation in a Minority Government: The Challenges of Product Delivery

Anna Esselment

Academic research in political marketing has led to the development of models that primarily apply its principles to how parties prepare for campaigns and less so to how marketing techniques can help maintain a party in power (Newman 1994; Ormrod 2005). In the political marketing model developed by Jennifer Lees-Marshment (2001b), however, stage eight of the process for a market-oriented party is delivery. In other words, should a market-oriented party (MOP) win an election and form government, it must deliver its product or risk losing re-election (Lees-Marshment 2009c, 209; see also Table 10.1). The achievability of the product is crucial to the market-oriented party, as over-promising and under-delivering can threaten a governing party's chances of remaining in power.

Since the early 1990s, delivering on election promises has gained greater currency among the public. This has resulted in party platforms with pledges or "contracts" for which voters can hold politicians directly accountable at the next election. Notable examples of such clear and transparent platforms include the Liberal Party of Canada's red book in 1993, the US House Republican's "Contract with America" in 1994, the Ontario Progressive Conservative Party's Common Sense Revolution in 1995, New Labour's 1997 "pledges" to Britons, and the Conservative Party of Canada's "five priorities" in 2006, to name just a few. Each of the aforementioned platforms was developed while the party was in opposition, however, and this has led some to conclude that a market orientation is more easily maintained out of power than as government (Lees-Marshment and Lilleker 2005, 32-33; Marland 2005). Nevertheless, the ability of political parties to do what they said they were going to do has heightened importance among the voting public, and, consequently, policy delivery has increased salience for governments and their leaders (Barber 2007). This has even led to the development of centralized policy implementation units within various jurisdictions (see Table 8.1) to

TABLE 8.1

Delivery and implementation units

	Created
Prime Minister's Delivery Unit (United Kingdom)	June 2001
Cabinet Implementation Unit (Australia)	October 2003
Queensland Implementation Unit (Australia)	March 2004

ensure emphasis and oversight of the delivery of key policy items (Richards and Smith 2006; Tiernan 2006; Wanna 2006). Maintaining a market orientation *after* the election, including a focus on delivery, is thus a key component of political marketing theory and practice (Lees-Marshment 2009b).

There are notable challenges to product delivery, however. Once a party wins power and takes over the machinery of government, daily crises and constraints with which the government must contend can bog down the larger strategic vision (Arterton 2007). Advisers, once critical and objective, become less willing to provide honest assessments to a prime minister. Experience in power, combined with a weak opposition, can lead a party toward arrogance and complacency with regard to the public (Kent 2006, 14). Similarly, the bubble in which the government operates has the effect of distancing it from citizens and their views. Governments can consequently become much less responsive than a market orientation requires, and this can hinder prioritizing time to consider future product development and possible adjustments. The latter is a critical exercise if a governing party wants to stay in touch with voters for the benefit of government decision making and planning the next campaign (Lees-Marshment 2009a, 533).

These challenges have a mixed impact on product delivery when, in a parliamentary system, the party is in a minority situation. Without majority control of a legislature, fulfilling policy platform items is not straightforward. Extra time and effort must be devoted to assessing the strategic goals of the opposition parties and reacting to them appropriately. At the same time, maintaining a market orientation and delivering on promises is critical for the party to grow its popular support and seat share in the next election. This can be problematic, as the governing party has limited control over the timing of a new campaign. A minority government is, rightly, at the mercy of the representative assembly through the vote of non-confidence. This has the dual effect of constraining a government's legislative manoeuvrability (which can adversely impact delivery) while also imposing a sense of urgency to move quickly on its key platform items in anticipation of the next election. In effect, the challenges to delivery (staying in touch with voters through market research, keeping the leader humble and responsive, encouraging critically objective opinions, setting aside time to think about future product development) are the very same components that are crucial to the success of a government in a minority parliament. The following case study examines how the Conservative Party of Canada (CPC) successfully steered its way through the first term of its minority government by remaining largely market-oriented.

Case Study: The Conservative Minority Government of 2006 to 2008

METHODOLOGY

This case study is informed by numerous primary and secondary sources, as well as interviews with two key political informants in the Stephen Harper minority government. Both were primary figures in the planning and execution of the 2006 campaign and in advising the prime minister during his first term in office. The semi-structured interviews were conducted in January 2006 and in May 2010 and lasted approximately ninety minutes each, with follow-up emails to clarify details. The author is grateful for the contribution of these former staff, and their anonymity has been respected.

DELIVERY SUCCESSES

In the 2006 federal election, the CPC managed to eke out only a minority government in spite of an almost perfectly executed market-oriented campaign against a wounded and maligned Liberal Party (Paré and Berger 2008; see also Chapters 4 and 5). The reason was readily apparent: the Liberal attack on Conservative leader Stephen Harper's "secret right-wing agenda" resonated with voters. Although they were tired and disillusioned with the Liberals, Canadians remained suspicious of the new Conservative Party and its leader. The main challenge for the government was to overcome this image of harbouring a hidden plan:

> How do you defeat that? Well, there are lots of ways to defeat that, but the core of it has to be, "This is what we ran on, this is what we said we were going to do, and when we go back to the polls this is what we did – we delivered." (personal interview with Harper strategist)

TABLE 8.2

"Stand Up for Canada" campaign platform, 2006

- Two-point reduction to the goods and services tax (from 7% to 5%)
- Child care allowance for families with children five years and under ($100 per month per child)
- Stronger government accountability measures
- Criminal justice reform
- Patient wait-times guarantee.

SOURCE: Conservative Party of Canada (2006, 30).

The Conservative platform focused on five main priorities (see Table 8.2) and, with a minority parliament, it was imperative they be delivered quickly and visibly. The Conservatives were able to implement two items from the platform shortly after their election, and this gave them some early "wins." In the May 2006 budget, Finance Minister Jim Flaherty announced that the first phase of a reduction in the goods and services tax (GST) from 7 percent to 6 percent would take effect that July (Canada, Department of Finance 2006a, 3). The second GST cut, reducing the tax from 6 percent to 5 percent, was made known on December 31, 2007. Both announcements came with much fanfare and visibility. The prime minister visited the same retail store in Mississauga, Ontario, where he had originally announced the tax policy in the 2006 campaign and, in an exemplary moment of marketing execution, slapped a large sticker reading "5%" onto the side of the cash register (*CityNews* 2007). Economists had panned the policy of cutting the GST, but it was an effective platform item, popular with the public, and a valuable contribution for the party's implementation record (Canadian Press 2007).

In the same budget speech, Minister Flaherty also announced the introduction of the child care allowance. This plan would provide $100 per month per child for families with children under the age of six (Canada, Department of Finance 2006a, 3). The aim of the annual $1,200 allowance was to help parents pay for child care, though how parents ultimately chose to spend the money was up to them. Like the GST cut, this came into effect on July 1, 2006. Every month since, families with children under six are "delivered" this care allowance, as $100 or more is deposited directly into their bank accounts or sent as cheques in the mail. Like the GST, it remains a solid pocketbook issue that the CPC can point to as a successful fulfillment of its 2006 campaign platform.

The third area of swift movement was on government accountability. As a result of the judicial inquiry into allegations of corruption by the former Liberal government (see Kirsten Kozolanka's preceding chapter), many Canadians were supportive of reforms that would prevent similar abuses of public money in the future. The Conservatives had highlighted this issue in the campaign and had promised a new Federal Accountability Act (FAA) to address numerous areas of concern. Demonstrating its commitment to the issue, the FAA was one of the first pieces of legislation introduced in the House of Commons by the new Conservative government. Among other changes, the new legislation reduced limits on financial donations to political parties, placed strict parameters and rules around lobbying the government, strengthened the role of the ethics commissioner and auditor general, made the procurement process for government contracts more transparent, and required that senior civil servants be more directly accountable to Parliament for the actions of their departments. The effectiveness of these particular measures has been questioned (Aucoin 2007), but the Tories clearly showed action where voters wanted it most. The FAA became a much-touted accomplishment for the CPC in its first term.

On these three items at least, the Conservative minority government embraced political marketing principles by efficiently and effectively delivering on its platform priorities as outlined in stage eight of the Lees-Marshment MOP model. This deliberate strategy gave the Conservatives early policy "wins," which they could easily highlight if an election was called.

Delivery Challenges

Despite the quick action on tax cuts, child care allowances, and accountability reform, the Conservative government had more challenges with the two remaining planks of its Stand Up for Canada platform: a patient wait-times guarantee and criminal justice reform. In Canada's federal system, powers are divided between the central and regional governments, and health care is primarily a provincial responsibility. The federal government's involvement in health care occurs through its spending power and through the enforcement of the Canada Health Act, which requires every province to maintain a universal, publicly funded system (see Chapter 9 by Lisa Birch for a related discussion). The Conservative pledge to reduce patient wait times for specific procedures was thus a more complicated promise, given that success was dependent on provincial cooperation. At the same time, the reduction of wait times had been a component of the 2004 health accord that had been negotiated between the previous Liberal government and the ten provinces and three territories. Both a plan and funding were thus already in place to work toward benchmarks for wait-times reduction when the Tories took office. The Conservative commitment, however, was for a "guarantee" – a *deadline* for Canadians to receive the medical treatment they needed in five areas: cancer care, hip and knee replacement, cardiac care, diagnostic imaging, and cataract surgeries. This was harder to achieve, and, within six months of taking office, the government began to distance itself from this platform priority (Wells 2006). More movement on this issue occurred in the 2007 budget, where a patient wait-times guarantee "trust" was put into place to advance the implementation of this promise (Canada, Department of Finance 2007). The government also scaled back certain requirements set out in the campaign platform and asked only that the provinces commit to a wait-time guarantee in one of the five priority areas. This was to be completed by March 2010 (S. Norris 2009, 8). When Health Minister Tony Clement secured the agreement of the provinces and territories to this budget item in early April 2007, Prime Minister Harper declared the campaign pledge fulfilled, although skepticism among some members of the public prevailed (CTV.ca 2007). Fortunately for the Conservatives, the failure to deliver cleanly on this priority did not become a major issue in the next election.

The Conservatives also had problems with efficient delivery of promised criminal justice reforms. In their first year of government, the Tories attempted to introduce changes to the criminal justice system incrementally by tabling eleven separate bills dealing with different areas of reform. These quickly became bogged down in the House of Commons justice committee, where opposition party members formed the majority. In the second session of Parliament (still in the government's first term), the Conservatives attempted a second tactic – they consolidated all of the violent crime bills into a single piece of legislation called the Tackling Violent Crime Act. The act included mandatory minimum sentences for firearms offences, raised the age of sexual consent, toughened provisions for sexual and violent offenders, and increased the penalties for impaired driving (Canada 2008). The government's strategy was to keep the focus on violent crime at the macro-level, and if the opposition parties again attempted widespread amendments, the government would accuse them of thwarting its efforts to keep Canadians safe. Furthermore, as a bread-and-butter issue of conservatives across Canada, the government made it clear that it was prepared to go to an election on this issue. One government insider noted that "that strategic ploy was successful ... we wanted to say we had made some progress on that, and we played a tougher hand, a much more brutal legislative hand, with that one than we had done in the first round right after 2006" (personal interview). The Tackling Violent Crime Act passed at the end of February 2008, and although it was a harder promise for the Conservatives to deliver, they were able to go into the subsequent fall 2008 election with that priority fulfilled.

Perhaps the biggest failure the Conservatives faced early in their mandate was a deliberate about-face on their promise not to tax income trusts. The campaign platform had specifically pledged to "preserve income trusts by not imposing any new taxes on them" (Conservative Party of Canada 2006, 32). On October 31, 2006, Finance Minister Flaherty reversed this decision. A steady number of businesses had turned to income trusts to avoid paying corporate taxes, and the government was unprepared to allow such vast sums of revenue go uncollected (Canada, Department of Finance 2006b). There was little the Conservatives could do to assuage this broken pledge and instead tried to address it directly:

> When we ultimately reneged on the income trust taxes, we were high profile about confronting the fact we were reneging on a promise. There was no discussion about how we could finesse this because we couldn't. There was no discussion about how to avoid facing up to the fact that what we said was "A" and then we were doing the opposite of "A." In an effort to contain the fact we were breaking a promise, we just tried to explain "here's why we did it and you can make your own judgment as to whether you are going to trust us again, but we aren't going to hide the fact that we did the opposite of what we told you we were going to do." (personal interview with Harper strategist)

Some finessing did occur, however, as members of the government – including the prime minister – tried to argue that the income security pledges were intended for seniors, not for Canadian corporations in general (Canwest News Service 2006). In an effort to explain its reasoning, however, the Department of Finance released detailed backgrounders describing how the financial picture had changed since the Conservatives had been elected nine months earlier. It appeared that a rethinking of the pledge, if not for reasons of good government, was required. Fortunately for the Conservatives, the political fallout from the income trust broken promise was not severe. Many Canadians indicated that their finances would not be negatively affected by the new tax (Aubry 2006), and although corporations were livid that this tax sanctuary had been terminated, campaign finance rules banning businesses from donating to political parties limited their avenues for effective retaliation.

To this point, the focus has been primarily on the five main planks of the CPC platform. Keen students of Canadian politics could note several other broken promises by the Stephen Harper government. Harper's first nominee for appointment to the Supreme Court was subjected to the new system of "parliamentary review," yet this process was bypassed for his second nominee, ostensibly because of a looming election campaign. Harper had championed Senate reform but immediately appointed a party insider to the second chamber in order to ensure the representation of Montreal in cabinet. The media's ability to keep the government accountable was limited by severe centralized communications control (see Chapter 7). The premiers of Newfoundland and Labrador and of Nova Scotia argued that the Conservatives reneged on their promise to keep the Atlantic Accord intact. Similarly, the prime minister orchestrated an early election call in 2008, despite legislating fixed election dates. On most of these issues, political expediency is an obvious explanatory factor. This suggests that shrewd political considerations (such as the perceived beneficial effect of a conservative judge on the Supreme Court) can occasionally undermine the delivery of campaign commitments. On others, such as the Atlantic Accord, more analysis is merited, but that is beyond the scope of this chapter.

CPC MINORITY GOVERNMENT AND FACTORS AFFECTING DELIVERY

Considering that most of the five priorities from the Stand Up for Canada platform were fulfilled within the first term of government, it would appear that delivery in this particular minority government was quite successful. Prime Minister Harper was in fact able to govern as though he had a majority of seats. What particular issues either challenged or facilitated policy delivery in this case?

A former member of the Prime Minister's Office noted that the inability to properly assess the relative strength or weakness of the opposition – particularly the Liberals – posed a problem for the government in terms of developing its overall strategy in the first term. The Liberal Party of Canada has been referred to as the country's "natural governing party" (Clarkson 2005), and its brand has deep roots in the minds of Canadians. Even though the Liberals had suffered major losses in the 2006 election and were distracted by a leadership race, their psychological impact on the Conservatives in terms of perceived strength initially played a large role on internal strategy:

> We overestimated the Liberals, or the relative Liberal strength, and underestimated our own. We underestimated the impact of our mandate and the amount of leeway we were going to get from the Liberals. It took us a while to figure out what a strong legislative hand that personally gave us. (personal interview with Harper strategist)

This overestimation of opposition strength was a challenge that had positive repercussions for the government. Political marketing principles suggest that a weak opposition can negatively impact the maintenance of a market orientation in government (Lees-Marshment 2009a, 533). Specifically, a weak opposition can facilitate victories for a government without it having to be "overtly responsive" to voters (ibid). In this case, at times the CPC minority government assumed opposition *strength;* as such, it operated with care in the legislature. This is unlike a coalition government where the parties forming the government have a majority of seats. In Canada, support for legislative initiatives by opposition parties is determined on a bill-by-bill basis. Reaching out to opposition parties, and by extension to their supporters, to smooth the legislative process is a key factor that encourages minority governments to stay market-oriented.

A greater challenge to delivery for the Conservative minority government was the legislative committee system, where proposed bills are thoroughly analyzed. When a government does not have a majority in Parliament, the opposition parties have the most members on the various committees. Consequently, the government has less control over amendments to its proposed laws, over committee wishes to allow witnesses or travel for hearings, or over whether the legislation will bear any resemblance to its original form after the committee process. This was the major stumbling block to the party's criminal justice reforms, but it was also a problem on other issues, to the point where the Conservatives developed a guide for Tory chairpersons on how to effectively manipulate committee procedures to the government's advantage (D. Martin 2007; see also Chapter 7). Consequently, committees were usually bitterly divided along partisan lines, leading to lengthy delays in the completion of work. The effect of this challenge in terms of remaining market-oriented is more difficult to assess. On the one hand, the Conservatives wanted to be sure that their priorities made it through the committee process. Many of the government's priorities were popular both with the public and with supporters of the party, and ensuring their successful implementation was a response to those needs. But working with opposition parties and being responsive to them also connects the government to the needs of Canadians who voted for other parties and who the governing party may want to capture in future elections. The delay-and-disrupt tactics used by government members suggest that the government became more frustrated and aggressive toward the opposition in these particular forums, contributing to committee dysfunction. This works against a market orientation by cutting the government off from an important segment of the market, one that could potentially be very important in the quest for majority status.

Despite these obstacles, there were also several issues that facilitated delivery in the Conservative minority government. The first was an abundance of financial resources. The government had a budgetary surplus that allowed for efficient implementation of certain commitments. Enough money was available to fulfill the child care allowance promise, the government could afford the two-point reduction in the GST, and resources could be put toward supporting the tough-on-crime and accountability measures. Delivery is easier when government finances are healthy.

Following through on commitments was also aided by the political salience of the particular promises; most were popular enough with the public that the opposition parties were unwilling to trigger an election over them. Even though the Liberals, NDP, and Bloc Québécois preferred a publicly funded child care system, it was hard to oppose a child care allowance because of its prominence with voters (in fact, in the 2008 election, the Liberals promised to double the child care allowance; see Canadian Press 2008). The GST cut, though probably worse public policy than income tax cuts, was also a measure that had public support, and there was little political gain in strenuous opposition.[1] Similarly, the Liberals would be supportive of strengthening accountability levers in the federal government by suggesting that the Conservatives did not go far enough with the FAA. Considering that the sponsorship debacle occurred under the previous Liberal government, to be against such reforms would certainly decrease that party's chances of reoccupying power in the near future. Lastly, opposing tough-on-crime measures is difficult when the issue is framed as criminals versus victims; it is much harder to explain, in digestible form, why getting tough on crime is a poor policy choice.

A third factor that assisted delivery was the recognition, ultimately, that the Opposition Liberals were much weaker than initially assumed. A leadership convention in December 2006 resulted in the election of Stéphane Dion as the replacement for outgoing leader and former prime minister Paul Martin. Dion had a track record as an aggressive and effective minister, but he faltered as leader of the Liberals. The party was in debt, its reputation was sullied, policy development was weak, and the Conservatives sought to ensure that Dion would be poorly received by voters in either English or French Canada. The CPC was able to mount an effective attack against Dion's leadership skills in advance of the 2008 election, including a negative advertising campaign. As a result of this dynamic, the Liberals were ill-prepared for an election, and, to delay one, they abstained from voting on bills rather than vote against the government (Jeffrey 2009, 78). This situation enabled the government to pass more of its legislative agenda through Parliament.

A former staffer in the Prime Minister's Office (PMO) also noted that the public service was an important player in the implementation of platform promises. In this case, the bureaucracy was given clear instructions on what policies to prioritize. The Privy Council Office (PCO) was particularly efficient in helping the government fulfill its commitments. When the Tories took office in 2006, they recruited Kevin Lynch, an experienced public servant, to head up the PCO. The PCO had been expanded under the previous Liberal government, and Lynch's first move was to scale back its size; people who had been brought in to manage different areas were returned to their ministries. Lynch then turned the core of the PCO into "an implementation-driving unit," which some viewed as more efficient than creating an internal "delivery unit" in the PMO itself (personal interview). The minority status of the government, furthermore, protected it from the malaise of the mid-term drift that can plague majority governments – in this case, both the political and public spheres were focused squarely on ensuring the successful delivery of its key policy items. When drift does occur, delivery is made more complicated, since a bureaucratic agenda may reshape the party's product in its own image. The Conservatives managed to avoid this in their first term.

Two final factors contributed to a productive first term in the minority government. One was the ability of the Tories to turn failures into successes, a clever political ploy that is obvious to other political parties but less so to the broader public. A good example is the patient wait-times guarantee. Because of the intergovernmental nature of the policy, delivery on that promise was difficult. Consequently, the government simply changed the priority by requesting that the provinces meet a maximum wait time for *one* of the five areas rather than for all five. When the provinces agreed, the government declared success and moved on.

The last factor that helped delivery was the use of public opinion research (POR) while in power. Between the 2004 and 2006 elections, market intelligence had primarily been used by the CPC to segment voters. This new "voter universe," as devised by party strategist Patrick Muttart, then informed the development of the 2006 platform (Flanagan 2007a, 223-25). After their electoral victory, many of the political professionals on the campaign accepted jobs in the PMO, and they recognized the value of gathering market intelligence in government. As a result, polling and focus group information was used extensively in the Harper government's first term – $31 million spent in the first full fiscal year alone (*Ottawa Citizen* 2007). This is a clear indicator of the importance the government placed on consulting with Canadians, and, with the added strength of public opinion behind them, the Tories were able to progress through their agenda.

The State of Political Marketing in Canada

From this analysis of the Conservative Party's first term in office, a few points must be raised that relate to the theory and practice of political marketing. This chapter has argued that the Conservative government attempted to maintain a market orientation in government. If we return to Lees-Marshment's tools that assist in this regard, there are a number that are applicable to the CPC government, such as the continued use of market research in government, the acknowledgement of mistakes, and facing a strong opposition (real or perceived) (Lees-Marshment 2009a, 533). For a government in a minority situation, the CPC experience in government has highlighted other important elements, discussed below.

ACHIEVABLE COMMITMENTS

Achievability is part of stage three in the political marketing process for a MOP, but its importance must be underscored. Designing a campaign document is a serious undertaking, considering the emphasis now placed on party commitments by the electorate. Achievability is a consideration of all parties, particularly if we consider some spectacular policy failures in other jurisdictions, such as US president Bill Clinton's health-reform initiative in his first term. But in Westminster systems, where minorities are possible, parties must design a product that can still be implemented from a weaker parliamentary position. This is especially important if that parliamentary system operates in a federal country. Policy priorities that involve cooperation from sub-national governments can be particularly tricky and should not dominate a campaign document. The CPC had to finesse its delivery on patient wait-time guarantees for exactly this reason.

"Quick Wins"

Because a minority government has less control over the legislative clock, implementing two or three policies quickly demonstrates its efficiency in power. Should Parliament dissolve and an election be called unexpectedly, the party will have successes to highlight during a campaign. Within the first six months of taking office, the CPC government could point to a tax cut and child care allowance and within the year had passed the Federal Account-ability Act and tabled numerous pieces of criminal justice–reform legislation. The tax cut and child care allowance alone would have served the Conservatives well in the event of an early election call.

Product Delivery Must Be Visible

All governments want visibility and credit for their popular initiatives, but this necessity is magnified for minority governments. The announcement of a platform item "delivered" should occur alongside a well-planned com-munications strategy. The placement of a bright blue "5%" GST sticker onto a cash register in a retail store is a strong marketing visual for a public that is notorious for its short memory.

Minority Governments Must Always Assume Opposition Strength

The CPC was aided by its assumption that the opposition parties were par-ticularly strong. This revealed itself to be an overestimation, yet the fact re-mained that the government held fewer seats in the House than the opposition parties combined – the government's fate was squarely in Parliament's hands. This fact of Westminster systems works in favour of maintaining a market orientation, as power is rarely taken for granted and government responsive-ness to voters tends to remain a salient feature of the party's larger strategic vision.

Caucus Consultation

Other scholars have noted the need for governments to engage in listening exercises to "get back in touch" with voters when they drift away from the market (Lees-Marshment 2009a, 528). The CPC did not engage in the same kind of consultation with the public as Tony Blair did in 2003 with his "Big Conversation," but Prime Minister Harper was keenly tuned in to his caucus. Many Conservative MPs were uncomfortable in Ottawa and suspicious of the Ottawa press gallery, preferring instead to spend time in their ridings, talking with constituents (personal interview with government insider). When Parliament convened, Tory members would return to Ottawa with good information about issues that were politically relevant in their constituencies. Caucus consultation is certainly not a new practice in politics, but CPC strategists were able to use MPs' input to inform the design and direction of their market research to determine whether constituent concerns were reflective of the broader public and, if so, how best to respond. For a minority government, the channel between elected representatives and the public is thus a valuable tool.

FUTURE PRODUCT DEVELOPMENT
With only a minority government, parties must find the time to engage in intense election preparations. The CPC was acutely aware of the need to make provisions for future campaigns. The caucus met quarterly for this purpose, although the bulk of campaign content was usually reserved for the summer and winter sessions. Slogans would be tested; campaign staff would present to the caucus on, among other matters, the plans for the election platform, leader's tour, communications strategy, and opposition research for the war room. Setting aside time for these preparations was an essential element of party strategy and contributed to their efforts for remaining market-oriented (personal interview with Harper strategist).

There are likely other elements that can help a minority government stay market-oriented, but these six components were particularly important to the Conservative government in its first term in power.

The logical next question is the extent to which the Conservatives will be able to maintain a market orientation as Canada's governing party. After winning a second minority government in October 2008, the CPC finally achieved its coveted majority status by securing 166 of 308 parliamentary seats in the May 2011 federal election. Evidence from elsewhere suggests that remaining market-oriented is more challenging both the longer parties are in government and when they have majority status. New Labour in the United Kingdom struggled to stay responsive to voters after its first term as a majority government, and New Zealand's Labour Party under Helen Clark shifted toward a product orientation within the span of six years (Lees-Marshment 2009a). In Canada, Alex Marland (2005, 74) has noted that the Liberal Party became more sales-oriented after holding power. There is a strong possibility that the Conservatives will follow a similar path. This is particularly true since the Liberal Party faced a significant decline in seats (winning only 34) and the NDP gained primarily in Quebec and thus has arguably only a temporary electoral hold in that province. Conservative seat strength overall may result in the party ignoring some of the fundamental elements that helped it remain market-oriented in the first place, particularly the assumption of a strong opposition. Future research could focus on minority status itself as a contributing explanatory variable for maintaining a market orientation in government.

Implications for the Quality of Democracy

Winning a minority government in Canada is akin to a "permanent campaign" (Blumenthal 1980). The government is acutely aware that it could be thrown into another election at any moment, and this situation acts as an incentive both to deliver on its promises as quickly as possible and to use market research to keep it responsive to citizens. What effect does this have on democracy in general? In one view, the development and design of the product have been grounded on citizen input, which creates an important and continuing dialogue between political elites and citizens. No longer is a political party trying to simply "sell" a position to the public; instead, the product itself is the result of what citizens have indicated they desire from government. Likewise, the emphasis on product delivery in the political marketing framework can enhance democracy, as it may revive voters' faith that political parties can be trusted to follow through on their commitments; governments will deliver the product once in power. As Royce Koop notes in Chapter 14, Canadian voters' sense of external efficacy increased between 2004 and 2008, and this measure of government responsiveness is encouraging.

In another view, heavy reliance on polls and focus groups that design a party's product, set government targets, define appropriate outcomes, and demand report cards on delivery progress has the effect of constraining government flexibility, and this squeezes the notion of democracy (Savigny 2008a). Political parties of the past eschewed written platforms because their focus was on good government. Good government meant the ability to respond to the changing needs of the country *in the absence* of rigid policy promises rather than the reverse.

Regardless, it is unlikely that parties will shed their campaign documents and even less likely that public opinion will not be sought to inform the design of the political product. This case study has demonstrated that the

Conservative Party of Canada delivered, to greater and lesser degrees, on its five priorities because it largely followed a market orientation in government. One might even venture to suggest that a minority government without a market orientation would be short-lived indeed.

NOTE

1 Because of procedural confusion in Parliament, all parties passed the 2006 federal budget unanimously on third reading.

9
Does Public Opinion Research Matter? The Marketing of Health Policy

Lisa Birch

Political marketing has focused on the use of marketing and public opinion research tools by political parties for political branding, communications, and election strategies. Political marketing specialists are now asking questions about the use of these tools by governments. How do governments use public opinion research (POR)? Is this research being used for policy development, social marketing, political marketing, or strategic communications? Is this research responding to the governing party's own needs or to those of the civil servants in policy and management? What are the implications of this for democracy?

Osborne and Gaebler's ideas (1993) about reinventing government sparked interest in applying political marketing and private-sector management to the public sector. Many authors claim that this will enhance government performance and accountability, as well as citizen satisfaction (Buurma 2001; Henneberg 2002; Madill 1998; Mintz, Church, and Colterman 2006; Serrat 2010). The opportunities for marketing in government arise in four specific contexts: (1) the marketing of public goods or services, (2) social marketing to obtain the voluntary behaviour changes required to achieve policy goals, (3) policy marketing to develop and "sell" policy packages to citizens, as well as to promote compliance, and (4) demarketing in cases where the government withdraws from a sector of activity (Madill 1998).

In each of these contexts, research (or POR) is an important tool for communications, market intelligence (policy knowledge), and product development (public policies). Lees-Marshment (2009b, 214) anticipated the considerable resources for POR to which a new government would have access should it choose to use political marketing once in power; she suggested that government POR could facilitate responsive, democratic leadership without falling into the traps of governing or manipulating by polls (see Manza and Lomax Cook 2002). Social marketing experts strongly recommend using POR to improve the effectiveness of policy instruments targeting voluntary behavioural changes (Hastings 2007; Kotler and Lee 2008). There are concerns about the use of public opinion research to inform government communications (see Chapter 7), but very little empirical work charts the use of marketing activities, including POR, and its effectiveness in improving public policies, their management, and democratic leadership. What exists focuses on government POR, not marketing. It offers inconclusive results and insufficient attention to applications in public administration. Some studies have reported on this in different policy contexts (see Hastak, Mazis, and Morris 2001 for the USA; Medlock 2005, and Page 2006 for Canada; Rothmayr and Hardmeier 2002 for Switzerland).

In practice, the public sector often displays elements of marketing, especially the promotion, monitoring, and evaluation aspects, without a global marketing vision (Serrat 2010). A survey of managers in the Canadian public and non-profit sectors has shown that respondents' understandings of marketing were limited to the promotion and communications aspects, largely to the exclusion of strategic marketing management (Mintz, Church, and Colterman 2006). Although the concept of political marketing seems abstract for respondents in this study, the production and utilization of POR by the Canadian government is part of regular operations. Starting in the mid-1990s, the Canadian federal government began institutionalizing opinion research as a policy tool. It was linked to the new governance mission of a results-oriented public service that considered citizen wants and needs (Canada, Treasury Board 2000). Various macro-level governance policies set the stage for the explosion in government POR at the federal level.[1]

Figure 9.1 depicts the evolution of public opinion research activity within the federal government from 1993-94 to 2009-10 by the yearly number of studies and the annual expenditures. The first decade shows how this activity expanded rapidly, with over six times more contracts and five times higher expenditures in 2003-4 than in 1993-94. Subsequently, the overall level of POR activity remains relatively high, with greater variability and a declining trend. The dramatic drop after 2007-8 reveals the combined effect of stricter rules and budget cuts imposed by the Harper government, in part out of fear of being accused of governing by polls. This context, where the entire POR budget equals what Health Canada used to spend in one year, spurred intense competition between and within ministries for access to POR funding. The apparatus adapted in creative ways: doing public environment monitoring by gathering data publicized by the media and by interest groups; redefining what it is doing as surveillance work; inserting questions that used to go into

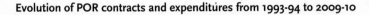

FIGURE 9.1

Evolution of POR contracts and expenditures from 1993-94 to 2009-10

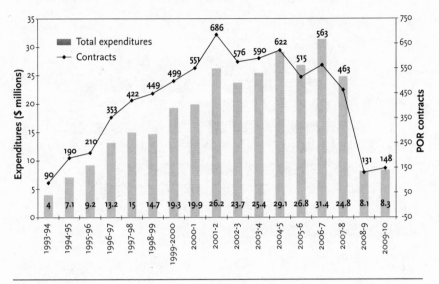

syndicated polls into authorized POR on other subjects instead; and substituting consultations with stakeholders. The potential of social media to identify the range of issues on the public agenda has also been examined, even though these media cannot indicate the prevalence of opinions on these issues among the general population. Since there are rules in the government's Communications Policy that oblige pre-testing and evaluations of advertisements and citizen input for regulatory impact assessments (RIAs), in recent years, most of the POR projects that are receiving ministerial approval concern advertising, and, to a lesser extent, substantive policy matters.

As André Turcotte explains in Chapter 5, there are various types of public opinion research. When clients commission such work, it can be done on a customized or omnibus basis; custom research is tailored to the specific needs of the department that commissions the research, whereas multi-client research involves the addition of questions to a syndicated poll. Up until 2007-8, custom research accounted for 87 percent of all such contracts; by 2010-11, custom research accounted for 100 percent of all government opinion research. Figure 9.2 shows the expenditures by type of research per fiscal year. The predominance of custom research indicates more comprehensive and tailored research activity than snap polling. It involves surveys and focus

FIGURE 9.2

Custom and syndicated government POR in Canada

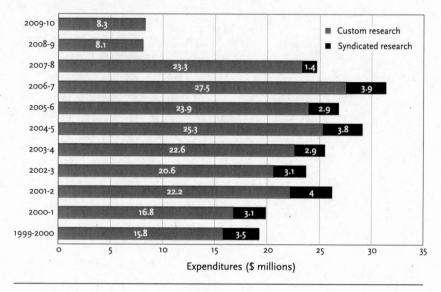

groups with samples from the general population and special target groups. This suggests more sophisticated and specialized studies to generate policy-relevant knowledge. Potentially, then, government has the capacity to produce market intelligence and to engage in quite extensive political marketing activities.

This potential capacity to use public opinion research for political marketing, however, is constrained by internal regulations, public scrutiny, and independent audits by government watchdogs. For example, public disclosure rules require federal agencies to deposit a copy of the final report with Library and Archives Canada within six months of completion. The rules governing POR forbid commissioning research for partisan purposes because government research is intended to meet the needs of federal civil servants in policy and management. Independent assessments of government POR activity confirm its non-partisan nature. Three reports of the auditor general of Canada (Canada, Auditor General of Canada 2003, 2005, and 2007) scrutinized opinion research for its management, quality, and value for money. These audits led to tighter rules regarding quality and commissioning procedures. The report of the independent adviser on public opinion research (Paillé

2007) found that this research largely complied with political neutrality guidelines and that there was no relationship between research volumes and election periods, even during the years of majority Liberal government from 1993 to 2003. The auditor general's reports and Paillé's report, however, raised questions about the actual use of data reports by federal departments. These questions about government POR and its utilization also remain an enigma for political marketing.

The following case study examines two stories of public opinion research and its utilization by Health Canada (the federal agency that commissions the most research): the future of the health care system (59 reports) and tobacco control (205 reports). They trace a profile of its production, its utilization, and the extent to which evidence reveals the presence of different political marketing activities. Through content analysis of these reports and their measurement instruments, along with document analysis and interviews, these case studies present a portrait of POR use by Health Canada.

Case Study: Public Opinion Research and Health Canada

Public opinion research commissioned by Health Canada for the health care system and tobacco policy reveals multifaceted uses of research for instrumental, conceptual, strategic, and managerial purposes. Instrumental use arises when the results contribute directly to decision making regarding policies and their instruments, whereas conceptual use denotes using POR to gain a better understanding of problems and their possible solutions. This may be linked to the ideas of product development and refinement. Strategic uses arise when opinion research results are mobilized to justify policy choices, promote policy options, or prepare communication plans. These uses may be linked to legitimization efforts. Finally, managerial uses entail POR utilization for tracking of opinion trends, benchmarking prior to implementation, monitoring, and evaluation. These uses are akin to continual market consultation. Each of the following cases tells a story about these types of utilization and similarities with political marketing.

UTILIZATION OF POR ABOUT HEALTH CARE

Given the importance of health care policy, it is not surprising that the government regularly solicits opinions about health care from thousands of Canadians in opinion surveys and focus groups. Although there is a match between the intended utilization suggested in research objectives and observable utilization for instrumental and conceptual uses to reform the health care system, close examination of this POR shows that the questionnaires and moderator guides contain questions of strategic interest and that the final reports include pollsters' commentaries of strategic nature. The research in this area can be divided into the following three distinct periods based on public perceptions about the state of the health care system and its perceived deterioration: the apprehended crisis from 1995 until 1997; the crisis period from 1997 until 2003 when the first health accord was reached; and the subsiding crisis from late 2003 until 2007. The focus of POR and its utilization vary throughout these phases.

The earliest research reports (1995-97) were essentially conceptual pieces to help decision makers get a grasp on the changing public mood and specific opinions about the health care system in the context of deficit reduction. Research hinted at a gradual shift of public opinion and behaviour toward a postmodern electorate that expects to be consulted and to have its opinions considered. In the study called *Rethinking Government*, the pollster suggested that the health care system, a symbol of national identity, would be a major challenge for the federal government (Ekos Research Associates 1995). One year later, in a quantitative and qualitative study, Ekos Research Associates (1996, 32) reported that Canadians in focus groups exhibited "combative resistance" to privatization and strong attachment to the principle of equality of access. At the outset of the second phase, POR by Pollara-Earnscliffe Research and Communications (1998) confirmed this strong adherence to equal access, with 85 percent of respondents willing to increase government spending to ensure this principle. However, this also showed that the perceived deterioration of the system was starting to shake confidence in the public system and especially in government.

In the second period (1997-2003), public opinion research reports captured snapshots of the growing anxiety and frustration Canadians felt toward the federal and provincial governments for failing to show leadership to protect the quality of the health care system and prevent further deterioration. Dissatisfaction rose as Canadians began blaming the federal budget cuts, not just provincial management. Initially, between 1998 and 2002, provincial and federal governments responded to criticism by using the tactics of "old style" politics with sterile public debates. Research revealed the futility of this approach. Focus group participants vociferously and cynically condemned intergovernmental bickering and wasted resources on advertising campaigns, given the perceived urgency of saving medicare. Quantitative data confirmed the public's desire for major improvements and new funding. Among the clear signals about the public mood, Pollara (2002a, 6) found that 56 percent of Canadians strongly agreed and 26 percent agreed that "the federal government should take a stronger stand in protecting public Medicare [sic] from profit-driven interests who have always opposed it." At least 85 percent of Canadians in all regions disagreed with the statement that "the Canada Health Act's five principles of universality, comprehensiveness, accessibility, portability and public administration, no longer reflect the values of Canadians" (Pollara 2002b, 73). Study after study confirmed the link between the health care system and national identity that was first suggested by Ekos Research in 1995.

During this period, a series of federal and provincial commissions investigated the future of the health care system and made recommendations on how to ensure the sustainability of the system. Beyond public audiences, during which the voices of organized interests including doctors, nurses, hospital cadres, and nongovernmental organizations were omnipresent, Quebec's Clair Commission, Saskatchewan's Fyke Commission, and Ottawa's Romanow Commission (Quebec 2000; Saskatchewan 2001; Romanow 2002) also resorted to collecting market intelligence to gather public input and to counter-verify the voices of organized interests. Health Canada assessed public reactions to reform proposals through its own POR, especially before and after the publication of the Romanow Report, by commissioning work from the Strategic Counsel (2002), Environics Research Group (2002a), and Ekos Research Associates (2003).

Additional government research was commissioned in preparation for federal-provincial conferences and was used to track opinion during and after the first ministers' meetings (FMMs). The Strategic Counsel (2003a, 2003b) conducted research before and after the meetings in September 2003 that led to the Health Accord. Other research firms were commissioned to research to prepare an information brochure promoting this accord and to evaluate the public's reaction. Similarly, in late August 2004, just prior to the upcoming FMM, the Strategic Counsel used focus groups to test public perceptions of government roles and responsibilities plus perceptions of the federal and provincial reform proposals. A formal exercise invited participants to define key expressions derived from federal and provincial positions in the debate. Respondents associated these expressions with the orders of government and discussed their feelings about their importance in the context of health care reform. Based on this and evaluations of participants' verbal and nonverbal reactions, the Strategic Counsel (2004a, 27) produced a concept map of the "most compelling communication messages" of each order of government. The most effective, emotionally appealing statements tended to be associated with the federal government's position, except for the provincial message favouring a national drug plan. During the week-long televised conference in September 2004, Earnscliffe Research and Communications/Veraxis (2004, 6) monitored the evolution of public opinion. This pollster found that "support for a broad federal role in a national Medicare [sic] program increased to 57 percent – an eight point increase by week's end," suggesting that the federal government was more effective in appealing to public opinion than the provinces, which proposed a narrower federal role with a national pharmacare plan. The ten-year plan to strengthen health care that came out of this meeting echoed the federal government's "compelling messages" through references to key terms such as "universality," "accessibility," "equal access," "financial sustainability," and "accountability" (Canada, Health Canada 2004). The Strategic Counsel (2004b, 35, 57) provided daily tracking information in the week after the conference regarding opinion about the quality of health care, the FMM, federal/provincial leadership, confidence in government, and reactions to proposed reform measures. The firm found that overall satisfaction with the agreement began at 76 percent and slipped to 71 percent one week later; however, the idea of asymmetrical federalism was less popular (64 percent approval), especially if the question referred only to Quebec (40 percent approval). Thus, the governments displayed responsiveness to citizens' demands about the health care system and showed leadership to accommodate Quebec's needs. Subsequent POR was used to develop and later evaluate promotional material about the ten-year plan that came out of this meeting (Ipsos-Reid 2004; Decima Research 2004).

In the third phase of POR (2003-7), the utilization pattern shifts and resembles more the pattern observed in tobacco control. The health accords provoked an opinion shift as public fears about system deterioration stabilized, then subsided gradually. Health Canada's public opinion research turned toward consulting citizens on how to implement elements of these accords, such as the electronic health record, wait-list management, and performance indicators for accountability. This POR examined the details of specific policy instruments and seems to fulfill instrumental and conceptual policy needs. For example, the choice and presentation of performance indicators to implement the accountability provision of the new health pact were tested in focus groups. The lists of indicators and the improvements in their presentation in subsequent performance reports reflected citizens' preferences for more "talkative" data. Some POR also tracked opinions about Health Canada, importance/performance gaps, and brand-loyalty issues (for more information about branding see Chapter 13, by Patricia Cormack).

The use of opinion research in this case shows a pattern that varies across three periods. In the first two periods, conceptual and strategic uses for policy positioning were followed by strategic use for communication purposes. The intense, high-stake debate on medicare and the quest for legitimacy seemed to guide POR. In the final period, once the policy direction was decided, attention shifted to implementation issues, and utilization seemed to be more instrumental and conceptual in nature. Some strategic issues revolved around the Health Canada "brand." Evidence shows some policy marketing using a selling approach during the first phase, followed by a shift to policy marketing through product development in the other phases. POR contributed to the development of the Health Accord and the ten-year plan in ways that resemble political marketing with a mix of responsiveness and leadership.

Utilization of POR in Tobacco Control

The case of government-sponsored opinion research in the tobacco control program contrasts sharply with the use pattern for medicare. In tobacco control, the policy makers and program managers are not marketing the idea of a restrictive tobacco control policy: they are mainly marketing the attitudinal and behavioural changes required to reduce smoking-related disease and death. Since tobacco control can be viewed as a counter-marketing effort against the tobacco industry that uses a variety of policy instruments, this case shows more extensive POR activity and utilization. It also reveals explicit social and policy marketing activity.

In the tobacco control program, the distinct pattern of opinion research reveals the presence of mini-research programs attached to specific tobacco issues and the policy instruments designed to address them. Whereas POR on the health care system constituted mainly a single-issue program until after the health accords, research on tobacco addresses many sub-issues, such as smoking cessation, "light and mild" descriptors, warning messages, and second-hand smoke. The research pattern for most sub-issues in tobacco control tends to follow the steps for social marketing: define the problem, learn about the target groups and barriers to change, design the instruments, and evaluate their impact. Public opinion research in tobacco control uses market segmentation, since it gathers information from particular policy targets – such as smokers, smokers of light and mild cigarettes, youth, parents who smoke, and opinion leaders – whereas POR on health care mainly addressed Canadians. This is directly linked to the development, implementation, and evaluation of regulatory and exhortation policy instruments. The finest details of policy instruments were designed through the intensive use of focus groups, often followed by large-scale validation with surveys (Birch and Pétry 2010, 2011). Surveillance and evaluation activities are built into each research program such that a baseline survey typically measures knowledge, attitudes, opinions, and behaviour prior to implementation, then subsequent surveys track for changes. Thus, POR in tobacco control more closely resembles applied social science and marketing research. Let's now consider two examples: the graphic health-warning messages and second-hand smoke.

A massive public opinion research effort on health-warning messages began with two studies by Environics Research Group (1997a, 1997b). By 1999, pioneering research explored a total of fifty-eight combinations of messages and images that helped design the final sixteen graphic health-warning messages (Environics Research Group 1999a, 1999b, 1999c, 1999d, 1999e, 2000). From 1995 to 2007, there were forty-eight POR studies regarding the size, verbal and visual content, and impact of health-warning messages on tobacco products. This work involved the general population and special subgroups, such as youth, smokers, non-smokers, recent quitters, First Nations people, and opinion leaders. Health-warning messages entailed recourse to 248 focus groups, mostly for the development, then the renewal, of this policy instrument. Survey instruments on this topic were administered to 39,313 people, mainly to track attitudes, behaviour, and opinions. This includes fourteen successive waves of surveys to monitor the impact of the health warnings on youth, adults, and adult smokers so that program managers could detect possible "wear-out" of the messages and plan a new round of research for the second generation of graphic warnings. POR contributed instrumentally and conceptually to the design, implementation, and monitoring of this internationally acclaimed policy instrument that brought counter-marketing messages to cigarette packages.

After the implementation of the health warnings in January 2001, attention turned to the issue of second-hand smoke. Opinion research was used to inform the design of a social marketing campaign calling for individual and collective action to reduce exposure to second-hand smoke and eventually to bolster support for comprehensive smoking bans by provincial governments. Research on second-hand smoke turned to 117 focus groups to design the tools for a social marketing campaign. Focus groups delved deeply into the knowledge, attitudes, behaviours, perceptions, and misperceptions that created barriers to action against second-hand smoke among adults and youth. They revealed how myths about ventilation and the risks of second-hand smoke, combined with the attitude of "live and let live," explained tolerance of smoking in public places. They inspired the creative concepts for the marketing campaign with three goals: (1) to reframe the debate in terms of the right to a smoke-free environment, with an emphasis on children and youth; (2) to debunk myths about second-hand smoke by enhancing citizens' understandings of the health risks; and (3) to empower citizens to act individually and collectively for a smoke-free environment (Pollara 2002d). Survey instruments, administered to 37,867 people, were used to validate ideas from focus groups with the general population, evaluate the impact of social marketing tools, or establish pre- and post-measures of public opinion following provincial smoking bans.

In 2002, the tobacco control program produced ten studies, with six focus group designs and four survey designs. The content of the Heather Crowe campaign and its success is linked to POR. A survey and a focus group convinced Health Canada that using celebrities such as figure skating champions Elvis Stojko or Josée Chouinard was ineffective compared with messages from real victims of second-hand smoke (Millward Brown Goldfarb 2002; Pollara 2002c). Health Canada acted on this and invited Crowe, a non-smoking waitress who was dying from lung cancer, to become that real human face. Public servants used these data to learn how Crowe could help drive home the message about the dangers of second-hand smoke by telling her story with the right dose of emotional intensity (Environics Research Group 2002b; Millward Brown Goldfarb 2003a, 2003b, 2003c, 2003d). Heather Crowe's story also facilitated the repositioning of the issue as one of workplace health and safety, as well as the rights of others to a smoke-free environment. In June and September of 2002, two baseline surveys on second-hand smoke in workplaces established reference points for the attitudes, behaviours, and opinions of adults and youth by which opinion shifts and behaviour changes could be observed (Decima Research 2002; Pollara 2002c). The first generation of messages aired in 2002. The second ones entered the movie theatres in 2003. Opinion research was then used to evaluate the impact of these messages (Millward Brown Goldfarb 2003a, 2003b). The taglines evolved from "Tobacco, we can live without it" at the outset of 2002 to "Second-hand smoke diseases: Are you a target?" and "Some tobacco companies say second-hand smoke bothers people. Health Canada says it kills" by 2003.

Before this campaign, which involved television and movie theatre advertisements as well as a pan-Canadian tour to meet premiers, health ministers, and representatives of nongovernmental organizations, survey data showed that support for a comprehensive smoking ban including bars and taverns was low (43.9 percent), especially among smokers (Decima Research 2002). Within a few years, general support for smoking bans soared into the 77 percent to 89 percent range depending on the province, and the opinion shifted to majorities of 59 percent to 78 percent of adults supporting bans in bars and taverns (Environics Research Group 2005a, 2005b, 2006). Qualitative assessments showed that opinion leaders supported bans and, later, that nine out of ten Canadians supported the right to a smoke-free environment for non-smokers (Environics Research Group 2004a, 2004b). This POR contributed to such an effective counter-marketing strategy that, within a few years, it unravelled the effects of twenty-five years of tobacco industry efforts to frame the second-hand smoke issue as one of freedom of choice (individual rights), smokers' etiquette (individual behaviour), and adequate ventilation systems (technological problems). It made pre-existing scientific evidence about the dangers of environmental smoke resonate with Canadians to the point that comprehensive smoking bans in public places became inevitable and acceptable, even to smokers.

These graphic warning messages and the second-hand smoke campaigns show the multifaceted utilization of opinion research for instrumental, conceptual, and strategic purposes to design, implement, and evaluate policy instruments. In tobacco control, there is a predominance of social marketing with some use for policy marketing. Whereas political parties often use opinion research to inform communications strategies and tactics that will sell their political product (see Chapter 4), strategic utilization of POR in tobacco control is not about selling policies to citizens. It is about producing solid evidence to support policy instruments should the tobacco industry launch another constitutional challenge. Given preponderance of proof rules and the nature of Article 1 Charter of Rights and Freedoms cases, POR can be introduced as evidence to demonstrate that the limits imposed on a right are reasonable and justified in a free and democratic society (Corbin, Gill, and Joliffe 2000, 136-37; Havighurst et al. 2001). Although very little POR in this sector is for public relations, some survey questions do address branding issues by asking people whether they associate a given policy instrument with Health Canada, whether they think that a government department should be engaging in such activities, and what message this sends about Health Canada. For the second-hand smoke issue, respondents interpreted Health Canada's actions as a sign of caring for the people's health (Environics Research Group 2002b).

The State of Political Marketing in Canada

By analyzing these case studies in light of data about public opinion research activity in other ministries, some preliminary insights are possible regarding political marketing and its forms in Canada. First, government POR activity may be a prerequisite for political marketing to occur, but it is not sufficient. Government-sponsored research may fulfill various needs for policy-relevant knowledge and lead to multifaceted utilization by government actors. The commissioned data reports may serve one of Madill's (1998) four political marketing activities (marketing public goods and services, social marketing, policy marketing, demarketing), whether or not policy makers and program managers actually employ political marketing vocabulary.[2]

Second, given the variations in the extent to which these political marketing activities can be observed at Health Canada, it is plausible to expect even greater variations across and within other departments. In the case of medicare, evidence suggests that some policy marketing, likely called by another name, was occurring to the extent that POR enabled some policy dialogue between policy makers and citizens about their preferences for the future of health care. This case also showed some use for communication strategies, but no social marketing or demarketing. By contrast, in the tobacco control case, POR is a policy tool mainly for social marketing, with some evidence of branding activity. The social marketing efforts against second-hand smoke included a form of policy marketing to build greater support for stronger restrictions. Little is known about government POR and its utilization in other departments beyond the differences in the volumes of research between departments. After Health Canada, the departments that used POR regularly were Human Resources and Skills Development Canada, Natural Resources Canada, National Defence, Foreign Affairs and International Trade Canada, Canada Revenue Agency, and Heritage Canada. It may be that the differences in the POR volumes and utilization in government departments depends on factors such as the nature of the policy issues or sub-issues, their salience, the controversy surrounding them, the types of policy instruments in the policy mix, the types of decisions to be made, and the legitimization needs. Since POR is a prerequisite for political marketing, these factors may also influence the nature and breadth of political marketing activities.

The long-term viability of public opinion research and, by implication, political marketing is also linked to funding issues, research contract rules, and their impact on the institutionalization of POR. Unstable funding hampers the sustainability and effectiveness of social marketing initiatives, as was noted in the evaluation of the tobacco control program (Ekos Research Associates 2006a, 2006b). Changes in macro-political conditions that modify government rules and affect funding can and do constrain the volume and the type of research activity (see Figures 9.1 and 9.2). For example, in February of 2008, the Conservative government introduced the requirement of ministerial approval for projects and imposed a freeze on syndicated research. It also cut an initial $10 million from the federal POR budget. This new political climate, coupled with the ideological orientation of the Conservative government and its tendency to equate government POR with political polling, has reduced and reconfigured government POR activity. Thus, even in states where opinion research has been institutionalized as a policy and governance tool, departments may face restrictions on their ability to mobilize resources for such purposes. In governments where institutionalization has not occurred, the production and utilization of such research may be far more elusive.

Lastly, the fine line between government and partisan POR seems clear in some cases and fuzzier in others. For example, although the research commissioned by Health Canada shows political neutrality from a purely partisan perspective, a close examination of reports and questionnaires reveals that the jurisdiction of the federal departments and their organizational needs for legitimacy tend to permeate the POR in subtle and not-so-subtle ways. In tobacco control, the content varies depending on whether the policy tool falls within federal jurisdiction or not. The cooperative interaction between the federal and provincial governments in tobacco control renders the quest for public loyalty less intense than in the case of medicare. Nonetheless, there are occasionally questions about whether Canadians recognize and approve of Health Canada's or the government's actions on a particular issue. Public opinion research on medicare regularly solicits views about the federal and provincial governments, about the attribution of blame for the state of health care, perceptions about government roles in health care, and approval ratings for each government's policy agenda, performance, and leadership. POR about Health Canada's stance and performance on medicare issues may act as a proxy for public perceptions of the governing party's performance on health care. Thus, on politically salient issues, the fine line between POR about a department or about a governing party may be blurred. This is akin to the old question about government advertising that Kirsten Kozolanka tackles in Chapter 7: At what point do state-citizen communications become a thinly disguised way to promote the governing party? In this case, we may ask: When is government POR a means of providing the state bureaucracy with policy-relevant knowledge, and when does it become a source of political information for the governing party?

Implications for the Quality of Democracy

The quintessential question about the multifaceted uses of POR concerns the implications for legitimacy and good governance. For any government, public approval depends on the cumulative efforts to legitimize the macro-political decisions of political authorities and the micro-political decisions of bureaucratic authorities with delegated powers. Macro-political decisions about policy orientations will have legitimacy in three cases: (1) the government makes a decision that respects the citizens' policy preferences, which shows democratic responsiveness; (2) the government explains clearly why it made a different choice, which demonstrates leadership; and (3) the government adopts measures within a range of acceptable interventions in cases where it benefits from a permissive consensus about the need for state action. The legitimacy of micro-political decisions about policy details is established when bureaucratic agencies respect required regulatory procedures; present a rationale for their decisions, preferably based on formal evidence (not anecdotes); and produce effective policy instruments that help attain policy objectives (Schrefler 2010, 311). For legitimization purposes at both decision levels, POR can provide valuable information about the following: citizens' preferences regarding policies and instruments; their receptivity to alternatives; the range of politically acceptable interventions; the attitudes, opinions, and behaviour of citizens and of special target groups; the likely effectiveness of policy instruments; and the actual impact of policy measures. Our cases provide different insights about the type of information found in government POR, its utilization, and the implications for legitimacy and democratic governance.

Public opinion research on the health care system suggests that governments can attempt to use such data collection methods instrumentally, conceptually, and strategically to enhance responsiveness, to lead opinion, or to achieve a combination of both. These data helped keep policy makers attuned to the worries and preferences of Canadians. It helped them design advertising campaigns and then informed them that old-style politics with negative advertising and federal-provincial finger pointing would not satisfy the public will. Only long-term, stable funding with major improvements to the system would quell public anxiety. So despite the early POR being associated with crafted talk, the cumulative impact of the research on subsequent policy actions suggests democratic responsiveness eventually occurred. Although POR gives voice to citizens, there is evidence of its use to market the federal government's preferred policy and to fine-tune communication strategies (see other chapters in this book for inquiries on these questions). The federal government used opinion research to develop and successfully promote its renewal proposal that sought to reinject funds with accountability mechanisms for the provinces; to focus on reducing wait times; to avoid expensive new programs, especially a national pharmacare plan; and to accommodate Quebec with asymmetrical federalism. Since the last two items went against majority opinion, the final policy product is a mix of public and government preferences – a mix of responsiveness and leadership. The competition between the federal and provincial governments and the salience of this issue for elections created an intense struggle for legitimacy. In the end, Health Canada reasserted its role as the guardian of medicare's fundamental principles, legitimizing the federal role in this provincial jurisdiction.

Public opinion research in tobacco control tells a different story. To the extent that the predominant uses of POR in this sector are to develop, implement, monitor, and evaluate policy instruments using a social marketing approach, this case speaks to the twin ideas of responsible government and results-based management. Opinion research contributed instrumentally and conceptually to the remarkable effectiveness of the tobacco control policy mix that attained policy targets in half the anticipated time. The policy mix reflects some responsiveness and some leadership with considerable efforts to ensure the legitimacy of bureaucratic decisions. Researching public opinion contributed much to the design and delivery of effective tobacco control instruments. However, if public opinion had trumped scientific research regarding graphic health-warning messages, Canada would never have innovated in this policy area, since survey respondents did not think such a policy instrument would be effective in reducing and preventing smoking. Health Canada sided with the scientific evidence to the contrary and then proceeded to use focus groups to determine the combinations of messages and images for cigarette packages. Now, international comparison research shows the superior effectiveness of the Canadian health warnings in reducing smoking and increasing quitting behaviour (Hammond et al. 2007). Would this result be the same without the POR? On the second-hand smoke issue, Health Canada's social marketing efforts were explicitly linked to a call for action that would culminate with majority support for smoking bans, which suggests some policy marketing. Thus, POR in tobacco control enhanced democratic governance through effective policy instruments designed with public input, but it also showed a mix of responsiveness regarding the fine details of policy instruments and leadership regarding major policy directions. Legitimacy questions in this area are less contentious due to federal-provincial cooperation and the existence of a "permissive consensus" in support of tobacco control, which leads to low public attentiveness as long as policy makers and managers act responsibly with public resources and reasonably with regulatory powers.

Since Health Canada clearly defined POR as a tool of democratic governance in its policy tool kit (Canada, Health Canada Corporate Consultation Secretariat 2000) and expressed commitment to citizens' involvement, there seems to be an organizational will to hear the public's voice. Politically, though, the legitimacy of government-sponsored opinion research as a policy and management tool will be secured more readily if such insights mainly provide policy or market intelligence that, along with other reputable sources of knowledge, contributes to responsive and responsible governance rather than pandering or image making.

NOTES

1   See key government documents that are available online, such as *Results for Canadians: A Management Framework for the Government of Canada* (Canada, Treasury Board 2000), *Evaluation Policy* (Canada, Treasury Board 2001), *Communications Policy of the Government of Canada* (Canada, Treasury Board 2006), and *Government of Canada Regulatory Policy* (Canada, Privy Council Office 1999).

2   In Chapter 11, Thierry Giasson shows that political marketing vocabulary is rarely used in the Canadian media.

10
Selling a Cause: Political Marketing and Interest Groups

...... *Émilie Foster and Patrick Lemieux*

Political marketing has established itself as one of the most fruitful fields of political communications in the last decade. However, researchers have tended to confine the study of concepts and techniques in political marketing to a simple framework of candidates and political parties, at a cost of neglecting the use of political marketing by other actors involved in politics, including interest groups (McGrath 2006, 106).

In the last few decades, we have seen a significant increase in the number of interest groups (especially citizens groups) in the United States (Berry 1999, Berry and Wilcox 2007). The same phenomenon is visible in Canada. The directory of Canadian associations (Canadian Almanac and Directory 2008) identifies almost twenty thousand active associations from coast to coast, compared with only eleven thousand in the 1984 edition. Political representation is changing: parties are no longer the only legitimate actors for ensuring citizens' representation in the political arena (Dalton and Wattenberg 2000; Hudon 2009; P. Norris 2002). The spectacular proliferation of interest groups places them at the centre of numerous mutations affecting democratic practices in Canada (Hudon 2009, 255).

Some scholars have noticed links between political marketing philosophy and lobbying by interest groups. For Mack (1997, 4), marketing and lobbying have a common objective: persuasion. Lock and Harris (1996a, 318) observe that lobbyists often use political marketing techniques but that this practice is still neglected by scholars. Andrews (1996, 79) argues that businesses are successful in influencing public policy not because they buy influence but because they apply marketing strategies in their lobbying activities. Meanwhile, McGrath (2006, 108) notes that "the persuasion function of lobbying can be bound into political marketing theory."

In Canada, political strategy practitioner Warren Kinsella (2007) has been approached by associations, corporations, and non-profit agencies to help them set up war rooms similar to those built by parties' political marketing professionals. He maintains that interest groups need war rooms because "big challenges don't simply happen to political parties and politicians anymore – they hit almost every company, non-governmental organization or group eventually" (34). He advises that ten lessons be followed on how to tell a story and how to attract people's attention: get organized, get the right story, get your story covered by reporters, get your message out by paying for it (advertising), get creative, get tough, get the facts and numbers, handle scandals, get modern, and get fighting (34-37).

There is little academic work available concerning Canadian interest groups in lobbying and political marketing literature. One is Seidle's analysis (1991) on the participation of interest groups in Canadian elections, which proposes an interesting overview of the groups' strategies and political activities at the federal and local level in an electoral context. We can mention too Montpetit's typology (2002) on communication between interest groups and the federal government. Montpetit rejects the notion that relations between the state and groups go beyond lobbying, and he sets out four types of activity that vary according to the scope (general or specific) and the form (knowledge and expertise or applications) of a group's communication activities: governance, public consumerism, self-regulation, and lobbying. In another study, Young and Everitt (2004) assess the contribution of interest groups to Canadian democracy from five standpoints: the nature of their participation, the form of engagement and composition of groups, the identification of groups' access to decision making, the strategies they implement, and their impact on democracy. Such research is quite general and does not systematically pose the question of which strategies are used by groups in their recruitment efforts and lobbying. This leaves the door open to discussing these dimensions further and to analyzing the cases of some Canadian interest groups.

To study the use of political marketing by interest groups in Canada, we follow the Lees-Marshment model of political marketing (2003, 2004), the only model in the literature to give an account of the political marketing efforts deployed by interest groups. Lees-Marshment applies the example of a political party that adopts a marketing approach (market-oriented party) to an interest group's recruitment strategy. She proposes a typology of three models of groups based on their use of political marketing: product-oriented, sales-oriented, and market-oriented groups. Other models (Henneberg 2002; O'Cass 2001; Ormrod 2007) apply to political parties only; the same is true

TABLE 10.1

Ideal types of political marketing by interest groups

Step	1. Product-oriented	2. Sales-oriented	3. Market-oriented
1	Product design	Product design	Market intelligence
2	Communication	Market intelligence	Product design
3	Campaign	Communication	Product refinement
4	Delivery	Campaign	Communication
5	–	Delivery	Campaign
6	–	–	Delivery

SOURCE: Lees-Marshment (2004).

of the typology outlined in Table 4.1. Lees-Marshment's comprehensive approach takes a look at the strategic thinking underlying the organization as a whole and does not leave us stuck with a single, inflexible model. The three orientations allow for groups to be classified according to their strategic thinking and the actions they take with regard to political marketing. Some groups can be more effective with a sales orientation, depending on the goals they aim to reach and the interests they defend. The model relies on ideal types (product-oriented, sales-oriented, market-oriented). This offers the analytical advantage of positioning groups and comparing them to each other using measurable indicators (different steps for each orientation). Table 10.1 presents Lees-Marshment's model.

The product orientation corresponds to interest groups that make minimal use of the concepts and techniques of political marketing, since the cause that they defend or promote is paramount. Dedication to the cause being defended or promoted delineates general guidelines for recruitment and lobbying. In fact, only limited resources are invested in communication efforts aimed at members, public office holders, and the general public. In the end, a product-oriented group makes an assessment of its efforts on the basis of what it considers to be best. Groups that match this profile are in a monopolistic position in terms of representation and are generally strong ideologically. Moreover, they receive their funding from a small number of donors and have only limited opportunities to expand their base of supporters and to influence government decision making (Lees-Marshment 2004, 98-99).

The second ideal type of sales-oriented groups corresponds to organizations that use political marketing in their recruitment efforts and lobbying. Although initially designing their products based on what they deem desirable, groups belonging to this category are innovative in comparison to product-oriented groups. They integrate market research in their activities, and this identifies other groups likely to support them, as well as the best ways of influencing government decisions. One such organization then moves into a phase of proactive communication to draw government attention and to raise money from potential supporters. It uses methods such as direct mail, direct dialogue with people in public positions, and television advertising. It delivers the final result to its members as it deems best, paying special attention to promotion. Although acknowledging the qualitative leap this approach makes in comparison with the first archetype of product orientation, Lees-Marshment (2004, 103-4) draws attention to various limitations, including ethical ones.

The first two cases attach great importance, respectively, to the justness of the cause and to the best methods and communication techniques for influencing government and recruiting new members; the third ideal type suggests that a group will attempt to advance its interests in line with its market, that is, its current and potential membership. An organization corresponding to the market-oriented group category generally proceeds in the same way as a market-oriented political party that applies the various stages of political marketing. First, it analyzes the characteristics of the environment in which it operates, such as political issues and competitors' positions, and then probes its market by identifying the needs of its supporters – past, present, and potential – through formal means (member surveys, focus groups, phone calls, national polls for the pulse population) as well as informal means (casual communication with members at public events), and it segments its potential members into different groups. From the data obtained, it then develops a product including the costs, the package provided to members, and campaign activities that may vary according to the segments identified and that may enable the group to distance itself from its competitors. This is followed by a refinement of the product in terms of various aspects: its appropriateness, the possibilities of cooperation with other organizations, and its potential for differentiation with respect to what is available from the competition and its potential support. The group then deploys a broad effort to refine its communications: it uses various channels (newspaper or television advertising, direct mail, direct dialogue) for each segment it wants to reach, and it tests its advertising to maximize its potential. The organization finally delivers from four dimensions: delivery of the package offered to supporters and an assessment of their satisfaction, delivery of the results of successful lobbying efforts, a focus on retention of new or existing members, and an update of members' contribution and involvement (Lees-Marshment 2004, 105-15).

Case Study: Business Groups, Trade Unions, and Social Groups

This chapter examines the use of political marketing by interest groups in Canada. More specifically, it investigates whether the nature of the interests defended by a group influences the use of political marketing. Yet, classifying interest groups is a challenge: "Attempting any classification of pressure groups is a difficult task ... There is such a multiplicity and diversity of associations and ... they vary enormously in their degree of organisation, durability, influence and status" (Watts 2007, 29). All classifications have their strengths and weaknesses, given that it is difficult to encompass all interest groups in pre-defined types.

Many writers (Berry 1999; Olson 1965) prefer the division between groups defending exclusive interests, variously known as interest, defensive, or sectional groups and those advancing a cause or a more inclusive interest, also known as social or citizen groups. Others, such as Grant (1989), divide groups as insiders or outsiders according to whether or not they have access to the corridors of power. We use the sectoral approach, which categorizes interest groups according to the sector in which they are active and which has been used by many studies (Finer 1966; Kollman 1998; Watts 2007). This provides the advantage of focusing on the sector in which groups perform their activities and their potential connection to marketing activities.

Moreover, Kollman (1998, 18) uses this classification to study the strategies of outside lobbying interest groups. From that point of view, we use the same categorization to compare the political marketing practices of three types of groups: business groups, trade unions, and social groups.[1] We emphasize that business groups and trade unions develop reflexes that orient them more toward a market approach than social groups, due to higher levels of centralization and hierarchy (in the case of trade unions) or their affinity with the business community and commercial marketing concepts and techniques (for business groups).[2] In the end, both types of groups are strongly associated with protection of their members' material interests, whereas social groups are associated more with the promotion of inclusive values such as social rights or the environment.

To study political marketing as used by interest groups in Canada, semi-structured interviews were conducted between January 2008 and November 2009 with professionals in charge of communications in nineteen organizations.[3] The interviews were audio recorded and interviewees were assured anonymity. Before being interviewed, participants received a summary stating the main research objectives and listing four broad questions: (1) the participant's professional profile and general information on the organization, (2) recruitment and funding, (3) direct and indirect lobbying, and (4) the participant's theoretical background in political marketing.

Although criticized for their shortcomings in terms of generalization, case studies represent an appropriate way of exploring understudied questions. The use of political marketing by interest groups is a good example of this type of subject matter. Greenwood (1997, 7) states that case studies are very useful for in-depth analysis of little-known phenomena. In addition, quantitative data and analyses become truly accessible only after case studies have enabled the phenomena coming under closer scrutiny to be typified. Furthermore, Greenwood believes that some of the most important contributions to political science have resulted from case studies.

Business Groups' Use of Political Marketing

Many authors have documented the lobbying tactics of different kinds of groups, but few of them, with some notable exceptions (see Schlozman and Tierney 1986), tried to browse an exhaustive portrait comparing types of interest groups and the different lobbying tools they tend to use, especially for the business groups. Kollman (1998, 18), for instance, showed that business groups were somewhat less likely than trade unions or public interest groups to use outside lobbying tactics, especially for advertising their policy positions and for protesting. This gives reason to believe that business groups would also tend to use less political marketing.

Business groups in Canada do not benefit from institutionalized mechanisms that enable them to obtain substantial ongoing funding. In this context, developing effective recruitment and funding strategies becomes a necessary condition for any hope of exerting influence on government and media representatives. Tools for assessing the composition and needs of a potential market or of current members are therefore critical to an organization. In developing their messages, many business groups pay plenty of attention to members and to larger socio-political movements, and they even take advantage of particular events to develop new issues. (In Chapter 13, Patricia Cormack describes how Becel, Dove, and Tim Hortons use political marketing to attach themselves to the consumer psyche.) Leading business groups survey their members to portray a more accurate picture of their respective clients and of their expectations for an organization representing the interests of entrepreneurs:

> Every two years, we conduct a survey of our members and companies in Quebec to find out which issues they want us to intervene in and what they think of our communications and our events. Otherwise, we try to maintain day-to-day contact with them and listen to what they say when they come to our activities. (respondent 2)[4]

However, some business groups make relatively limited use of these tools because of a lack of resources. They seem to focus more on informal methods to determine their members' needs: for example, on the occasion of the various events they organize or the comments they may receive. However, the intention of taking members' opinions into consideration remains important to them.

Employers' organizations share a relatively small market of members and donors. As a result, they must conduct a rigorous and detailed segmentation of the various companies and business associations in Canada. This represents a crucial step in their initial strategy:

> We keep a detailed database that is updated regularly with information on our members' profile: company turnover, number of employees, sector of activity, etcetera. This is very useful for following up with them when the time comes to renew their membership and to meet their expectations more effectively. (respondent 3)

However, the use of search tools is not yet fully incorporated by all business groups. At most, respondents indicated that they rely on their association to calibrate their recruitment strategy with a general picture of what they believe to be the market representing the interests of business, without adopting a systematic and rigorous process of producing detailed and reliable data. However, a clear desire to work toward a segmentation model emerged from participants' comments.

The employers' associations' recruitment strategy corresponds perfectly to the ideal type of political marketing deployment: it moves upstream following an almost surgical segmentation of the various characteristics of its market, with careful targeting to identify the companies or other business associations most likely to join and therefore the most profitable in terms of financial, human, and organizational resources. Again, although maintaining some strategic thinking in their recruitment efforts, business groups do not conduct a systematic targeting of potential members for recruitment. They identify some players generally regarded as potential members, or they adopt a broader strategy through which they hope to recruit a variety of organizations with interests that are sometimes at odds. At best, the groups they surveyed offer a more general portrait of their target market (for example, small and medium enterprises, large companies, specific industries).

In terms of positioning, business organizations in Canada do not correspond perfectly to their members' needs and wants. Yet, it would be wrong to believe that these groups are disconnected from their members' concerns and needs. The resources awarded to these organizations are concentrated in a relatively small pool of corporate members and associations; they have an incentive to stay informed of those members' expectations by various means (for example, phone calls, email messages, meetings with their leaders, private events) to know how to position themselves on various issues relevant to their members:

We have regular discussions with most of our members. They call us regularly if they have problems or concerns. They also call us for answers to questions or for assistance in specific cases. (respondent 23)

The cost of going against the wishes of some members may be relatively high. This feedback is even more significant in the case of business groups or associations in a specific industry niche, characterized by smaller stakes, a recurring agenda, and greater knowledge by organizations of their members' public policy needs and preferences over the years.

Considering the specific conditions that characterize business groups, it is particularly interesting to analyze their communications strategies in recruiting new members. These organizations often take a targeted approach to persuading potential members to join their ranks. Group leaders can contact prospective members through their social networks to persuade them to join; of course, social networking is moving increasingly online (see Tamara Small's chapter, Chapter 12, on relationship marketing), but in-person networking remains essential. These group leaders also produce promotional material outlining the benefits of membership and distribute it at corporate events or send information by mail. These groups also have employees whose jobs revolve around member recruitment and retention. They devote substantial lobbying efforts to attracting policy makers and also to convincing current and prospective members of their strength and political influence as an organization, thereby encouraging them to join or to renew their memberships:

> We defend companies from our sector ... This involves participating in parliamentary committees when a bill is presented and to lobby the government and the public constantly on issues that affect them directly. (respondent 1)

Trade Unions' Use of Political Marketing

Trade unions seem more inclined to use outside lobbying tactics and grassroots activities, especially protesting (Kollman 1998; Schlozman and Tierney 1986), though some authors have identified several factors that could give them a significant advantage in the lobbying process. Watts (2007), for instance, identifies some key characteristics of influential interest groups, the main one being the group's resources – namely members, staff and leadership, financing, organization, and ability to make strategic alliances with other groups. From many perspectives, this group's resources seem particularly relevant to more effective use of political marketing by trade unions.

With unions, the issue of recruitment and funding is somewhat different from that of business groups and social groups. We might expect organizations on the left of the political spectrum, such as trade unions, to be less willing to embrace a market orientation than are organizations on the right, such as businesses (see Alex Marland's discussion at the beginning of Chapter 4). However, unlike business associations, where membership is voluntary, unions have a structural advantage over other types of groups. This is because of the Rand formula, a clause in collective agreements allowing a union representing a bargaining unit to request that the employer collect compulsory union dues paid by all employees who are members of a given unit, even those who do not wish to become union members. Thus, even if labour groups must strive constantly to recruit and retain their membership base, especially during raiding periods when organizations compete to encourage some union locals to change their affiliation, they nevertheless enjoy a valuable asset that has a significant impact on the effectiveness of their upstream strategy.

Labour groups consist of unions representing employees in various sectors, with the market they seek to conquer usually being relatively large.

Although in many cases recruitment is done in collaboration with the unions concerned, their high degree of centralization means that strategy coordination is typically handled at the highest hierarchical level of an organization. Thus, labour groups frequently conduct research to obtain a detailed and accurate picture of the vast pool of existing and potential members, focusing recruitment efforts on the basis of their needs and expectations: "In our survey, we will see what our members want. How and what? What do we know? What do we need to know?" (respondent 20).

They also analyze the political and social environment, as well as the labour movement in general. Unions seem to use more respondents in their various public opinion research (POR) tools (see Chapters 5 and 9 for discussions of POR). The strategy development process does not seem to have penetrated very deeply into the strategy that these groups apply. Thus, the use of market segmentation is barely higher than in the case of employers' organizations.

The degree of correspondence between the ideal type of political marketing deployment by interest groups and effective targeting efforts by labour groups varies substantially, depending on the organization. However, data collected during our interviews suggest that the gap is significantly higher, which leads us to give trade unions a score ranging from low to moderate in this regard. Indeed, although in some campaigns it is possible to identify workers to be recruited in specific industrial sectors, these choices do not seem to result from systematic strategic thinking following the segmentation process.

Because members of labour organizations are individuals, the positioning process carried out by these groups is usually more elaborate than for other types of organizations and is very similar to the process conducted by political parties during their permanent campaign efforts. Labour groups are organizations that are more centralized and hierarchical than other types of interest groups, yet they usually try to position themselves on issues where their leaders believe there is a target market from which they can gain members: "For one of our campaigns, we wanted to try to get young people, because they are less unionized. So we did some research, and this helped build an argument which touched on issues that directly affected them" (respondent 9).

Trade unions deploy a range of tools to recruit new members and generate a sense of belonging among those who have already joined. These methods take different forms: communication campaigns, promotional items, group insurance, wage gains, background papers and periodicals, involvement within the organization, and opportunities for mobilization. Some groups are more creative. For example, one group had a caravan touring the province to visit different festivals over a period of more than five years. It worked very well, and the group is thinking of repeating the experience: "A caravan painted with our colours and logo was doing regional tours every year. This caravan stopped by different festivals with hosts, singers, and actors. We transmitted a lot of information about our organization by this means" (respondent 19).

In addition, unions are now increasingly using the web in their recruitment efforts. It is very easy for those who wish to organize online to use an electronic forum, an avenue that has not been explored up to now by employers' organizations. Moreover, the frequent use by labour groups of various outside lobbying tactics also provides significant exposure to workers, thereby promoting their organizations indirectly with a view to maximizing the short-term pool of potential supporters.

SOCIAL GROUPS' USE OF POLITICAL MARKETING

Finally, it may seem that social groups could be viewed as the interest groups most predisposed to use outside lobbying tactics and political marketing, but certain factors appear to invalidate this idea. In his study, Nownes (2006, 95-100) gives six tips for lobbyists to increase their influence on policy makers: avoid asking too much at once, have plenty of resources, do not go against public opinion, act defensively by not going on the offensive, present reliable information to the government, and mobilize members at the grassroots level (a practice that stimulates participation by conducting grassroots advocacy). Apart from some major social groups, many of these organizations face a shortage of resources and other factors that could be expected to limit their capacity to make regular use of research tools (for example, opinion polls) and communication techniques (for example, advertising) that the political marketing approach requires.

In general, social groups make little use of systematic research tools in gauging their pool of current and potential members. Their thinking often suggests that the cause they espouse is good enough to win supporters. For social groups, message delivery is determined on the basis of the values they stand for and the ideas they believe in. Social organizations are not prone to alter their messages, since they are fighting for causes they consider just and are afraid of diluting the messages they defend. Whenever they adjust a communication strategy, the core of the message remains unaltered: "We are more in a logical message campaign. If we must say something specific to the Quebec government or the public, we will get the message. We won't refine it" (respondent 14). However, in recent years, some social organizations have recognized the strategic importance of their membership bases and have made substantial efforts to develop sophisticated methods of analysis to get further support from their bases.

Targeting does not appear to be a strategic priority of the social groups surveyed. Because of the collective nature of the interests they represent, these organizations seem to believe that all potential members will join for the same reasons: the group's values and mission. Therefore, focusing on certain segments they could win over in the vast interest-representation market is not a priority. However, organizations that have relatively well-delineated membership bases occasionally target certain categories of potential members as part of specific campaigns. But these are essentially ad hoc approaches rather than a systematic process: "Sometimes we run our campaigns by trying to reach some specific publics. We target issues that are crucial to them. But most of the time, we seek to reach as many people as possible in order to gain influence with public authorities" (respondent 11).

The positioning of the groups interviewed is determined only rarely by a systematic consultation of their members' needs and preferences. Obviously, these organizations take pride, with good reason, in their democratic character and participatory practices. However, a lack of standardized mechanisms can bring group leaders to position themselves more in terms of their cause without necessarily taking account of the expectations of current and potential members, further reducing their ability to attract and retain publics. However, organizations that have associations as members can be positioned according to the information they receive from their member associations. These associations may, depending on their resources, conduct consultation with association members and individual units in a more formal way.

In terms of communication tactics, the social groups studied put significant energy into developing tactics that are varied, proactive, and attractive. These organizations rely mostly on in-house journals, toll-free phone numbers, email updates, and websites. In conducting indirect lobbying, social organizations use a broad array of means to build their profiles and credibility, making particular use of press releases, press conferences, advertising (print, web, radio, or television), open letters, fundraising activities, websites, and social media (Facebook, Twitter). Some groups establish partnerships with well-known retail businesses to distribute promotional material: "For a non-profit organization, marketing is a major development. We try to create partnerships with retailers, to make things more dynamic and original" (respondent 18). In the end, social groups are constantly seeking something new to stand out among the general public and to raise their profiles:

> In order to gain critical strength, we must be able to sell our cause successfully and seek those who believe in what we do. That's why we try to spread our message as widely as possible: we want to tackle the problem ... of getting people to join us. (respondent 13)

The State of Political Marketing in Canada

We have suggested that business groups and trade unions, traditionally associated with the protection or promotion of their members' material interests, have reflexes that guide them toward a greater market orientation than social groups, which advocate a more inclusive orientation associated with the common good, such as the environment or social rights. Therefore, on the basis of our observations, our hypothesis is partially confirmed.

The differences between business groups, trade unions, and social groups can be noted mainly at the level of upstream political marketing, in how they approach their members. In comparison with social groups, business groups and trade unions get their members more involved in the development of the message. In the same vein, these latter groups pay greater attention to refining the messages sent to their members as a way of maximizing their loyalty.

First, business groups and trade unions end up being slightly more market-oriented. The difference with social groups lies mainly in the deployment of a marketing approach toward their members (upstream political marketing). Compared with social organizations, there is an increasing adherence by business groups, and by trade unions in particular, to the idea that research among members must precede any action put forward by the group. This leads business groups and trade unions to involve their members more in developing the message. Similarly, business organizations and trade unions are more sensitive to the notion of refining the message, again involving their members, to ensure that they satisfy these members and maximize member retention. In short, the nature of the relationship between business groups or trade unions and their members seems more advanced and personalized than the situation that prevails between social groups and their bases.

Among social groups, the message remains the glue of the organization and is not diluted to appeal to members or the public. The message is central to social groups and is determined by the values they uphold and the ideas they believe to be sound. Research, often informal, comes after the message. It supports the message and is used primarily in positioning communication strategies.

However, beyond these differences, our research found that most Canadian interest groups belong to the sales-oriented group model described by Lees-Marshment. We stress that our three categories of groups are predominantly persuasion-oriented. Indeed, the three categories of groups develop their actions with persuasion as their intention, aiming for audiences that are potentially reactive to the message circulated. Communications from all groups are generally diversified, proactive, and designed to attract attention. Moreover, the traditional differences are not fixed realities: for instance, although business groups and trade unions devoted significant resources to direct lobbying in the past, they are now as active as social groups in addressing the general public. It follows from this that our three categories of groups aim to increase their visibility and, after that, to persuade public office holders.

Implications for the Quality of Democracy

The democratic nature of interest groups has been a central question studied by many authors since the first studies about groups in the United States. Representatives of the pluralist school (Dahl 1961; Key 1942; Truman 1951), for example, first defended the idea that power within a society does not lie solely in the hands of government or the electorate but is also distributed among a multitude of groups and associations. This competition between groups of somewhat equal strength would give fair representation to all actors in civil society, safeguard the democratic political system, and ensure the common good. However, some authors in the early 1960s questioned this view, criticizing in particular the idea that all groups had equal weight and asserting that this representation was tainted by greater political influence on the part of certain groups, including business associations. This finding has led some to conclude that "the flaw in the pluralistic heaven is that the heavenly chorus sings with a strong upper-class accent" (Schattschneider 1960, 35). The publication of *The Logic of Collective Action* by Mancur Olson (1965) substantially undermined the theoretical and empirical hypotheses of the pluralist school by offering a new perspective, inspired by economics and followed by many authors (for reviews, see Mitchell and Munger 1991; Mueller 2003), setting the groundwork for an analysis of associations as rational actors representing specific interests and deploying strategies for promoting them.

Studying the use of political marketing by Canadian interest groups necessarily raises new questions and reflections as to the role and impact of interest groups in the democratic system. It is legitimate to ask whether an organization managing a market orientation, as in the Lees-Marshment model, could be a threat to democracy, since it may be capable of manipulating its membership or public opinion. Rather than this pessimistic vision, we believe instead that democracy has much to gain from the application of the marketing approach to recruitment efforts by lobbying groups. The marketing approach, by definition, brings the leaders of an organization to build its strategy around consumers. An interest group with a marketing approach would not only be more sensitive to the needs of its current and potential members, which would also help it maximize its resources, but would also pay attention to movements in public opinion in order to increase its support among the population and its influence with policy makers. Far from the stereotype of lobbyists and interest groups pulling strings in the dark corridors of power, the marketing approach necessarily implies transparency and ethics on the part of the organizations that apply it in order for it to be effective. (For a discussion of the ethical implications of political marketing, see Henneberg 2004.) From our point of view, it can answer concerns as to the importance of maintaining relatively strong civil associations to counterbalance the power of the state in a democratic system.

This chapter has aimed to paint a picture of the use of political marketing by Canadian interest groups. Political marketing remains practically unexplored in relation to interest groups. This study represents an initial contribution at explaining how these organizations use political marketing practices. Therefore, theoretical gaps remain in this subfield of political science, but our contribution offers an initial interdisciplinary look that provides for opening up the study of the practice of political marketing, which is usually confined to political parties. It also gives impetus to further analyses of interest groups.

NOTES

1   For the purpose of this chapter we considered only groups representing a significant number of people or organizations and not single-person advocacy groups (also called astroturf groups in the literature; see Kollman 1998, 5) like Ezra Levant in

Canada or Ann Coulter in the United States, even though they can make extensive use of political marketing methods.

2   Scammell (1995) and Kavanagh (1995), for example, noted that the more centralized and hierarchical nature of the British Conservative Party and its closeness with the business community made the party more open to the integration of a marketing approach in its electoral campaigns.

3   Lemieux (2008) interviewed twelve spokespersons from various interest groups in January 2008. The business groups he met with were the Fédération des chambres de commerce du Québec, the Fédération canadienne de l'entreprise indépendante, Manufacturiers et exportateurs du Québec, and the Conseil de l'industrie forestière du Québec. As for trade unions, he conducted interviews with representatives of the Fédération des travailleurs et des travailleuses du Québec (FTQ), the Confédération des syndicats nationaux (CSN), the Centrale des syndicats du Québec (CSQ), and the Centrale des syndicats démocratiques (CSD). Regarding social groups, he conducted interviews with people from Greenpeace Québec, the Front d'action populaire en réaménagement urbain (FRAPRU), and the Fédération étudiante universitaire du Québec (FEUQ). Foster (2010) conducted interviews with members of ten interest groups. The social groups she met were Greenpeace Québec, Option consommateurs, UNICEF, the FEUQ, and La Société de l'arthrite. In terms of trade unions, Foster conducted interviews with the Fédération des producteurs de porc du Québec (FPPQ), the Syndicat de la fonction publique du Québec (SFPQ), and the Fédération des médecins spécialistes du Québec (FMSQ). For business groups, Foster interviewed representatives of the Conseil du patronat du Québec (CPQ), and the Association provinciale des constructeurs d'habitations du Québec (APCHQ). Lemieux and Foster chose these groups for their high public profiles and their representativeness in their own fields.

4   Anonymity was guaranteed to all interviewees. Accordingly, they are presented as "respondent 1" to "respondent 24." With all interviews having been conducted in French, all quotes are free translations by the authors.

PART 3
The Media and Citizens ....

11
As (Not) Seen on TV: News Coverage of Political Marketing in Canadian Federal Elections

Thierry Giasson

This chapter looks at the understudied relationship between political marketing and media coverage of politics. This interest gap in political marketing research seems preoccupying, considering the central role of intermediary and interpreter that the news media plays in democratic politics. Furthermore in Canada, as in many other post-industrial democracies, press coverage of politics during and between elections has evolved considerably (Nadeau and Giasson 2003; Nadeau et al. 2001; P. Norris 2000; Norris et al. 1999; Pratte 2000; Sabato 1991; Taras 1999; Wagenberg et al. 1988). According to Sabato (1991), political journalism has moved away from its previous role of watchdog toward a more confrontational model of attack journalism. This new brand of political journalism now shows citizens what really goes on "behind the scenes" of politics. It frames the political process as a competition with winners and losers, highlights scandals and abuses of power implicating politicians, and speculates about actors' motives, interests, and intentions. This ultimately reduces the public policy process to a rather critical, if not cynical, negative image of tactical partisan strategies carried out during campaigns.

Simultaneously, other analyses (Cappella and Jamieson 1996, 1997; de Vreese 2005; Patterson 1994) have looked at the relationship that this new political reporting might have with the democratic malaise that many post-industrial societies have been said to experience in the last decade. A cynical media generates a cynical citizenry, as this spiral-of-cynicism argument goes, and Canada's political system is suspected to suffer from the same democratic uneasiness (Nadeau 2002). Canadian electoral studies and public opinion polls conducted in the last twenty years reveal declines in voter turnout and fluctuations in levels of public trust toward political and government actors and institutions (Angus Reid 2010; Gidengil et al. 2004, 104-7; Léger Marketing 2006, 2007; Nevitte 1996, 54-58; see also Chapter 3 for an overview of this issue).

Yet, very little attention has been directed to the way the news media covers political marketing practice. Since the mid-1990s, the bulk of contributions in political marketing research have been dedicated to conceptualizing theoretical models of market-oriented political marketing or discussing how parties follow or digress from these archetypes (Johansen 2005; Lees-Marshment 2004, 2008; Marland 2005; O'Cass 1996, 2003; Ormrod 2007; Ormrod and Henneberg 2006). This market-orientation ethos imposes that parties put the voters' demands and expectations first when designing their political offer. As Strömbäck, Mitrook, and Kiousis (2010, 75; emphasis added) reiterate, "Marketing essentially is about identifying, responding to and satisfying the needs and wants of selected groups and people in society. Thus it is not only about campaigns. Rather political marketing and market orientation is about the *relationship.*" Addressing this relationship ideal, more recent contributions now insist on the importance that notions of confidence building and trust building in citizens must play in political marketing. For instance, Johansen (2005) reminds us that marketing politics is similar to the marketing of service businesses such as financial institutions or insurance companies. They both offer their consumers an intangible product, and the benefits associated with its consumption cannot be immediately evaluated. The transaction between producer and consumer is therefore immersed in uncertainty. Organizations that share these characteristics, like political parties, should ground their product conception and delivery processes in relationships stimulating trust and confidence in their actual and potential consumers. Confidence building could therefore alleviate consumer uncertainty and facilitate the political/electoral transaction.

In a political market like Canada, where product offerings are numerous and brand loyalty has reached new lows, according to the democratic malaise theory, consumers are difficult to attract and retain. Scholars like Johansen (2005) see in confidence building and relationship marketing potential solutions to these challenges. Relationship marketing puts consumers at the centre of product design and makes them active participants in the process. By being actively involved, consumers gain confidence in the producer. This new philosophy differs somewhat from its commercial cousin, where product design and communications are controlled, *marketers-only* experiences. Relationship marketing imposes a co-production, a *consumer/marketer* experience, in which a constant contact is secured between both actors (Johansen 2005, 95). Yet, the reality of political marketing shows otherwise, as it still remains a *marketers-only* experience.

This represents a strong challenge for political parties conducting political marketing and which must generate trust in the electorate in order to alleviate uncertainty and stimulate support. This impacts both the product design sequence and the product communication and promotion steps of the process. But parties are not the only ones speaking publicly about their offers. The news media is another key player in the public deliberation process of political products. It carries its own opinion on the matter.

Political Marketing in the Media: A Discreet Dynamic

In Canada as elsewhere, elections are first and foremost communication campaigns. In the course of an electoral campaign, product promotion is done both directly and indirectly toward targeted voters. Efforts of direct communication will take the form of advertising activities (both paid and the free advertising minutes allocated in election campaigns in the Canadian case). These promotional tools allow the organization to communicate a partisan message – the content and exact time of diffusion of which are controlled by the producer – to specific voters without having it reinterpreted or commented on by any third party.

However, such paid promotional activities are expensive and usually represent the bulk of electoral expenditures for parties. A more affordable compromise then comes in the form of public relations activities. This is the classic two-step flow of communication. By speaking first to the news media, parties can access voters indirectly, through the press coverage of their campaign activities. Therefore, putting together a leader's campaign tour, staging daily pseudo-events, and holding press conferences allow a political party to keep the media's attention on its message and to promote its product to their audiences.

As communication and political marketing scholars have previously stated (Johansen 2005, 94-95; Strömbäck, Mitrook, and Kiousis 2010, 76, 83-84, 87; Washbourne 2010), the relationship that unites political marketing practice and the media is undeniable. Parties need the news media to convey their messages to voters and to promote their respective electoral offers. However, O'Shaughnessy (2002, 211) has reminded other scholars that "political marketing, and political communication phenomena, are distinguished from consumer marketing also by the arbitration of an independent communication power centre – the mass or 'free' media that they may be able to influence but cannot control."

Political communication research has demonstrated that the media selects, interprets, and comments on the message political parties present to voters during elections. Strategic news framing can transform and alter the initial message a party tries to convey by focusing on campaign organization, strategies, tactics, and motives. O'Cass (2003, 90) posits that "the messages reaching the public about a commercial product are largely marketer-controlled, whereas the messages reaching the public about a political candidate and party are largely controlled by the news media." Such a conclusion is echoed by O'Shaughnessy's comment (2002, 215) that "we can speak not of political marketing, but of a media-arbitrated image of political marketing."

Yet, until recently, no one had investigated these media-controlled images of political marketing in the literature. The initial groundbreaking came from Savigny and Temple (2010), who indicate that the theoretical perspective currently dominating political marketing research – imported from management and which considers parties and voters as near-perfect equivalents of commercial businesses and consumers – limits knowledge production on the dynamics uniting political marketing and the mediation of politics. According to the authors, political marketing literature usually treats the media like a "dog that isn't barking" (7-8). So far, political marketing research has considered the product-communication stage as just another step to follow in the marketing process, similar to what would be achieved in a commercial advertising strategy. Such a mechanistic conception fails to address a core aspect of the democratic political market: the existence of a free news media. Savigny and Temple remind readers that the news media's raison d'être in democratic regimes is to analyze and make sense of the political elite's messages to help citizens produce informed decisions. They are neither neutral nor passive conduits.

How then does the Canadian news media cover political marketing practices in its overwhelmingly strategic framing of electoral politics? Does it mention it? If so, on which aspects of political marketing during elections does the news media direct its attention? And finally, could this coverage affect the relationship- and confidence-building exercises that market-oriented parties must engage in with citizens to alleviate the inherent uncertainty of the electoral transaction?

Case Study: News Coverage of Political Marketing

Addressing three specific questions can help us better understand how the news media depicts political marketing practices in Canadian political parties: What is the proportion of electoral news coverage dedicated to political marketing practice in Canadian federal parties? Which aspects of political marketing practice are highlighted in the coverage? How does the news media associate political marketing use in parties with the broader subject of democratic life in Canada?

Three hypotheses, built from previous conclusions presented in electoral coverage studies, such as the dominance of horserace journalism and the potential existence of a spiral of cynicism (Cappella and Jamieson 1997; de Vreese 2005), will be tested in the ensuing analysis.

Hypothesis 1: In its coverage of campaign activities, the Canadian media will dedicate an important part of its news items to the practice of political marketing the federal parties are conducting.

From this significant proportion of news items dedicated to political marketing, it is expected that:

Hypothesis 2: The Canadian news media will dedicate a larger proportion of its coverage to aspects of tactical marketing than to aspects of strategic marketing, since tactical marketing is implemented in the course of the campaign the media covers.

Strategic marketing refers to the initial phase of political marketing conducted by parties prior to an election call, during which they define and refine their respective political offers based on market intelligence, segment the electorate, target specific groups of electors to reach, and devise a promotion/ communication strategy. Tactical marketing refers to the implementation, during the campaign, of the communication strategy promoting the political offer. This second phase of political marketing is carried through advertising and public relations activities held during the leaders' electoral tours and aimed specifically at the news media covering the campaign.

The third hypothesis looks at the association reporters make in their electoral stories between the practice of political marketing and its impact on the quality of democratic life in Canada. Therefore, it is expected that:

Hypothesis 3: In its coverage of political marketing practices, the news media will associate negatively the use of political marketing with democratic vitality in Canada.

These propositions were tested by analyzing the content of transcripts from all electoral news items presented in the evening newscasts of

Radio-Canada, CBC, and CTV and in the daily editions of four national broadsheet newspapers (La Presse, Le Devoir, the Globe and Mail, the National Post) during the federal election campaigns of 2000, 2004, 2005-6, and 2008. The dataset comprises 10,720 electoral news items, including news reports, analyses, commentaries, citizen forums, features, and op-ed pieces produced during the four election campaigns in the seven news outlets.[1] This sample of the Canadian news media is representative but not exhaustive. Radio news, online reporting, and periodicals are not included in the analysis, but the selected corpus offers a representative portrait of what a significantly large portion of the Canadian news industry, both private and public, written and electronic, and French and English, presented in its electoral coverage for nearly a decade. The selected seven outlets are also part of large media enterprises that on any given day share or redistribute political content on their other news platforms, including their radios or websites. In addition, recent studies indicate that the leading source of political information for Canadians continues to be television news, with newspapers a distant second, ahead of radio and the Internet (Centre d'études sur les médias 2010; Gidengil et al. 2004; Marcotte and Bastien 2010). Finally, these news outlets all produce comparable political content during elections, engage similar amounts of resources in campaign coverage, and share a broad reach in audiences.

The corpus was analyzed with Lexicoder, an open-source software that conducts deductive automated content analysis of large bodies of written documents.[2] This software searches the documents for predetermined expressions and keywords listed in categories that are grouped in dictionaries. The tool calculates the total occurrences of each word or expression mentioned in a category within the studied corpus. Seven dictionaries, both in French and English versions, were designed for this study in order to measure all the variables in the research hypotheses.[3]

The content analysis was conducted in four distinct phases. Table 11.1 presents a summary of the categories each dictionary contained, examples of keywords and expressions associated with those categories, and the size of each analyzed sample of news items per dictionary. Since most analyses of electoral content in news conducted in Western democracies indicate an increase in horserace coverage in the last thirty years, the initial round of analysis looked at the distinction between campaign coverage (horserace) and stories dedicated to electoral issues (issue). The "Horserace" category contained expressions and terms associated with all matters of campaigning, such as electoral polls, the leaders' tours, campaign incidents or gaffes, political marketing activities, and televised debates. On the other hand, the

Table 11.1

Summary of automated content analysis procedure

Rounds of analysis	Categories in dictionary	Examples of key words	Sample size
1. Horserace vs. issue	1. Horserace (107 words) 2. Issue (82 words)	*Horserace:* campaign trail, debate, ads, strategy, tour, press conference, polls, race *Issue:* health care, daycare, economy, public finance, environment, national unity, defence	10,720 election news items
2. Aspects of the campaign covered	1. The race (19 words) 2. The tour (5 words) 3. Gaffes (5 words) 4. Strategy (4 words) 5. Political marketing (79 words) 6. Televised debates (7 words)	*The race:* survey, poll, battleground *The tour:* tour, campaign trail *Gaffes:* gaffe, campaign problem *Strategy:* strategic, campaign strategy *Political marketing:* targets, opinion research, image, brand *Televised debates:* leaders debate, televised debate	6,075 horserace news items
3a. Strategic vs. tactical marketing	1. Strategic marketing (42 words) 2. Tactical marketing (36 words)	*Strategic:* market research, segmentation, targeting, campaign strategy *Tactical:* damage control, spin, press release, press conference, briefing	2,875 strategy and political marketing news items
3b. Aspects of political marketing practice	Twenty-nine categories, such as market research, segmentation, targeting, strategy, positioning, ads, media and communication, spin, tactics	Same key words and expressions used in the previous dictionary but grouped differently under the twenty-nine categories	2,875 strategy and political marketing news items
4. Association between political marketing practices and democratic life	1. Positive association (36 words) 2. Negative association (35 words)	*Positive:* higher turnout, deliberation, active participation, have a say, listening to *Negative:* secrecy, pandering, low turnout, cynical, turned off	2,875 strategy and political marketing news items

"Issues" category listed different policy themes frequently debated during Canadian elections, such as health care, the economy, and national unity.

The second wave of coding investigated the different aspects of the campaign that were most prevalent in the horserace coverage. In order to discriminate between polling activities conducted for market research purposes by parties from polls sponsored by the media during the campaign, the words "polls" and "surveys" were included in "The race" category, since they focus mainly on vote intentions as the campaign progresses. To get a sense of public opinion research done by parties, different keywords and expressions were used, such as "party pollster," "market research," "opinion research," "market intelligence," and "focus group." The third sequence of analysis unveiled how the media referred to different concepts associated with political marketing. The dictionary also contained synonyms of "political marketing" that the media might use, such as "electioneering," "campaign management," "marketing," and "electoral marketing." Finally, the fourth content analysis sequence investigated the type of association the news media made between political marketing and the quality of democracy in Canada. This dictionary looked at the occurrences of keywords associated positively or negatively with democratic life.

All keywords and expressions contained in the dictionaries were selected from pre-existing open-source dictionaries on Lexicoder's website and its word count tool indicating the frequency of occurrences for specific expressions in the corpus. All of them are associated with concepts and terms commonly used in the literature on political marketing, on democratic malaise theory, and in traditional media electoral coverage. Therefore, other researchers familiar with these bodies of literature could produce similar lists. All of the dictionaries, which are available for consultation or use on request, were constructed in such a way as to ensure the highest levels of internal and external validity. Yet, we must recognize that these tools might generate a selection bias, as they cannot claim to be entirely exhaustive in nature and they solely address the specific research objectives of this project.

RESULTS

The seven studied Canadian news outlets confirm what studies of electoral coverage conducted in Canada and other Western democracies have revealed in the past thirty years: that horserace journalism dominates electoral news. The majority of coverage in the studied period was dedicated primarily to stories of campaign activities as opposed to electoral issues. In general, English-language newspapers tended to cover electoral issues such as health

TABLE 11.2

Horserace coverage in Canadian electoral news

Horserace topic	2000 (%)	2004 (%)	2006 (%)	2008 (%)	2000-8 (%)
Political marketing	34.7	34.5	35.4	36.9	35.3
The race	30.8	31.7	27.4	28.9	29.6
The tour	21.6	19.2	22.6	18.2	20.5
Strategy	5.5	6.1	7.0	7.0	6.5
Televised debates	5.4	6.7	5.8	6.6	6.2
Gaffes	2.0	1.8	1.8	2.4	1.9
Total mentions	100	100	100	100	100
Mentions (*n*)	(12,809)	(16,739)	(18,133)	(14,090)	(61,771)

NOTE: Total number of news items analyzed: 6,075. See Table 11.1 for examples of keywords and expressions within each topic.

care, the economy, or the environment slightly more than did television news or French-language dailies. Nevertheless, all outlets followed similar coverage trends, with horserace dominating throughout these four election cycles.

As Table 11.2 indicates, horserace coverage in the Canadian news media during these four elections reported mostly about voting intentions and electoral battles, the leaders' tours, and campaign organization activities. The data show that mentions of keywords related to the categories "The race," "Political marketing," and "The tour" dominated. All things being equal, electoral news items covered fewer campaign gaffes and leaders debates. In addition, mentions made to concepts that could be associated with political marketing dominated the horserace coverage. This conclusion is in line with the first theoretical proposition.

However, the number of mentions in a given category could hide the fact that high occurrences of mentions might be expressed in a limited number of news items. Therefore, looking at the number of news items that are primarily dedicated to strategy and political marketing could offer a clearer picture of this category's position in electoral coverage. "Strategy" and "Political marketing" mentions were combined into a new single category to identify the relative importance of strategic framing in the Canadian media. This more robust indicator does not support Hypothesis 1. As Figure 11.1 indicates, although a large proportion of the coverage deals with it, the majority of horserace news does not refer mainly to strategic framing. On average,

FIGURE 11.1

Evolution of strategic framing in Canadian electoral news

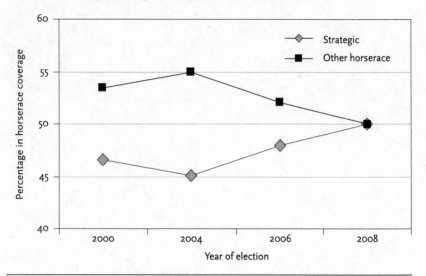

NOTE: See Table 11.1 for examples of keywords and expressions within each topic.

in the four election cycles investigated, 47 percent of electoral horserace news focused on strategic issues such as political marketing concepts, campaign organization, and strategies. This proportion is nevertheless important, as electoral coverage does indeed frequently mention party strategies and organizational effort invested in campaigns. However, the data also indicate that, in the course of these four federal elections, the media preferred covering the electoral fight in battleground ridings and the movement in voting intentions (The race) or campaigning activities from the leaders (The tour).

POLITICAL MARKETING ... WHAT POLITICAL MARKETING?
The second research proposition poses that, during elections, the news media will report more often on tactical marketing than on strategic marketing. According to theoretical models of political marketing (see Lees-Marshment 2008; Newman 1999a), strategic marketing usually follows five stages that help craft the offer and the communication strategy: (1) market research, (2) segmentation of the market, (3) targeting attractive market segments, (4) positioning and product design, and (5) conception of promotional/communication strategy. Political parties undertake this process many months prior to the election call. On the other hand, tactical marketing consists of

Figure 11.2

Evolution of political marketing coverage in Canadian electoral news

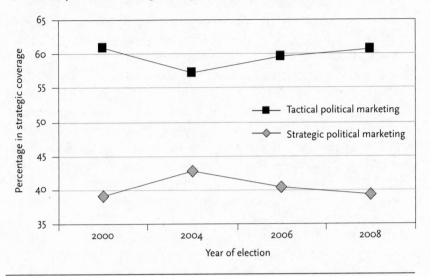

NOTE: See Table 11.1 for examples of keywords and expressions within each topic.

implementing the product's promotional strategy in the course of the election campaign. It deals with the public relations efforts directed toward the different publics of the political party (citizens, interest groups, party members, the media), and it includes the organization of pseudo-events (for example, staged visits, town hall meetings, or partisan rallies) and media management activities (e.g., news conferences, scrums, interviews). Finally, it also includes the tactical exercises of message-adjustment carried out during the campaign in reaction to opponents' offers and messages.

The second hypothesis was tested on the subsample of 2,875 news items primarily dedicated to marketing and party strategy, which is referred to here as the strategic framing in election coverage. This phase of the analysis was conducted with a dictionary comprising the categories "Strategic PM" and "Tactical PM" that each listed keywords and expressions depicting their proper stages in the political marketing process. Figure 11.2 indicates the evolution of both categories in the news media. The data support the second research hypothesis and indicate that news items more frequently mention concepts and expressions associated with tactical marketing, such as public relations exercises, pseudo-events, debate preparation, and message control (with terms such as "spin," "on message," and "damage control"). Over the studied period, the Canadian news media devoted 53 percent of its strategic coverage to stories focusing on tactical marketing practices. Such a situation should not be surprising, since a political reporter's daily routine during an election is to follow the leaders' tours' activities – mostly tactical experiences – and report on them. Political journalists are front-line witnesses and targets of tactical public relations exercises aimed specifically at ensuring an efficient and ef- fective product communication with the media.

Significantly, the analysis did uncover that the expression "political marketing" is virtually absent from electoral coverage in the Canadian media, appearing just twice in *Le Devoir* throughout the eight-year period. The syn- onymous concepts of electioneering, campaign management, and marketing were mentioned in the overall 10,720 electoral news items only three, eleven, and thirty-three times respectively. The media might mention "strategies," "organizations," and "tactics," but during the period in question, they did not call it "political marketing."

Three potential justifications could explain this silence. First, the political marketing process and its inherent conception of the politics-as-product might not be perceived positively in general by the news media. Political marketing may evoke to some a demeaning merchandising of the political, a victory of image over substance (Egan 1999, 496; Lock and Harris 1996b, 22). This social taboo explanation would bring the media to openly mention concepts and realities evoking political marketing, such as "strategy," "spin," or "tactics," but would simultaneously impose a ban on the use of "political marketing." Yet, it could be argued that these synonyms, especially the term "spin," also carry a negative stigma. Regardless, the media could fear that the label might cast a negative image of the political process in the population. Another explication could reside with a possible confusion that members of the press corps might experience between what political marketing really is (a process) and some specific promotional activities of political messages they witness during campaigns, such as public relations, pseudo-events, TV spots, or leaders' tours (tactics). By restrictively equating political marketing to communicative dimensions, the news media would therefore not have to refer to it as "political marketing" but rather as "political communication." This also makes sense, since the media covers more extensively the official campaign than the pre-campaign phase, where parties conduct market intel- ligence, segmentation, targeting, and product development. And unless a campaign is not running smoothly, reporters will therefore witness tactics and not the process that generated them.

Finally, one last hypothesis that could explain the media's silence is its ignorance of the very existence of the political marketing process and of the extent of its application in Canadian parties. Such a proposition does indeed sound more improbable, since recent political analyses and journalistic accounts of Canadian party organizations or electoral strategies making direct references to political marketing practices – most of them dealing specifically with the Conservative Party of Canada – were written by prominent political pundits and commentators (Castonguay 2010; Hébert 2007; Valpy 2008; Wells 2006). It should be more probable that these portrayals of political marketing have circulated among the journalistic community and would have contributed to better informing its members on the extent to which political marketing has been integrated in partisan organizations. Therefore, the collective ignorance hypothesis could probably be lifted.

Then again, the fact that the expression "political marketing" is mostly used by academics (few of them Canadians) and some practitioners (but very few politicians) does not mean that it will be widely known in the media and the general public. As Marland (2005) uncovered in his interviews with Canadian political strategists, many of them were unfamiliar with the expression, and those who were more knowledgeable about it mostly viewed the term negatively. Therefore, this terminology might be rarely used outside of closed, specialized circles. The data presented here nevertheless inform us that electoral coverage does indeed speak a lot about different aspects of organization and strategies. Whether it is labelled "political marketing," "electioneering," or "campaign management" might ultimately be irrelevant to political reporters and citizens. Our analysis indicates that the media does tell citizens that parties strategize, conduct polls, spin information, and organize events to persuade them to go out and vote.

The State of Political Marketing in Canada

The analysis of the two first research hypotheses indicates that the media speaks at length of campaign organizations and that it is aware that parties do practice marketing activities. The press does not tend to call it political marketing, but it still refers to many aspects of the process in its electoral coverage.

So far, press coverage of political marketing has been understudied in the discipline, and this omission seems preoccupant because it fails to understand a central and distinct aspect that the political market does not share with its commercial counterpart: the active role of interpreter of the electoral game that the news media plays in democratic systems. The fact that the data indicate a terminological silence in the news media about political marketing during the Canadian elections sampled does not imply that it refuses to comment on and interpret the political products (for example, policy positions, leaders, and party images), strategies, and electoral tactics. This analysis indicates quite the contrary, with seven leading Canadian news organizations speaking at length to their respective audiences of these realities in their election news. Therefore, as Savigny and Temple (2010) reminded other scholars, the media must be considered as a filtering device through which political marketing is reinterpreted and presented to the population, not as a quiet lapdog.

This is why Canadian parties invest significant resources during elections in developing extensive public relations and media-management activities aimed at defining and adjusting what the political press tells citizens about them. Investing in leaders' tours, giving press conferences and interviews, and having public relations personnel readily accessible to the media are all important aspects of the political marketing process for parties engaging in an election. Message cohesiveness is paramount as each party fights daily with its opponents to be positioned favourably in the news agenda regarding its stand on issues and its positive advantages on the competition. But message cohesiveness should not equal media control. Any attempt at this by an organization could result in a media backlash that could compromise or derail a campaign (for some discussion about this post-election, see Chapters 7 and 8).

The close scrutiny of the press also means that parties are not completely free in their positioning, branding, or even rebranding exercises. A product incoherent with previous offers or that departs too much from a party's historical ideological stand would be spotted by the press and presented to voters as pander, a flip-flop, or manipulative. Political parties have learned to navigate the animated waters of democracy, often shaken by an independent news media acting as moderator of public affairs, highlighting motives and interests of all those involved. Thus, parties should implement political marketing openly, even in regard to highly strategic activities like market research, targeting, or positioning. Insiders' accounts of such practices exist in Canada (Bernier 1991; Flanagan 2009, 2010a; see also Chapter 6). The media will report on it anyway; the secret is out.

Furthermore, open use of political marketing would help parties broker a better relationship with electors and could help alleviate uncertainty in the electoral transaction. The strategic/negative/interpretative coverage that the media generates during elections by focusing on tactics, intentions, and motives certainly will not help. Politicians and parties alike are frequently depicted in electoral news as implementing elaborate schemes aimed at bettering their electoral fates. As the data analysis presented here indicates, policy, issue positions, and electoral engagements receive less media attention, especially in television news, which remains the dominant source of political information for a majority of Canadians (Marcotte and Bastien 2010; see also Chapter 3).

Implications for the Quality of Democracy

This study finally looks at the association that the media makes between political marketing and the state of democracy in Canada. The spiral of cynicism theory (Cappella and Jamieson 1997; de Vreese 2005) maintains that by framing politics strategically, the news media stimulates political disengagement and cynicism in the electorate. Alternative viewpoints (Norris 2000) state the opposite effect but have failed to look specifically at how the media refers to democracy when speaking of concepts of political marketing such as market research, spin, or targeting. The third hypothesis tested here poses that electoral news will mention more frequently a negative association between political marketing and the quality of democratic life. The proposition was analyzed on the 2,875 strategic news items by using dictionaries containing lists of positive and negative expressions and keywords that are commonly associated with democratic vitality, such as "cynicism," "participation," "low turnout," "undemocratic," "propaganda," "have a say," "mobilization," "increase turnout," and "civic engagement."

Figure 11.3 shows that few news stories mention either positive or negative expressions associated to democracy. Only 566 stories contained such mentions (422 news items with negative mentions and 114 with positive mentions), which represent just over 19 percent of all strategic news. Although all types of news media presented a majority of negative mentions in their news (English-language newspapers being more negative and French-language newspapers somewhat more positive), which supports the research proposition put to test, their rather low occurrences in the entire strategic coverage do not permit a solid validation of the negative association hypothesis.[4]

This study indicates that Canadian news media covers political marketing practices widely during federal elections without referring directly to these as "political marketing." It also reveals that when news reports associate

FIGURE 11.3

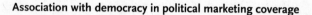

Association with democracy in political marketing coverage

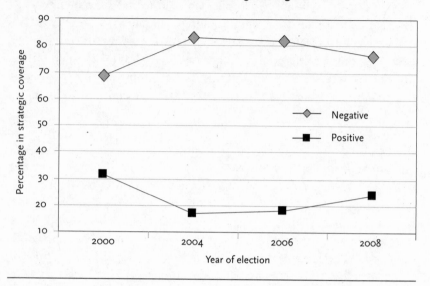

concepts of political marketing to Canadian democracy, the expressions commonly used are mostly negative. We have not investigated the tone of coverage dedicated to parties' strategic activities, and further analyses should be undertaken in order to better understand the relationship uniting political marketing, the media, and the citizenry. New research should also look at what is said of the more discreet and thus more widely unknown phases of strategic marketing during which consultants, advisers, and politicians jointly develop the political product.

Understanding the nature of the association that the media makes between political marketing and democratic life is paramount, since market-oriented parties, not unlike service businesses, must generate confidence in their potential consumers in order to facilitate a positive transaction. The way that the news media will frame its discourse on a given party's promotional practices might therefore have significant implications on the conclusion of the transaction because it could alter the level of trust and confidence that the elector feels toward the party. This fundamental and quite distinctive aspect of the political market should generate more interest in political marketing research than has been the case so far. Such efforts would enable future models to provide better understanding of the active role that the news media plays in the political marketing process, its potential impact on the reception of political messages, and more broadly, on how Canadians understand and evaluate its contribution to the political system.

NOTES

1 Media outlets and programming regularly change; what follows is an overview of the media studied as it existed in 2010 to provide some context for the reader. CTV is a private television network owned by Canadian media giant Bell Media. Its evening newscast, *CTV National News,* is broadcasted daily at 11 p.m. and gets the highest ratings in viewership for prime-time news programs. *CTV National News* has a format of thirty minutes, including advertisements. The Canadian Broadcasting Company (CBC) is Canada's English public network. Its daily evening newscast, *The National,* is broadcasted on the network at 10 p.m., usually in a sixty-minute format, from Sunday to Friday. On Saturday, its format varies from ten to thirty minutes because of special sports programming. Radio-Canada is the country's French-language public broadcaster. Like CBC, its daily newscast, *Le Téléjournal,* is presented at 10 p.m. in a sixty-minute format. Its weekend edition usually lasts thirty minutes. It should be noted that Radio-Canada's transcripts for the 2000 newscast were not produced due to a labour conflict. It should also be noted that the private French-language network TVA, whose daily newscast, *Le TVA 22 heures,* gets the highest viewership for French-language newscasts, does not produce transcripts of its programs and it was therefore not possible to include it in our corpus. *La Presse* is a broadsheet newspaper produced in Montreal and is a property of Gesca, which owns six other French-language dailies publishing in all large cities in Quebec, and is one of the only French-language dailies available throughout Canada. *Le Devoir* is an independent broadsheet newspaper published in Montreal and available throughout Quebec and in most large Canadian markets. Its circulation is limited, but it is considered to be one of the more influential papers in the country. Finally, Canada's two national English-language newspapers, the *Globe and Mail* (owned by the Woodbridge Company) and the *National Post* (formerly part of the Canwest Global empire, but currently owned by Postmedia Network), were also included in the sample. All transcripts from televised newscasts were obtained from the following public databases: ProQuest (CBC 2000; CTV 2006, 2008), Eureka (CBC 2004, 2006, 2008; Radio-Canada 2004, 2006, 2008), and LexisNexis (CTV 2000, 2004). French-language newspapers' electoral reporting was accessed via the Repère database. English-language newspapers' electoral coverage was provided by the Media Observatory of the McGill Institute for the Study of Canada. The size distribution of all outlets in the sample was CTV, 628 items (5.9 percent); CBC, 798 items (7.4 percent), Radio-Canada 633 items (5.9 percent),

La Presse 1,108 items (10.3 percent), *Le Devoir*, 721 items (6.7 percent); the *Globe and Mail*, 4,035 items (37.6 percent); and the *National Post*, 2,797 items (26.1 percent).

2 Lexicoder was developed at McGill University by Stuart Soroka, Lori Young, and Mark Daku. The author wishes to thank Soroka and his team for the great technical support they provided for this research. The author also thanks Martin Quirion and Mélanie Verville for their research assistance on this project. For a broader methodological discussion on automated content analysis and Lexicoder see Daku et al., 2009.

3 Dictionaries designed for Lexicoder are long lists of words grouped in categories written in xml format. Word count limitation therefore prohibits their inclusion in this chapter. However, on request, the author will gladly provide the dictionaries.

4 This situation could have resulted from a methodological flaw in the study. This portion of the content analysis was conducted with dictionaries, each containing less than forty words and expressions. More exhaustive categories of positive and negative terms associated with democratic life might generate more valid data.

12
Are We Friends Yet?
Online Relationship Marketing
by Political Parties

Tamara A. Small

Canadian political parties have been online for almost two decades. Without a doubt, the strategic value of digital technologies has increased. The Internet presences of Canada's parties have become more technologically sophisticated and more integrated into the overall communication strategy. The online world of Canadian parties is vast. Parties publish internal and external e-newsletters and operate Facebook pages, YouTube channels, and Twitter feeds in addition to official party websites. Although there is a burgeoning literature on Internet politics, there is little research on the topic from a political marketing perspective in Canada, and indeed the world. This chapter seeks to address this knowledge gap through an analysis of Internet marketing by Canadian political parties.

Internet marketing refers to the use of digital technologies, including the web, mobile devices, and email, to achieve marketing objectives. With 80 percent of Canadians aged sixteen and older using the Internet for personal reasons in 2009 (Canada, Statistics Canada 2010), Internet marketing has become a vital part of marketing communications in many organizations. More specifically, this chapter assesses whether Canadian political parties use the popular social networking site Facebook as part of a relationship marketing strategy.

Coined in 1983, relationship marketing differs from the traditional, transactional approach to marketing. Relationship marketing recognizes "the importance of sustaining mutually satisfying exchanges and the building of customer relationships as central to generating loyalty and repeat business" (Bannon 2005b, 74). Rather than a one-off exchange between a business and a consumer, relationship marketing is concerned with establishing long-term associations. This relationship is akin to a marriage. Scholars use terms such as "trust," "commitment," "loyalty," "mutual benefit," and "long term" in describing this marketing theory. The sale is just the beginning, for customer retention is a fundamental principle (Christopher, Payne, and Ballantyne 2002). Applied to party politics, relationship marketing offers parties a potentially effective means of mobilizing long-term support. Henneberg and O'Shaughnessy (2009, 10) suggest that "political parties and candidates, and also voters and citizens, perceive political exchanges not merely as isolated transactions (like the episode of actually voting for a party or a candidate) but as an enduring social process of interactivity within which they live their daily lives." Party politics does not only exist during election campaigns. Thus, instead of engaging with voters only at election time, it is believed that "continuous contact with voters over a period of time may be as persuasive" (Jackson 2006a, 154). Politicians and parties have always engaged in activities meant to strengthen relationships with citizens, though, as Henneberg and O'Shaughnessy (2009) point out, most do not conceptualize such behaviours as relationship marketing. Direct-mail, newsletters, town hall meetings, and politicians contributing regularly to the mass media, such as writing a weekly newspaper column, are relationship-building activities.

Technology is crucial to the implementation of a relationship marketing strategy. Technology enables two-way dialogue between consumers and organizations from which relationships can emanate (Baker, Buttery, and Richter-Buttery 1998). More specifically, the Internet offers organizations unique opportunities to put into practice a relationship marketing approach. Compared with traditional media channels, the Internet is more interactive. Online interactivity "concerns the relationship of the user with the communication supply and the relationships among the users themselves" (Bentivegna 2002, 54). Not only does the Internet create a two-way communication channel for dialogue, it does so in a cost-effective manner. Within politics, Williams, Aylesworth, and Chapman (2002) argue that "websites are an excellent opportunity to establish and maintain such long-term relationships" (44) between candidates and voters. Email, too, can be used in relationship marketing. Jackson (2005) suggests that e-newsletters may help build long-term relationships between politicians and their constituents because they are interactive and can be targeted.

There is a small body of literature that explores online relationship marketing by political parties.[1] In one of the earliest studies on the topic, Williams, Aylesworth, and Chapman (2002) assessed websites in the 2000 US Senate races and found that most candidates did not employ a relationship marketing strategy. Although many candidates engaged in recruitment activities, most did not exploit interactivity. Overall, the study concludes that "the needs of candidates and voters have not been joined, at least as yet, by this new Internet technology" (56). British politics are the focus of Bowers-Brown (2003) and Jackson (2005, 2006a, 2006b). Jackson's study (2005) explored legislative email. Similar to the findings of Williams, Aylesworth, and Chapman (2002), he concludes that email did not simulate a relationship marketing approach by British Members of Parliament. Instead of seeing email as an opportunity for building relationships, Jackson concludes that MPs simply reacted to the demands of their constituents. Jackson (2006a) came to a more positive conclusion in a study on British party e-newsletters. He found that most parties had used a relationship marketing approach with internal audiences, though few had used it with external audiences. Online campaigning is the context of two other studies. First, Bowers-Brown (2003) explored relationship marketing on campaign websites in the 2001 British election. Examining the three major parties, he concludes that "all three parties' websites conform to a commercial web-marketing model and demonstrate some use of relational strategy" (113). Jackson's study (2006b) of the 2005 election came to similar results. Although there was some evidence of a relationship marketing strategy, party sites were "weak" on interactivity. Although the literature is scant, research indicates that an online relationship marketing approach has become more common in party politics despite the lack of interactivity.

Political relationship marketing research so far has focused on websites and email. However, the Internet has moved beyond these applications. The term "web 2.0" is used to describe this shift: "Web 2.0 harnesses the web in a more interactive and collaborative manner, emphasizing peers' social interaction and collective intelligence, and presents new opportunities for leveraging the web and engaging its users more effectively" (Murugesan 2007, 34). Web 2.0 incorporates a number of various applications, including social networking (for example, Facebook), blogs, microblogs (for example, Twitter), online video sites (for example, YouTube), wikis (for example, Wikipedia), and social bookmarking (for example, Digg). It is not that participation and collaboration were non-existent in the pre-2.0 period. Rather, web 2.0 is characterized by "easiness in content production and publication on the internet" (Breindl and Francq 2008, 19). It is argued that web 2.0 creates a new landscape for relationship marketing (Meadows-Klue 2008). This is because collaboration and interactivity is inherent in the infrastructure of web 2.0 applications. Nevertheless, this chapter presents a mixed picture of the use of relationship marketing on Facebook by Canadian political parties.

Even though thousands of individuals have become "friends" with a Canadian party, many parties are not reciprocating this relationship; indeed, as other chapters in this book have indicated, Internet communications and online relationship marketing have thus far not been much of a priority in Canadian politics.

Case Study: Facebook and Relationship Marketing

This case study focuses on the use of the Internet in the inter-election period. This focus is important for several reasons. First, this is an understudied area, as Canadian studies of political e-marketing focus on election campaigns. Although the use of the Internet ramps up during elections, Canadian parties have always maintained their online presences between elections. Next, studying the inter-election period has become even more important given that Canadian politics has evolved into a permanent campaign. Campaign techniques that once defined elections, such as polling, marketing, and fund-raising, are now increasingly a feature of everyday politics. According to Flanagan and Jansen (2009, 207), one reason for the development of the permanent campaign in Canada is the frequency of minority government, which requires that political parties "remain campaign ready." Scholars argue that political marketing is crucial in the era of the permanent campaign (Sparrow and Turner 2001). Finally, assessing the inter-election period is crucial because relationship marketing requires a long-term perspective. Canadian parties have made extensive use of websites and social networking sites during election campaigns. If relationship building is to occur, parties cannot simply use the Internet as a one-off tool to attract votes. The Internet must be used year-round.

Facebook is the focus of this analysis. Founded in February 2004, Face-book is a social utility that helps people communicate more efficiently with others. Not only is Facebook currently the most popular social networking site, it is one of the world's most trafficked websites. As of 2010, Facebook had more than 500 million active users (Facebook 2010), around 16 million of whom were Canadian (Canadian Press 2010). A study by Zinc Research (2009) found that despite a broad cross-section of Canadians using Face-book, users tend to be younger (eighteen to thirty-four years) – but that usage has "exploded" among the thirty-five years or older segment. What started out as a site for American college students is now propagated by people of all ages, as well as groups, celebrities, and organizations worldwide.

An individual creates a profile, whereas a brand, whether it is a company, celebrity, organization, or politician, creates a page. Pages allow for the broadcasting of "information to fans in an official, public manner" (Facebook n.d.-b). Pages and profiles have similar functionality. Like any Facebook user, brands can provide information about themselves, post photographs or videos, post notes, and interact with followers. However, whereas on profiles both parties must agree to be friends with one another, pages are non-reciprocal. As such, the term "friend" is not used, as Facebook pages are visible to everyone, but profiles are visible only to friends. To enter into a relationship with a brand, the user clicks on the "Like" button. This enables content published by the brand to go directly to the user's news feed, and the user may also post comments on the brand's page.[2]

In 2006, Facebook allowed politicians to create pages and buy ad space. Facebook has even published a how-to guide for politicians (Facebook n.d.-a). Small (2010) has identified four potential benefits for political parties using Facebook for election campaigning, which also seem relevant to employing a relationship marketing strategy. First, it can increase unmediated exposure at low or no cost. Second, Facebook provides access to the millennial generation, those born between 1980 and 2000, the members of which are less likely to be interested or involved in politics. Third, a database can be created, which may allow parties to raise contributions, recruit volunteers, and send targeted messages. Finally, Facebook is interactive, and this could potentially allow communication between voters and the party and between voters and other voters. Perhaps the key benefit of using Facebook as part of a relationship marketing strategy is that those who become friends are basically saying they want to enter into a relationship with the brand. The user is interested in receiving information and content from the organization. According to Sweetser and Weaver Lariscy (2008, 193) in their analysis of Facebook and the 2006 American mid-term elections, many who become friends with the candidate "treat him or her just like any other Facebook friend." Thus, one-half of the relationship is already in place.

Politicians all around the world are using Facebook. US president Barack Obama is currently the most popular politician, amassing some 12 million friends at the time of writing. By comparison, as Table 12.1 shows, more than 120,000 people in total were friends with the major Canadian political parties and/or their leaders as of August 2010. This is a far cry from the number of Obama's friends; indeed, globally, politicians' Facebook popularities range. For instance, in September 2010, French president Nicolas Sarkozy had around 315,000 friends, British prime minister David Cameron had around 87,000 friends, and German chancellor Angela Merkel had about 46,000 friends. Comparatively, Canada's parties and leaders were quite popular on Facebook.

TABLE 12.1

Number of Facebook friends (June 1 to July 30, 2010)

Political party	Party page	Leader page
Bloc Québécois	n/a	4,599
Conservative	3,986	34,557
Green	692	7,121
Liberal	7,356	31,237
NDP	n/a	30,631
Total	12,034	108,145

In 2009, Sysomos released a report based on analysis of nearly 600,000 Facebook pages. Only 23 percent of pages had more than 1,000 friends, whereas 4 percent of pages had more than 10,000 friends (Sysomos 2009). Hence, Canadian parties have the opportunity to create relationships with many individuals.

This case study is based on a framework adapted from Jackson's analyses (2006a, 2006b) of online relationship marketing by British political parties. Williams, Aylesworth, and Chapman (2002) and Bowers-Brown (2003) also employed similar categories. Table 12.2 lists the criteria used to assess whether Canadian parties use Facebook as part of a relationship marketing approach.

Content published on Facebook pages belonging to the Bloc Québécois (BQ), Conservative Party (CPC), Green Party (GPC), Liberal Party (LPC), and New Democratic Party (NDP) between June 1 and July 30, 2010 (sixty-one days), were examined.[3] The period of analysis can be considered a limitation of this case study, given that relationship marketing is about long-term relationship building. However, Jackson (2006b, 64) suggests that this framework is effective in assessing "whether parties seek and have in place the basis of the relationship marketing approach." This period of analysis may present a second limitation, given that the House of Commons was in recess. Yet, if a relationship marketing approach is in place, assessing the parties' online behaviour during a recess is ideal because whereas we would expect considerable communication when the House is meeting, to find evidence of it in the summer months is a good indication of whether parties engage with citizens continuously. Moreover, one benefit of Facebook is that it can be accessed anywhere with an Internet connection. Therefore, Facebook can still be used even if leaders or party staffers are away from Ottawa. With

TABLE 12.2

Relationship marketing criteria for Facebook

Continuous	Updated at regular intervals	Yes/No
Value	Information not easily available elsewhere	Yes/No
	Information of relevance to non-members	Yes/No
Recruitment	Membership	Yes/No
	Donations	Yes/No
	Volunteer	Yes/No
	E-newsletter sign-up	Yes/No
	Events	Yes/No
Interactivity	Feedback (Like or Comment)	Yes/No
	Wall post	Yes/No
	Discussion board	Yes/No

the rise of social networking, Canadian party leaders have begun to establish separate Internet presences from the parties they represent. In cases where the party and leader both operate a Facebook page, both were included. A total of eight pages were analyzed.

The first factor that is required for a relationship marketing approach is for Facebook to be used continuously. All and Armstrong (2009, 19) advise political actors to engage their friends every day; they write, "Adding new content every day means visitors see fresh content, and current fans are brought back to your page on a regular basis." To assess this, the number of days in which the party or leader posted an update on the wall during the analysis period was recorded. The wall is the main page of a Facebook account. Updates published on the wall by the party or leader will show up on the news feed of all of their friends. Moreover, the wall is also a public writing space where friends can post comments online.

Overall, Canadian parties did not update their Facebook pages with great regularity (Table 12.3). On average, new content was added to the Facebook walls of parties and leaders every three days (32 percent of analysis period). Although no page was even remotely close to meeting the recommendation of All and Armstrong (2009), the Facebook pages belonging to the Liberal Party and leader Michael Ignatieff published new content on the wall about every other day. During the analysis period, the Liberal Party was engaged in a participatory process dubbed the "Liberal Express," where Ignatieff visited every province and territory to meet with citizens. The Liberal Express started

Table 12.3

Publishing of new Facebook content (June 1 to July 30, 2010)

Political party	Party page (%)	Leader page (%)
Bloc Québécois	n/a	29.5
Conservative	34.4	11.5
Green	1.6	37.7
Liberal	72.1	68.9
NDP	n/a	4.9

N = 61

unofficially on July 10 and officially on July 13, representing 36 percent of the analysis period. New content was published continuously throughout the analysis period. A relationship marketing approach was evident on the two Liberal Party pages prior to the Liberal Express. At the other end of the spectrum, NDP leader Jack Layton and the Green Party rarely posted new wall content during the analysis period. Perhaps the lack of updates could be attributed to the summer recess of the House of Commons? A brief examination of other party Internet presences, including Twitter and official websites, shows that this is not the case. For instance, Layton's Twitter feed was updated thirty-two times during the analysis period, compared with three wall posts on Facebook. With the exception of the Liberals, it is difficult to suggest that the first criterion of a relationship marketing approach is met.

The second criterion of Jackson's relationship marketing framework is value. According to Jackson (2006a), value is a subjective assessment of whether politicians provide content that is useful, especially content that is not readily available. So what is published on Facebook? In general, party and leader Facebook walls consist of links to party-related information found elsewhere on the web. This includes news releases and stories from official websites, videos on YouTube, and tweets from Twitter. For instance:

Stephen Harper Launched Small and Medium Enterprise Finance Challenge http://bit.ly/9kiB1W.

This post by Stephen Harper (or rather, by one of his communications personnel) linked to a press release on the prime minister's official website. It is also a Twitter tweet. Whereas all the posts on Harper's Facebook page were from a single site, other Facebook pages featured more diverse content from several sites. Green Party leader Elizabeth May's page, for instance, featured selected comments from her Twitter feed and posts from her blog. This finding is consistent with other Canadian research. Since the early 1990s, parties have always attempted to leverage existing offline and online content (see Chapter 4). For instance, in recent election campaigns, television ads have been uploaded to YouTube and to party websites during campaigns. As noted, the online world of Canadian parties is vast, and content is often shared between sites. For instance, a Twitter post that links to a policy state-ment on the party website will also be posted on Facebook. Overall, there were very few instances of content on Facebook that was not readily available elsewhere.

This said, it is arguable that the value of content on Facebook comes not only from its source but also from Facebook as an application. That is, the infrastructure of Facebook overcomes one major limitation of the Internet for political marketing. Bowers-Brown (2003, 103) rightly points out that the Internet "is a 'pull' technology rather than a 'push' technology such as television and, as such, is reliant on members of the public actively seeking out websites rather than being passively open to receiving political informa-tion or party PR that typically may occur in the offline media." This means that if someone wanted information from a political party, the person would have to know the URL of the site or search for it, and then locate the relevant information. However, on Facebook, the user needs to be active only one time – the first time. Once the user clicks on the "Like" button, content is streamed to him or her every time he or she logs on. Facebook is more pas-sive than other aspects of the Internet. Given that the average Facebook user spends about seven hours per month on the site (Nielsen Wire 2010), there is a lot of opportunity to establish relationships by continuously publishing updates. This is because Facebook users log on and off several times a day, whether parties post content or not. Recall that content on Facebook typically comes from elsewhere on the web; given that all parties have to do is merely link content that already exists (i.e., Jack Layton's thirty-two tweets), parties and leaders that do not continuously upload content truly miss out on an opportunity to engage with their friends.

Recruitment is the third factor that needs to be considered to determine whether Facebook is part of a relationship marketing strategy of Canadian political parties. As Bowers-Brown (2003, 102-3) points out, an online pres-ence should aim to convert people into customers; this "conversion efficiency"

may "include membership and registration facilities as well as the encourage-
ment of an 'offline' customer relationship." Christopher, Payne, and
Ballantyne's "ladder of loyalty" (2002) is useful here. According to the model,
by building sound relationships, a customer will progress up the five stages
or rungs of the ladder. In the final rung, the customer is an "advocate,"
"someone who actively recommends [the business] to others, who does your
marketing for you" (48). Thus, one goal of online relationship marketing for
political parties is to get citizens to move up the loyalty ladder by encouraging
greater involvement in party activities, including donating, volunteering, and
membership.

Overall, Facebook plays a very minimal role in recruitment in Canadian
politics. Only two Facebook pages, that of the Liberals and the Greens, made
any mention of recruitment in summer 2010. Both pages featured a "Take
Action" tab that provided links to actions such as donations, memberships,
e-newsletter sign-up, event calendars, and connecting with local party organizations. These links would take the friends to the official website of the party
to complete the action. The lack of recruitment on Facebook is surprising.
Both Bowers-Brown (2003) and Jackson (2006b) found that British party
websites presented users with a number of recruitment opportunities, as did
Williams, Aylesworth, and Chapman (2002) in the United States. Furthermore,
recruitment was evident on the websites of all five major Canadian political
parties in previous elections (Small 2004). In the 2004 election, users could
join the party, volunteer to help with the campaign, or donate money with
a few strokes of a keyboard. Parties also encouraged viral campaigning by
providing online tools that make it easy for supporters to pass along campaign
messages to others, including sending e-postcards. So Canadian parties do
recruit online; most are just not using Facebook. Arguably, a Facebook friend
would be the very type of person who would be willing to donate or become
a party member. By becoming friends in the first instance, these individuals
had already begun their assent up the rungs. Parties forwent the opportunity
in encouraging friends to move up the loyalty ladder.

The final criterion examined is interactivity, which Williams, Aylesworth,
and Chapman (2002, 42) describe as one of the holy grails of e-marketing.
This is because relationship marketing is based on two-way communication.
Despite this, we have seen that although political actors have engaged in
some aspects of relationship marketing, interactivity is typically not employed.
However, like the pull/push technology distinction, Facebook seemingly
overcomes a major barrier to the use of interactivity. Facebook, as part of web

TABLE 12.4

Use of interactive features on Facebook pages (2010)

	Bloc Québécois	Conservative		Green		Liberal		NDP
	Leader	Party	Leader	Party	Leader	Party	Leader	Leader
Feedback	✓	✓	✓	✓	✓	✓	✓	✓
Wall posting	✓	✓		✓	✓	✓		
Discussion board			✓			✓	✓	

2.0, has interactivity built directly into the application. As Facebook's how-to guide for politicians points out, the site "is a culture of conversations, giving politicians and political campaigns/organizations a huge opportunity to get immediate feedback on various issues" (Facebook, n.d.-a). There are three ways that a friend can interact with a Facebook page. First, friends can provide feedback to content published by the party or leader. The friend can either click on the "Like" button or post a comment. Second, friends can contribute to a wall by posting their own content, including links, photos, and videos. Unlike the previous category, this type of interaction is not initiated by the brand. Finally, a page can have a discussion board. These provide political actors with a variety of ways to engage in two-way communication.

Table 12.4 reports the ability of a friend to engage in Facebook inter-activity. Feedback, in the form of comments or likes, was available on all eight of the pages analyzed for each party. Comments included posts of support, criticisms, questions, broader discussion of posts, and responses to previous comments. For instance, eighty comments were received in response to the above-mentioned Harper post, including "strong ideas from a strong leader ... way to go prime minister harper" and "Why did we have to spend a billion dollars to decide to cut the deficit?" Overall, Facebook friends contributed more than nine thousand comments or likes on the eight pages during the analysis period, though a considerable five thousand of these came from a single page, that of Liberal leader Michael Ignatieff. However, even though there was two-way communication, this could not be described as a conversation between parties and users. Parties tended not to respond to the comments left by friends on the walls. Indeed, Sweetser and Weaver Lariscy (2008) make a distinction between a responsive and unresponsive wall. Like their study of American candidates, the unresponsive wall was more common on Canada's party Facebook pages. They write, "Sadly, this represents another case where campaigns integrate a dialogic interactive technology as a façade" (193).

The latter two types of interactivity were employed less frequently. Only six pages allowed friends to post their own comments on the wall, and only three pages operated a discussion board. The findings on the latter two categories are telling because page administrators have the option to disable these functions, and clearly most of the Facebook pages did. One user even expressed dissatisfaction about this, writing on Harper's wall: "I wish your wall was open for 'Open Discussion' ... or that you had the 'discussion tab' enabled for us to discuss the issues that are Important ... to US." There is precedence for disabling interactive features on social networking sites. During the 2008 election, comments were disabled on Stephen Harper's Facebook page and YouTube channel; only the Twitter pages of Elizabeth May and Bloc Québécois leader Gilles Duceppe allowed for follower comments to be posted (Small 2010). Despite the evolution to web 2.0, the findings here mirror previous research. Only two pages, those of the Liberal Party and the Conservative Party, provided friends with all three options. Unresponsive walls and disabled interactive features certainly call into question any meaningful relationship building between most parties or leaders with friends.

The question guiding this case study was whether Canadian political parties use Facebook as part of a relationship marketing strategy. Based on this assessment, the Facebook pages of the Liberal Party correspond most to a relationship marketing approach (Table 12.5). Both the party and leader

TABLE 12.5

Use of Facebook as part of relationship marketing strategy (2010)

	Bloc Québécois	Conservative		Green		Liberal		NDP
	Leader	Party	Leader	Party	Leader	Party	Leader	Leader
Continuous	✓	✓			✓	✓	✓	
Value	✓	✓			✓	✓	✓	
Recruitment				✓		✓		
Interactivity	✓					✓	✓	

pages were used continuously, publishing content almost every other day. The pages were valuable to friends, given the regularity and the diversity of content published. The Liberals' pages were one of two that actually attempted to turn friends into supporters by offering recruitment facilities. Although the walls of the leaders and the party were unresponsive, the Liberals were still the most open to interactivity. Both pages featured discussion boards, and the party page also allowed friends to post their own content. During the analysis period, there were more than fifty-five hundred likes or comments and more than a hundred wall postings on the two Liberal pages. As with the first category, likes and comments on these pages were spread evenly over the analysis period. One-half of comments and likes on the party and leader pages came from the Liberal Express period; however, the relationship marketing approach of the Liberals was not limited to a period otherwise marked by reduced politicking. It is more difficult to see the basis of a relationship marketing strategy on other pages. Indeed, barely a single criterion of a relationship marketing approach was met on the Facebook pages of Conservative Stephen Harper and of Jack Layton of the NDP. Both pages were used in the 2008 federal election (Small 2010), but less so in the inter-election period. It is possible that these pages focused more on a one-off exchange with voters rather than a long-term association with citizens. Overall, this presents a mixed picture of whether Canadian political parties follow a relationship marketing strategy in their use of Facebook. Some parties are trying to create friendships; others are not.

The State of Political Marketing in Canada

This case study has contributed to a small literature on online relationship marketing. One area of congruence is on the issue of interactivity. Despite that two-way communication is essential to the relationship marketing approach and is a fundamental feature of Internet technology, political actors continue to eschew it. In 2000, one American researcher concluded that political actors avoid interactivity because it is burdensome and they risk losing control of the communication environment (Stromer-Galley 2000). These conclusions appear to remain relevant today and highly applicable to Canada. This creates a real problem for the development of an online relationship marketing strategy. Indeed, Jackson (2006b, 177; emphasis added) questions whether political actors can ever truly engage in relationship marketing "if they are not focusing on *the key element* of a relationship marketing approach." Whereas two-way communication was avoided in previous studies,

American and British political actors did engage in recruitment and provided far more content than did Canadian parties. The findings of this case study are more pessimistic than those studies preceding it, with very few Canadian parties using any aspect of relationship marketing on Facebook, indicating that Canadian parties are Internet laggards or that they do not prioritize relationship marketing, or both.

This said, it is very difficult to conclude that Canadian parties do not engage in relationship marketing or other types of marketing online. It is extremely important for researchers to remember that Facebook, while currently very popular, is just one aspect of online politics. As noted, Canadian parties operate numerous Internet presences, including websites, email, and social networking sites. Each has a very different communication purpose. Therefore, it is quite possible that Canadian parties may be employing a relationship marketing approach elsewhere on the Internet. Indeed, our understanding of online political marketing is challenged by the technology itself. Hence, we should see this case study as the starting place for understanding political marketing online in Canada rather than the final word.

Implications for the Quality of Democracy

In advanced industrial nations, there has been a decline in the confidence in, and attachment to, governmental and non-governmental institutions. In Canada, the majority of citizens have little confidence in their political leaders, few Canadians are members of political parties (Cross and Young 2004), and voter turnout is low (see Elisabeth Gidengil's and Royce Koop's chapters in this book). Parliament, parties, and the electoral system are all sources of a democratic deficit. Given these circumstances, it must be asked if, and in what ways, online political marketing affects the quality of democracy in Canada. We argue that it could potentially affect democracy in two interrelated ways.

First, the Internet, especially compared with older media, is considered a democratic technology. This intersection between democracy and the Internet can be seen in the development of terms like "e-democracy" and "e-engagement." E-democracy is defined as "efforts to broaden political participation by enabling citizens to connect with one another and with their representatives via new information and communication technologies" (Chadwick, 2006, 84). Obviously, interactivity is especially relevant to the concept of e-democracy. Bentivegna (2002) lists interactivity first in her list of the Internet's "democratic potentials." Other democratic features include the varied and unlimited information found online. Access to political information has the capacity to create an educated and active citizenry. The cost-effectiveness of the Internet has the capacity to increase participation by lowering barriers into politics. As a decentralized space, the Internet is also considered to be a new place for marginalized voices. Web 2.0 is considered to have even more of a connection with democracy than the early web; Breindl and Francq (2008, 21) argue that both web 2.0 and e-democracy "stress the importance of enhancing the role of internet users. As e-democracy wishes to involve increasingly cyber-citizens in the political process, new web 2.0 applications may contribute to augment the impact of internet users in the democratic system." Overall, increased and varied opportunities for political participation are potentially created by the inclusion of the Internet in politics. As such, the Internet is seen as a remedy for the "procedural and institutional flaws" that plague modern government (Margolis and Moreno-Riaño 2009, 7).

The theory of relationship marketing also intersects with democracy. Whereas "traditional political marketing activities contribute to voter apathy ...[,] It is political relationship marketing that might claim to combat that apathy, since the essence of what it offers is a social connection and involvement" (Henneberg and O'Shaughnessy 2009, 20). A relationship marketing strategy may be a means to achieve engagement or re-engagement in politics. Indeed, Henneberg, Scammell, and O'Shaughnessy (2009) argue that relationship marketing is compatible with a particular model of democracy: deliberative democracy, defined by Gutmann and Thompson (2004, 7) as "a form of government in which free and equal citizens (and their representatives), justify decisions in a process in which they give one another reasons that are mutually acceptable and generally accessible, with the aim of reaching conclusions that are binding in the present on all citizens but open to challenge in the future." Rational, collective decision making among all stakeholders is central to this model. According to Henneberg, Scammell, and O'Shaughnessy (2009, 179), relationship marketing "emphasizes the need to pay attention to the core (supporters and members) as well as the periphery of target floating voters and other societal stakeholders, and thus provides incentives to develop political interest and engagement on an enduring basis." Relationship marketing's focus on building long-term associations and dialogue fits with the deliberative democracy model.

Put together, the Internet and relationship marketing may provide political parties with potentially powerful democratic tools. This said, it all depends on how political parties take advantage of such tools. Henneberg, Scammell, and O'Shaughnessy (2009, 170) warn that for a political relationship marketing strategy to be operational, "it has to go beyond the cosmetic and the superficial." This must also be said of the Internet. It is easy for political parties to appear democratic by establishing an Internet presence. This is especially true with web 2.0, where interactivity and collaboration are built directly into the application. But as this case study shows, e-democracy requires more than simply having a Facebook page. A "façade of interactivity" (Stromer-Galley and Baker 2006, 120) is easy to perpetrate, as many of the Facebook pages examined here demonstrated. Neither the Internet nor relationship marketing are panaceas to the democratic deficit. Yet, as in the case of the Liberal Party, both of these forms of political marketing may be used to create a foundation for relationship building and, ultimately, for democratic engagement.

NOTES

1   There is also a literature on Internet marketing by political parties that utilize other marketing concepts and theories.
2   The News Feed aggregates content that friends post. Content can be organized by popularity (Top News) or in real time (Most Recent).
3   Despite not having a seat in the House of Commons at the time of the study, the Green Party is still considered a significant party in Canadian politics. In the past four federal elections, the Greens had run a full slate of candidates. In 2008, the party leader was included in the televised leaders' debates. At the time of writing, polls showed the party receiving around 10 percent of support. For these reasons, the Green Party was included in the analysis.

13
Double-Double: Branding, Tim Hortons, and the Public Sphere

Patricia Cormack

What is branding? The notion of the branding of commodities and companies reflects the root meaning of the word – to burn or mark in a distinct and unique way. This may include a company name, usually written in an identifiable style and colour and pronounced in a uniform way, or a logo, signage, a slogan, or a combination of these things. Coca-Cola, for example, uses a stylized cursive script that dates back to the company's origin in the nineteenth century. It is so recognizable that the characters used here to represent it may look odd to the reader. Behind this identifier is a constellation of meanings and ideas. For Coca-Cola, this set of meanings has also existed for almost a century (after first being marketed as a health tonic) – leisure, companionship, well-being.

Branding of a commodity or company is complex because it depends on consumers' willingness to recognize and support the set of meanings, ideas, and associations the brand is trying to establish. A whole subsection of the study of marketing is given over to understanding the art and science of branding. Branding plays on deeply psychological and social meanings that consumers get from products – personal identity, distinction from others, social class, and taste standings. Consumers can become extremely loyal to a particular brand and continue to consume it over decades. This is more than a matter of habit. From the point of view of the marketer, the consumer should come to think of himself or herself as a branded "type" – for example, as a life-long Chevy driver. As Kotler and Gertner (2002, 249) put it, "Brands differentiate product and represent a promise of value." James Barnes (2003, 184) argues that "the brand or company 'borrows' or trades on the meaning in the relationships that customers have with others." All branding is rooted in notions of community, he argues: "Those with whom we share a common history, values, interests, culture and beliefs" (182). In fact, customers themselves use brands to create their own "brand communities" (Muniz and O'Guinn 2001) and to "produce a common social world" (Arvidsson 2005, 235).

Branding, then, is a kind of contract between consumer and company. While the customers consume and display the brand for various reasons, the company becomes highly accountable to public scrutiny (labour practices, quality of product, and customer service become central). Thus, a brand is more than just the company name or logo. It rolls together the logo, products, advertising, image, customer service, investment opportunities, and production practices into one integrated and recognizable whole. Hence, branding promises a consistency through all these layers. The bigger the brand name, the more open the company becomes to action on the part of the consumer-citizen. Companies like Nike, Coca-Cola, and McDonald's have had to reform their practices in response to the bad publicity arising around their products. So while branding is often considered the ultimate form of commoditization, the brand puts a face and identity to otherwise faceless production and consumption by virtue of its breadth. Oddly, it seems to break down the social hieroglyphic of the commodity form, as Marx called it (1967), that classically has appeared to the consumer as if it has no production history. Anti-brand guru Naomi Klein has conceded this point (and proven it by the influence of her book *No Logo*):

> Nike, Shell, Wal-Mart, Microsoft and McDonald's have become metaphors for a global economic system gone awry, largely because, unlike the back-door wheeling and dealing at NAFTA, GATT, APEC, WTO, MA1, the EU, the IMF, the G-8 and the OECD, the methods and objectives of these companies are plain to see. (Klein 2000, 441)

But can politics itself be branded? Should politics be branded? The academic discussions of political branding run in many directions, rooted in various assumptions. They can be collected into three general camps: (1) branding is a limited analogy when applied to politics, (2) politics and branding share an inherent pre-existing affinity, and (3) branding brings the values of the market into the political sphere and changes politics in fundamental ways. As an example of the first position, G. Smith (2001) argues that handling the welter of unforeseeable events faced by politicians and their parties once in office is critical to ongoing success, which is not true of the branded commodity (which only occasionally faces an "event" like a tainted product). So, as much as party handlers may try to conflate politics and branding, a distinction still exists. And, even if there is a somewhat strong connection between branding and politics, branding – moving away from an ideologically based party to a branded one – risks bringing the party's reputation into question. For example, as other chapters in this book have remarked on, the rebranding of the United Kingdom's leftist Labour Party into "New Labour" raised the question of how far to the right this party had moved such that it would consider using the market notion of branding at all. White and de Chernatony (2002) conclude that the New Labour government was seen as lacking in coherent values and was more concerned with spin than policy once in power. In the context of Canada, a 2010 comedy production called *Stephen Harper! The Musical* told the fictional story of a hapless prime minister losing control of his party to spin doctors after the (real) attention he received in October 2009 performing a Beatles' song.

An example of the second position is held by Needham (2006), who points out that loyalty to a political party, like that to a brand, relies on predictability and coherence of product over time. Hence, parties are very much like brands in that they make big promises of quality and consistency, and offer a vision of the "good life" that they have to deliver on. This position often focuses on the contract between company and consumer, party and citizen, and uses the notions of citizen and consumer almost interchangeably. Needham (2006) asserts that branding allows parties to do well especially with "charismatic leaders" – a somewhat disquieting comment, considering that charismatic leaders have so often been associated with tyranny and manipulation of mass sentiment. Other literature in this vein uncritically accepts the conflation of social good and immediate consumer-citizen demand. In their discussion of "building a political brand," Reeves, de Chernatony, and Carrigan (2006, 419) propose that "political marketing is, in general, a force for good within society, given that political marketing is concerned with the satisfaction of the electorate." Jerry Palmer (2002) points to a number of positive effects of political marketing that resonate with branding. He argues that political marketing of parties and candidates forces them to take seriously issues of accountability and trust. As discussed by Lilleker (2005a), marketing of political parties as brands is far more than superficial packaging – it includes the history of the party as core, its unalterable principles as middle, and publicity as outer layer.

The third position treats branding as a new influence on politics and usually views it as deeply detrimental to the democratic process. Collins and Butler (2003, 52) note that if political branding involves responding to immediate consumer demand, then this has profound implications for the whole of politics and democracy:

The features of liberal representative democracy, particularly the role of deliberation, informed assent and accountability, have been neglected. Speed of response has been emphasized to the cost of democratic filters and checks on public opinion.

Reg Whitaker (2001), like Collins and Butler, argues that the branded party's primary strategy is the immediate gratification of the citizen/consumer. Hence, the branded political party becomes organized around gaining office, eroding notions like long-standing general beliefs about the common good over which a party may both win and fail. Traditionally, he says, it is the party's job when it fails to gain office to work harder to convince the electorate that its political ideology is correct, not to spend time on the packaging of an image. In terms of the language of branding, the party name used to, he says, stand for loyalty and allegiance (think of a flag, for example) rather than a brand (a promise to an individual to provide something pleasing). In short, it is a cynical and instrumental relationship to the citizen and civic life. On the right side of the Canadian ideological spectrum, the rebranding of the old Reform Party (associated with a grassroots populism rooted in western Canada) into the Canadian Alliance in 2000 meant that party members began to be treated as consumers rather than "learning the norms and practices [of the party], its sense of collective memory and shared identity" (Whitaker 2001, 20; see also Chapter 5). Similarly, in the attempt to rebrand Reform, the Canadian Alliance struggled with a new leader, Stockwell Day, and with its policies and platform. For Whitaker (2001, 21), it suffered from its own "flight from principle" in its conversion from traditional party to brand. Nevertheless, once the Alliance merged with the old Progressive Conservative Party in 2003, it did make inroads in the federal Parliament, forming a Conservative Party minority government in 2006 and eventually a majority in 2011. Anchoring itself with the old Tory party surely afforded a needed legitimacy.

Hence, the literature on political branding moves in diverging directions. Nevertheless, all sides of this debate acknowledge that the language of branding is now used by parties (effectively or ineffectively, rightly or wrongly) to organize campaigns and party promotion. The language of brand recognition, loyalty, equity, and the like are now part of the language of politics in Canada. Many of the contributors to this book pursue important questions about marketing and politics in various ways. Other Canadian scholars have done so less directly, such as Carty's discussion (2002) about the franchising of party brands in electoral districts. In the following case study, I discuss branding as a specific marketing strategy that is now used by political parties and by commercial companies alike. I argue that although politics can be affected by branding tactics used by political parties, conversely, the branding practices used by commercial enterprises can re-establish the grounds of politics. Political branding is, then, a two-way street in terms of its influence on political life in Canada – political parties take up the market strategies of branding, and branded companies become political players in public life. Specifically, I discuss the remarkable success of Tim Hortons branding in Canada and ask how it becomes a public site in which politics and politicians appear.

Case Study: Tim Hortons and the Public Sphere

As branding makes companies accountable and visible in ways that non-branded production does not, it also opens up huge possibilities in terms of its place in public life. After all, if they are being asked to shape their labour, production, distribution, and advertising practices to public opinion, they are being invited to participate in the public sphere. This invitation has been eagerly taken up. Jürgen Habermas (1989) famously described the modern or "bourgeois" public sphere as a place where people come together to discuss matters of common concern in a way that ignores social standing and is inclusive of its members. According to Habermas, this sphere arose with the decline of feudal social relations and was supported by the rise of the British coffee house and the free press. For Habermas, the public sphere should exist outside both state and market control.

Branding, especially, allows companies to gain access to or even *define* the public sphere, its issues, and how these issues are understood. Hence, health issues such as heart disease are taken up by companies like Becel (Canada) to emphasize their brands' links to health and their more general corporate images as public actors. As its website explains, "Becel has always believed in the importance of caring for your heart. That's the reason Becel margarine was made, and that's the reason we are dedicated to educating Canadians about the importance of heart healthy living" (Becel 2010). This helps distance this product from its mother company, Unilever, the Dutch-based multinational corporation. Becel is the "founding sponsor" of the Heart and Stroke Foundation of Canada, whose "health check" logos are supported by fees (up to $180,000) from branded companies to appear on their products. This campaign also has other political effects – it highlights one disease as deserving of public attention, resources, and action (heart disease being a non-controversial and democratic problem that cuts across race, ethnicity, sexuality, and social class, although not equally) and frames it in particular ways (as in need of scientific research and personal lifestyle choices rather than, for example, social, environmental, or political action) and moves the debate about health care out of Parliament and into the marketplace. It is interesting to note in this context that Canadian film director Sarah Polley produced a two-minute short film to be aired during the Oscar awards television broadcast but pulled her name from it when she learned that this promotion for the Heart and Stroke Foundation was also a promotion for Becel.

Similarly, Dove beauty company (like Becel, owned by Unilever) has a stated "social mission" that has reframed feminist political issues (systemic poverty, institutionalized discrimination, family violence) into a personalized problem of self-esteem treated through its Self-Esteem Fund campaign (begun in Canada in 2006) that encourages girls to use pamphlets and sleepovers that purportedly develop their self-image. This fund is a part of its larger international Campaign for Real Beauty begun in 2004.

With political action more and more directed by branded companies, it takes on the look of donning ribbons, coloured T-shirts and bracelets, and activities like walking to raise money for specific projects. Indeed, many products are advertised around their promise to donate money toward a particular cause, such that even shopping becomes a form of political action. Debate and politicization of issues become redirected toward personal consumer practices. But if much corporate branding turns complex political issues into personal matters, other corporate brands reach much further into the formation of political sentiment, even colonizing the public sphere. In Canada, the Tim Hortons coffee chain is the best example of this phenomenon.

Tim Hortons has a formidable political role in Canadian politics. Politicians regularly flock to the restaurants; Stephen Harper in particular has publicly linked himself to the brand (for example, Marland 2008). Moreover, the Conservative Party has targeted Tim Hortons consumers. According to Flanagan (2009, 224) and as described in Chapters 5 to 7 in this volume, after delivering a presentation in 2005 on segmentation analysis (i.e., dividing up the electorate based on their propensity to support the party on the grounds of socio-economic and values research) to party strategists, the Conservatives' political marketer "summed it up" by saying, "You buy your coffee at Starbucks, but these people [i.e., members of the Tories' targeted elector segments] get their coffee at Tim Hortons."

The status of Tim Hortons as a branded company in Canada is unquestionable – it is the king of the Canadian coffee scene. It has over twenty-eight hundred outlets in Canada and over five hundred in the United States (by comparison, Starbucks has just under eight hundred outlets in Canada). As a purveyor of coffee and quick food, it has insinuated itself into the everyday life of Canadians equally in the urban and rural areas. Moreover, it has, more than any other company, managed to align itself with Canadian identity, history, and culture. As political commentator Rex Murphy (2009) has stated, "Outside of *Hockey Night in Canada* and – with reverence – Don Cherry, there are few institutions or companies that have blended into the character of the nation so completely as Tim Hortons." Tim Hortons has long been recognized by the business community in Canada for its admirable brand management. For three consecutive years, readers of *Canadian Business* magazine deemed it Canada's "best managed brand" (Gray 2004, 2005, 2006). *Advertising Age* included Tim Hortons in its 2010 list of thirty "World's hottest brands" (Advertising Age 2010). Tim Hortons' domestic marketing differs radically from its exported marketing, playing on notions of Canada and Canadianness at home, but not doing so abroad. (For instance, its US marketing focuses on themes like the quality and value of its food). In marketing language, it is a "local brand." Tim Hortons is certainly not the only branded company to do this – in the 1980s, Roots branded Canadian nationalism (in the context of NAFTA debates and general anti-Americanism) even though the company was run by Americans (Carstairs 2006). But whereas Roots put general signifiers on sweatshirts – canoes, beavers, maple leaves – Tim Hortons promotes a set of more explicitly political values. This is part of its distinct claim on the public sphere.

The Canadian media, especially, treat Tim Hortons as a Habermasian public sphere. When an employee is fired (*Toronto Star* 2008) or a customer banned (T. Fletcher 2010), it becomes a national media story, almost as if the company does not have the right to exclude anyone from patronage or employment. This puts the company in the quasi-political position of having to publicly defend actions that other companies could get away with outside of public scrutiny. Certainly, as a coffee shop, Tim Hortons is socially like a public space or village square where people congregate and talk, argue, and debate. From this notion of the coffee shop as a public space, it can offer itself also as a public sphere. It does this by helping to direct the ways Canadians are to think about themselves and the collective good.

Tim Hortons is held to account in terms of its inclusivity partly because it markets itself as inclusive. It is the down-to-earth, unpretentious coffee chain in the marketplace filled with pseudo-Italian/French coffee names that are challenging to pronounce without an undergraduate course in Romance languages (for example, Starbucks' "Cinnamon Dolce Crème Frappuccino" comes in sizes "tall," "grande," and "venti"). So while customers at Starbucks are invited to toss around their sophistication as they consume coffee, Tim Hortons' customers are invited to display their lack of pretension – their inclusiveness toward others rather than elitist exclusiveness – in their "double-double" coffees.[1] Generally, coffee seems to be a commodity fraught with meaning for its consumers. Some display their geo-political commitments by consuming fair trade coffee, others show urban sophistication by consuming Italian-style coffee, and still others choose Tim's as a statement (or counterstatement) about their identities. As will be discussed, Tim Hortons' marketing plays on long-standing Canadian values that are tied to notions like inclusion, community, collectivism, and sacrifice.

Is it valid to claim that Tim Hortons is a part of the Canadian public sphere? Consider a few examples, including those in which agents of government and state come to Tim Hortons to gain legitimacy. When US secretary of state Condoleezza Rice visited Canada in 2006, she was taken to a Tim Hortons in the home riding of the foreign affairs minister, Peter MacKay. This produced a huge media response, even provoking rumours in the Canadian and American press of a budding romantic relationship. Presumably, MacKay felt that this coffee chain could do the work of representing Canadian hospitality and reflect well on him as a political figure. Since then, politicians have also used Tim Hortons outlets to make political announcements. For example, in 2009, Finance Minister Jim Flaherty used a Tim's location in London, Ontario, to announce his plans to reign in public spending, but the media picked up on his renting of a plane at public cost and undermined his bid at the down-to-earth common sense he was trying to portray (Whittington 2010). In 2010, Prime Minister Harper was widely criticized in the press and by political opponents for choosing to visit Tim Hortons' headquarters in Oakville, Ontario, rather than attend an address to the United Nations by US president Obama. Harper defended his decision by pointing out that he was celebrating the repatriation of Tim Hortons to Canada (which had been bought in 1995 by the American Wendy's corporation). Politically, the prime minister was choosing to make domestic affairs more symbolically important than international affairs, opening himself and his party to the charge that Canada's status on the world stage is at risk, while further publicly linking the Conservative brand with the Tim Hortons brand.

Other agents of state, most notably the military, get lots of support and positive publicity from Tim Hortons. When the first poppy coin was minted for Remembrance Day in 2004, Tim Hortons was named its exclusive distributor. The Royal Canadian Mint and the Royal Canadian Legion both supported this plan because the company was "a distinctive Canadian enterprise." This support of the military also comes from Tim Hortons itself, with Remembrance Day commemoration treated seriously and sombrely in its own promotions that feature artifacts and photographs depicting soldiers, medals, clothing, and photos. For years, Tim Hortons has sent coffee to peacekeeping troops posted outside Canada as part of its True Stories campaign that include soldiers writing to Tim's to ask for a "taste of home." Perhaps the most famous link between Tim's and the military is the opening of the outlet in Kandahar city, Afghanistan, in 2006. The troops had been lobbying for this outlet and also for a buy-a-coffee-for-a-soldier promotion. They did get their outlet in Kandahar, but Tim Hortons has been careful not to develop an explicit coffee-for-troops campaign at home. Nevertheless, when the former chief of the defence staff of the Canadian Forces, General Rick Hillier, announced the opening of the Kandahar outlet, he described it as the strengthening of "an already superb relationship between two great Canadian institutions" (Tim Hortons 2006).

Even at its inception in 1964 as a coffee and donut shop, Tim Hortons already had a claim on the Canadian imagination by way of its co-founder and namesake, NHL hockey player Tim Horton. Earlier advertising played on this celebrity until his sudden death in 1974. As Steve Penfold (2002, 48) has argued, not all NHL stars could parlay their status into a coffee chain, and the image of Horton "had all the trappings of the classic myth of white Canadian manhood." Here we begin to see an earlier linking of the coffee chain to a set of values Canadians could recognize as their own. This is the key to understanding Tim Hortons' success. It makes a claim on the public sphere by promoting recognizable Canadian values.

Tim Hortons could not long depend on this linkage of the hockey player with the company because, after his death, his widow required that his image be removed from advertising and store interiors. The company does, importantly, retain a link with sports, especially kids' and amateur hockey. This association also makes sports and hockey into quasi-political themes of inclusion (of girls and poor children, for example), fair play, non-violence, and community spirit. Timbits (in this case, not a reference to their tiny pieces of fried dough but to the sponsored children of the same name) ads focus on these themes and their role as socializing the next generation of Canadians into a shared identity.

If the modern public sphere is inclusive, then it seeks out new members. Historically, the early modern public sphere established the grounds for its own expansion – that is, its Enlightenment notions of debate and reason as the basis of citizenship allowed thinkers like Wollstonecraft and Paine to argue for the inclusion (and education) of women and working men. This sentiment is played up at Tim Hortons by way of its celebration of immigration. The much-discussed (again, in the media) immigration ad aired on television during the Canada-hosted 2010 Winter Olympics in Vancouver featured the story of the reunion of an African immigrant with his wife and children. In this advertisement, the man hands his wife a cup of Tim's coffee as she comes off her plane and says, "Welcome to Canada." Clearly, this ad boldly announces Tim Hortons as the primary signifier of Canada, but it also celebrates the reunion of families through Canadian immigration policy and law. These people are not visitors but new Canadians, that is, citizens (or future citizens). As Citizenship and Immigration Canada explains, immigrants are expected to learn the culture, language, values, and habits of their new home. This new Canadian has had her first such lesson.

Significantly, Tim Hortons' product advertising plays on the presumed collective values of community, sacrifice, and collectivism. Take, for example, a TV spot that aired in the early 2000s that showed a man arriving at a rural hockey arena on a frigid winter morning before dawn. With his cup of Tim's coffee, he readies the arena for the children who will soon hit the ice. They will not think about the hours of labour that went into preparing the arena for their enjoyment. Nevertheless, this man's labour has set the stage of the ongoing ritual of hockey play in the rural arena. These themes of hockey and the rural outpost are extremely clichéd, yet note how this ad also plays on notions of unsung sacrifice, hard work, and continuity of culture. The first Tim Hortons True Story television advertisement, made in the mid-1990s, told of an old woman walking up a hill each day with her cane and purse to have her cup of Tim's coffee. The campaign has very much played on this notion of the integrity, sacrifice, and ruggedness of its customers. Metaphorically, the Tim Hortons customers featured in these advertisements are all Tommy Douglases (voted number one in CBC's 2004 Greatest Canadian contest) in their character and mentality.

Finally, like any good public sphere, Tim Hortons provides a place for people to talk and share stories. Both its True Stories campaign and its subsequent Every Cup Tells a Story campaign are rooted in stories that come from and feature its customers, even in the most mundane pursuits. The Every Cup campaign makes use of its company website to allow all customers to post their own stories in a display of web 2.0 interactivity that Canada's political parties have been slow to embrace (see Tamara Small's preceding chapter). There have been thousands of such postings to the site, with stories ranging from the most mundane to heart-wrenching, but all speaking in some manner to the sense of political identity that the Tim Hortons brand conveys. One story is told by a widow who has little time to spend with her young daughter since the premature death of her husband. Their weekly visit together to Tim Hortons is apparently the highlight of their busy lives. Other stories tell about engagements, medical procedures, departures (especially of troops), the birth of babies ... almost anything. What is interesting in the context of this discussion is that other social networks are available to these users of the Tim Hortons site. Why are people seeking to share such stories there? Perhaps it is the apparent reach of this site, but it is likely far more. After all, these personal and often deeply private stories all involve the Tim Hortons product (usually coffee) woven into the narrative. Certainly, a common theme in these stories is ritual (the consumption of the coffee being used to structure and punctuate daily life) and comfort. Many stories involve some fear and trepidation – including rites of passage like marriage or leaving home – and the coffee works almost as a magical object of luck or comfort. These stories seem to call up the earlier True Stories ads in which ordinary people display courage and tenacity.

Implications for the Quality of Democracy

How does Tim Hortons' claim on the public sphere affect political life in Canada? Much has been written on the issue of marketing politics – that is, turning the citizen into a consumer; considerably less has been written on the opposite move – turning the consumer into a citizen. In this chapter, we have considered what it means to invoke collective national values by way of a branded commodity – that is, to come to political life by way of the branded commodity. As political marketing experts argue, politics and branding link together because they both offer a set of values and allow a kind of contract with the citizen-consumer. As others have pointed out in this book, political parties now think of their constituents in terms of their consumer habits because there seems to be a strong predictive value of political leaning and consumption practices. This in itself is not too surprising. Consumer objects and products are selected and valued because they seem to speak about who we are or want to be. Consumption becomes a way of appearing both to ourselves and to others in a meaningful way. Values are embedded and displayed in these objects. As we have seen, coffee is especially evocative in this way – with sophistication, labour politics, and environmentalism all available for display with one's choice of coffee. Branding adds to this value because it gives a personality to a company and it establishes a kind of contract with the consumer.

Tim Hortons has managed to establish a contract with its Canadian customers that extends into the public sphere. It offers politicians and agents of state more than just a friendly place to glad-hand during elections or to seek free positive publicity. Tim Hortons offers a social and political site through which these agents and actors can place themselves within a romantic set of values – collectivism, community, sacrifice, inclusion. As discussed, the strategies by which Tim Hortons accomplished this remarkable status are complex and sophisticated. Tim Hortons plays on much deeper social values than most branded commodities, touching more directly on national character and national history. Hence, Canadian political actors, from party leaders to candidates, make the pilgrimage to the site to benefit from the feelings it can generate.

This case study raises a number of important issues: (1) Is the two-way influence between branding and politics increasing?; (2) Does this mutual influence wear down the distinction between politics and private, corporate interests (allowing corporations to appear as public actors and public interests to appear as brandable issues)?; and (3) Does this conflation of politics and brands play up sentiment over reason and undermine the classic Enlightenment notion of the citizen? The answer to these questions seems to be yes, at least in Canada. As Flanagan (2009) notes, the Conservative Party has recognized that Tim Hortons, especially, does the work of collecting its constituents around a set of sentiments. This is more than a correlation between consuming habits and voting tendencies. These political marketers have recognized that this particular company helps articulate a set of values and organize their constituents. Nimijean (2006) also recognizes that Canadian political parties have taken up what he calls "brand Canada" to sell themselves by playing on general nationalistic sentiments about Canadian values while implementing policies that have little ideological coherence. As mentioned, Prime Minister Stephen Harper makes good use of Tim Hortons for image building both during and between election campaigns.

The Conservative Party is the first federal party to have systematically studied the correlation between Tim Hortons customers and citizen sentiment. And while they are keen to promote the image that the Tim's drinker is a Tory, survey data do not support this contention. A Harris/Decima poll conducted in 2009 found almost equal political support for the three major parties among Tim Hortons customers (Grenier 2010). This research also looked at factors like age and income, and found that Tim Hortons collects its customers very broadly from the general population. This capacity to unite a politically diverse customer base runs parallel to its populist image. Just as populist movements and leaders in Canadian politics – such as CCF socialism, Québécois nationalism, Alberta and Newfoundland regionalism, and Social Credit conservatism – have united a broad electorate, the Tim Hortons brand employs a mass market approach that appeals to a wide range of consumers and which is contingent on its public image of embodying the political identity of its customers. In seeking to attach themselves to this mass commercial brand, the Harper Tories have therefore attempted to overcome some of the limitations of their market segmentation, narrowcasting, and leader's charisma.

Other parties, most notably the Liberals, are also trying to make use of Tim Hortons. Having been accused of appealing to a "Starbucks" constituency of elitists, in 2010, Liberal leader Michael Ignatieff toured the country, with many visits to Tim's outlets. Crossing the country by bus and stopping at Tim's was meant to recast his image away from Harvard intellectual and into the Canadian Everyman. Again, the Liberals were doing more than simply going to a place where people are likely to congregate, such as a shopping mall. It is a strategically preferred location that allows a particular version of the party and its leader to be reflected. In other words, Tim Hortons' commercial branding strategies provide the ground for the political branding strategies of Canada's political parties. As it has made itself a part of the public sphere, political life has necessarily adjusted to Tim Hortons' branded image, which has attracted politicians seeking to benefit from being associated with the organization's positive brand attributes in the broader consumer and media marketplace.

If Tim Hortons has made a claim on the public sphere, Habermas would have us recognize that this is not a public sphere in any deep sense. In fact, he would call it the "refeudalization" of the public sphere by private interests. Although a set of arguably laudable values are defended at this site, they are not themselves debated or *made* debatable. These values circulate as collective feelings, associated with the particular ways Canadians have been taught to think of themselves since at least the 1970s – multicultural, inclusive, tolerant, etcetera. These images are in fact supportive of federal government policies that are used to organize and administer the populace.

At least in principle, a citizen and a consumer are different things, just as a body politic and a corporation are different things. As discussed, typically when corporations (like Unilever with its Becel or Dove labels) come into the public sphere, they simplify and individualize collective problems so that their solutions can be easily packaged – for example, raising money or self-esteem. Their goal is to sell their products and raise profits for shareholders. They achieve this hard-nosed goal by way of claiming to care about the customer. Our collective capacity to think of health and gender as highly political issues of institutionalized power, resource distribution, and policy threatens to be eroded by the busywork that these companies elicit in their customers, who also seem to be interested in demonstrating that they care about various things. Tim Hortons' marketing and advertising are far more subtle than these campaigns of caring. This particular branded commodity and company employs the notion of caring in a broader and deeper way than most others by playing on care for the newcomer, tradition, the warrior, and so on. In short, it plays on the complex and emotional notion of the patriotic Canadian (who seems to stand in quiet certainty and coherence compared with the more atomized and even hysterical social actor induced by the caring campaigns). Patriotic caring cannot care about everything (as is possible with the care campaigns, given enough will and time on the part of the citizen-consumer) but must exclude some values and ideas as non-Canadian. Hence, this type of caring on the part of Tim Hortons lends itself directly to political life and a claim on the public sphere.

All of us are both citizens and consumers, yet this does not mean that these social roles are easily reconciled. The obligation of the citizen is to maintain an imaginative or thoughtful relationship to the notion of the common good. The consumer is not a political actor in this sense, at least not without a huge degradation of the notion of the political. As Hannah Arendt (1958) has argued, to be a citizen is to act in a public way that offers oneself into debate and thought. The consumer is ultimately a private actor, a "householder" in Arendt's terms, who does not have to produce a coherent and explicit notion of the common good in his or her actions. If the communitarian and patriotic sentiments celebrated and supported by Tim Hortons work to enhance democratic life by providing an identity for the contemporary citizen, democracy nevertheless still relies on politicians and their parties to organize general sentiment into concrete and explicit policy. Although policy can be said to follow from general values (found at Tim Hortons, perhaps), policy is also the implementation of values into practice. Practice, rather than sentiment, allows debate about what the Canadian common good is. Politicians and parties may try to make the most of sentiment, but their actual policies make them appear on the political scene and gain meaning for citizens. Hence, despite its successful use of political marketing, Tim Hortons remains, or should remain, a limited part of the Canadian public sphere.

NOTE

1   This expression, meaning two creams and two sugars, arises from Anglo-Canadian slang but has become popularly associated with Tim Hortons in English Canada.

14
Marketing and Efficacy: Does Political Marketing Empower Canadians?

Royce Koop

Does political marketing empower Canadians? One way to address this question is to explore how the use of political marketing techniques by political parties affects the efficacy of citizens. Political efficacy is classically defined as citizens' feelings that individuals can bring about political and social change (Campbell, Gurin, and Miller 1954, 187-89). Citizens with high degrees of efficacy are optimistic about their own utility in politics, whereas citizens with low degrees of efficacy feel hopeless in this respect. Parties are the crucial linkage between the citizens of democracies and their political institutions (Chandler and Siaroff 1992, 192). When parties are accessible and responsive, then citizens' senses of external efficacy are likely to be high. But when parties are unresponsive and seemingly impermeable to the wishes of citizens, then their feelings of external efficacy may be low.

Marketing consists of "identify[ing] and respond[ing] to customer needs and wants in the way they design, produce and deliver their goods" (Lees-Marshment 2009c, 23). Although the academic literature on marketing has developed in response to the use of these practices by business organizations, marketing techniques are also employed by non-business organizations such as charitable groups (Wood, Snelgrove, and Danylchuk 2010), governments (Page 2006), and, more precisely, government bureaucracies (Proctor 2007). The application of a marketing understanding to political parties makes sense, since parties, like these other organizations, are also concerned with issues such as product branding and marketing strategy; however, the application of marketing principles to political parties involves a substantial degree of conceptual stretching (Scammell 1999, fn 50). A number of theoretical frameworks have accordingly been developed to account for the use of marketing techniques by political parties (for example, Newman 1999a; Wring 2002), most notably Lees-Marshment's eight-stage process for the development of market-oriented parties (MOPs; see Table 10.1).

It is understood that the use of marketing techniques by political parties impacts the political efficacy of citizens. However, the literature on political marketing provides conflicting accounts of the impact of political marketing on feelings of efficacy. On the one hand, there are both theoretical reasons and empirical evidence that suggest that political marketing does indeed boost political efficacy and, in so doing, empower Canadians (see Lees-Marshment 2008, 273-74). Indeed, the use of marketing techniques by political parties was originally viewed as an effort by parties to reconnect with the public (Bowler and Farrell 1992). On the other hand, political marketing may lead to the development of elitist political parties willing to ignore entire segments of the voting population, as well as their own loyalists and members.

Table 14.1 draws on this literature to list several consequences – positive, mixed, and negative – of political marketing for the efficacy of citizens. First, there is an argument to be made that the development of marketing orientations causes parties to become more responsive to citizens' wishes. Since marketing techniques allow parties to (1) more clearly understand the concerns of citizens and (2) integrate public concerns into their own campaign appeals, it is reasonable to expect that MOPs will be less likely than other parties to espouse the out-of-date ideas of party elites (Lees-Marshment 2011). "Part of the use of polls," note Bowler and Farrell (1992, 231), "is not only that parties learn about the issues and concerns of the voters whom they seek to represent, but also that parties can be responsive ... to public preferences and concerns." The result is that a MOP "takes into account the electorate's needs and wants" in order to "achieve a high level of satisfaction" (Henneberg

Table 14.1

The impact of political marketing on citizen efficacy

Positive	Mixed	Negative
Parties are more responsive to citizens	Political marketing brings about an end to ideology	Parties are responsive to the target market but unresponsive to other citizens
Parties are more responsive to minorities and to previously marginalized groups	Political marketing disempowers party activists, members, and supporters	Political marketing feeds cynicism about the political process

and Eghbalian 2002, 74). The efficacy of citizens is likely to be low in the face of non-responsive, elite-dominated parties; in contrast, citizen efficacy is more likely to be high when parties are tuned into citizen concerns through political marketing techniques and are responsive to those concerns.

The use of marketing techniques also allows parties to tune into the concerns of minorities and previously marginalized groups (Lees-Marshment 2011, 42-43). Elite parties with roots in only small segments of Canadian society are unlikely to be attuned to these concerns. The use of voter segmentation techniques – the method of dividing heterogeneous citizenries into targeted homogenous groups (Baines et al. 2003, 225-26) – is oftentimes viewed as exclusionary, yet segmentation in fact allows parties to recognize the concerns of such minority groups. Whereas small or emerging groups previously had to fight to gain the attention of parties, segmentation techniques allow parties to isolate, recognize, and reach out to those groups through their own appeals. More importantly, marketing techniques allow parties to understand the concerns of these citizens. The result is that previously alienated groups of citizens that were left out of the political process may develop a new sense of efficacy.

On the other hand, there is good reason to expect that the use of political marketing techniques by parties will lead to decreased citizen efficacy. Market segmentation of citizens, for example, allows parties to target and actively pursue the support of some groups over others. Responsiveness to citizens in this sense is not the goal in and of itself, but rather is a means for parties to accomplish their real objective of electoral victory (Savigny 2006, 83). The result is that segmentation techniques, particularly the use of focus groups, create incentives for parties to pursue certain groups within society while altogether ignoring others (Wring 2006, 87). In particular, parties pursue the support of uncommitted voters in contrast to partisans. Lilleker (2005a, 18) memorably refers to such a strategy as "narrowing the market share to swingers." In this way, segmentation and targeting lead to "a division in society: those to whom politics belongs and those whom politics has abandoned" (Lilleker 2005a, ibid.). The use of focus groups is particularly well suited to such a strategy, since demographic equality is neither ensured nor typically desired in focus group research (Savigny 2008a, 54-55). So, while some citizens encounter very responsive MOPs and as a result may be quite efficacious, others may find parties unresponsive and their senses of efficacy will consequently be low.

Party elites may also make use of focus groups not to learn about the concerns of any group of citizens, but rather to find ways of presenting their own preconceived policies and ideas in such a way as to boost the likelihood of electoral success. In the terminology developed by Lees-Marshment, these parties would resemble product-oriented or sales-oriented parties rather than true MOPs. Focus groups may be used to refine the presentation of these preconceived ideas or allow elites to pick and choose among the more popular policies. Focus groups employed for the UK Labour Party, for example, were designed to test existing ideas rather than generate new policies or listen to the electorate (Gould 1998, 328). And such qualitative research is a useful way for parties to demonstrate that they are "listening" to the electorate when this is in fact not taking place (Savigny 2007, 130). This may ironically boost the efficacy of citizens, as these groups create the image of responsive parties. But this is a mirage, and party policies in government may eventually betray this reality, with deleterious consequences for the efficacy of citizens.

There is also the possibility that political parties, by embracing a sales- and marketing-oriented approach to campaigning that eschews sound principles, may contribute to Canadians' cynicism regarding politics (Delacourt and Marland 2009, 47). Market research allows parties to tailor policies to particular segments of the population, but such policies may not be in the wider public interest. Furthermore, market research illuminates the aspects of party policies to emphasize and downplay; for example, Paré and Berger (2008) emphasize the importance of this approach to the Conservative Party of Canada's electoral victory in the 2006 national election. As a result, marketing may encourage the perception that politicians are interested in power for power's sake, without any fundamental principles underlying that pursuit. And cynicism is, of course, related to low feelings of efficacy.

Two further consequences of political marketing techniques appear to have mixed consequences for the political efficacy of citizens. Several scholars argue that political marketing brings about an end to ideology. With the ability to identify with great precision the concerns of citizens, parties now have little use for employing ideological appeals in order to mobilize supporters (see, for example, Lees-Marshment 2004, 8). In practice, this tendency may have both positive and negative consequences for the efficacy of citizens. On one hand, ideology functions to constrain the actions and appeals of parties. By shedding ideological constraints, parties may become more accessible to previously disenfranchised citizens. But on the other hand, ideological parties provided excellent outlets for certain groups within society; ideological mass parties, for example, greatly increase the efficacy of working-class citizens. These citizens' sense of efficacy is therefore likely to decrease when parties shed their ideological orientations. Furthermore, the jettisoning of ideological principles may lead to what the public perceives as opportunistic parties. However, Scammell (1999, 730) persuasively argues that this particular argument – that political marketing brings about an end to ideology – is unconvincing, given that some of the earliest practitioners of marketing techniques were strongly ideological parties, including Margaret Thatcher's Conservative Party (also see Wring 1997, 660).

A similar concern relates to party supporters, activists, and members. Much of the literature on party democratization speculates on how party elites may remake their parties in order to be more responsive to the concerns of party members and activists (Young and Cross 2002b). But the use of political marketing techniques by party elites is likely to curtail the influence of party members within the party. Since MOPs are actively concerned with identifying and responding to the concerns of citizens, the concerns of party members may be shuffled aside, with alienation among party members resulting (Lilleker 2005b). At the very least, the concerns of party members will be given second-rate status to those of party pollsters and market researchers. The result is that previously influential "party people" may find their influence decrease substantially, and their senses of political efficacy will accordingly decline.

Such reforms may actually be an important aspect of parties' marketing strategies, partly because they allow the parties to portray themselves as accessible to citizens (Lees-Marshment and Quayle 2001, 208-9). However, members may find in reality that such parties are quite inaccessible. The Canadian Reform Party provides a good example of how this occurs. The Reform Party sparked the trend of plebiscitary democracy in Canadian parties (Young and Cross 2002b, 678). However, it became clear that the party leader, Preston Manning, was adept at manipulating delegates at party policy conventions to arrive at conclusions that he himself favoured (see, for example, Ellis 2005, 74).

Case Study: Political Marketing and Efficacy in Canadian Party Politics

Are these theoretical arguments concerning the relationship between political marketing techniques and the efficacy of citizens borne out in the Canadian experience? To what extent have Canadian parties adopted these techniques, and what do the consequences of these techniques appear to be for Canadians' political efficacy?

Has political marketing brought about an end to ideology among Canadian parties? At least among the major parties, the question is moot because the Liberal and Conservative Parties have generally been non-ideological for most of their histories. In this sense, the major parties conform to Otto Kirchheimer's 1966 expectations of catch-all parties: in sharp contrast to mass parties, they are rooted in neither particular ideological traditions nor socio-economic groups for support (Henneberg and Eghbalian 2002). Although these parties may operate within an ideological range (Christian and Campbell 1990), they have shifted their appeals substantially over time. In the vocabulary of the political marketing literature, Canada's major parties can long be understood as MOPs that have been "ideologically adaptable" in order to exploit "strategic opportunities" (Delacourt and Marland 2009, 48; Scott 1970, 57).

Canada's brokerage parties (the Liberals and Conservatives) appear to be well-adapted to experimenting with new techniques of political marketing (see Chapters 1 and 15, by the editors of this book). Whereas previous party leaders relied on contacts throughout the country to attempt to piece together ideas about what was required in terms of policy, party leaders can now rely on a more sophisticated arsenal of marketing techniques to adapt their activities and promotions to the targeted market. But the consequences of such a market orientation for Canadians and their efficacy is not likely to be substantial; brokerage parties have never been particularly product-oriented, so new political marketing techniques have not brought about a significant change among the parties in ways that would impact how Canadians view their accessibility. This suggests that the evolution of Canada's major parties into full-fledged MOPs is unlikely to exercise a deleterious effect on the efficacy of Canadians. The situation is somewhat different for the ideological New Democratic Party, but activists even in this party have long tolerated the sales orientations of leaders (Marland 2005).

In any case, political marketing techniques can allow parties to reach out to non-loyalists even without jettisoning unpopular policies. Since Canada's two major brokerage parties have not generally been ideological, the utility of marketing techniques has not always consisted of adapting party policies to the wishes of a wider market share. Instead, careful massaging of previous policies combined with rebranding, particularly with respect to party leaders, have characterized Canadian parties. This is to be expected, since party leaders have dominated Canadian parties since Siegfried's observations (1978) of the nation's politics while Wilfrid Laurier was prime minister.

The next question is whether the parties' embrace of political marketing techniques has contributed to a disenfranchisement of party activists and supporters. Recent research provides the confounding result that Canadian federal parties were democratizing their internal structures in order to accommodate greater member input as they were simultaneously embracing marketing techniques (Young and Cross 2002b).

One alteration to party structures that is likely to see more party actors embrace marketing techniques, and in so doing benefit Canadians, is in the realm of leadership selection. The party caucus and later indirect conventions traditionally selected the leaders of Canadian parties, but the parties have seen a democratization of these processes over the course of the twentieth century, culminating in direct election methods, which allow all party members to vote for the leader (Cross 2004, chap. 5). This method empowers individual Canadians by giving them a low-cost opportunity to vote for a party leader. Such selection methods also provide incentives for leadership candidates to employ marketing techniques to lure new voters into the party. However, party elites are disadvantaged by these arrangements because they are no longer privileged with the task of leadership selection, as they are under the caucus and convention selection methods.

It is also important to note that it is not clear that individual party members would have their senses of efficacy sapped by the increasing adoption of marketing techniques by party executives. This is because members of Canada's brokerage parties have never had a substantial say in the formulation of party policies or campaign themes. Instead, their real place of influence has been in the constituencies. Carty (2002) argues that the internal arrangements of Canadian parties are governed by a "franchise bargain" between party leaders and members: leaders are relatively free to determine party policy, particularly during election campaigns, whereas party members are provided with the right to select party candidates in the constituencies. With some exceptions, this franchise bargain has been maintained in the major national parties, and party members have retained their traditional right to candidate selection. This bargain suggests that party members have always understood that their role has not been to formulate policy, and so the embrace of political marketing by party leaders would not impact their sense of efficacy – market orientation at the national level is unlikely to matter to party members as long as they can continue to select local candidates and also leaders (see Young and Cross 2002a, Table 2). So in this sense, at least, the use of political marketing techniques by party elites is unlikely to impact the efficacy of party members and activists.

Has political marketing caused Canadian parties to become more responsive to Canadians, particularly to minorities? Political marketing techniques have allowed parties to identify and reach out to different groups within Canadian society. More generally, all Canadian parties began in the 1990s to tailor their messages to certain segments of society, experimenting with direct mail and other such appeals to specific groups (Carty, Cross, and Young 2000, chap. 5; also see Chapters 1 and 4). And the regionalization of Canadian election campaigns reflected a segmentation strategy as well, as parties focused their efforts on winnable regions and neglected non-winnable regions. This even manifested itself in parties playing regions off one another. The result is that increased contact with and response from Canadian parties should be accompanied by an increase in the political efficacy of those groups.

It is also important to ask whether the use of political marketing by party elites has caused the parties to ignore certain segments of Canadian society, with a resulting decline in efficacy among the neglected groups. Market segmentation inevitably involves some segments of society being ignored, and political efficacy is likely to decline as a result. As Flanagan (2009) and other contributors to this volume (particularly Chapters 4 to 6, and 8) have described, the Conservative Party has gone to great lengths to segment the Canadian population into winnable and non-winnable votes. Armed with this information, the party has not wasted resources on electors who were deemed likely to be entirely impervious to its appeals. At the same time, however, leader Stephen Harper has attempted to minimize the fears of such skeptics by portraying the Canadian Alliance and later the Conservative Party as mainstream.

The problem of ignored segments may be more pronounced in states like Canada where single-member plurality electoral systems are used (see Karp and Banducci 2008; also Chapters 2 and 3). This system tends to provide a bonus in seats to the party that wins the most votes and penalize smaller parties. The result is that parties can form majority or single-party minority governments with only a small percentage of the overall popular vote. The Conservative Party, for example, formed a minority government following the 2008 national election despite having received only 37.6 percent of the popular vote, and a majority government after the 2011 election despite having increased its vote share only 2 percent from the previous election. The problem is that if parties are employing marketing techniques to segregate voters into groups and then ignoring those less likely to be receptive to party appeals, the overall legitimacy of the government that results is diminished. So too is the political efficacy of the Canadians who have been ignored by the winning party, as their own influence over the government and its policies are thought to be non-existent.

However, the negative impact of such segmentation should not be overstated. If the citizenry is a market and parties are segmenting that market in order to successfully sell a product, then it is reasonable to expect that other parties will move to embrace some segments of the electorate that are ignored. So a Conservative opponent's sense of efficacy may certainly have been stung by Stephen Harper's refusal to address the issues that matter to him or her; however, other parties address many such issues. Political marketing allows parties to segment the market, but the nature of electoral competition ensures that Canadians will in many cases be able to identify a party that is sympathetic to their interests, and their efficacy will respond accordingly.

The State of Political Marketing in Canada

For some time, scholars have recognized that political efficacy in fact contains two components: internal and external efficacy. Internal efficacy refers to individuals' views about their own ability to understand and participate effectively in politics. External efficacy refers to views concerning the responsiveness of political institutions and actors to their own demands (Niemi, Craig, and Mattei 1991, 1407-8). Citizens with high internal and external efficacy are confident in both their ability to engage in politics and the responsiveness of the political system. In contrast, citizens with low internal and external efficacy lack confidence in their own ability to participate and, anyway, political actors and institutions are not responsive. Other citizens may differ on these measures. A citizen with high internal but low external efficacy is highly confident in herself and her own abilities, but disillusioned with institutions and political actors that appear to be unresponsive to her. In contrast, some citizens may find institutions responsive but nevertheless not be confident themselves.

The question then is whether new marketing techniques employed by Canadian parties have been associated with any shifts in the political efficacy of citizens. Marshalling evidence from the Canadian Election Study (CES), Nevitte traced trends in the external and internal efficacy of Canadians from the 1965 to the 1993 general elections. The 1984 election marked the beginning of what Nevitte refers to as the efficacy gap: whereas rates of internal efficacy remained relatively steady, rates of external efficacy began to drop, reaching a low in the 1993 election. "As people's sense of their own subjective political competence has been sustained, their evaluations of the responsiveness of their own political system have been declining," Nevitte (2002, 22) reports.

The prognosis for the use of political marketing techniques by political parties on levels of external efficacy is not bright: just as scholars began to observe the use of such techniques in developed democracies, a Canadian efficacy gap came into existence. The overall efficacy of Canadians did not decline; their senses of political confidence did not change markedly. However, their senses of the responsiveness of political institutions and actors did decline. This suggests that the embrace of political marketing techniques by parties has caused those parties to be seen as more elite and less responsive to citizens. There is much theoretical support for this argument, and we should be open to the view that political marketing has contributed to a feeling of hopelessness about the political process.

In order to explore this efficacy gap following the 1993 election, I examined external and internal efficacy in the 1997, 2000, 2004, and 2008 elections using CES data (Figure 14.1). For the 1997 survey, the questions used to measure efficacy are different, so these results should be interpreted with caution. Each data point is the percentage of respondents returning low or very low levels of efficacy.

In all of these elections, more Canadians lacked internal efficacy than they did external efficacy. This gap was very wide in 1997 and 2004. However, the gap narrowed in both 2000 and 2008. The result for 2008 suggests that Nevitte's efficacy gap has narrowed considerably. To the extent that this gap still exists, its nature has been reversed; whereas Canadians between 1984 and 1993 were more likely to lack external efficacy, from 1997 to 2008 more Canadians lacked internal efficacy.

What can then be said about the impact of political marketing techniques on citizens' senses of efficacy? If there is such an effect, then the adoption of political marketing techniques appears to have produced more Canadians who have confidence in their parties instead of themselves. Furthermore, the total percentages of Canadians with low levels of efficacy – particularly external efficacy – are objectively low; with the exception of the 1997 election, the percentage of Canadians feeling low or very low levels of efficacy never exceeds 25 percent.

This result that the development of political marketing has been accompanied by fewer Canadians with low external rather than internal efficacy is surprising and counterintuitive, as politicians who rely on public opinion research, voter segmentation, and other marketing techniques are unlikely to be chained to clear policy positions or permeable to citizens' concerns. However, it may be the case that the adoption of marketing techniques has

FIGURE 14.1

Canadians lacking internal and external efficacy, 1997-2008

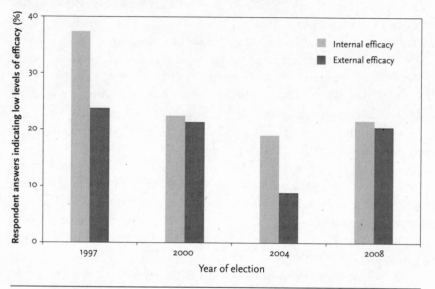

NOTE: For each statement, respondents were asked whether they strongly agree, somewhat agree, somewhat disagree, or strongly disagree. Internal efficacy: "Sometimes politics and government seem so complicated that a person like me can't really understand what's going on" and "People like me don't have any say about what the government does." External efficacy: "I don't think the government cares much what people like me think" and "Those elected to Parliament soon lose touch with the people." The figure summarizes the percentage of respondents giving answers that indicate low or very low levels of efficacy. These questions were not included in the 2006 CES.

created the perception that parties have opened themselves up to the concerns of citizens. This may be especially true in Canada, where the two historically dominant parties, the Conservatives and the Liberals, have never been associated with clear policy positions. When it comes to elite brokerage parties such as Canada's major national parties, it may be the case that focus groups and other marketing techniques have opened the party up to citizen input. And citizens themselves appear to know this.

However, this narrative should not be extended too far. It appears that the efficacy gap has tightened in recent elections. And it is also important to remember that the 1990s were a period of upheaval in Canadian politics, particularly in how the parties viewed themselves in relation to Canadian society and how they approached campaigning (Carty, Cross, and Young

2000). The efficacy gap may be attributed to the many other pressures facing Canadian politics at the time, not simply political marketing. It is clear that Canadian parties emerged from the 1990s with a greater willingness to embrace marketing techniques, and the efficacy gap in this period appears to be narrowing.

This chapter began by asking whether political marketing has empowered Canadian citizens. Put another way, this question might be, has political marketing enhanced Canadians' senses of internal efficacy? This does not appear to be the case. Canadians have had fairly steady levels of internal efficacy for some time – political marketing does not appear to have impacted internal efficacy positively or negatively. Political marketing techniques allow parties to reach out to Canadians, tune into their concerns, and formulate policy and electoral appeals in response to those concerns. However, the use of these techniques does appear to have seen an overall decrease in the number of Canadians with low or very low levels of external efficacy. Perhaps it is the case that political marketing has empowered Canadians by creating the perception that the use of such techniques has opened up parties and made them more responsive to citizens' wishes.

In order to explore further this uncertain verdict regarding the relationship between political marketing and citizen efficacy, it is necessary to explore findings in other similar democracies. Political marketing research has been conducted mostly in the United Kingdom and the United States – indeed, Scammell (1999, 730) argues that such techniques were used first and most extensively by the UK Conservative Party and the American New Right movement (see also Chapter 7). The question is what effect the use of such techniques has held for the efficacy of these states' citizens.

Lilleker (2005a) makes a powerful argument that the rebranding of the Labour brand in the United Kingdom and the use of marketing techniques by that party has led to a "democratic deficit." In particular, Lilleker draws on interview data to demonstrate that Labour, by focusing on "swingers," confused and in some cases alienated traditional Labour supporters, who were unfriendly to the new party brand developed during and after the 1997 election. Of primary importance is the impact of the party's rebranding exercise on the external efficacy of traditional Labour supporters: of those surveyed, 61 percent agreed that "people like me have no say in government actions" (Lilleker 2005a, 19). Lilleker demonstrates the negative impact that rebranding and the embrace of marketing techniques have exercised on the political efficacy of citizens, particularly party loyalists. The result was that party membership dropped from 420,000 after the 1997 election to 320,000 by mid-1999, a remarkable decline accompanied by a new-found listlessness in the party membership (Lees-Marshment and Lilleker 2005, 25). Moreover, the use of such techniques cannot be said to have helped Labour win, as victory in the 1997 and 2001 elections was "inevitable" (Lilleker 2005a, 17).

Has the embrace of marketing techniques by Canadian political parties led to a similar disenchantment on the part of party activists and loyalists? The Conservative Party and its predecessors – the Reform Party and the Canadian Alliance – demonstrate that exercises in rebranding have resulted in backlash among party loyalists. The transition from the Reform Party to the Canadian Alliance through the United Alternative process following the 1997 election was an explicit attempt at rebranding the party in order to appeal to a wider range of voters (see Chapter 5 by André Turcotte). In so doing, the party alienated a segment of its Reform Party supporters (Ellis 2005, 171-72). However, it is not clear that a significant segment of the party's supporters were disenchanted by the party's transition.

It is more difficult to detect backlash to the party's transition from the Alliance into the rebranded Conservative Party prior to the 2004 national election, and more difficult still to detect backlash in response to the party's moderation while in government. It is likely that since the Conservative Party, like the Liberal Party, allows activists to exercise significant freedoms in their constituency organizations, the response to rebranding exercises and marketing techniques has not been as pronounced as was the case in the Labour Party following the 1997 election.

It is certainly true that candidates in American elections employ political marketing techniques (for example, O'Shaughnessy 1990), but it is less clear that American parties can adopt market orientations, given the decentralized nature of their organizations. Nevertheless, Knuckey and Lees-Marshment (2005) apply the political marketing framework to the candidacy of George W. Bush prior to, during, and following the 2000 presidential campaign. In this case, the adoption of a marketing orientation helped the candidate. However, following the 2000 election, segmentation of the electorate by the Republican Party into sympathizers and non-sympathizers is likely to have contributed to significant polarization based on partisanship, state of residence, and religion versus secularism (see, for example, Abramowitz and Saunders 2005). In this case, the use of marketing techniques had overall negative consequences for the electorate.

A recurring theme in the literature on political marketing is the relationship between marketing and voter turnout. If marketing consists in part of engaging voters and allowing parties to connect with previously disenfranchised citizens, then it is reasonable to expect that voter turnout would in response increase or at least remain steady. But this has not been the case in the United Kingdom and the United States. For example, New Labour perfected its marketing techniques between the 1997 and 2001 elections, yet turnout markedly declined from 71.4 percent in 1997 to 59.4 percent in 2001. More damningly, turnout in Labour's "heartland constituencies" was a mere 24 percent (Lilleker 2005a, 18). Although turnout rebounded to 65 percent in the 2010 election, it is still significantly lower than was the case prior to Labour's first election win. Turnout in US presidential elections has not declined significantly, instead remaining steady, suggesting that parties' embrace of political marketing techniques has not led to the more synergistic relationship between electors and elected promised by proponents of the marketing approach. Indeed, a common criticism of the marketing approach in the American context relates to the impact of negative advertising on voter turnout, though this relationship is far from clear (Ansolabehere and Iyengar 1995; Wattenberg and Brians 1999).

In terms of turnout in Canada, the situation has not been significantly different from that of the United Kingdom and United States (on this point see Marland 2005, 59; also Chapter 3). From a 75.3 percent turnout rate in the 1984 general election, the turnout rate has steadily declined until just 58.8 percent of eligible Canadians turned out to vote in the 2008 election, with a slight rebound to 61.1% in 2011. Lilleker (2005a) argues that declining turnout in the United Kingdom can be traced back to the democratic deficit created in part by political marketing. Perhaps the same argument can be made with respect to Canada.

Implications for the Quality of Democracy

How does the quality of democracy change, if at all, when party elites embrace political marketing techniques? This concluding section draws together some of the tentative findings of this chapter on the relationship between political marketing and the efficacy of citizens.

First, however, it is important to note the crucial nature of citizens' efficacy for the healthy functioning of democracy. Internal efficacy is related to political participation and external efficacy is related to voting (Finkel

1985; 1987, 444). Given the importance of high rates of efficacy for the healthy functioning of democracies, we need to pinpoint the impact of the use of political marketing techniques on citizens' efficacy. If marketing does indeed empower Canadians, it should be lauded. But if the opposite is true, then scholars should question the consequences of political marketing techniques for the democratic vitality of the state.

This is a particularly valid consideration in Canada, where citizens' lack of interest in and engagement with the political process has long been bemoaned. Gidengil et al. (2004, 19) describe Canadians' interest in the political process as "middling": in the 2000 CES, respondents returned an average of 5.5 on a scale from zero to 10 for interest in politics generally. By 2008, that average had increased only slightly to 5.8 out of 10. Furthermore, few Canadians participate in Canadian politics by taking out memberships in parties, and those who do are not particularly committed to their parties (Cross and Young 2004). And, as already noted, voter turnout in Canadian federal elections is low.

Has the quality of Canadian democracy changed with parties' increasing use of political marketing techniques? This is, of course, a difficult question to answer with certainty. There are several theoretical reasons for suspecting that the use of marketing techniques by political parties has not affected the efficacy of Canadians, since Canada's brokerage parties have not traditionally been rooted in clear ideologies. However, the development of the efficacy gap does appear to suggest that marketing has resulted in Canadians who are less confident in their ability to affect politics, although this gap does appear to be correcting itself in more recent years. We should be open to the possibility that by adopting marketing techniques, Canada's traditionally elite brokerage parties have opened themselves up to input from citizens.

PART 4

Conclusion

15
Challenges for Democracy

Thierry Giasson, Jennifer Lees-Marshment, and Alex Marland

Political marketing is ubiquitous around the world, and technological advancements are spurring more sophisticated practices of monitoring, communicating with, and responding to the electorate. Canada is no exception to this. Political marketing pervades decision making, policy making, party organization, and government. This book has provided a rich insight into a wide range of political marketing activity, including the use of market research, its impact on leadership, strategy formation, communication, and delivery management. This concluding chapter synthesizes the findings to provide a perspective on Canadian political marketing as a whole so as to enable a comprehensive debate on how marketing and political marketers may be changing Canadian politics and democracy.

The Nature of the Political Market in Canada

Canada presents both similarities and differences with other Western liberal democracies such as the United States and United Kingdom. Socially and politically, it has experienced significant transformations in recent decades, with electoral volatility rising and positive evaluation of parties and politicians falling. Given that party attachments are flexible, parties have a realistic prospect of being able to attract new support if they design a product offering that addresses the needs and wants of those most likely to consider switching votes. However, the Canadian market also has strong regional and linguistic cleavages; different regions have different political priorities and may want different political products – but a party can offer only one. A political party has to consider traditional supporters as well as new ones or it risks losing its core constituency, and it thus cannot move its positioning too far away from its base. Parties also have to work harder to communicate with target voters who have low levels of political awareness. Market segmentation may therefore become a more important political marketing tool in Canada, at a basic level, to understand the different cleavages, but also as a potential means to create new segments that can cut across regional differences without sending conflicting messages.

Canadian political parties need to adapt and work within the geographic clustering in the marketplace in order to be effective, whether this involves designing policy proposals to reflect regional variations in elector preferences, or perhaps pitching to metropolitan, urban, suburban, or rural values. Using technology, Canadian practitioners have identified new target groups that cut across such physical divides, such as Tim Hortons coffee drinkers, Canadian Tire shoppers, and the hockey moms of suburbia. This may mean greater resources need to be spent on voter profiling, segmentation, micro-targeting, and get-out-the-vote efforts. The nature of Canadian media and academia is such that observers give more focus to tactical political marketing such as public relations exercises, pseudo-events, debate preparation, and message control (with terms such as "spin," "on message," and "damage control") rather than more sophisticated strategic political marketing, such as segmentation and positioning. This may encourage greater use of marketing tools rather than of concepts. Overall, we would therefore expect to see a wide range of political marketing practice in Canadian politics but also potential tensions as to how to reconcile the conflicting demands of different market segments, of core and target voters, of listening and leading the public, and of repositioning but also maintaining authenticity.

The Use of Political Marketing in Canada

Market intelligence and marketing strategy are used in Canadian politics in varying ways. Political parties adopt a range of strategies, including all three product, sales, and market orientations, and they have utilized market research to different degrees to inform communication, the allocation of research, positioning, and sometimes, the design of the political product. With significant political changes occurring after the formative 1993 federal election, we have seen considerable progress in the use of political marketing in Canadian politics, and yet a constant preoccupation with persuasion tactics.

The 1993 election marked the ushering in of a new party system in Canadian federal politics, meaning that political parties had entered a period of transformative change whereby competitive pressures would force them to undergo introspection, rebuilding, and innovation. The technological sophistication of that election now seems to represent a bygone era, what with the Liberal war room scoring a competitive edge by installing extra phone lines and coordinating the broadcast faxing of its news releases. The collection and analysis of market intelligence was likewise primitive compared with today's technology. In 1993, the NDP used public opinion research to inform communication only by testing slogans and messaging, whereas the Liberals used research, including "oppo," to inform strategy. By comparison, the governing PCs succumbed to public pressure to withdraw negative advertising that had passed research tests. In contrast, the Reform Party went ahead with policies that it knew would lack pan-Canadian appeal because it believed in the resonance of its policies with its core supporters, indicating a product orientation. However, when Reform wanted to broaden its base of support in British Columbia and Alberta to other areas of Canada, the party adopted a more positive attitude toward market research, resulting in the rebranding of the party as the Canadian Alliance, and eventually as the Conservative Party. This evolution to a sales-oriented and then to a market-oriented party (albeit one with ideological underpinnings) involved using methods such as benchmark surveys, strategic polls, focus groups, segmentation, targeting, competition analysis, test marketing, and voter profiling. The change in approach drew some internal opposition, as is typical of parties that move toward the market-oriented model, such as UK Labour under Neil Kinnock and then Tony Blair in the 1990s, and this limited the effectiveness of the tools somewhat. But after the 2004 general election, Conservative strategists brought all market intelligence under the party and hired marketing staff, including Patrick Muttart, who used it proactively to test policies and inform communication, and adopted micro-targeting (also known as hyper-segmentation). This responded to the values held broadly by the median voter at the time (for example, cleaning up Ottawa), but focused research and communication on a tiny segment of the electorate: an estimated 500,000 electors out of 23 million.

Although it is difficult to determine the causal factors for electoral outcomes, political marketing suggests that the greater the use of and responsiveness to research, the greater success that parties have in winning support, just as in commerce, where market research is used to inform smarter business decisions. Increasing commitment to marketing professionalism and the move away from social conservatism was one of the key factors of success in the evolution of the Reform–Canadian Alliance Parties between the 1993 and 2000 elections, and for the Conservative Party in the four elections from 2004 to 2011, when it used market intelligence in a more market-oriented approach, albeit without shedding the party leader's conservative and libertarian ideological leanings. As it created a more coherent message, the party also used segmentation to both maintain core voter support and reach out to new potential markets to be able to win power. Segmentation and research have affected policy focus, with the Conservatives developing policies intended to appeal to working people, families, married women, and Roman Catholics. Voter profiling identified those voters who had a propensity to vote Conservative, even stereotyping and giving names – such as Dougie, Eunice, and Zoë – to micro-targets so as to achieve buy-in within the party for research-based decisions that focused on targeting segments of the elector market while ignoring others.

Canadian practitioners see market research as being valuable in politics because it provides accurate information that politicians can then use when making decisions; it also helps to ensure that politicians talk about what the public – not the political or media elite – is concerned with. The data need to be of high quality and rigorous, of course, and when any data collection innovations are imported from other countries, they need to be relevant to the Canadian situation. Market research is used in a range of ways: to inform politicians of public demands, to help identify regional differences, and to pinpoint what drives voters, including their key values. This informs position, policies, and communication. However, research is also used to help polit-icians change those demands or views, or to understand opposition and find a way to move opinion toward progress and development on important issues. There is also awareness among Canadian consultants that if politicians change their positions too much, they can lose support for not being authentic and genuine. Politicians, after all, are humans who are obviously less malle-able than commercial products are, especially in the case of an experienced rather than new candidate. Therefore, a balance is important. Strategists who have worked with Canada's political leaders, including heads of government, recalled how market research has limitations. Public opinion research (POR) has to be interpreted and does not always suggest a final decision; it can only inform the latter.

It is not just political parties and politicians that utilize market research but also government departments, which commission studies to inform policy development and decisions. Health Canada, for example, makes substantial use of POR, including surveys and focus groups. As with its use by politicians, it has multiple objectives, including instrumentally to directly contribute to decision making, and strategically to communicate, justify, and promote policy. Market research is also used to track trends in policy and to measure progress after policy implementation, to market government services, to change behaviour through social marketing, and to demarket (i.e., reduce demand for services). It can be also used as a means to enable dialogue between policy makers and citizens about priorities for future health care.

Voter profiling helps parties build databases that can be used in communication, especially direct mail, including electronic mail. Communication is geared to suit the different market segments, regions, and cultural communities in Canada with the leaflets and ads conducted by parties in both official languages. Smaller niche parties obviously appeal to their particular markets, like the Bloc Québécois using slogans such as *"Ici, c'est le Bloc"* (Here, it's the Bloc) and *"Parlons QC"* (Let's speak about Quebec) to convey its political uniqueness. The Bloc's successful positioning as defenders of Quebeckers' interests for nearly two decades until it was overwhelmed by the NDP's "orange wave" in 2011 speaks to the difficulties faced by political marketers who cannot "solve" the depth of support for a party that concentrates its efforts on a geographically concentrated market. It also illustrates the need for parties to respond to elector desires for change. As the Progressive Conservative Party and NDP discovered in 1993 and the Bloc found out in 2011, the preferences of target markets must be constantly monitored, and party elites must respond to changing market needs and wants.

Effective campaigns build on strong and clear organizational structures. This means that technological knowledge and skill are important ingredients in electoral success in Canada. Control is also an aspect of this. The Harper government created a highly centralized communications system and attempted to control and formalize how ministers, parliamentarians, and staff communicated publicly, reducing media access. Moreover, the Conservatives sought new oversight of POR. The aim has been to reach regional and local media and to communicate successful delivery – both goals being part of a political marketing approach. However, as with campaigning tools, this has resulted in an increase in tactical rather than strategic communication.

Political marketing doesn't just offer politicians a means of understanding and connecting with electors; it encourages them to be in touch. Relationship marketing seeks to develop a long-term connection with citizens, which builds trust and loyalty. In an era of permanent campaigning, this has involved personal interactions, such as town hall meetings, or the use of technology to reach out, such as direct mail. Newer technologies are enabling personalized interactions through social networking websites, file sharing, and micro-blogging, whereby two-way relationships are cultivated. Pessimists lament that social capital is fragile because people increasingly interact with others who live outside their communities and whom they may never meet. An optimist's view, on the other hand, may point to e-democracy and e-engagement as signs of an emerging deliberative democracy.

Technology can only support, not replace, the democratic value of people interacting with each other in person, such as by having coffee house chats about politics. In Canada, the people's coffee shop, Tim Hortons, offers politicians a physical place to convey a symbolic relationship with citizens and to position themselves as onside with the masses as compared, say, with being associated with the bourgeoisie's fondness for Starbucks. The Tim Hortons restaurant franchise has become a part of branding communication whereby politicians can place themselves within a social sphere that conveys values that appeal to the public, such as community and belonging. Increasingly, political parties and their leaders, governments, and interest groups all come to think of themselves as brands, the compilation of all of their communications activity, and their image positioning vis-à-vis competitors. Branding is not in itself a panacea, but a damaged brand does take some time to regain public confidence. In the case of political parties, it may take several election cycles to earn favourable media and, most importantly, require that a leader be committed to political marketing principles.

Canadian interest groups also use political marketing, and they may take different approaches. Business-related organizations and trade unions tend toward a stronger market orientation than community-based interest groups do. Business groups and organized labour get their members more involved in the development of the message, whereas social advocacy groups focus their efforts on the messages sent to their members to increase their loyalty and are driven more by their values and ideals. Research is simply used in strategic communication. Overall, as with political parties, most Canadian interest groups are sales-oriented and focus on using marketing to persuade.

The last aspect of political marketing is delivery management. The Conservative Party of Canada has focused on this, creating specific priorities before the 2005-6 election campaign, and successfully acted on two of these priorities (government reform and tax reductions) quickly after getting into power, followed by steps on two others (tough on crime and child care allocations). However, the remaining one (health care) was more of a challenge, which highlights the practical problems with creating contract or pledge-like promises before getting into government and the need to adjust the product to make it achievable – especially any pledges that involve intergovernmental relations. One response to failing to deliver such promises was simply to be honest about it, to explain why delivery was not achieved, and to invite the public to judge the governing party as to whether that was reasonable or not. The Conservatives' delivery success was possibly helped along by its status as a minority government, given that they had to reach out to opposition parties and their supporters to enable legislation and delivery. These decisions were reinforced with effective communications, such as by using visible symbols and appropriate locations, with the prime minister slapping a bright blue "5%" GST sticker onto a cash register in a retail store where the initial promise to reduce the sales tax was made.

Political Marketing and the Canadian Party System

The Americanization and "presidentialization" of Canadian politics have been furthered by the political marketing evolution. A credible political party seeking to form government no longer designs and promotes a political product without the benefit of opinion research. In the brokerage and pan-Canadian party systems, a big tent party may have been contented to under-stand electors' viewpoints at a macro level, such as impressions about the parties, leaders, and major policies and issues. In the post-brokerage era, pol-itical marketers develop a complex understanding of the electorate that is informed by identifying clusters of electors based on profiles of their values and beliefs rather than foremost on the geographical region they inhabit. Market intelligence also includes non-political consumer behaviours, such as which retail shops and restaurants a citizen visits, as the same sophisticated data modelling used in the commercial marketplace is applied with a pol-itical lens. With political marketing, a federal party leader is less beholden to the demands of a premier or regional minister, for – unless conceding to those demands is likely to deliver votes from the targeted segments of the electorate and/or marginal seats – the leader has some reassurance that it is potentially more profitable to withstand such political pressure and to stay focused on the implementation of a research-based strategy.

The role of political marketing in sustaining the period of successive federal minority governments from 2004 to 2011, and then enabling the Conservatives to win a majority of seats, should not be underestimated. Canadian political parties have, to varying degrees, used political marketing to solidify their base. It has become very difficult for opponents to convert partisans, whose loyalty is cultivated through targeted communications, and it is thus quite challenging to attract new supporters. The battleground is, perhaps more than ever, floating voters: those whose partisan attachments are flexible and/or who are undecided. With political marketing, parties can simultaneously reinforce their core support and nibble away at the edges of their opponents' support by using research to introduce targeted policy proposals, to reposition the organization and leader's image, and to promote it all using messages and media designed to resonate with segments of the electorate. There is homogeneity in a political environment where there is widespread agreement on many major public issues. This sees political parties promote median voter positions on issues that otherwise seem at odds with their usual image positioning, such as the NDP advocating tax cuts while the Conservatives promote stronger public health care, the Bloc avoiding public discussion about separatism, or the Liberals endorsing military intervention in Afghanistan rather than peacekeeping. Leadership variables and heuristic cues become more pronounced, as does balancing the internal ideological pressures of party membership with the wants and needs of narrow market segments. Researching and monitoring electors' viewpoints, and using media technology to communicate with them, is an increasingly competitive business.

Our knowledge of political marketing can help us reflect on what others have concluded about the state of Canadian party politics. We now know that Carty, Cross, and Young (2000, 211) were correct in predicting that the post-1993 party system would feature the Conservative and Liberal Parties redefining themselves. In the past decade, we have seen these parties undergo internal and external renewal through rebranding, repositioning, and reinvigoration. The rules of the game have changed, requiring parties to adapt to significant fundraising restrictions that place an emphasis on mobilizing grassroots donations while responding to the monetary incentive of winning the votes that were used to calculate quarterly allowances. Likewise, governance has changed and is becoming ever more deliberative with the maturation of e-politics. Although Canadian party politics is no longer as regionalized as it was in the 1990s, nor are political parties as diverse or democratized as Carty, Cross, and Young (2000, 222-27) forecast, we have seen in this book that their predictions of a fragmented electorate and of parties guided by professional political marketers has materialized. We likewise have every reason to believe that the professionalization exhibited by the Harper Conservatives, itself inspired by political marketing in other countries, will trickle over to the other Canadian parties, as well as to market leaders and challengers in the provinces.

Canadian Political Marketing in Comparative Context

The growing use and importance of market intelligence in Canadian politics follows global trends, in particular the move toward greater use of voter profiling and segmentation as seen in the United States since 2004 and the United Kingdom since 2005. We do note that global tools are adapted to the Canadian market and that there is limited political marketing innovation in Canada. Although there is a strong literature in political science on Americanization and the import of US political consultants to countries in the rest of the world (Johnson 2007; Medvic 2001; Plasser and Plasser 2002; Thurber and Nelson 2000), not all influence in Canadian politics has been directly from the United States. For instance, Muttart, who has advised the Conservative Party's campaign strategy, took ideas such as identifying and responding to core public values, and focusing on micro-segments, from Australia's Liberals, as well as older examples from other right-wing parties appealing to the middle class, such as the 1979 Margaret Thatcher Conservatives. Indeed, although Canadian practitioners are globally aware, they take ideas from a range of countries and are aware of the need for a "local lens" when taking ideas back to Canada. As such, political marketing in Canada follows international trends in its own unique national version. Although the American influence on politics is formidable, Canadian practitioners do look for tools from a range of countries, notably those with parliamentary systems, and pick out different elements to suit the Canadian market.

In addition, Canadian practitioners are also utilizing market research to inform a range of decision making and leadership positions, taking an approach that has developed beyond the market-driven orientation of early Tony Blair/New Labour and Bill Clinton's New Democrats to one where vision is also a part of political marketing strategy. This development is just starting to appear in comparative research, and thus Canada would seem to be very much part of this maturing of political marketing practice. Political leaders and advisers in Canada use market analysis more proactively to identify current public concerns as well as to explore ways to change opinion and achieve change. Market analysis results are not just taken and followed: they are interpreted and considered in relation to policy, leadership, and party goals. The use of market intelligence is thus more nuanced and complex now.

Strategically, the same variations of product, sales, and market orientation are in Canada as elsewhere. In terms of communication, locally driven means are favoured, however, with the Conservative government seeking to communicate through local and regional rather than national media, and politicians from all parties placing themselves in mainstream Canada's coffee shop to brand themselves as being in touch with the common folk. The same growth in focus on delivery both pre- and post-election has occurred in Canada as in Australia and the United Kingdom, as well as in the United States under Barack Obama.

The Implications of Political Marketing for Canadian Democracy

Political marketing is said to have both positive and negative implications for democracy. The actual democratic outcome of the process depends on the way that political organizations choose to use the tools and concepts it offers. Simply using it to sell the political product is unlikely to help broker a strong, sustainable, and positive citizen-government relationship. This is particularly the case if we accept that most market leaders and followers are self-interested actors rather than unselfish heroes, and that they will therefore use those methods that are most likely to propel them to power, including negative communications. However, a more market-oriented approach, where citizens' needs are answered and where the political marketer looks to build trust and confidence with citizens, could theoretically combat political apathy and dissatisfaction. Conclusions presented in many chapters of this book and elsewhere indicate that Canadian political parties and actors still tend to be viewed negatively. This poses a problem for democracy, given that these organizations are "the central linkage of a democratic system between the society and its governing institutions" (Carty, Cross, and Young 2000, 212). If all Canadian political parties are using political marketing, and yet most citizens still express distrust in them, then how is political marketing helpful to democracy?

Again, the answer to this question resides with the democratic enhancement possibilities of political marketing done in a market-oriented way. As a theoretical model, market orientation presents the opportunity to craft a political product that responds to electors' demands, which may be beneficial for citizens whose needs and interests are therefore better represented. The process is also conceived as an ongoing enterprise during which political actors engage in a conversation with citizens by implementing and maintaining consultation and co-production in the product definition or redefinition. If branding and positioning are used effectively to create differentiated products, disaffection with politics might be reduced. Segmentation could be used to identify the needs of minorities that have previously been neglected, which would be particularly important in a multicultural society like Canada, which experiences ideological, constitutional, and regional tensions, and where participation in elections has been declining over the last two decades.

Nevertheless, if these principles of market orientation are not followed during campaigns or maintained once in government and product delivery is not ensured, citizens' disillusionment with politics will be encouraged.

Similarly, interest groups adhering to a market orientation could become more democratic. Doing so would entail being more sensitive to the needs of current and potential members but also incurring organizational changes in response to public opinion in order to increase the group's support among the population and its influence with policy makers. Pressure groups would also encourage greater transparency and less reliance on lobbying behind the scenes, and they would hold the potential to help maintain strong civil associations to counteract the power of the state.

The use of market intelligence for political purposes is also said to have implications for democracy. On one hand, qualitative and quantitative data help politicians understand and reach voters more effectively, and they may provide a means for electors to get their views across to elites continuously instead of just during elections. However, the concern expressed by Savigny (2008a) that micro-targeting and segmentation may lead to some electors' views becoming more important than others because they encourage elites to focus on a small group in society that may affect the election is also potentially true for Canada and was conceded by the Canadian practitioners who have engaged in this type of work. Furthermore, the individualistic rationality postulate inherent to political marketing theory also poses a problem to many scholars.

Critics say that any expected democratic enhancements are linked to a simplistic and idealistic view of the actions of citizens and, mostly, of political actors involved in the political marketing process. First, as critical theory would suggest, considering political elites as genuinely altruistic or inherently preoccupied with the fluctuating state of democratic vitality is nothing short of naive. Political actors use political marketing tools and tactics to gain and retain power. Electoral tactics too often trump deliberation, consultation, and relationship building with citizens. A true market orientation is not implemented. Second, the presupposed rationality of citizens presented by political marketing theorists to justify the expected democratic benefits might be off the mark too. Rational choice imposes that citizens are able to identify their needs, are able to make a near-perfect evaluation of the cost-benefit implications of their choices, and have access to and use appropriate information to make a decision. Canadians have a much greater opportunity to access information about politics and public policy than they ever have before, but their decision-making process may not fit the economic rationality model.

When Canadians are polled, or when they participate in focus groups put together by parties in order to gather market data, do they know where their interests lie? Do they inevitably prioritize imagery over political substance? What do they make of the larger Canadian common good? Moreover, there remains the dilemma of how to reconcile political wants with policy needs when these conflict, as they often do.

Then again, any apprehension that such research is of low quality or used for nefarious purposes seems unfounded in Canada: practitioners are aware of the need for it to be accurate and appropriate. Furthermore, the way that market intelligence is used varies, and thus it does not always lead to politicians pandering to public opinion. Such data can be used to help sell an unpopular position, to understand opposition, and to adjust the original position, as well as to change in response to citizen viewpoints. Listening does not mean following at all times, and, as such, caution should be taken before supporting claims that political marketing is going to be damaging to democracy by leaving no room for leadership. This more positive analysis reflects a very recent maturation of political practice, but we cannot claim that Canadian political marketing is inherently good for democracy, either. Rather, there is understanding among political elites of the need for a balance between political leaders listening to public views, and then taking appropriate decisions, which can include following but also overriding citizens' demands. Market research can elevate electors' concerns, and politicians may design a market-oriented product in response to those concerns, but research can also guide leaders in how to introduce new ideas to the public. In this way, political marketing could therefore be used both to win elections and to enhance democracy.

What adds further support to this argument is that government opinion research is also used in multifaceted ways. Public opinion research can provide valuable information about citizens' preferences, their potential to accept policy that intervenes in their lives, how they are likely to behave, and how effective policy may be in improving a problem. It can thus help to ensure that policies align with public priorities and give voice to citizens. It helps increase the likelihood that policies will actually work when implemented, and it can even make them work better or more quickly. Nevertheless, this does not mean that it is always democratically positive; there can appear to be a fine line between government POR and partisan POR. There are occasionally questions that measure the public's support for government action on an issue and how it assesses blame, and research is also used to create communication to justify government decisions against public opinion. This is also true of government communication, such as when the governing Conservatives attempted, beginning in late 2008, to portray a positive image of their plans to manage the global economic recession and were criticized for using party colours, logos, and labels on the government website and advertising that would promote Canada's Economic Action Plan and stimulus spending. Such situations are preoccupying. Is blurring the line of governance and partisanship good for democracy?

Nevertheless, in opinion research terms, the final policy product can become a mix of public and government preferences, which suggests, as with partisan research, that there is more balanced use of market intelligence, and in this way it can become a tool of democratic governance. The thinking behind political marketing – the concepts, rather than the tools – is perhaps crucial for a more mature, responsible, and thus positive form of political marketing to emerge. One concern is that the growing need for technological innovation and segmentation tools, combined with the centralization and control of government over communication strategies, will encourage reliance on marketing tactics rather than a market-orientation philosophy. This would not connect governments to citizens effectively or ensure that leaders respond appropriately to voter demands. A full market orientation imposes a way of thinking, not just doing, and an appropriate judgment in response to research, not just good research itself. Furthermore, the emphasis on product delivery in the political marketing framework can enhance democracy, as it may revive electors' faith that political parties can be trusted to follow through on their commitments once elected. This is where the process of building trust and developing confidence with citizens should begin. Based on what political parties offer during a campaign, governments are given mandates by citizens with the understanding that a governing party will need some flexibility in order to respond to emerging situations. Governments must then reasonably deliver the expected product once in office unless there is room for them to change position when necessary and it is justifiable. Failing to do so will contribute to democratic malaise.

The impact of political marketing is also affected by the relationship between the citizen and the state, and thus more deliberative market research, or consultation, may help expand the one-way information occurring behind closed doors through formal market intelligence into a transparent two-way communication. Citizens of this country have had fairly steady levels of internal efficacy (the perception of their potential impact on politics) for some time. Therefore, political marketing does not appear to have affected internal efficacy positively or negatively, though there has been an overall decrease in the number of Canadians with low levels of external efficacy (their perception of the responsiveness of governments to their needs). Therefore, political marketing could be seen to have empowered Canadians by creating the perception that the use of such techniques has opened up parties and made them more responsive to citizens' wishes. The more market-oriented that Canada's political elites become, the more open they are to input from citizens, which could theoretically have positive implications for democratic life. Yet, when thinking of the potential for democratic empowerment of political marketing, we must also consider the association between marketing and electoral participation. If marketing consists, in part, of engaging voters and allowing parties to connect with previously disenfranchised citizens, then it is reasonable to expect that voter turnout would increase in response or at least remain steady. In Canada, as elsewhere, there has been a worrying trend of declining electoral participation in elections, as indicated by turnout figures. Lilleker (2005a) argues that declining turnout in the United Kingdom can be traced back to the democratic deficit created in part by political marketing. Perhaps the same argument can be made with respect to Canada. This conclusion raises an interesting alternative hypothesis to democratic malaise to consider, that of the "marketing malaise." Is the diffusion of the practice of political marketing by political actors and institutions contributing to citizens' uneasiness, distrust, and cynicism toward politics in general and liberal representative democracy in particular? How aware are Canadians of the implementation of these strategic practices by parties and governments? Regardless of the extent of the public's awareness of political parties' selective use of political marketing, is its practice affecting Canadians' evaluations of the political system?

Thus far, the Canadian news media, in its role as a relationship mediator between citizens and their political institutions, has taken some notice of political marketing practices in parties and has relayed the information to Canadians during electoral campaigns. True, the term "political marketing" is hardly ever mentioned by journalists, but they do regularly report on campaign strategy and tactics. The implication for democracy is unfavourable, given that such media coverage tends to be negative. This reflects the lack of awareness that political journalists have about the potential positive aspects of political marketing but also their rightful concern about political parties' attempts at persuasion rather than responsiveness.

Conclusion

Overall, we can arrive at the conclusion that political marketing is being used in Canada, that it is changing the nature of politics, and that this has implications for Canadian democracy. Whether such change is positive or not in democratic terms depends partly on how political marketing is implemented by political actors and institutions. The utilization of market research provides elites with a greater understanding of the public, but, of course, they have to decide how to use that knowledge. Communication is still used to persuade the public, and research can help make it more effective and ensure that it reaches the right people through segmentation. This can include unpalatable strategies and tactics that include weakening the brand values of opponents through attack ads that not only aggravate a hostile political environment but also deflect public attention from evaluating the substance of the sponsor's offering. Nevertheless, research also informs politicians' decisions and contributes to their responses to public demands. This can help elevate electors' role in the democratic system, which is a positive development as long as there is still room for politicians to make necessary decisions against public opinion and to explain their reasons for doing so. Overall, there may be a growing sense of a much closer dialogue and connection between citizens and government in Canada through the use of political marketing, or its use could in fact be entrenching distances. A maturation of political marketing practice means that, in time, political actors should be able to reduce their emphasis on salesmanship and pandering as they move toward more of a deliberative, dialogue-seeking citizen-state relationship.

Glossary

Attack ad: Negative advertising that emphasizes the personal characteristics of an opponent, rather than just political or policy aspects. A notorious Canadian example is the Jean Chrétien face ads of the 1993 campaign.

Branding: The overall perception of a product or organization, but less tangible and specific than the product, which is often connected with familiar logos or slogans that evoke meanings, ideas, and associations in the consumer. In politics, branding involves creating a trustful relationship with electors that can be sustained over the long term. A Canadian example of rebranding occurred after the late 2003 merger of the Canadian Alliance party with the federal Progressive Conservative Party to become the "new" Conservative Party.

Brokerage politics: A Canadian term for successful big tent parties that embody a pluralistic catch-all approach to appeal to the median voter and to broker regional tensions, particularly those emanating from Quebec. This involves adopting centrist policies and electoral coalitions to satisfy the short-term preferences of electors who are not located on the ideological fringes.

Canada Elections Act: Legislation that is intended to encourage fairness, facilitate democratic access, and limit excesses during federal election campaigns. Aspects that influence political marketing include the Register of Electors, the rules surrounding communications, and financing and spending regulations.

Canadian Election Study (CES): A publicly available dataset of Canadian attitudes and opinions. Survey data are collected at each federal general election.

Citizen efficacy: Citizens' feelings that individuals can bring about political and social change.

Democratic malaise: Reduced civic engagement, interest, and confidence in politics and government exhibited by electors. This is often measured through declines in voter turnout and fluctuations in levels of public trust toward political and government actors and institutions.

Direct marketing: The precise communication of messages directly to individuals, thereby bypassing other filters such as the mass media, conducted by a range of communication methods, including direct mail, telemarketing, direct dialogues, personalized emails, or texts to portable communications devices. Direct marketing relies on lists of consumers generated by companies that collect data on individuals on a range of factors, such as geographical location, age, and lifestyle, and is often used in conjunction with segmentation. In politics, informal lists have been generated via door-to-door or phone canvassing that records voting intentions, but the process is becoming more complex and commercial lists are often bought, or databases used, to build up voter profiles. List management software is often employed, which in Canada tends to draw on the Register of Electors.

Election platform/manifesto: A document identifying a political party's commitments and policy proposals that, if the party forms government, will be used to guide the government's agenda. A notable Canadian example is the Liberal red book.

Election turnout: The proportion of registered electors, such as those on the Register of Electors, who voted in an election. Over time, turnout has been trending downward in Canada.

Franchising: Permission granted to a local unit to represent the central organization responsible for most strategic and tactical decisions, including branding. The centre provides equipment, coordinates staff training, manages communications, and offers head office support. A Canadian political example is an election candidate or elected official who is authorized by the party leader to represent the New Democratic Party. This should not be confused with "the franchise," which refers to the right to vote.

Get out the vote (GOTV): Mobilization strategies and tactics designed to ensure that supporters will turn out to cast a ballot on polling day. GOTV uses segmentation and voter profiling to identify who to target, and direct marketing is often employed to key segments.

Horserace journalism: The tendency of news media to prioritize reporting on the latest opinion poll and on the market leader.

Hypersegmentation: see *Micro-targeting.*

Inter-election period: The time between official election campaign periods. In Canada, the inter-election period, unlike campaign periods, is not regulated by extraordinary limitations on fundraising activities, spending, or political communications.

Internet marketing: The use of digital technologies, including the web, mobile devices, and email, to achieve marketing objectives. Electronic communications tactics include websites, e-newsletters, texting, social networking, online file sharing, wikis, social bookmarking, and microblogging. In political marketing, this is sometimes referred to as e-marketing, but it involves more than just online communication. Instead, concepts such as market orientation and relationship marketing are added so that the message suits the receiver, not just the producer; enables two-way communication between political elites and the public; and builds a long-term relationship.

Market challenger: A political candidate or party that has less public support than the market leader does but that is not satisfied as a runner-up and aspires to become the market leader.

Market-driven: A heavy reliance on consultation as opposed to dialogue, such as relying on polling data as a proxy for market demand.

Market follower: A political candidate or party with less public support than a market challenger but that is not sufficiently competitive to be positioned to replace the market leader.

Market intelligence: Empirical data about the political marketplace and public views, also called "market research." The collection of market intelligence involves quantitative and qualitative methods such as polls, opinion surveys, focus groups, role play, co-creation, and consultation, as well as analysis of existing public data such as census data and election records. Politicians and political parties rely on market intelligence to decide on issue priorities, develop communication strategies, and help present themselves as the most competent to address those issues.

Market leader: The political candidate or party with the most public support, as determined by vote share in the last election, seat count in the legislature, and/or standing in recent public opinion polls.

Market nicher: A political candidate or party that has a small but dedicated base of public support and that defends the priorities of this base over broader market growth. An excellent example is the Bloc Québécois.

Market positioning: The use of market segmentation and analysis of the competition to indicate that candidates and parties can occupy a distinctive and superior place in the political market from which they can attract support.

Market research: see *Market intelligence.*

Market-oriented party (MOP): A political party that actively engages in efforts to identify and incorporate electors' concerns and priorities into the design of the party's product offerings, using market intelligence to understand those concerns before finalizing politician decisions. A MOP therefore engages in far more consultation and dialogue with the electorate than POPs or SOPs do.

Median voter: An elector whose views are positioned in the political mainstream, or centre, rather than the ideological fringes of the political left or right.

Micro-targeting: A strategic use of resources designed to focus efforts on small segments of the electorate, uncovered through market intelligence, whose socio- and geo-demographic profiles indicate a propensity for supporting the sponsor; sometimes called hypersegmentation. It relies on complex voter profiling or databases. A Canadian example is the Conservatives' use of micro-policies such as boutique tax credits targeted at construction workers and truck drivers.

Narrowcasting: The selection of media communications that is most likely to reach targeted market segments. A Canadian example is the Conservatives seeking to reach targeted groups by advertising on The Sports Network (TSN) instead of via the broader mass media.

Partisanship: A person's psychological ties to a political party. Every party has a core of strong partisans who may or may not publicly self-identify as such.

Permanent campaigning: Sustained electioneering after the conclusion of an election campaign and throughout the inter-election period. In the Canadian parliamentary system of government, this is more prevalent during a period of minority government because of the proximity to, and uncertainty of, the next election campaign.

Policy marketing: The use of marketing to develop and promote policy packages to citizens, as well as to encourage compliance.

Political advertising: Paid political communications, such as a newspaper ad, billboard, radio commercial, TV spot or website, whereby the sponsor controls all aspects of the communication.

Political advisers: People who provide political advice on the daily decisions made by elected officials and non-governmental organizations in relation to their potential impact on public opinion. In Canadian politics, advisers tend to be party insiders whom the party leader trusts and who are on the party payroll, are a member of caucus, or are employed in the leader's or a parliamentarian's office. An example is a senator who doubles as a fundraiser or campaign co-chair. See also *Political consultants.*

Political consultants: For-hire professionals such as communications experts, advertising agencies, direct marketing and fundraising specialists, and opinion researchers who may or may not have a proprietary relationship with a political party. Political consultants are common in the United States, but they are less common in the parliamentary system of government because of the infrequency of elections. In Canada, they include outside experts who provide advice to the party leadership circle, sometimes on a pro bono basis. Consultants are also hired by government departments and by non-governmental organizations such as interest groups. Examples include pollsters, image consultants, and lobbyists.

Political marketing: The application of business marketing concepts to the practice and study of politics and government. With political marketing, a political organization uses business techniques to inform and shape its strategic behaviours that are designed to satisfy citizens' needs and wants. Strategies and tools include branding, e-marketing, delivery, focus groups, GOTV, internal marketing, listening exercises, opposition research, polling, public relations, segmentation, strategic product development, volunteer management, voter-driven communication, voter expectation management, and voter profiling.

Product-oriented party (POP): A party that employs a marketing strategy that is guided by the assumption that electors will recognize the normative value of the party's ideas and so will vote for it. Little consideration is given to gathering and using market intelligence to design or communicate the party's product offering.

Public opinion research (POR): The collection of intelligence from a sample of the population designed to measure the public's views, such as on issues, policies, leaders, and parties. The most common form of POR is opinion surveys and focus groups, which can be purchased on a customized or omnibus basis.

Register of Electors: A list of eligible voters maintained by Elections Canada and that includes an elector's name, sex, date of birth, and address. Although it is foremost used for election administration purposes, it is also available to political parties, elected officials, and election candidates for communications purposes.

Relationship marketing: The use of marketing to build customer relationships and long-term associations that are sustained through commitment, loyalty, mutual benefit, and trust.

Sales-oriented party (SOP): A party that relies on the use of market intelligence to design strategies for selling its product offerings to targeted segments of the electorate. Emphasis is placed on research for advertising and message design as opposed to the design of the party's actual product offering.

Segmentation: Division of individuals into new groups, to allow more efficient targeting of resources, and also creation of new segments, such as ethnic minorities or seniors, as society evolves. Segments can be targeted by policy, communication, or GOTV, or to encourage greater volunteer activity. See also *Micro-targeting.*

Single member plurality (SMP): The electoral system in which the candidate with the plurality of votes in an electoral district is the winner. This is also known as first-past-the-post in recognition that the winner needs just one more vote than the runner-up. In Canadian elections, this tends to exaggerate the seat counts of regional-based niche parties as compared with their total share of the vote overall.

War room: The nucleus of a campaign team's headquarters, often staffed by a small task force dedicated to information management and rapid response.

References

Abad, Mercedes, and Ophelia Ramirez. 2008. "Polling in Developing Democracies – the Case of the Philippines." In *Public Opinion Polling in a Globalized World*, ed. Marita Carbello and Ulf Hjelmar, 267-80. Berlin: Springer-Verlag.

Abramowitz, Alan, and Kyle Saunders. 2005. "Why Can't We All Just Get Along? The Reality of a Polarized America." *The Forum* 3(2): 1-22. DOI: 10.2202/1540-8884. 1076.

Adams, Michael. 2003. *Fire and Ice: The United States, Canada and the Myth of Converging Values*. Toronto: Penguin.

Advertising Age. 2010. "A World of Inspirational Problem-Solving, Savvy Brands and Smart Marketing." http://adage.com/globalnews/.

Alford, Robert. 1963. *Party and Society: The Anglo-American Democracies*. Chicago: Rand-McNally.

All, David, and Jerome Armstrong. 2009. "Ten Ways to Use Facebook to Get Your Message Out." *Politics*, August 1, 18-19. http://www.politicsmagazine.com/.

Andrews, Leighton. 1996. "The Relationship of Political Marketing to Political Lobbying: An Examination of the Devenport Campaign for the Trident Refitting Contract." *European Journal of Marketing* 30(10/11): 68-91.

Angus Reid. 2010. *Charest's Image Tarnished in Quebec over Allegations of Influence Peddling*. http://www.visioncritical.com/.

Ansolabehere, Stephen, and Shanto Iyengar. 1995. *Going Negative: How Political Advertisements Shrink and Polarize the Electorate*. New Haven, CT: Free Press.

Arendt, Hannah. 1958. *The Human Condition*. Chicago: University of Chicago Press.

Arterton, F. Christopher. 2007. "Strategy and Politics: The Example of the United States of America." In *The Strategy of Politics: Results of a Comparative Study*, ed. Thomas Fischer, Gregor Peter Schmitz, and Michael Seberich, 133-72. Gütersloh, Germany: Verlag, Bertelsmann Stiftung.

Arvidsson, Adam. 2005. "Brands: A Critical Perspective." *Journal of Consumer Culture* 5(2): 235-58.

Aubry, Jack. 2006. "Majority Opposes Income Trust Levy." *Winnipeg Free Press*, November 8.

Aucoin, Peter. 2007. "After the Federal Accountability Act: Is the Accountability Problem in the Government of Canada Fixed?" *Financial Management Institute Journal* 18(2): 12-15.

Axworthy, Thomas S. 1991. "Capital-Intensive Politics: Money, Media and Mores in the United States and Canada." In *Issues in Party and Election Finance in Canada,* ed. F.L. Seidle, 157-234. Toronto: Dundurn.

Baines, Paul R. 1999. "Voter Segmentation and Candidate Positioning." In *Handbook of Political Marketing,* ed. Bruce I. Newman, 403-20. Thousand Oaks, CA: Sage.

Baines, Paul R., Robert M. Worcester, David Jarrett, and Roger Mortimore. 2003. "Market Segmentation and Product Differentiation in Political Campaigns: A Technical Feature Perspective." *Journal of Marketing Management* 19(1-2): 225-49.

Baker, M.J., E.A. Buttery, and E.M. Richter-Buttery. 1998. "Relationship Marketing in Three Dimensions." *Journal of Interactive Marketing* 12: 47-62.

Bannon, Declan. 2005a. "Electoral Participation and Non-Voter Segmentation." In *Current Issues in Political Marketing,* ed. Jennifer Lees-Marshment and Walter Wymer, 109-28. Philadelphia: Haworth.

–. 2005b. "Relationship Marketing and the Political Process." *Journal of Political Marketing* 4(2): 73-90.

Barber, Michael. 2007. *Instruction to Deliver: Fighting to Transform Britain's Public Services.* London: Politicos.

Barnes, James G. 2003. "Establishing Meaningful Customer Relationships: Why Some Companies and Brands Mean More to the Customers." *Managing Service Quality* 13(3): 178-86.

Becel. 2010. "About Becel." http://www.becel.ca/en_ca/.

Bélanger, Éric, and Richard Nadeau. 2006. "The Bloc Québécois: A Sour-Tasting Victory." In *The Canadian Federal Election of 2006,* ed. Jon H. Pammett and Christopher Dornan, 122-42. Toronto: Dundurn.

Bentivegna, Sara. 2002. "Politics and the New Media." In *The Handbook of New Media,* ed. Leah A. Lievrouw and Sonia M. Livingstone, 50-61. London: Sage.

Bernard, André. 1994. "The Bloc Québécois." In *The Canadian General Election of 1993,* ed. Alan Frizzell, Jon H. Pammett, and Anthony Westell, 79-88. Ottawa: Carleton University Press.

Bernier, Robert. 1991. *Gérer la victoire? Organisation, communication, stratégie.* Montreal: Gaëtan Morin Éditeur.

Berry, Jeffrey M. 1999. *The New Liberalism: The Rising Power of Citizen Groups.* Washington, DC: Brookings Institution Press.

Berry, Jeffrey M., and Clyde Wilcox. 2007. *The Interest Group Society.* New York: Longman.

Bickerton, James, Alain C. Gagnon, and Patrick J. Smith. 1999. *The Ties That Bind: Parties and Voters in Canada.* Don Mills, ON: Oxford University Press.

Birch, Lisa, and François Pétry. 2011. L'utilisation des entretiens de groupe dans l'élaboration des politiques de santé. *Recherches qualitatives* 29(3): 103-32.

–. 2010. "The Multifaceted Uses of Public Opinion Research (POR) in Canadian Tobacco Control." *Alert!* 50(3): 25-27.

Blais, André, Elisabeth Gidengil, Agnieszka Dobrzynska, Neil Nevitte, and Richard Nadeau. 2003. "Does the Local Candidate Matter?" *Canadian Journal of Political Science* 36(3): 657-64.

Blais, André, Elisabeth Gidengil, Richard Nadeau, and Neil Nevitte. 2001. "Measuring Party Identification: Canada, Britain, and the United States." *Political Behavior* 23: 5-22.

–. 2002. *Anatomy of a Liberal Victory: Making Sense of the 2000 Canadian Election.* Peterborough, ON: Broadview.

Blais, André, Mathieu Turgeon, Elisabeth Gidengil, Richard Nadeau, and Neil Nevitte. 2004. "Which Matters Most? Comparing the Impact of Issues and the Economy in American, British, and Canadian Elections." *British Journal of Political Science* 34: 555-63.

Blake, Donald E. 1982. "The Consistency of Inconsistency: Party Identification in Federal and Provincial Politics." *Canadian Journal of Political Science* 15(4): 681-710.

Blanchfield, Mike, and Jim Bronskill. 2010. "Documents Reveal Extreme Steps Conservatives Use to Control All Federal Events, Announcements." *Toronto Star,* June 7, A1.

Blumenthal, Sidney. 1980. *The Permanent Campaign: Inside the World of Elite Political Operations.* Boston: Beacon.

Blumler, Jay G. 1997. "Origins of the Crisis of Communication for Citizenship." *Political Communication* 14(4): 395-404.

Bowers-Brown, Julian. 2003. "A Marriage Made in Cyberspace? Political Marketing and UK Party Websites." In *Political Parties and the Internet: Net Gain?* ed. Rachel Gibson, Stephen Ward, and Paul Nixon, 98-119. London: Routledge.

Bowler, Shaun, and David M. Farrell, eds. 1992. *Electoral Strategies and Political Marketing.* Basingstoke, UK: Palgrave Macmillan.

Breindl, Yana, and Pascal Francq. 2008. "Can Web 2.0 Applications Save E-Democracy? A Study of How New Internet Applications May Enhance Citizen Participation in the Political Process On-line." *International Journal of Electronic Democracy* 1(1): 14-31.

Brodie, Ian. 2010. Phone interview with André Turcotte, March 30.

Brodie, Janine, and Jane Jenson. 2007. "Piercing the Smokescreen: Stability and Change in Brokerage Politics." In *Canadian Parties in Transition*, 3rd ed., ed. A. Brian Tanguay and Alain-G. Gagnon, 33-55. Peterborough, ON: Broadview.

Brodie, Janine, and Linda Trimble, eds. 2003. *Reinventing Canada: Politics of the 21st Century.* Toronto: Prentice Hall.

Brooke, Jeffrey. 2009. "Missed Opportunity: The Invisible Liberals." In *The Canadian Federal Election of 2008*, ed. Jon H. Pammett and Christopher Dornan, 63-97. Toronto: Dundurn.

Burt, Sandra. 2002. "The Concept of Political Participation." In *Citizen Politics: Research and Theory in Canadian Political Behaviour*, ed. Joanna Everitt and Brenda O'Neill, 232-46. Oxford: Oxford University Press.

Butler, Patrick, and Neil Collins. 1994. "Political Marketing: Structure and Process." *European Journal of Marketing* 28(1): 19-34.

–. 1996. "Strategic Analysis in Political Markets." *European Journal of Marketing* 30(10/11): 25-36.

–. 1999. "A Conceptual Framework for Political Marketing." In *Handbook of Political Marketing*, ed. Bruce I. Newman, 55-72. Thousand Oaks, CA: Sage.

Buurma, Hans. 2001. "Public Policy Marketing: Marketing Exchange in the Public Sector." *European Journal of Marketing* 35(11/12): 1287-1300.

Cairns, Alan C. 1968. "The Electoral System and the Party System in Canada." *Canadian Journal of Political Science* 1(1): 55-80.

Campbell, Angus, Philip E. Converse, Warren Miller, and Donald Stokes. 1960. *The American Voter*. New York: Wiley.

Campbell, Angus, Gerald Gurin, and Warren E. Miller. 1954. *The Voter Decides*. Evanston, IL: Row Peterson.

Canada. 1966. *Report of the Committee on Election Expenses*. Ottawa: Queen's Printer.

–. 1991. *Reforming Electoral Democracy: Final Report*. Vol. 1. Royal Commission on Electoral Reform and Party Financing. Ottawa: Supply and Services.

–. 2005. *Who Is Responsible? Phase 1 Report: Commission of Inquiry into the Sponsorship Program and Advertising Activities*. (Gomery Report.) Ottawa: Public Works and Government Services.

–. 2008. *Canadian Communities Now Safer as Tackling Violent Crime Act Receives Royal Assent*. Ottawa: Department of Justice. http://www.tacklingcrime.gc.ca/.

Canada. Auditor General of Canada. 2003. "Management of Public Opinion Research." Chap. 5 in *November Report of the Auditor General of Canada*. Ottawa: Minister of Public Works and Government Services. http://www.oag-bvg.gc.ca/.

–. 2005. "The Quality and Reporting of Surveys." Chap. 2 in *November Report of the Auditor General*. Ottawa: Minister of Public Works and Government Services. http://www.oag-bvg.gc.ca/.

–. 2007. "Advertising and Public Opinion Research." Chap. 1 in *February Status Report of the Auditor General of Canada*. Ottawa: Minister of Public Works and Government Services. http://www.oag-bvg.gc.ca/.

Canada. Communication Canada. N.d. *Sponsorship Canada: Reaching Canadians through Cultural, Sports and Community Events across the Country*. Information kit. Ottawa: Communication Canada.

Canada. Communications Community Office. 2008. *2007-08 Benchmarking Review of Federal Government National Headquarters and Regional Office Communications Branches*. Ottawa.

Canada. Department of Finance. 2006a. *Focusing on Priorities: Canada's New Government Turning a New Leaf.* Budget Speech 2006. Ottawa: Her Majesty the Queen in Right of Canada.

–. 2006b. *Canada's New Government Announces Tax Fairness Plan.* News release, October 31. http://www.fin.gc.ca/.

–. 2007. "The Budget Plan." Chap. 3 in *Aspire to a Stronger, Safer, Better Canada.* Ottawa: Her Majesty the Queen in Right of Canada.

–. 2009a. *Budget 2009: Canada's Economic Action Plan.* News release, January 27, p. 1. Ottawa: Department of Finance.

–. 2009b. *Canadians Can Track Progress of Economic Action Plan: Website Helps Hold Governments and Parliamentarians Accountable.* News release, March 11, p. 1. Ottawa: Department of Finance.

Canada. Health Canada Corporate Consultation Secretariat. 2000. *Health Canada Policy Toolkit for Public Involvement in Decision-Making.* Ottawa: Minister of Public Works and Government Services.

–. 2004. *A 10-Year Plan to Strengthen Health Care.* http://www.hc-sc.gc.ca/.

Canada. House of Commons. 2007. *House of Commons (Debates): Official Report (Hansard).* 39th Parliament, 1st Session. Number 157. May 18. http://www2.parl.gc.ca/.

Canada. Office of the Conflict of Interest and Ethics Commissioner. 2010. *The Cheques Report: The Use of Partisan or Personal Identifiers on Ceremonial Cheques or Other Props for Federal Funding Announcements.* Ottawa: Parliament of Canada.

Canada. Office of the Information Commissioner. 2010. *Out of Time: 2008-2009 Report Cards; Systemic Issues Affecting Access to Information in Canada.* Special report to Parliament. www.infocom.gc.ca/eng/.

Canada. Privy Council Office. 1999. *Government of Canada Regulatory Policy.* www.tbs-sct.gc.ca/.

–. 2010. *Report on Plans and Priorities 2010-11.* www.tbs-sct.gc.ca/.

Canada. Public Works and Government Services. 2009a. *Public Opinion Research in the Government of Canada: Annual Report, 2008-2009.* Ottawa: Public Works and Government Services. http://www.tpsgc-pwgsc.gc.ca/.

–. 2009b. Government Electronic Directory. Prime Minister's Office. http://sage-geds.tpsgc-pwgsc.gc.ca.

Canada. Statistics Canada. 2010. "Canadian Internet Use Survey." *The Daily.* May 10. http://www.statcan.gc.ca/.

Canada. Treasury Board. 1990. *Federal Identity Program Policy.* Ottawa: Treasury Board.

–. 2000. *Results for Canadians: A Management Framework for the Government of Canada.* http://www.tbs-sct.gc.ca/.

–. 2001. *Evaluation Policy.* http://www.tbs-sct.gc.ca/.

–. 2003a. *2002-2003 Estimates: Part III – Report on Plans and Priorities.* http://dsp-psd.pwgsc.gc.ca/.

–. 2003b. *Values and Ethics Code for the Public Service*. Ottawa: Canadian Government Publishing.

–. 2006. *Communications Policy of the Government of Canada*. http://www.tbs-sct.gc.ca/.

Canadian Almanac and Directory. 2008. *Associations Canada: An Encyclopedic Directory*. Toronto: Canadian Almanac and Directory.

Canadian Association of Journalists. 2010. "An Open Letter to Canadian Journalists." June 22, 1. http://www.caj.ca/.

Canadian Marketing Association. 2010. "Code of Ethics and Standards of Practice." http://www.the-cma.org/.

Canadian Press. 2007. "Poll Suggests Canadians Like Tory Mini-Budget." CTV, November 9. http://toronto.ctv.ca/.

–. 2008. "Dion Fires Back at Harper, Promises to Double Child Care Allowance." Citytv, September 9. http://www.citytv.com/.

–. 2010. "Canadian Facebook Users Now 16 Million Strong." CTV, June 2. http://www.ctv.ca/.

Canwest News Service. 2006. "Income Trust Decision Not a Broken Promise, Harper Says." Canada.com, November 2. http://www.canada.com/.

Cappella, Joseph N., and Kathleen Hall Jamieson. 1996. "News Frames, Political Cynicism and Media Cynicism." *Annals of the American Academy of Political and Social Science* 546: 71-74.

–. 1997. *Spiral of Cynicism: The Press and the Public Good*. New York: Oxford University Press.

Carballo, Marita, and Ulf Hjelmar, eds. 2008. *Public Opinion Polling in a Globalized World*. London: Springer.

Carstairs, Catherine. 2006. "Roots Nationalism: Branding English Canada Cool in the 1980s and 1990s." *Histoire Sociale/Social History* 39(77): 235-55.

Carty, R. Kenneth. 2001. "Three Canadian Party Systems: An Interpretation of Development of National Politics." In *Party Politics in Canada*, 8th ed., ed. Hugh G. Thorburn and Alan Whitehorn, 16-35. Toronto: Prentice-Hall.

–. 2002. "The Politics of Tecumseh Corners: Canadian Political Parties as Franchise Organizations." *Canadian Journal of Political Science* 35(4): 723-45.

–. 2004. "Parties as Franchise Systems: The Stratarchical Organizational Imperative." *Party Politics* 10: 5-24.

Carty, R. Kenneth, William Cross, and Lisa Young. 2000. *Rebuilding Canadian Party Politics*. Vancouver: UBC Press.

Castonguay, Alec. 2010. "Comment la droite s'organise." *Le Devoir*, May 22, A1.

Centre d'études sur les médias. 2010. *Comment les Québécois s'informent-ils?* Quebec: Centre d'études sur les médias et Consortium Canadien de recherche sur les médias.

Chadwick, Andrew. 2006. *Internet Politics: States, Citizens, and New Communication Technologies*. London: Oxford University Press.

Chandler, William M., and Alan Siaroff. 1992. "Parties and Party Government in Advanced Democracies." In *Canadian Political Parties*, ed. Herman Bakvis, 191-264. Toronto: Dundurn.

Cheadle, Bruce. 2010. "Elections Canada to Contend Tories Are Subverting Parliament on Campaign Finance." *Globe and Mail*, June 9. http://www.theglobeandmail.com/.

Christian, William, and Colin Campbell. 1990. *Political Parties and Ideologies in Canada*. 3rd ed. Toronto: McGraw-Hill Ryerson.

Christopher, Martin, Adrian Payne, and David Ballantyne. 2002. *Relationship Marketing: Creating Stakeholder Value*. Oxford: Butterworth Heinemann.

CityNews. 2007. "Harper Ends Year by Cutting GST to 5 Per Cent." Citytv, December 31. http://www.citytv.com/.

Clarke, Harold D., Jane Jenson, Lawrence LeDuc, and Jon H. Pammett. 1984. *Absent Mandate: The Politics of Discontent in Canada*. Toronto: Gage.

–. 1991. *Absent Mandate: The Politics of Discontent in Canada*. 3rd ed. Toronto: Gage.

Clarke, Harold D., and Allan Kornberg. 1993. "Evaluations and Evolution: Public Attitudes toward Canada's Federal Political Parties, 1965-1991." *Canadian Journal of Political Science* 26(2): 287-311.

Clarke, Harold D., Allan Kornberg, and Thomas J. Scotto. 2009. *Making Political Choices: Canada and the United States*. Toronto: University of Toronto Press.

Clarke, Harold D., and Marianne Stewart. 1992. "Canada." In *Electoral Change: Responses to Evolving Social and Attitudinal Structures in Western Countries*, ed. Mark N. Franklin, Thomas T. Mackie, and Henry Valen, 123-44. Cambridge: Cambridge University Press.

Clarkson, Stephen. 2005. *The Big Red Machine: How the Liberal Party Dominates Canadian Politics*. Vancouver: UBC Press.

–. 2006. "How the Big Red Machine Became the Little Red Machine." In *The Canadian Federal Election of 2006*, ed. Jon H. Pammett and Christopher Dornan, 24-57. Toronto: Dundurn.

Cohn, Daniel. 2003. "Changing Conceptions of the Public Interest." In *Reinventing Canada: Politics of the 21st Century*, ed. Janine Brodie and Linda Trimble, 67-71. Toronto: Prentice Hall.

Collins, Neil, and Patrick Butler. 2002. "Market Analysis for Political Parties." In *The Idea of Political Marketing*, ed. Nicholas J. O'Shaughnessy and Stephan C. Henneberg. London: Praeger.

–. 2003. "When Marketing Models Clash with Democracy." *Journal of Public Affairs* 3(1): 52-62.

Conservative Party of Canada. 2006. *Stand Up for Canada*. (Federal election platform.) http://www.cbc.ca/.

Corbin, Ruth M., L.A. Kelly Gill, and R. Scott Joliffe. 2000. *Trial by Survey: Survey Evidence and the Law*. Scarborough, ON: Carswell Thomson Professional.

Cosgrove, Kenneth. 2007. "Midterm Marketing: An Examination of Marketing Strategies in the 2006, 2002, 1998, and 1994 Elections." Paper presented at the annual meeting of the American Political Science Association, Chicago, August 30-September 2. http://www.allacademic.com/.

Cross, William. 2004. *Political Parties*. Vancouver: UBC Press.

Cross, William, and Lisa Young. 2004. "The Contours of Political Party Membership in Canada." *Party Politics* 10: 427-44.

CTV.ca. 2007. "Critics Say Wait-Times Deal Falls Short of Promise." *CTV News*, April 4. http://www.ctv.ca/.

Cunningham, Stanley B. 1999. "The Theory and Use of Political Advertising." In *Television Advertising in Canadian Elections: The Attack Mode, 1993*, ed. Walter I. Romanow, Michel De Repentigny, Stanley B. Cunningham, Walter C. Soderlund, and Kai Hildebrandt, 11-25. Waterloo, ON: Wilfrid Laurier Press.

Dahl, Robert A. 1961. *Who Governs? Democracy and Power in an American City*. New Haven, CT: Yale University Press.

Daku, Mark, Adam Mahon, Stuart Soroka, and Lori Young. 2009. "Media Content and Election Campaigns: 2008 in a Comparative Context." Paper presented at the annual conference of the Canadian Political Science Association, Ottawa, May 27-29.

Dalton, Russell J. 1996. "Comparative Politics: Micro-Behavioral Perspectives." In *A New Handbook of Political Science*, ed. Robert E. Goodin and Hans-Dieter Klinge-mann, 336-52. New York: Oxford University Press.

–. 2010. "Ideology, Partisanship, and Democratic Development." In *Comparing Democracies 3: Elections and Voting in the 21st Century*, ed. Lawrence LeDuc, Richard G. Niemi, and Pippa Norris, 143-64. Los Angeles: Sage.

Dalton, Russell, and Martin Wattenberg, eds. 2000. *Parties without Partisans: Political Change in Advanced Industrial Democracies*. New York: Oxford University Press.

Davidson, Scott. 2005. "Grey Power, School Gate Mums and the Youth Vote." *Journal of Marketing Management* 21(9): 1179-92.

Davis, Jeff. 2010a. "Opposition Parties Attack Feds: $89 Million Advertising Strategy." *Hill Times*, April 5, A1.

–. 2010b. "Bureaucrats Chafing under 'Unprecedented' PMO/PCO Communications Control." *Hill Times*, April 26, A1.

de Vreese, Claes H. 2005. "The Spiral of Cynicism Reconsidered." *European Journal of Communication* 20(3): 283-301.

Decima Research. 2002. *Second-Hand Smoke in the Workplace*. Ottawa: Health Canada.

–. 2004. *ACET Application Post-FMM Advertising: Final Report and Banner Tables*. Ottawa: Health Canada.

Delacourt, Susan, and Alex Marland. 2009. "From Sales to Marketing: The Evolution of the Party Pitch." *Policy Options*, September: 47-52.

Donsbach, Wolfgang, and Michael W. Traugott. 2008. *The SAGE Handbook of Public Opinion Research*. Thousand Oaks, CA: Sage.

Downs, Anthony. 1957. *An Economic Theory of Democracy*. New York: Harper and Row.

Doyle, Simon. 2007. "U.K. Public Service Expert Says 'The Centre' Is a Good Thing." *Hill Times*, June 25, A1.

Earnscliffe Research and Communications/Veraxis. 2004. *Report on the First Ministers' Meeting on the Future of Health Care: Monitoring Changes in Public Opinion*. Ottawa: Health Canada.

Egan, John. 1999. "Political Marketing: Lessons from the Mainstream." *Journal of Marketing Management* 15(6): 495-503.

Ekos Research Associates. 1995. *Rethinking Government 1995*. Ottawa: Ekos Research Associates.

–. 1996. *Research on Canadian Values in Relation to Health and the Health Care System: Final Report*. Ottawa: Health Canada, Values Working Group, National Forum on Health.

–. 2003. *Romanow Tracking Poll: Romanow Report in One-Year Rear View Mirror*. Ottawa: Health Canada.

–. 2006a. *Public Perceptions of the Relevance and Progress of Tobacco Control in Canada*. Ottawa: Health Canada.

–. 2006b. *Evaluation of the Relevance and Design and Delivery of the Federal Tobacco Control Strategy (FTCS)*. Ottawa: Health Canada.

Election Almanac. 2010. "Canada Federal Election 2010: Public Opinion Polls." Electionalmanac.com.

Elections Canada. 2010. *Estimation of Voter Turnout by Age Group at the 2008 Federal General Election*. www.elections.ca/.

Elkins, David J., and Richard Simeon. 1980. *Small Worlds: Provinces and Parties in Canadian Political Life*. Toronto: Methuen.

Ellis, Faron. 2005. *The Limits of Participation: Members and Leaders in Canada's Reform Party*. Calgary: University of Calgary Press.

Ellis, Faron, and Keith Archer. 1994. "Reform: Electoral Breakthrough." In *The Canadian General Election of 1993*, ed. Alan Frizzell, Jon H. Pammett, and Anthony Westell, 59-77. Ottawa: Carleton University Press.

Ellis, Faron, and Peter Woolstencroft. 2004. "New Conservatives, Old Realities." In *The Canadian General Election of 2004*, ed. Jon H. Pammett and Christopher Dornan, 66-105. Toronto: Dundurn.

–. 2006. "A Change of Government, Not a Change of Country: The Conservatives and the 2006 Election." In *The Canadian Federal Election of 2006*, ed. Jon H. Pammett and Christopher Dornan, 58-92. Toronto: Dundurn.

Environics Research Group. 1997a. *Public Attitudes toward Toxic Constituent and Health Warning Labelling on Cigarette Packaging: Qualitative Research Report Phase 1*. Ottawa: Health Canada.

–. 1997b. *Public Attitudes toward Tobacco Advertising Warning Labels and Tobacco Packaging: Phase II Qualitative Research Report*. Ottawa: Health Canada.

–. 1999a. *Health Canada–Office of Tobacco Control Qualitative (Focus Group) Report Regarding Health Warning Labels and Images on Cigarette Packages*. Ottawa: Health Canada.

–. 1999b. *Qualitative (Focus Group) Report Regarding Health Warning Labels and Images on Print Advertisements for Cigarettes*. Ottawa: Health Canada.

–. 1999c. *Health Warning Testing Final Report*. Ottawa: Health Canada.

–. 1999d. *Canadian Adult and Youth Opinions on the Sizing of Health Warning Messages*. Ottawa: Health Canada.

–. 1999e. *Smoking Risk Assessment and Sizing of Health Warning Messages: Canadians North of 60*. Ottawa: Health Canada.

–. 2000. *Canadian Opinion on the Size of Health Warning Messages: A Validation Survey*. Ottawa: Health Canada.

–. 2002a. *Post-Romanow Commission Report, Daily Tracking Report: December 1 to 12*. Ottawa: Health Canada.

–. 2002b. *Report to Health Canada: Focus Group Findings; Final Test on Second Hand Smoke in the Workplace Ad*. Ottawa: Health Canada.

–. 2004a. *"Heather" Television and Transit Ads: Recall Survey with Opinion Leaders*. Ottawa: Health Canada.

–. 2004b. *Ad Recall Survey of Movie-Goers: Heather/Barb Cinema Ad*. Ottawa: Health Canada.

–. 2005a. *Smoking in Public Places: Manitoba and New Brunswick*. Ottawa: Health Canada.

–. 2005b. *Smoking in Public Places: Quebec, Ontario and Saskatchewan*. Ottawa: Health Canada.

–. 2006. *Smoking in Public Places: Saskatchewan*. Ottawa: Health Canada.

Facebook. 2010. *Facebook Statistics*. http://www.facebook.com/.

–. n.d.-a. *Facebook Guidebook: Politics*. http://www.facebook.com/.

–. n.d.-b. *Facebook Pages*. http://www.facebook.com/.

Farrell, David. 1996. "Campaign Strategies and Tactics." In *Comparing Democracies: Elections and Voting in Global Perspective*, ed. Lawrence LeDuc, Richard G. Niemi, and Pippa Norris, 160-83. Thousand Oaks, CA: Sage.

Finer, Samuel E. 1966. *Anonymous Empire: A Study of the Lobby in Great Britain*. London: Pall Mall.

Finkel, Steven E. 1985. "Reciprocal Effects of Participation and Political Efficacy: A Panel Analysis." *American Journal of Political Science* 29: 891-913.

–. 1987. "The Effects of Participation on Political Efficacy and Political Support: Evidence from a Western German Panel." *Journal of Politics* 49: 441-64.

Flanagan, Tom. 2001. "From Riel to Reform (and a Little Beyond): Politics in Western Canada." *American Review of Canadian Studies* 31(4): 623-38.

–. 2007a. *Harper's Team: Behind the Scenes in the Conservative Rise to Power*. Montreal and Kingston: McGill-Queen's University Press.

–. 2007b. "Thou Shall Not Lean Too Far to the Right." *Globe and Mail*, September 22, A1.

–. 2009. *Harper's Team*. 2nd ed. Montreal: McGill-Queen's University Press.

–. 2010a. "Campaign Strategy: Triage and the Concentration of Resources." In *Election*, ed. Heather MacIvor, 155-72. Toronto: Emond Montgomery.

–. 2010b. Phone interview with André Turcotte, April 9.

Flanagan, Tom, and Harold J. Jansen. 2009. "Election Campaigns under Canada's Party Finance Laws." In *The Canadian Federal Election of 2008*, ed. Jon H. Pammett and Christopher Dornan, 194-216. Toronto: Dundurn.

Fletcher, Frederick J. 1994. "Media, Elections and Democracy." *Canadian Journal of Communication* 19: 131-50.

Fletcher, Joseph F., Heather Bastedo, and Jennifer Hove. 2009. "Losing Heart: Declining Support and the Political Marketing of the Afghanistan Mission." *Canadian Journal of Political Science* 42(4): 911-37

Fletcher, Thandi. 2010. "Patron Makes a Double-Double Take over Ban." *Vancouver Sun*, February 8.

Foster, Émilie. 2010. "Political Marketing and Interest Groups in Quebec." MA thesis. Quebec: Université Laval.

Fournier, Patrick. 2002. "The Uninformed Canadian Voter." In *Citizen Politics: Research and Theory in Canadian Political Behaviour*, ed. Joanna Everitt and Brenda O'Neill, 92-109. Don Mills, ON: Oxford University Press.

Fournier, Patrick, André Blais, Richard Nadeau, Elisabeth Gidengil, and Neil Nevitte. 2004. "Time-of-Voting Decision and Susceptibility to Campaign Effects." *Electoral Studies* 23: 661-81.

Franklin, Bob. 1994. *Packaging Politics*. London: Hodder Arnold.

–. 2004. *Packaging Politics: Political Communications in Britain's Media Democracy*. 2nd ed. London: Hodder Arnold.

Franklin, Mark N. 1985. *The Decline of Class Voting in Britain*. Oxford: Clarendon Press.

–. 1992. "The Decline of Cleavage Politics." In *Electoral Change: Responses to Evolving Social and Attitudinal Structures in Western Countries*, ed. Mark N. Franklin, Thomas T. Mackie, Henry Valen, and Clive Bean, 383-431. Cambridge: Cambridge University Press.

Friesen, Joe. 2011. "Micro-targeting Lets Parties Conquer Ridings, One Tiny Group at a Time." *Globe and Mail*, April 22. http://www.theglobeandmail.com/.

Galbraith, John Kenneth. 1992. *The Culture of Contentment*. Boston: Houghton Mifflin.

Gibson, Rachel, and Andrea Römmele. 2001. "Changing Campaign Communications: A Party-Centred Theory of Professionalized Campaigning." *Harvard International Journal of Press/Politics* 6: 31-43.

Gidengil, Elisabeth. 1992. "Canada Votes: A Quarter Century of Canadian National Election Studies." *Canadian Journal of Political Science* 25(2): 219-48.

–. 2002. "The Class Voting Conundrum." In *Political Sociology: Canadian Perspectives*, ed. Douglas Baer, 274-87. Don Mills, ON: Oxford University Press.

Gidengil, Elisabeth, André Blais, Joanna Everitt, Patrick Fournier, and Neil Nevitte. 2006. "Back to the Future? Making Sense of the 2004 Canadian Election outside Quebec." *Canadian Journal of Political Science* 39(1): 1-25.

Gidengil, Elisabeth, André Blais, Neil Nevitte, and Richard Nadeau. 1999. "Making Sense of Regional Voting in the 1997 Federal Election: Liberal and Reform Support outside Quebec." *Canadian Journal of Political Science* 32(2): 247-72.

–. 2001. "The Correlates and Consequences of Anti-Partyism in the 1997 Canadian Election." *Party Politics* 7: 491-513.

–. 2004. *Citizens.* Vancouver: UBC Press.

Gidengil, Elisabeth, Matthew Hennigar, André Blais, and Neil Nevitte. 2005. "Explaining the Gender Gap in Support for the New Right: The Case of Canada." *Comparative Political Studies* 38: 1-25.

Goot, Murray. 1999. "Public Opinion, Privatization and the Electoral Politics of Telstra." *Australian Journal of Politics and History* 45(2): 214-38.

Gosselin, André, and Walter C. Soderlund. 1999. "The 1993 Canadian Federal Election: Background and Party Advertising Strategies." In *Television Advertising in Canadian Elections: The Attack Mode, 1993,* ed. Walter I. Romanow, Michel De Repentigny, Stanley B. Cunningham, Walter C. Soderlund, and Kai Hildebrandt, 27-48. Waterloo, ON: Wilfrid Laurier Press.

Gould, Philip. 1998. *The Unfinished Revolution: How the Modernisers Saved the Labour Party.* London: Little, Brown.

Grant, Wyn. 1989. *Pressure Groups, Politics and Democracy in Britain.* London: Philip Allan.

Gray, Brendan, Sheelagh Matear, Christo Boshoff, and Phil Matheson. 1998. "Developing a Better Measure of Market Orientation." *European Journal of Marketing* 32(9/10): 884-903.

Gray, John. 2004. "King of the Cruller." *Canadian Business* 77(12): 45-48.

–. 2005. "Canadian Icons." *Canadian Business* 78(12): 32-33.

–. 2006. "Staying Power: Strong Brands." *Canadian Business* 79(22): 73-74.

Greenwood, Justin. 1997. "Representing Interests in the European Union: The Contribution of Case Study Methods." *Current Politics and Economics of Europe* 7(1): 1-33.

Grenier, Eric. 2010. "Does Easy Access to Starbucks Latte Really Make You Vote Liberal?" *Globe and Mail,* November 14. http://www.theglobeandmail.com/.

Grönroos, Christian. 1998. "Marketing Services: The Case of a Missing Product." *Journal of Business and Industrial Marketing* 13: 322-38.

Gutmann, Amy, and Dennis Thompson. 2004. *Why Deliberative Democracy?* Princeton, NJ: Princeton University Press.

Habermas, Jürgen. 1989. *The Structural Transformation of the Public Sphere.* Cambridge, MA: MIT Press.

Hammond, David, Geoffrey T. Fong, Ron Borland, K. Michael Cummings, Ann McNeill, and Pete Driezen. 2007. "Text and Graphic Warnings on Cigarette Packages: Findings from the International Tobacco Control Four Country Study." *American Journal of Preventive Medicine* 32(3): 202-9.

Harris, Phil. 2001. "To Spin or Not to Spin, That Is the Question: The Emergence of Modern Political Marketing." *Marketing Review* 2: 35-53.

Harris, Phil, Andrew Lock, and Patricia Rees, eds. 2000. *Machiavelli, Marketing and Management.* London: Routledge.

Hastak, Manoj, Michael B. Mazis, and Louis A. Morris. 2001. "The Role of Consumer Surveys in Public Policy Decision Making." *Journal of Public Policy and Marketing* 20(2): 170-85.

Hastings, Gerald. 2007. *Social Marketing: Why Should the Devil Have All the Best Tunes?* Burlington, MA: Elsevier.

Havemann, Paul. 1998. "Social Citizenship, Re-Commodification and the Contract State." In *Communitarianism and Citizenship,* ed. Emilios Christodoulidis, 134-57. Aldershot, UK: Ashgate.

Havighurst, Clark C., Peter Barton Hutt, Barbara J. McNeil, and Wilhelmine Miller. 2001. "Evidence: Its Meanings in Health Care and in Law." *Journal of Health Politics, Policy and Law* 26(2): 195-215.

Hébert, Chantal. 2007. *French Kiss: Le rendez-vous de Stephen Harper avec le Québec.* Montreal: Les éditions de l'Homme.

Hellwig, Timothy. 2010. "Elections and the Economy." In *Comparing Democracies 3: Elections and Voting in the 21st Century,* ed. Lawrence LeDuc, Richard G. Niemi, and Pippa Norris, 184-201. Los Angeles: Sage.

Henderson, Ailsa. 2004. "Regional Political Cultures in Canada." *Canadian Journal of Political Science* 37(3): 595-615.

Henneberg, Stephan C. 2002. "Understanding Political Marketing." In *The Idea of Political Marketing,* ed. Nicholas J. O'Shaughnessy and Stephan C. Henneberg, 93-171. Westport, CT: Praeger.

–. 2004. "The Views of an *Advocatus Dei:* Political Marketing and Its Critics." *Journal of Public Affairs* 4(3): 225-43.

–. 2008. "An Epistemological Perspective on Research in Political Marketing." *Journal of Political Marketing* 7(2): 151-82.

Henneberg, Stephan C., and Stefan Eghbalian. 2002. "Kirchheimer's Catch-All Party: A Reinterpretation in Marketing Terms." In *The Idea of Political Marketing,* ed. Nicholas J. O'Shaughnessy and Stephan C. Henneberg, 67-91. Westport, CT: Praeger.

Henneberg, Stephan C., and Nicholas J. O'Shaughnessy. 2007. "Theory and Concept Development in Political Marketing: Issues and an Agenda." *Journal of Political Marketing* 6(2/3): 5-31.

–. 2009. "Political Relationship Marketing: Some Macro/Micro Thoughts." *Journal of Marketing Management* 25(1): 5-29.

Henneberg, Stephan C., Margaret Scammell, and Nicholas J. O'Shaughnessy. 2009. "Political Marketing Management and Theories of Democracy." *Marketing Theory* 9: 165-88.

Hillwatch. 2006. "Still Virtually Lawn Signs: Benchmarking Canadian Political Web Sites during the 2006 Campaign." *Hillwatch,* January 10. http://www.hillwatch.com/.

Hood, Christopher, and Martin Lodge. 2006. *The Politics of Public Service Bargains*. Oxford: Oxford University Press.

Hudon, Raymond. 2009. "Les groupes d'intérêt ... au coeur de mutations démocratiques." In *Le Parlementarisme Canadien*, ed. Réjean Pelletier and Manon Tremblay, 197-242. Quebec: Presses de l'Université Laval.

Hughes, Andrew, and Stephan Dann. 2009. "Political Marketing and Stakeholder Engagement." *Marketing Theory* 9: 243-56.

Inglehart, Ronald, and Pippa Norris. 2003. *Rising Tide: Gender Equality and Cultural Change around the World*. New York: Cambridge University Press.

Ipsos-Reid. 2004. *Testing of Follow-Up Materials to the 2004 First Ministers' Meeting: Final Report*. Ottawa: Health Canada.

Jackson, Nigel A. 2005. "Vote Winner or a Nuisance: Email and Elected Politicians' Relationship with Their Constituents." In *Current Issues in Political Marketing*, ed. Walter Wymer and Jennifer Lees-Marshment, 91-108. Binghamton, NY: Haworth.

–. 2006a. "Political Parties, Their E-Newsletters and Subscribers: 'One-Night Stand' or a 'Marriage Made in Heaven'?" In *Winning Elections with Political Marketing*, ed. Philip Davies and Bruce I. Newman, 149-75. London: Haworth.

–. 2006b. "Banking Online: The Use of the Internet by Political Parties to Build Relationships with Voters." In *The Marketing of Political Parties*, ed. Darren G. Lilleker, Nigel A. Jackson, and Richard Scullion, 157-82. Manchester: Manchester University Press.

–. 2009. "UK MPs and the Marketing of Their Websites." In *Political Marketing: Principles and Applications*, ed. Jennifer Lees-Marshment, 183-85. New York: Routledge.

Jackson, Nigel A., and Darren G. Lilleker. 2004. "Just Public Relations or an Attempt at Interaction? British MPs in the Press, on the Web and 'In Your Face.'" *European Journal of Communication* 19(4): 507-33.

Jacobs, Lawrence R., and Robert Y. Shapiro. 2000. "Polling and Pandering." *Society* 37(6): 11-13.

Jamieson, Kathleen Hall. 1992. *Dirty Politics: Deception, Distraction, and Democracy*. New York: Oxford University Press.

Jaworski, Bernard J., and Ajay K. Kohli. 1996. "Market Orientation: Review, Refinement, and Roadmap." *Journal of Market-Focused Management* 1: 119-36.

Jeffrey, Brooke. 2009. "Missed Opportunity: The Invisible Liberals." In *The Canadian Federal Election of 2008*, ed. Jon H. Pammett and Christopher Dornan, 63-97. Toronto: Dundurn.

Johansen, Helene P.M. 2005. "Political Marketing: More than Persuasive Techniques, an Organizational Perspective." *Journal of Political Marketing* 4(4): 85-105.

Johnson, Dennis W. 2007. *No Place for Amateurs*. 2nd ed. New York: Routledge.

Karp, Jeffrey A., and Susan A. Banducci. 2008. "Political Efficacy and Participation in Twenty-Seven Democracies: How Electoral Systems Shape Political Behaviour." *British Journal of Political Science* 38: 311-34.

Kavanagh, Dennis. 1995. *Election Campaigning: The New Marketing of Politics*. Oxford: Blackwell.

Kent, Tom. 2006. "The Pearson Decade: How Defeat Foretold Victory." *Policy Options* 27(2): 13-17.

Kesteloot, Soetkin, Philippe De Vries, and Christ'l De Landtsheer. 2008. "Branding the Mayor: Introducing Political Consumerism in Belgian Municipal Elections." In *Voters or Consumers: Imagining the Contemporary Electorate*, ed. Darren G. Lilleker and Richard Scullion, 73-96. Newcastle, UK: Cambridge Scholars.

Key, Valdimer Orlando. 1942. *Politics, Parties, and Pressure Groups.* New York: Crowell.

Kinsella, Warren. 2001. *Kicking Ass in Canadian Politics.* Toronto: Random House.

–. 2007. *The War Room: Political Strategies for Business, NGOs, and Anyone Who Wants to Win.* Toronto: Dundurn.

Kippen, Grant. 2000. *The Use of New Information Technologies by a Political Party: A Case Study of the Liberal Party in the 1993 and 1997 Federal Elections.* Vancouver: SFU-UBC Centre for the Study of Government and Business.

Kirchheimer, Otto. 1966. "The Transformation of the Western European Party Systems." In *Political Parties and Political Development*, ed. Joseph LaPalombara and Myron Weiner, 177-200. Princeton, NJ: Princeton University Press.

Klein, Naomi. 2000. *No Logo.* New York: Picador.

Knuckey, Jonathan, and Jennifer Lees-Marshment. 2005. "American Political Marketing: George W. Bush and the Republican Party." In *Political Marketing: A Comparative Perspective*, ed. Darren G. Lilleker and Jennifer Lees-Marshment, 39-58. Manchester: Manchester University Press.

Kohli, Ajay K., and Bernard J. Jaworski. 1990. "Market Orientation: The Construct, Research Propositions, and Managerial Implications." *Journal of Marketing* 54: 1-18.

Kollman, Ken. 1998. *Outside Lobbying: Public Opinion and Interest Group Strategies.* Princeton, NJ: Princeton University Press.

Kotler, Philip, and David Gertner. 2002. "Country as Brand, Product, and Beyond: A Place Marketing Management Perspective." *Brand Management* 9(4/5): 249-61.

Kotler, Philip, and Nancy R. Lee. 2008. *Social Marketing: Influencing Behaviours for Good.* Thousand Oaks, CA: Sage.

Kozolanka, Kirsten. 2006. "The Sponsorship Scandal as Communication: The Rise of Politicized and Strategic Communications in the Federal Government." *Canadian Journal of Communication* 31: 343-66.

–. 2009. "Communication by Stealth: The New Common Sense in Government Communication." In *How Ottawa Spends, 2009-2010: Economic Upheaval and Political Dysfunction*, ed. Allan M. Maslove, 222-40. Montreal and Kingston: McGill-Queen's University Press.

Kraus, Sidney. 2000. *Televised Presidential Debates and Public Policy.* 2nd ed. Mahwah, NJ: Lawrence Erlbaum Associates.

Kuper, Ayelet, Lorelei Lingard, and Wendy Levinson. 2008. "Critically Appraising Qualitative Research." *British Medical Journal* 3(37): 687-89.

Lafferty, Barbara A., and G. Tomas M. Hult. 2001. "A Synthesis of Contemporary Market Orientation Perspectives." *European Journal of Marketing* 35(1/2): 92-109.

Lambert, Ronald D., James E. Curtis, Steven D. Brown, and Barry J. Kay. 1986. "In Search of Left/Right Beliefs in the Canadian Electorate." *Canadian Journal of Political Science* 19(3): 541-63.

Laschinger, John, and Geoffrey Stevens. 1992. *Leaders and Lesser Mortals: Backroom Politics in Canada*. Toronto: Key Porter.

Lebel, Gregory G. 1999. "Managing Volunteers: Times Have Changed – or Have They?" In *Handbook of Political Marketing*, ed. Bruce I. Newman, 129-42. Thousand Oaks, CA: Sage.

LeDuc, Lawrence. 1984. "Canada: The Politics of Stable Dealignment." In *Electoral Change in Advanced Industrial Democracies: Realignment or Dealignment?* ed. Russell J. Dalton, Paul Beck, and Scott Flanagan, 402-24. Princeton, NJ: Princeton University Press.

LeDuc, Lawrence, Jon H. Pammett, Judith Mackenzie, and André Turcotte. 2010. *Dynasties and Interludes*. Toronto: Dundurn.

Lees-Marshment, Jennifer. 2001a. "The Marriage of Politics and Marketing." *Political Studies* 49(4): 692-713.

–. 2001b. *Political Marketing and British Political Parties: The Party's Just Begun*. Manchester: Manchester University Press.

–. 2003. "Marketing Good Works: New Trends in How Interest Groups Recruit Supporters." *Journal of Public Affairs* 3(4): 358-70.

–. 2004. *The Political Marketing Revolution: Transforming the Government of the UK*. Manchester: Manchester University Press.

–. 2006. "Political Marketing Theory and Practice: A Reply to Ormrod's Critique of the Lees-Marshment Market-Oriented Party Model." *Politics* 26: 119-25.

–. 2008. *Political Marketing and British Political Parties*. 2nd ed. Manchester: Manchester University Press.

–. 2009a. "Managing a Market-Orientation in Government: Examples from Tony Blair and Helen Clark." In *The Routledge Handbook of Political Management*, ed. Dennis W. Johnson, 524-36. New York: Routledge.

–. 2009b. "Marketing After the Election: The Potential and Limitations of Maintaining a Market Orientation in Government." *Canadian Journal of Communication* 34: 205-27.

–. 2009c. *Political Marketing: Principles and Applications*. New York: Routledge.

–. 2011. *The Political Marketing Game*. Hampshire, UK: Palgrave Macmillan.

Lees-Marshment, Jennifer, and Darren G. Lilleker. 2005. "Political Marketing in the UK: A Positive Start but an Uncertain Future." In *Political Marketing: A Comparative Perspective*, ed. Darren G. Lilleker and Jennifer Lees-Marshment, 15-38. Manchester: Manchester University Press.

Lees-Marshment, Jennifer, and Stuart Quayle. 2001. "Empowering the Members or Marketing the Party? The Conservative Reforms of 1998." *Political Quarterly* 72: 204-12.

Lees-Marshment, Jennifer, Jesper Strömbäck, and Chris Rudd. 2010. "Global Political Marketing: Analysis and Conclusions." In *Global Political Marketing*, ed.

Jennifer Lees-Marshment, Jesper Strömbäck, and Chris Rudd, 278-97. New York: Routledge.

Léger Marketing. 2006. *Baromètre des professions: Rapport OmniCan*. March 9, 3-54. http://www.legermarketing.com/.

-. 2007. *Baromètre des professions: Rapport OmniCan*. May 15, 1-11. http://www.leger-marketing.com/.

Lemieux, Patrick. 2008. *Du recrutement au lobbying: L'utilisation du marketing politique par les groupes d'intérêt au Québec*. Montreal: Université de Montréal, mémoire de maîtrise.

Leslie, Larry Z. 2010. *Communication Research Methods in Postmodern Culture*. Boston: Allyn and Bacon.

Lilleker, Darren G. 2005a. "Political Marketing: The Cause of an Emerging Democratic Deficit in Britain?" *Journal of Nonprofit and Public Sector Marketing* 14(1-2): 5-26.

-. 2005b. "The Impact of Political Marketing on Internal Party Democracy." *Parliamentary Affairs* 58: 570-84.

Lilleker, Darren G., and Jennifer Lees-Marshment. 2005. "Introduction: Rethinking Political Party Behaviour." In *Political Marketing: A Comparative Perspective*, ed. Darren G. Lilleker and Jennifer Lees-Marshment, 1-14. Manchester: Manchester University Press.

Lilleker, Darren G., and Richard Scullion, eds. 2008. *Voters or Consumers: Imagining the Contemporary Electorate*. Newcastle, UK: Cambridge Scholars.

Lloyd, Jenny. 2005. "Square Peg, Round Hole? Can Marketing-Based Concepts Such as the 'Product' and the 'Marketing Mix' Have a Useful Role in the Political Arena?" *Journal of Nonprofit and Public Sector Marketing* 14(1-2): 27-46.

Lock, Andrew, and Phil Harris. 1996a. "Machiavellian Marketing: The Development of Corporate Lobbying in the UK." *Journal of Marketing Management* 12(4): 313-28.

-. 1996b. "Political Marketing - Vive la Difference!" *European Journal of Marketing* 30(10/11): 14-24.

MacCharles, Tonda. 2010. "Former Top Aide Criticizes PM for Leadership Style." *Toronto Star*, June 2, A13.

Mack, Charles S. 1997. *Business, Politics, and the Practice of Government Relations*. Westport, CT: Quorum.

Macleod, Harris. 2009. "$34-Million Ad Campaign for Economic Action Plan Priming Voters for Election." *Hill Times*, August 17, 1.

Madill, Judith J. 1998. "Marketing in Government." *Optimum Online: The Journal of Public Sector Management* 28(4): 9-18.

Manheim, Jarol B., Richard C. Rich, Lars Willnat, and Craig Leonard Brians. 2008. *Empirical Political Analysis*. 7th ed. New York: Pearson Longman.

Manning, Preston. 2002. *Think Big*. Toronto: McClelland and Stewart.

-. 2010. Phone interview with André Turcotte, April 13.

Manza, Jeff, and Fay Lomax Cook. 2002. "The Impact of Public Opinion on Public Policy: The State of the Debate." In *Navigating Public Opinion: Polls, Policy and the*

Future of American Democracy, ed. Jeff Manza, Fay Lomax Cook, and Benjamin I. Page, 17-32. Oxford: Oxford University Press.

Marcotte, Philippe, and Frédérick Bastien. 2010. *L'influence du mode de financement des médias sur le cadrage des campagnes électorales: Le cas des élections fédérales de 2005-06 et 2008*. Paper presented at the annual meeting of the Société québécoise de science politique, Quebec.

Margolis, Michael, and Gerson Moreno-Riaño. 2009. *The Prospect of Internet Democracy*. Farnham, UK: Ashgate.

Marland, Alex. 2005. "Canadian Political Parties: Market-Oriented, or Ideological Slag-brains?" In *Political Marketing in Comparative Perspective*, ed. Darren G. Lilleker and Jennifer Lees-Marshment, 59-78. Manchester: Manchester University Press.

–. 2008. "Promotional and Other Spending by Party Candidates in the 2006 Canadian Federal Election Campaign." *Canadian Journal of Media Studies* 3(1): 57-89.

Martin, Don. 2007. "Tories Have Book on Political Wrangling." *National Post*, May 17. http://www.canada.com/nationalpost/.

Martin, Lawrence. 2010. *Harperland: The Politics of Control*. Toronto: Viking.

Marx, Karl. 1967. *Capital*. Vol. 1. New York: International Publishers.

May, Kathryn. 2007. "Accountability Act Creates PS 'Dilberts.'" *Ottawa Citizen*, October 5, A1.

McGough, Sean. 2009. "Political Marketing, Democracy and Terrorism: Ireland Highlights the Dangers." In *Political Marketing: Principles and Applications*, ed. Jennifer Lees-Marshment, 288-90. London: Routledge.

McGrath, Conor. 2006. "Grass Roots Lobbying: Marketing Politics and Policy 'Beyond the Beltway.'" In *Winning Elections with Political Marketing*, ed. Philip J. Davies and Bruce I. Newman, 105-30. New York: Haworth.

McGregor, Glen. 2009. "Tory Ridings the Winners from Stimulus: Analysis Reveals More than Half of Big-Money Projects Went to Blue Districts." *Ottawa Citizen*, October 20, A1.

McLaughlin, David. 1994. *Poisoned Chalice: The Last Campaign of the Progressive Conservative Party?* Toronto: Dundurn.

Meadows-Klue, Danny. 2008. "Falling in Love 2.0: Relationship Marketing for the Facebook Generation." *Journal of Direct, Data and Digital Marketing Practice* 9(3): 245-50.

Medlock, Jennifer. 2005. *The Role of Public Opinion Research in Federal Public Policy Development*. Calgary: University of Calgary.

Medvic, Stephen K. 2001. *Political Consultants in U.S. Congressional Elections, Parliaments and Legislatures Series*. Columbus: Ohio State University Press.

Meisel, John. 1975. *Working Papers on Canadian Politics*. 2nd enlarged ed. Montreal: McGill-Queen's University Press.

Millward Brown Goldfarb. 2002. *Youth Second-Hand Smoking Focus Groups*. Ottawa: Health Canada.

–. 2003a. *Qualitative Evaluation of the Second Series of "Heather Crowe" Commercials and Second-Hand Smoke Stories*. Ottawa: Health Canada.

–. 2003b. *Qualitative Evaluation of "Heather Crowe" Commercials and Second-Hand Smoke Stories*. Ottawa: Health Canada.

–. 2003c. *Final Review of Heather Crowe/Barb Tarbox Creative Concept 2003*. Ottawa: Health Canada.

–. 2003d. *Heather Crowe/Barb Tarbox test #2 (French)*. Ottawa: Health Canada.

Mintz, John H., Doug Church, and Bernie Colterman. 2006. "The Case for Marketing in the Public Sector." *Optimum Online: The Journal of Public Sector Management* 36(4): 40-48.

Mitchell, William C., and Michael C. Munger. 1991. "Economic Models of Interest Groups: An Introductory Survey." *American Journal of Political Science* 35(2): 512-46.

Montpetit, Éric. 2002. "Pour en finir avec le lobbying: Comment les institutions canadiennes influencent l'action des groupes d'intérêt." *Politique et Sociétés* 21(3): 91-112.

Moore, James, and Wayne Slater. 2004. *Bush's Brain*. New York: Wiley.

Mortimore, Roger. 2003. "Why Politics Needs Marketing." *International Journal of Non-Profit and Voluntary Sector Marketing* 8(2): 107-21.

Mosco, Vincent. 2009. *The Political Economy of Communication*. 2nd ed. London: Sage.

MRIA. 2007. "Code of Conduct and Good Practice for Members of the Marketing Research and Intelligence Association." http://www.mria-arim.ca/.

Mueller, Dennis C. 2003. *Public Choice III*. New York: Cambridge University Press.

Muniz, Albert M. Jr., and Thomas C. O'Guinn. 2001. "Brand Community." *Journal of Consumer Research* 27(4): 412-32.

Murphy, Rex. 2009. *Canada and Other Matters of Opinion*. Toronto: Doubleday.

Murray, Shoon-Kathleen. 2006. "Private Polls and Presidential Policymaking: Reagan as a Facilitator of Change." *Public Opinion Quarterly* 70(4): 477-98.

Murugesan, San. 2007. "Understanding Web 2.0." *IT Professional* 9(4): 34-41.

Muttart, Patrick. 2011. Personal correspondence with Alex Marland, August 1.

Nadeau, Richard. 2002. "Satisfaction with Democracy: The Canadian Paradox." In *Value Change and Governance in Canada*, ed. Neil Nevitte, 7-71. Toronto: University of Toronto Press.

Nadeau, Richard, André Blais, Elisabeth Gidengil, and Neil Nevitte. 2001. "Election Campaigns as Information Campaigns: The Dynamics of Information Gains, the Knowledge Gap, and Vote Intentions." Paper presented at the annual conference of the American Political Science Association, San Francisco, August 30-September 2.

Nadeau, Richard, and Thierry Giasson. 2003. "Canada's Democratic Malaise: Are the Media to Blame?" *Choice* 9(1): 3-32.

Needham, Catherine. 2003. *Citizen-Consumers: New Labour's Marketplace Democracy*. London: Catalyst.

–. 2005. "Brand Leaders: Clinton, Blair and the Limitations of the Permanent Campaign." *Political Studies* 53(2): 343-61.

–. 2006. "Brands and Political Loyalty." *Journal of Brand Management* 13(3): 178-87.

Negrine, Ralph M. 2008. *The Transformation of Political Communication: Continuities and Changes in Media and Politics.* New York: Palgrave Macmillan.

Negrine, Ralph M., and Darren G. Lilleker. 2002. "The Professionalization of Political Communication: Continuities and Change in Media Practices." *European Journal of Communication* 17(3): 305-23.

Neuman, W. Laurence, and Karen Robson. 2009. *Basics of Social Research.* Canadian ed. Toronto: Pearson.

Nevitte, Neil. 1996. *The Decline of Deference: Canadian Value Change in Cross-National Perspective.* Peterborough, ON: Broadview.

–. 2002. "Introduction: Value Change and Reorientation in Citizen-State Relations." In *Value Change and Governance in Canada,* ed. Neil Nevitte, 3-35. Toronto: University of Toronto Press.

Nevitte, Neil, André Blais, Elisabeth Gidengil, and Richard Nadeau. 2000. *Unsteady State: The 1997 Canadian Federal Election.* Don Mills, ON: Oxford University Press.

Newman, Bruce I. 1994. *The Marketing of the President: Political Marketing as Campaign Strategy.* Thousand Oaks, CA: Sage.

–. 1999a. *The Mass Marketing of Politics: Democracy in the Age of Manufactured Images.* Thousand Oaks, CA: Sage.

–, ed. 1999b. *Handbook of Political Marketing.* Thousand Oaks, CA: Sage.

Nielsen Wire. 2010. *Facebook Users Average 7 Hrs a Month in January as Digital Universe Expands.* http://blog.nielsen.com/.

Niemi, Richard G., Stephen C. Craig, and Franco Mattei. 1991. "Measuring Internal Political Efficacy in the 1988 National Election Study." *American Political Science Review* 85: 1407-13.

Nimijean, Richard. 2006. "Brand Canada: The Brand State and the Decline of the Liberal Party." *Inroads* 19: 84-93.

Noel, Sid. 2007. "Leaders' Entourages, Parties, and Patronage." In *Canadian Parties in Transition,* 3rd ed., ed. Alain-G. Gagnon and A. Brian Tanguay, 197-213. Peterborough, ON: Broadview Press.

Norris, Pippa. 2000. *A Virtuous Circle: Political Communications in Postindustrial Societies.* Cambridge: Cambridge University Press.

–. 2002. *Democratic Phoenix: Reinventing Political Activism.* Cambridge: Cambridge University Press.

Norris, Pippa, John Curtice, David Sanders, Margaret Scammell, and Holli A. Semetko. 1999. *On Message: Communicating the Campaign.* London: Sage.

Norris, Sonya. 2009. *The Wait Times Issue and the Patient Wait Times Guarantee.* Ottawa: Library of Parliament.

Nownes, Anthony J. 2006. *Total Lobbying: What Lobbyists Want (And How They Try to Get It).* Cambridge: Cambridge University Press.

O'Cass, Aron. 1996. "Political Marketing and the Marketing Concept." *European Journal of Marketing* 30(1): 37-53.

–. 2001. "The Internal-External Marketing Orientation of a Political Party: Social Implications of Political Marketing Orientation." *Journal of Public Affairs* 1(2): 136-52.

–. 2003. "An Exploratory Assessment of the Political Product: Proclamation of the Faithful." *Journal of Nonprofit and Public Sector Marketing* 11(2): 67-98.

–. 2009. "A Resource-Based View of the Political Party and Value Creation for the Voter-Citizen: An Integrated Framework for Political Marketing." *Marketing Theory* 9(2): 189-208.

O'Shaughnessy, Nicholas J. 1990. *The Phenomenon of Political Marketing*. Basingstoke, UK: Macmillan.

–. 2002. "The Marketing of Political Marketing." In *The Idea of Political Marketing*, ed. Nicholas J. O'Shaughnessy and Stephan C. Henneberg, 209-20. London: Praeger.

–. 2004. *Politics and Propaganda: Weapons of Mass Seduction*. Ann Arbor: University of Michigan Press.

Olson, Mancur. 1965. *The Logic of Collective Action: Public Goods and the Theory of Groups.* Cambridge, MA: Harvard University Press.

Ormrod, Robert P. 2005. "A Conceptual Model of Political Market Orientation." *Journal of Nonprofit and Public Sector Marketing* 14(1/2): 47-64.

–. 2006. "A Critique of the Lees-Marshment Market-Oriented Party Model." *Politics* 26: 110-18.

–. 2007. "Political Market Orientation and Its Commercial Cousin: Close Family or Distant Relatives?" *Journal of Political Marketing* 6(2/3): 69-90.

Ormrod, Robert P., and Stefan C. Henneberg. 2006. "'Are You Thinking What We're Thinking,' or 'Are We Thinking What You're Thinking?'" In *The Marketing of Political Parties: Political Marketing at the 2005 British General Election*, ed. Darren G. Lilleker, Nigel Jackson, and Richard Scullion, 31-58. Manchester: Manchester University Press.

Osborne, David E., and Ted Gaebler. 1993. *Reinventing Government: How the Entrepreneurial Spirit Is Transforming the Public Sector*. New York: Plume.

Ottawa Citizen. 2007. "Record-Spending Tories Review Polling Contracts." December 5. http://www.canada.com/.

Page, Christopher. 2006. *The Roles of Public Opinion Research in Canadian Government*. Toronto: University of Toronto Press.

Paillé, Daniel. 2007. *Public Opinion Research Practices of the Government of Canada, Independent Advisor's Report*. (Paillé Report.) Ottawa: Minister of Public Works and Government Services. http://www.tpsgc-pwgsc.gc.ca/.

Palmer, Jerry. 2002. "Smoke and Mirrors: Is That the Way It Is? Themes in Political Marketing." *Media, Culture and Society* 24(3): 245-363.

Paltiel, Khayyam Zev. 1989. "Political Marketing, Party Finance, and the Decline of Canadian Parties." In *Canadian Parties in Transition*, ed. Alain-G. Gagnon and A. Brian Tanguay, 332-53. Scarborough, ON: Nelson.

Pammett, Jon H., and Christopher Dornan. 2006. "From One Minority to Another." In *The Canadian Federal Election of 2006*, ed. Jon H. Pammett and Christopher Dornan, 9-23. Toronto: Dundurn.

Pammett, Jon H., and Lawrence LeDuc. 2003. *Explaining the Turnout Decline in Canadian Federal Elections: A New Survey of Non-Voters*. Ottawa: Elections Canada. http://www.elections.ca/.

Paré, Daniel J., and Flavia Berger. 2008. "Political Marketing Canadian Style? The Conservative Party and the 2006 Federal Election." *Canadian Journal of Communication* 33: 39-63.

Patterson, Thomas E. 1994. *Out of Order*. New York: Vintage.

Pedersen, Mogens N. 1979. "The Dynamics of European Party Systems: Changing Patterns of Electoral Volatility." *European Journal of Political Research* 7: 1-26.

Penfold, Steve. 2002. "'Eddie Shack Was No Tim Horton': Donuts and the Folklore of Mass Culture in Canada." In *Food Nations: Selling Taste in Consumer Societies*, ed. Warren James Belasco, 48-66. New York: Routledge.

Plamondon, Bob. 2008. "The Aim Is a Conservative Dynasty." *Globe and Mail*, September 15, A15.

–. 2009. *Full Circle*. Toronto: Key Porter.

Plasser, Fritz. 2009. "Political Consulting Worldwide." In *Routledge Handbook of Political Management*, ed. Dennis W. Johnson, 24-41. New York: Routledge.

Plasser, Fritz, and Gunda Plasser. 2002. *Global Political Campaigning: A Worldwide Analysis of Campaign Professionals and Their Practices*. Westport, CT: Praeger.

Pollara. 2002a. *Quantitative Research among Canadians: Testing Arguments Pertaining to the Reform of Health Care in Canada: Final Report*. Ottawa: Health Canada.

–. 2002b. *Public Input on the Future of Healthcare*. Ottawa: Health Canada.

–. 2002c. *Attitudes and Behaviours of Canadians Regarding Second-Hand Smoke in the Workplace*. Ottawa: Health Canada.

–. 2002d. *Qualitative Research with Focus Group Testing of Social Marketing Creative Concepts for the Second Hand Smoke Campaign: Final Report of Focus Group Findings*. Ottawa: Health Canada.

Pollara-Earnscliffe Research and Communications. 1998. *National Health Survey: Summary of Quantitative Research Findings*. Ottawa: Health Canada.

Pratte, André. 2000. *Les oiseaux de malheur*. Montreal: Boréal.

Proctor, Tony. 2007. *Public Sector Marketing*. Harlow, UK: Financial Times/Prentice-Hall.

Pross, A. Paul. 1975. "Pressure Groups: Adaptive Instruments of Political Communication." In *Pressure Group Behaviour in Canadian Politics*, ed. A. Paul Pross, 1-26. Toronto: McGraw-Hill Ryerson.

Putnam, Robert. 2000. *Bowling Alone*. New York: Simon and Schuster.

Quebec. 2000. Les Solutions Émergentes: Annexe Groupes nationaux, résumés des mémoires à la Commission. *Commission d'étude sur les services de santé et les services sociaux*. (Clair Report.) Quebec: Government of Quebec.

Rademacher, Eric W., and Alfred J. Turchfarber. 1999. "Pre-Election Polling and Political Campaigns." In *Handbook of Political Marketing*, ed. Bruce I. Newman, 197-221. Thousand Oaks, CA: Sage.

Reeves, Peter, Leslie de Chernatony, and Marylyn Carrigan. 2006. "Building a Political Brand: Ideology or Voter Driven Strategy?" *Journal of Brand Management* 13(6): 418-28.

Richards, David, and Martin Smith. 2006. "Central Control and Policy Implementation in the UK: A Case Study of the Prime Minister's Delivery Unit." *Journal of Comparative Policy Analysis: Research and Practice* 8(4): 325-45.

Roberts, Alasdair, and Jonathan Rose. 1995. "Selling the Goods and Services Tax: Government Advertising and Public Discourse in Canada." *Canadian Journal of Political Science* 28(2): 311-30.

Robinson, Claire. 2010. "Political Advertising and the Demonstration of Market Orientation." *European Journal of Marketing* 44(3/4): 451-60.

Robinson, Daniel J. 1999. *The Measures of Democracy*. Toronto: University of Toronto Press.

Romanow, R. 2002. *Building on Values: The Future of Healthcare in Canada; Final report of the Royal Commission on the Future of Healthcare*. (Romanow Report.) Ottawa: Public Works and Government Services.

Romanow, Walter I., Michel de Repentigny, Stanley B. Cunningham, Walter C. Soderlund, and Kai Hildebrant, eds. 1999. *Television Advertising in Canadian Elections: The Attack Mode, 1993*. Waterloo, ON: Wilfrid Laurier Press.

Rose, Jonathan. 2000. *Making "Pictures in our Heads": Government Advertising in Canada*. Westport, CT: Praeger.

Rothmayr, Christine, and Sybille Hardmeier. 2002. "Government and Polling: Use and Impact of Polls in the Policy-Making Process in Switzerland." *International Journal of Public Opinion Research* 14(2): 124-40.

Rove, Karl. 2010. *Courage and Consequence*. New York: Simon and Schuster.

Rubin, Ken. 2010. "Access Act Big Loser in Fight over Afghan Documents." *Hill Times*, April 5, 2.

Rubin, Ken, and Kirsten Kozolanka. 2010. "Hide and Seek Ottawa-Style: Managing Access to Information in the Publicity State." Unpublished paper.

Sabato, Larry. 1991. *Feeding Frenzy: How Attack Journalism Has Transformed American Politics*. New York: The Free Press.

Sarantakos, Sotirios. 2005. *Social Research*. Basingstoke, UK: Palgrave Macmillan.

Saskatchewan. 2001. *Caring for Medicare: Sustaining a Quality System*. Commission on Medicare. (Fyke Report.) Regina: Government of Saskatchewan.

Savigny, Heather. 2006. "Political Marketing and the 2005 Election: What's Ideology Got to Do with It?" In *The Marketing of Political Parties*, ed. Darren G. Lilleker, Nigel A. Jackson, and Richard Scullion, 81-97. Manchester: Manchester University Press.

–. 2007. "Focus Groups and Political Marketing: Science and Democracy as Axiomatic?" *British Journal of Politics and International Relations* 9: 122-37.

–. 2008a. *The Problem of Political Marketing*. London: Continuum International.

–. 2008b. "The Construction of the Political Consumer (Or Politics: What Not to Consume)." In *Voters or Consumers: Imagining the Contemporary Electorate*, ed. Darren G. Lilleker and Richard Scullion, 35-50. Newcastle, UK: Cambridge Scholars.

Savigny, Heather, and Mick Temple. 2010. "Political Marketing Models: The Curious Incident of the Dog That Doesn't Bark." *Political Studies* 58(4): 1049-64.

Savoie, Donald J. 1999. *Governing from the Centre: The Concentration of Power in Canadian Politics*. Toronto: University of Toronto Press.

–. 2003. *Breaking the Bargain: Public Servants, Ministers, and Parliament*. Toronto: University of Toronto Press.

–. 2010. *Power: Where Is It?* Montreal and Kingston: McGill-Queen's University Press.

Scammell, Margaret. 1995. *Designer Politics: How Elections Are Won*. New York: St. Martin's.

–. 1999. "Political Marketing: Lessons for Political Science." *Political Studies* 47(4): 718-39.

–. 2008. "Brand Blair: Marketing Politics in the Consumer Age." In *Voters or Consumers: Imagining the Contemporary Electorate*, ed. Darren G. Lilleker and Richard Scullion, 97-113. Newcastle, UK: Cambridge Scholars.

Scarrow, Susan E. 2010. "Political Parties and Party Systems." In *Comparing Democracies 3: Elections and Voting in the 21st Century*, ed. Lawrence LeDuc, Richard G. Niemi, and Pippa Norris, 45-64. Los Angeles: Sage.

Schattschneider, Elmer E. 1960. *The Semi-Sovereign People: A Realist's View of Democracy in America*. New York: Holt, Rinehart and Winston.

Schlozman, Kay Lehman, and John T. Tierney. 1986. *Organized Interests and American Democracy*. New York: Harper and Row.

Schrefler, Lorna. 2010. "The Usage of Scientific Knowledge by Independent Regulatory Agencies." *Governance: An International Journal of Policy, Administration, and Institutions* 23(2): 309-30.

Scott, Andrew M. 1970. *Competition in American Politics: An Economic Model*. New York: Holt, Rinehart and Winston.

Seawright, David. 2005. "On a Low Road: The 2005 Conservative Campaign." *Journal of Marketing Management* 21(9/10): 943-57.

Seidle, F. Leslie, ed. 1991. *Interest Groups and Elections in Canada*. Vol. 2 of the research studies of the Royal Commission on Electoral Reform and Party Financing. Ottawa and Toronto: RCERPF/Dundurn.

Serrat, Olivier. 2010. *Marketing in the Public Sector*. Manila: Asian Development Bank. http://www.adb.org/.

Sherman, Elaine, and Leon Schiffman. 2002. "Trends and Issues in Political Marketing Technologies." *Journal of Political Marketing* 1(1): 231-33.

Siegfried, Andre. 1978. *The Race Question in Canada*. Toronto: Macmillan.

Simpson, Jeffrey. 2001. *The Friendly Dictatorship*. Toronto: McClelland and Stewart.

Slater, Stanley F., and John C. Narver. 1998. "Customer-Led and Market-Oriented: Let's Not Confuse the Two." *Strategic Management Journal* 19: 1001-6.

—. 1999. "Market-Oriented Is More than Being Customer-Led." *Strategic Management Journal* 20: 165-68.

Slocum, Rachel. 2004. "Consumer Citizens and the Cities for Climate Protection Campaign." *Environment and Planning* 36: 763-82.

Small, Tamara A. 2004. "parties@canada: The Internet and the 2004 Cyber-Campaign." In *The Canadian General Election of 2004*, ed. Jon H. Pammett and Christopher Dornan, 203-34. Toronto: Dundurn.

—. 2010. "Still Waiting for an Internet Prime Minister: Online Campaigning by Canadian Political Parties." In *Election*, ed. Heather MacIvor, 173-98. Toronto: Emond Montgomery.

Smith, Denis. 1997. *Rogue Tory.* Toronto: Macfarlane, Walter and Ross.

Smith, Gareth. 2001. "The 2001 General Election: Factors Influencing the Brand Image of Political Parties and Their Leaders." *Journal of Marketing Management* 17(9): 989-1006.

Smith, Gareth, and Alan French. 2009. "The Political Brand: A Consumer Perspective." *Marketing Theory* 9(2): 209-26.

Smith, Jennifer, and Herman Bakvis. 2000. "Changing Dynamics in Election Campaign Finance: Critical Issues in Canada and the United States." *Policy Matters* 1(4): 1-40.

Sniderman, Paul M., H.D. Forbes, and Ian Melzer. 1974. "Party Loyalty and Electoral Volatility: A Study of the Canadian Party System." *Canadian Journal of Political Science* 7(2): 268-88.

Sparrow, Nick, and John Turner. 2001. "The Permanent Campaign." *European Journal of Marketing* 35(9/10): 984-1002.

Stanbury, W.T. 1991. *Money in Politics: Financing Federal Parties and Candidates in Canada.* Vol. 1 of the research studies of the Royal Commission on Electoral Reform and Party Financing. Ottawa and Toronto: RCERPF/Dundurn.

—. 2010. "PM Harper's Playbook for Dealing with Critics." *Hill Times*, April 5, 18.

Stanyer, James. 2007. *Modern Political Communication: Mediated Politics in Uncertain Times.* Cambridge, UK: Polity.

Steeper, Fred. 2008. "The Use of Voter Research in Campaigns." In *The Sage Handbook of Public Opinion Research*, ed. Wolfgang Donsbach and Michael W. Traugott, 594-602. Thousand Oaks, CA: Sage.

Steinberg, Arnold. 1976. *The Political Campaign Handbook.* Lexington, MA: D.C. Heath.

Stevenson, H. Michael. 1987. "Ideology and Unstable Party Identification in Canada: Limited Rationality in a Brokerage Party System." *Canadian Journal of Political Science* 20(4): 813-50.

Strategic Counsel. 2002. *Health Care: Views on Current State and Options for Reform: Highlights from Focus Groups.* Ottawa: Health Canada.

—. 2003a. *Attitudes towards Health Care and Health Care Reform: National Polling Pre-First Ministers' Meeting.* Ottawa: Health Canada.

—. 2003b. *Attitudes towards Health Care and Health Care Reform: National Polling Post-First Ministers' Meeting.* Ottawa: Health Canada.

–. 2004a. *Canadians' View on the First Ministers' Meeting on Health Care*. Ottawa: Health Canada.

–. 2004b. *Attitudes towards Health Care and Health Care Reform: Report on Findings from a Rolling National Poll, Post-First Ministers' Meeting*. Ottawa: Health Canada.

Strömbäck, Jesper. 2007. "Political Marketing and Professionalized Campaigning." *Journal of Political Marketing* 6(2): 49-67.

–. 2010. "A Framework for Comparing Political Market-Orientation." In *Global Political Marketing*, ed. Jennifer Lees-Marshment, Jesper Strömbäck, and Chris Rudd, 16-33. New York: Routledge.

Strömbäck, Jesper, Michael Mitrook, and Spiro Kiousis. 2010. "Bridging Two Schools of Thought: Applications of Public Relations Theory to Political Marketing." *Journal of Political Marketing* 9(1): 73-92.

Stromer-Galley, Jennifer. 2000. "Online Interaction and Why Candidates Avoid It." *Journal of Communication* 50(4): 111-32.

Stromer-Galley, Jennifer, and Andrea B. Baker. 2006. "Joy and Sorrow of Interactivity on the Campaign Trail: Blogs in the Primary Campaign of Howard Dean." In *The Internet Election: Perspectives on the Web in Campaign 2004*, ed. Andrew Paul Williams and John C. Tedesco, 111-31. Lanham, MD: Rowman and Littlefield.

Sweetser, Kaye D., and Ruthann Weaver Lariscy. 2008. "Candidates Make Good Friends: An Analysis of Candidates' Use of Facebook." *International Journal of Strategic Communication* 2(3): 175-98.

Sysomos, Inc. 2009. *Inside Facebook*. http://sysomos.com/.

Taras, David. 1999. *Power and Betrayal in the Canadian Media*. Peterborough, ON: Broadview.

Teinturier, Brice. 2008. "The Presidential Elections in France 2007 – the Role of Opinion Polls." In *Public Opinion Polling in a Globalized World*, ed. Marita Carballo and Ulf Hjelmar, 135-52. London: Springer.

Temple, Mick. 2010. "Political Marketing, Party Behaviour and Political Science." In *Global Political Marketing*, ed. Jennifer Lees-Marshment, Jesper Strömbäck, and Chris Rudd, 263-77. New York: Routledge.

Thurber, James, and Candice Nelson, eds. 2000. *Campaign Warriors: Political Consultants in Elections*. Washington, DC: Brookings Institution Press.

Tiernan, Anne. 2006. "Working with the Stock We Have: The Evolving Role of Queensland's Implementation Unit." *Journal of Comparative Policy Analysis: Research and Practice* 8(4): 371-91.

Tim Hortons. 2006. "Joint Operation: Tim Hortons and Canadian Forces Announce Opening in Afghanistan." Press release, March 8. www.timhortons.com/.

Toronto Star. 2008. "Tim Hortons Fires Single Mom over Free Timbit." TheStar.com, May 8. http://www.thestar.com/.

Truman, David B. 1951. *The Governmental Process: Political Interests and Public Opinion*. New York: Knopf.

Tupper, Allan. 2003. "New Public Management and Canadian Politics." In *Reinventing Canada: Politics of the 21st Century*, ed. Janine Brodie and Linda Trimble, 231-42. Toronto: Prentice Hall.

Turcotte, André. 2005. "Different Strokes: Why Young Canadians Don't Vote." *Electoral Insight*, January: 12-15.

–. 2007. "'What Do You Mean I Cannot Have a Say?' Young Canadians and Their Government." *Canadian Policy Research Networks* 48799: 1-23.

–. 2009. "Polling as Modern Alchemy." In *Elections*, ed. Heather MacIvor, 199-217. Toronto: Emond Montgomery.

Valpy, Michael. 2008. "The Federal Election: Demographics." *Globe and Mail*, September 13, A11.

Verba, Sidney, and Norman Nie. 1972. *Participation in America*. New York: Harper and Row.

Wagenberg, R.H., W.C. Soderlund, W.I. Romanow, and E.D. Brigg. 1988. "Campaigns, Images and the Polls: Mass Media Coverage of the 1984 Canadian Election." *Canadian Journal of Political Science* 21(1): 117-29.

Walsh, Kieron. 1994. "Marketing and Public Sector Management." *European Journal of Marketing* 28(3): 63-71.

Wanna, John. 2006. "From Afterthought to Afterburner: Australia's Cabinet Implementation Unit." *Journal of Comparative Policy Analysis: Research and Practice* 8(4): 347-69.

Ward, Ian. 1999. "The Early Use of Radio for Political Communication in Australia and Canada: John Henry Austral, Mr. Sage and the Man from Mars." *Australian Journal of Politics and History* 45(3): 311-29.

Washbourne, Neil. 2010. *Mediating Politics: Newspapers, Radio, Television and the Internet*. Maidenhead, UK: Open University Press.

Wattenberg, Martin P., and Craig Leonard Brians. 1999. "Negative Campaign Advertising: Demobilizer or Mobilizer?" *American Political Science Review* 93: 891-99.

Watts, Duncan. 2007. *Pressure Groups*. Edinburgh: Edinburgh University Press.

Wells, Paul. 2006. *Right Side Up: The Fall of Paul Martin and the Rise of Stephen Harper's New Conservatism*. Toronto: McClelland and Stewart.

Wheeler, Michael. 1976. *Lies, Damn Lies and Statistics*. New York: Dell.

Whitaker, Reg. 2001. "Virtual Political Parties and the Decline of Democracy." *Policy Options*, June: 16-22.

–. 2008. "Politics versus Administration: Politicians and Bureaucrats." In *Canadian Politics in the 21st Century*, ed. Michael Whittington and Glen Williams, 54-77. Toronto: Thomson Nelson.

White, Jon, and Leslie de Chernatony. 2002. "New Labour: A Study of the Creation, Development and Demise of a Political Brand." *Journal of Political Marketing* 1(2/3): 45-52.

White, Theodore H. 1961. *The Making of the President, 1960*. New York: Atheneum.

Whitehorn, Alan. 1994. "The NDP's Quest for Survival." In *The Canadian General Election of 1993*, ed. Alan Frizzell, Jon H. Pammett, and Anthony Westell, 43-58. Ottawa: Carleton University Press.

–. 2006. "The NDP and the Enigma of Strategic Voting." In *The Canadian Federal Election of 2006*, ed. Jon H. Pammett and Christopher Dornan, 93-121. Toronto: Dundurn.

Whittington, Les. 2010. "Jim Flaherty Blasted for $3,100 Flight." *Toronto Star*, March 9. http://www.thestar.com/.

Williams, Christine B., Andrew Aylesworth, and Kenneth J. Chapman. 2002. "The 2000 E-Campaign for U.S. Senate." *Journal of Political Marketing* 1(4): 39-63.

Wlezien, Christopher, and Stuart Soroka. 2007. "The Relationship between Public Opinion and Policy." In *Oxford Handbook of Political Behavior*, ed. Russell Dalton and Hans-Deiter Klingemann, 801-17. New York: Oxford University Press.

Wood, Laura, Ryan Snelgrove, and Karen Danylchuk. 2010. "Segmenting Volunteer Fundraisers at a Charity Sport Event." *Journal of Nonprofit and Public Sector Marketing* 22(1): 38-54.

Woolstencroft, Peter. 1994. "Doing Politics Differently: The Conservative Party and the Campaign of 1993." In *The Canadian General Election of 1993*, ed. Alan Frizzell, Jon H. Pammett, and Anthony Westell, 9-26. Ottawa: Carleton University Press.

Wring, Dominic. 1997. "Reconciling Marketing with Political Science: Theories of Political Marketing." *Journal of Marketing Management* 13(7): 651-63.

–. 2002. "Conceptualising Political Marketing: A Framework for Election-Campaign Analysis." In *The Idea of Political Marketing*, ed. Nicholas J. O'Shaughnessy and Stephan C. Henneberg, 171-85. Hampshire, UK: Palgrave Macmillan.

–. 2006. "Focus Group Follies? Qualitative Research and Labour Party Strategy." *Journal of Political Marketing* 5(4): 71-97.

Young, Lisa, and William Cross. 2002a. "Incentives to Membership in Canadian Political Parties." *Political Research Quarterly* 55: 547-69.

–. 2002b. "The Rise of Plebiscitary Democracy in Canadian Political Parties." *Party Politics* 8: 673-99.

Young, Lisa, and Joanna Everitt. 2004. *Advocacy Groups*. Vancouver: UBC Press.

Young, Lisa, Anthony Sayers, and Harold Jansen. 2007. "Altering the Political Landscape: State Funding and Party Finance." In *Canadian Parties in Transition*, 3rd ed., ed. Alain-G. Gagnon and A. Brian Tanguay, 335-54. Peterborough, ON: Broadview.

Zinc Research. 2009. *Almost 80% of Canadians Use Social Networking Sites*. News release, October 2, p. 1. Calgary. http://zincresearch.files.wordpress.com/.

Contributors

Lisa Birch (Université Laval) has published articles about evaluation and the use of survey and focus group research in health policy. Her research interests include the utilization of public opinion, evaluation and scientific research, political and social marketing, the role of epistemic communities in policy, and comparative public policy.

Patricia Cormack (St. Francis Xavier University) has published on Tim Hortons and nationalism in *Cultural Sociology* and co-authored research about the CBC and popular nationalism in *Topia*. Her interests include Canadian nation building, nationalism, and commercial culture.

Yannick Dufresne (University of Toronto) has diverse interests that include electoral behaviour in Canada and market research methodologies, which he has drawn upon as associate director of analytics for Vote Compass. His research has focused on the relationship between the stability of voting patterns and floating voters.

Anna Esselment (University of Waterloo) has published about parties, elections, and partisanship in the *Canadian Journal of Political Science* and *Canadian Public Administration*. Her research interests include political parties, campaigns and elections, Canadian institutions, and the role of partisanship in intergovernmental relations in Canada.

Émilie Foster (Université Laval) has presented papers about the use of political marketing by interest groups at academic conferences such as the Atlantic Provinces Political Science Association and Canadian Political Science Association. Her research interests include political communication by pressure groups and the impact of political marketing practices on democratic disaffection.

Thierry Giasson (Université Laval) has published about televised political debates in the *Canadian Journal of Political Science*, political journalism in the *Canadian Journal of Communication*, and politicians' image management in *Questions de communication*. His research interests include new forms of online political communication, biopolitics, Quebec politics, and democratic malaise in Canada.

Elisabeth Gidengil (McGill University) is director of the Centre for the Study of Democratic Citizenship. Her research focuses on voting behaviour and public opinion. She was a member of the Canadian Election Study team from 1992 to 2008 and was principal investigator for the 2008 study.

Royce Koop (Simon Fraser University) is the author of *Grassroots Liberals: Organizing for Local and National Politics in Canada* (UBC Press) as well as articles in *Canadian Journal of Political Science*, *Representation*, and the *Journal of Elections, Public Opinion, & Parties*. His research focuses on political parties, federalism, and Canadian politics.

Kirsten Kozolanka (Carleton University) is the author of *The Power of Persuasion: The Politics of the New Right in Ontario* (Black Rose, 2007) and the co-editor of *Alternative Media in Canada* (UBC Press), and has published in the *Canadian Journal of Communication*, *Studies in Political Economy*, and *How Ottawa Spends, 2009-2010*. Previously, she has worked in political offices and in government communication.

Jennifer Lees-Marshment (Auckland University) is a leading comparative researcher in political marketing. Her books include *Political Marketing: Principles and Applications* (Routledge), *Global Political Marketing* (Routledge), and *The Political Marketing Game* (Palgrave Macmillan). Her research interests include political marketing, consultation, leadership, and deliberative democracy.

Patrick Lemieux is a practitioner of communications and public relations. He has worked for many interest groups and research organizations, notably the Quebec Employers Council and the Institute for Research on Public Policy. His research interests include political marketing by non-party political organizations, especially for fundraising, growing their membership, and government relations.

Alex Marland (Memorial University) has published work on political marketing, election campaigning, political talk radio, and nationalism. His research interests include political communication, electioneering, and democracy in Canada.

Tamara A. Small (University of Guelph) has published work on online election campaigning in *Party Politics* and in the *Canadian Journal of Political Science* and about Internet regulation in *Election Law Journal*. Her research interests include digital politics in Canada, political communications, and party politics.

André Turcotte (Carleton University) has written extensively on voting behaviour in Canada and public opinion polling. He specializes in the design of social inquiry and the study of image, politics, and persuasion. He has also provided strategic public opinion advice to several politicians and major corporations.

Index

1993 federal election: efficacy gap and, 232-33; electoral system significance in, 61; electoral volatility and, 41, 44-45; influence on future politics, 14, 242; negative advertising and, 11; Reform Party and, 72, 80

2000 federal election, 82, 86, 236, 243

2004 federal election: Conservative Party strategy and, 83, 86-87; electoral volatility and, 43, 54; hypersegmentation in, 86; relationship marketing, 202

2006 federal election: Conservative Party and, 130; the evolution of campaigns and, 61; results of, 125

2008 federal election: efficacy gap and, 233, 237; electoral volatility and, 44-45; negative advertising in, 133; party platforms in, 132; relationship marketing during, 204-5; turnout during, 237

2011 federal election: Conservative Party and results of, 136; electoral volatility and, 45; micro-targeting in, 101; regionalized voting in, 45

Access to Information Act, 30, 111, 113

accountability: attack ads and, 12; centralization of communications and, 109; as a Conservative party policy, 66, 110-11, 115-17, 126(f), 127, 132; ethics and, 116; Federal Accountability Act and, 110, 119, 127, 132, 135; health care and, 146; importance of, 25; political marketing and, 139, 211-12; public opinion research and, 30, 154

advertising. See political advertising

Americanization, 36, 247, 249

attack ad, 11-12, 67, 255

Blair, Tony, 7, 28, 87, 91, 121, 123, 136, 243, 249

Bloc Québécois: attack ads and, 100; Canadians' knowledge of, 42(f); election platform of, 67; the Elections Act and, 32-33, 68; market intelligence, 63; niche marketing, xi, 16, 27(t), 61, 245; regional advertising and, 68; relationship marketing, 198(t), 200(t), 203(t), 204

branding: characteristics of, 209-10, 212; concerns about, 120, 211-12; democratic implications of, 220, 250; differences with the USA in, 101; media effects on, 188; as a part of political marketing, 9(f); the public sphere and, 213-14, 220-21, 246; rebranding and efficacy, 235-36; rebranding of right wing, 73, 75n3;

theory as strategy, 10; Tim Hortons and, 213-14, 219-21, 246; value of for political parties, 211, 213

Brodie, Ian, 83-84, 86, 88, 90, 93(t), 94, 100-1

brokerage politics, 24-25, 80, 101; political marketing and, xii, 11, 13-15

Bush, George W., 87, 236

business: direct marketing and, 69; as a framework to study political parties, 26; marketing research and, 178, 224, 243; party financing and, 33-34, 130; political marketing and, 4, 8, 160-64, 246; political parties and, 71, 73; political strategy and, 26; practices used in politics, xi, 8, 15, 176; public policy and, 156; regulations of, 29; relationship marketing and, 202; social groups and, 167-69; Tim Hortons as a, 215

Campbell, Kim, 62(t), 64

Canada: electoral rules of, 29, 30-33, 68, 130; electoral system effectiveness, 48, 49(t), 50(t), 51(t); electoral system and turnout, 48; significance of single-member plurality (SMP) system in, 61. See also electoral system; rules

Canada Elections Act: election expenses and, 31; regional advertising and, 68

Canadian Alliance Party: market intelligence, 82-83, 86-87; market positioning of, 27(t); rebranding of, 15, 75n3, 212, 236, 243; segment marketing, 84

Canadian Election Study (CES), 40, 41(f), 42(f), 43(f), 232

Chrétien, Jean: 11, 67-68, 72-73

citizen efficacy, 234(t)

class: branding and, 209, 214; decline of class cleavage, 52, 56n5; self image and, 95-96; strategy for marketing to, 66, 70, 249; vote choice and, 23, 46, 53

cleavages: decline of, 23, 35(t), 52; effects on strategy, 23, 54; elections and, 39; political marketing and, 22; segmentation and, 242; strength of regional, 241

Clement, Tony, 128

Clinton, Bill, 28, 64, 69-70, 87, 91, 134, 249

Communication Canada, 109-10, 119

Conservative Party of Canada (CPC): branding, 212, 214, 216, 220-21; brokerage politics and, 13; Canadians' knowledge of, 42(f), 43(f); centralized control of, 70, 107; constituent information management system (CIMS), 69; creation of Federal Accountability Act, 127, 132; democracy and, 243-49, 253; efficacy and, 227-29, 231-32, 234-36; election platform of, 123, 126-29, 133, 135, 137-38; electoral rules and, 32-34; electoral volatility and, 44, 56n3; Internet marketing, 12, 73, 198, 200, 203-5; market communications and, 107, 109-12, 114-20; market intelligence, 76, 79-80, 83-89, 91, 93, 95, 100-1; market positioning of, xi, xii, 27(t), 28; as a market-oriented party (MOP), 127-29, 131-38; media management, 70, 111; micro-targeting, 26, 66, 243; negative advertising, 11, 12, 73; policy development of, 66; political journalism and, 187; political marketing techniques, 15-16, 20; public opinion research and, 134, 152;

regionalized voting and, 45; relationship marketing, 198, 200, 203-5; religious voting and, 47; segmentation, 26, 72, 85-87, 243-44; targeting, 18, 20, 23, 26
constituent information management system (CIMS), 26, 32, 69, 72
content analysis, 143, 180, 181(t), 182
Coulter, Ann, 170n1

Day, Stockwell, 82, 212
Delacourt, Susan, 4, 11
democracy. See political marketing, democratic implications
democratic malaise, 175-76; political marketing and, 19, 182, 253-54
Democratic Party (USA), xii, 28, 91, 249
Dion, Stephane, 11, 28, 73, 133
direct marketing, 69, 79, 81-82, 86-87
Donolo, Peter, 45
Duceppe, Gilles, 62(t), 63, 73, 204
Duffy, John, 93(t), 94, 96-97
Durdin, Martha, 93(t)

e-marketing. See Internet marketing; relationship marketing
Earnscliffe Research and Communications, 144, 146
Economic Action Plan 2008, 107, 116-17, 119, 122, 253
Ekos Research Associates, 144-45
election: 1993 federal election, 14, 39, 46, 59, 61, 62(t), 63, 68, 72, 79-80, 232, 242; 1997 federal election, 82; 2000 federal election, 82, 86; 2004 federal election, 83, 86, 202, 243; 2006 federal election, 59, 61, 62(t), 63, 67, 130; 2008 federal election, 45, 97, 204-5; 2011 federal election, xi-xii, 4, 45, 101; efficacy gap in federal elections, 232-33, 234(t);

Election Expenses Act, 31; electoral volatility in, 44, 45(t), 51; expenses of, 88; increasing competitiveness of, 40; inter-election period, 29; issue importance in, 25, 47; media coverage of federal election campaigns, 180, 181(t), 183-84, 185(f), 188, 190(f); negative advertising and turnout, 12; permanent campaign and proximity of, 73; political advertising and strategy, 11; provincial election spending regulations, 37n6; regulations of election campaigns, 29-34; strategies for electioneering, 9; turnout in federal elections, 19, 40-44, 48, 89, 238, 254
election platform, 65, 110, 115, 136
electoral system: democratic malaise and, 55; effectiveness of, 48, 49(t), 50(t), 51(t), 231; significance of, 61; single-member plurality (SMP) and regionalism, 13; tactical implications of, 30-31, 71; turnout and, 48
electoral volatility, 22, 24, 39, 45, 51, 241. See also turnout
engagement: citizen efficacy and, 75; democratic malaise, 19; interest groups and, 157; Internet marketing and, xii, 206-8, 246; measurement of, 50(t); the media and, 189; political strategy and, 37; technology and, 74; United States and, 94; voting and, 120
Environics Research Group, 81, 145, 148
Evershed, Alexandra, 93(t), 96, 102

Facebook: democratic implications of, 208; political advertising on, 12; political parties, 193, 195-206, 208; relationship marketing and, 193,

197-201; as a source of market intelligence, 77; status of, 196. *See also* relationship marketing

Flaherty, Jim, 115, 126, 129, 216

Flanagan, Tom: campaign strategy of, 118, 196, 214, 220, 231; market intelligence, 81, 83-86, 90

franchising, 13, 212. *See also* branding

fundraising: constituent information management system (CIMS) for, 69; direct voter contact program (DVC) for, 86; electoral rules effects on, 29, 33, 36, 248; institutional regulations on, 33, 36; permanent campaign and, 73; targeting tactics used for, 15

Gallup, 83

Get out the vote (GOTV): xii, 8, market intelligence and, 83, 86-87, 242

Green Party of Canada (GPC), 208n3; Canadians' knowledge of, 42(f); market positioning and, 27(t); relationship marketing, 198, 200-2, 203(t), 204(t); the single-member plurality system (SMP) and, 72

Gregg, Allan, 84, 94

Hamm, John, 93t, 98

Harper, Stephen: Conservative Party platforms and, 81, 128, 130, 136; difficulties in policy development, 97-100; and efficacy, 231-32; Facebook, 200, 203-5; image of, 11; media management, 70; party discipline, 83; proroguing of parliament, 73; Tim Hortons and, 214, 216, 220

Harris-Decima, 221

Health Canada: branding and, 147; the federal government and, 154-55; political marketing and, 151; public opinion research, 109, 140, 143,

145-55, 244; reform and, 145; tobacco control and, 149. *See also* health care system

health care system: deterioration of, 144; Health Canada and, 143; national identity and, 145; public opinion research and, 143-47, 153; reforms to, 143-44

horserace journalism, 179, 182

householder, 109, 222

Howard, John, 66, 86, 105

Hyder, Goldy, 93(t), 105

hypersegmentation, 85-87, 89. *See also* micro-targeting

ideology: branding and, 212; citizen efficacy and, 225, 227-28; marketing as an end to, 225, 227-28; the New Right, 107, 122n1; political marketing and, 8, 25, 35(t); as a political product, 28; types of campaigns and, 60, 62

Ignatieff, Michael, 11, 12, 45, 64, 73, Facebook, 199, 203; and Tim Hortons, 221

inter-election period, 29, 196, 205

interest groups: branding and, 246; classification of, 160-61, 164; democracy and, 156, 169, 170, 251; electoral participation of, 157; party financing and, 34, 36(t); the party system and, 14; political marketing and, xi, 4, 8, 15-16, 20, 156-57, 158(t), 160-61, 165, 170; the proliferation of, 156; public opinion research and, 140; regulations to, 29, 33; social groups as, 166; as sales oriented groups, 169; war rooms, 157

Internet: campaigns and, 116; as an information source, 42, 180; political parties and, 193-201, 205; relationship marketing and, 194-201, 205-8; for surveys, 78

Internet marketing, 193, 208n1

Kinsella, Warren, 156

Lavigne, Brad, 93(t)

Layton, Jack, 62(t), 66-67, 73; relationship marketing, 200-1, 205

leadership: the Federal Accountability Act and, 119; leadership goals and public opinion, 105; market analysis, 17, 37, 76, 91, 97, 99, 104, 106, 241, 249; political marketing and, 4; public opinion research and, 139-40, 144, 146-47, 152-55; strategies based on, 24

legitimacy: the Conservative Party and, 212; Health Canada and, 154-55; marketing techniques and, 231; policy orientation and, 153; public opinion research and, 147, 152-53, 155; Tim Hortons and, 216

Leslie, Noble, 93(t), 97

Levant, Ezra, 170n1

Levin, Ben, 93(t)

Liberal Party of Canada: branding and, 130-33, 136, 143; Canadian's knowledge of, 42(f), 43(f); centralized communication and, 107-8; election platform of, 13, 66, 72, 123, 125, 133, 229, 234, 236; electoral rules and, 32-33; electoral volatility and, 39; involvement with sponsorship scandal, 110, 117, 127; loss of party identifiers, 54; market positioning of, xi, 27(t), 62, 84; micro-targeting, 28; negative advertising and, 11, 29, 67, 68; political marketing, 15, 64, 69-70, 241-42, 248;

regionalized support of, 44-45 ,47; relationship marketing, 198(t), 199, 200, 202-5

lobbying: business groups and, 161, 169; democratic implications of, 251; interest groups and, 157-58, 161; political marketing and, 156; recruitment and, 170; regulations to, 29, 30, 127; sales-oriented groups and, 157-60; social organizations and, 167; Tim Hortons and, 217; trade unions and, 164, 169

Lynch, Kevin, 133

MacKay, Peter, 216

Manning, Preston, 62(t), 73, 75n3, 81-82, 228

market challenger, xii, 62, 67

market driven, 7-8, 56, 120, 249

market follower, xi, 13, 61-62

market intelligence: Canadian Alliance Party, 82; citizen efficacy and, 253; Conservative Party, 80, 83-89, 134, 243; democracy and, 56, 89-90, 251-53; evolution of, 249; global, 249; government, 94, 134, 142, 145, 155; Health Canada, 155; influence on political decisions, 94; Liberal Party, 62, 243; market-orientation and, 6-7; media coverage of, 186; NDP, 243; policy and, 65; political marketing and, 10, 22; political parties, 63, 80, 242-43; political strategy and, 59, 62-63, 76-77, 80, 83; purpose of, xiii, 3; Reform Party, 81-82; techniques used for, 76-78; and segmentation, 23, 87-90, 179, 247, 249

market leader, xi, 13, 248, 250; political strategy of, 27(t), 35(t), 62

market nicher, 26, 27(t), 35(t), 62. *See also* niche marketing market orientation: American parties and, 236; business groups and, 168, 246; Canada's use comparatively, 249; challenges for parties using, 52, 122-24; characteristics of, 7; the Conservative Party and, 136-38; democracy and, 56, 170, 250-51, 253; effects of government on, 131-32; effects on turnout, 55; and efficacy, 229-30; the electoral system and, 135; importance of maintaining, 124; incentives to adopt a, 52-53, 54(f); permanent campaign and, 75

market positioning, xi, 9-10; types of, 27(t)

market research. See market intelligence

market segmentation. See segmentation

market-oriented party (MOP), characteristics of, 7; the Conservative Party as, 85, 123, 157; ideology of, 28; strategy of, 67

Martin, Paul, 62(t), 66, 68, 97, 133

May, Elizabeth, 201, 204

McGuinty, Dalton, 97

McLaughlin, Audrey, 62(t)

media: accountability and, 130; concerns about, 74; Conservative Party management of, 70, 111-12, 117-19, 121, 245; coverage of election campaigns, 186-87; coverage of political marketing, 176-80, 181(t), 182-90, 242; coverage of Tim Hortons, 215-16; earned and paid campaign, xii; effects on branding, 188, 221; Elections Act and, 32-33; influence of, 52-53; polls in, 76, 87-88; relationship between political marketing and, 177, 188-89, 246; role of in politics, 175-77, 254

media coverage: attack ads and, 12; the importance of, 111; influence of,

52-53; of political marketing, 4, 175, 254; the Reform Party and, 70. See also media

media management: Conservative Party, 70, 111-12, 117-19, 121, 245

median voter, 65, 84, 95, 105, 243

micro-targeting: as alternative to brokerage politics, 101; concerns about, 251; Conservative Party, 26, 66, 243; constituent information management system (CIMS) for, 26; See also narrowcasting; niche marketing; segmentation

minority government: challenges for, 124; the Conservative Party as, 119, 125, 127, 130-33, 136-38; the legislative process and, 131; permanent campaigning and, 34, 73, 118, 137, 196; product delivery and, 130-32, 135-36, 247

Mulroney, Brian, 61, 65

Muttart, Patrick: campaign strategy of, 64, 66, 84, 86, 94-95, 249; market intelligence, 99-102, 104, 134, 243; political marketing and, xii-xiii

Nanos, 93(t)

Nanos, Nik, 93(t), 96, 98-99, 103-4

narrowcasting, 67, 70, 221

national unity: and brokerage politics, 13; the Liberal Party red book and, 65; media content and, 181(t), 182; as a product, 91

negative advertising: association with political marketing, 28; Conservative Party, 11, 133; election turnout and, 12, 237; Internet for, 11; Liberal Party, 68

New Democratic Party of Canada (NDP): Canadians' knowledge of, 42(f), 43(f); democracy and, 245, 248; election platform of, 67; electoral rules and, 33; market intelligence, 63, 69; market orientation of, 132, 137; market positioning of, xi, xii, 27(t); member efficacy of, 229; political advertising, 68; pollsters, 63; relationship marketing, 198, 200, 203-5; results of in federal elections, 45, 61, 62(t), 72; targeting, 66, 68

New Labour Party (UK): branding and, 211; democracy and, 249; efficacy and, 237; market intelligence and, 89, 91-92; market orientation and, 123, 136; and market positioning, 7, 28

new public management (NPM), 108, 117

new right: definition of, 122n1; the economy and, 115; efficacy and, 235; ideological influence of, 107-8; new public management (NPM) and, 108; the public service and, 117; state minimization and, 107, 109; stress on accountability, 109

niche marketing, xi, 16, 72

Obama, Barack, 26, 94, 197, 216, 250

Paille Report, 110. See public opinion research (POR)

parliament: accountability and, 127; branding and, 213; citizen efficacy and, 234; committees of, 112-13, 164; criminal justice reforms and, 128; democratic malaise and, 41, 206; Elections Act and, 32-33; in a minority government, 124-26, 131, 133-36; political marketing and, 15; prorogation of, 73; public service independence and, 108; and state minimization, 108

parliamentary press gallery, 111, 112, 136

participation: citizen efficacy and, 237; democracy and, 19, 120, 250, 254; Internet marketing and, 195, 206-7; of interest groups, 157, 166; of party members, 13-14; political marketing and, 17; public attitude towards, 181(t)

partisanship, 44, 53, 236, 253

party activists, 229, 236

party members: branding and, 212; brokerage politics and, 15; Canada Elections Act and, 32; citizen efficacy and, 19; election platforms and, 65; influence of, 212, 218, 230, 236; political marketing and, 8, 17

permanent campaign: Canadian politics and, 196; causes of a, 34; as a concern of political marketing, 17; democratic implications of, 70, 120, 137; effects of, 34, 120; hypercentralization and, 119; minority government and, 32, 118-19; relationship marketing and, 196, 245; strategic and tactical marketing during, 35(t), 36(t); as a type of political campaign, 60(t)

permanent campaigning. See permanent campaign

policy: influence of business on, 156, 161, 164, 166; influence of interest groups on, 170, 251; influence of party members on, 230; market intelligence and design of, xiii, 8, 23, 34, 84, 96-97, 103-4, 107, 229, 233, 235, 241, 244-45, 248-49; media and the policy process, 175, 182, 189; policy as a product, 5, 15, 23, 65-66, 123-24, 126-27; 130, 133-35, 139, 253; and political advertising, 12; political strategy and, 35; pollster impact on, 17; media management and, 70, 72; public opinion research impact on, 20, 30, 37, 63, 104, 139-40, 142-43, 146-48, 151-55, 233; segmentation and, 85

policy marketing, 139, 147, 150-51, 154

political advertising: characteristics of, 11; Chrétien face ads, 67; criticism of, 12, 67; differences between political marketing and, 11-12; the Elections Act and, 32; market intelligence and, 77; as a part of political marketing, 9-10; targeting and, 68

political advisers, 20, 119

political awareness, 42-43, 53-54, 241

political consultants, 3, 16, 59, 68, 75, 249

political disaffection, 40, 50. *See also* democratic malaise; turnout

political marketing: citizen efficacy and, 224-28, 231-38, 254; democratic implications, xii, 16-19, 29, 36, 54-56, 89, 102, 104, 106-7, 170, 189, 206-8, 211, 219, 237, 241-43, 245, 250-55; electoral rules and, 29, 32, 36; electoral system, 71; evolution of in Canada, 4, 10-11, 20, 72, 83, 121, 134, 242, 247-49; federal government, 110-11, 114-15, 118, 122, 127, 139-40, 142-43, 151; interest groups, 156-57, 158(t), 160-61, 165, 170, 246; Internet, 201, 206-8; news media coverage of, 176-78, 182, 183(t), 184, 187-90

political product: advertising and, 13; brokerage politics and, 25; contents of, 8; delivery of, 241; democracy and, 250; ideology and, 28; information technology and, 74; market research and, 91; the media and, 177, 188; political marketing and, 5, 8, 13; public opinion research and,

137, 150, 247; strategic marketing and, 22, 25, 190, 242

Pollara, 144

polling: Conservative Party, 84-86, 88, 89, 134; different types of, 79(f); government, 17; hypersegmentation and, 84-86; as an indicator of market demand, 7, 55; Labour Party (UK), 7; as market intelligence, 64, 74, 84; in policy development, 63, 74; political party, 14, 111; question wording and, 96; role in election campaigns, 78; value of, 94, 104-5; voter tracking programs and, 79(f)

pollster: Conservative Party, 83-84; importance of to political parties, 228; Reform Party, 81; role in campaign strategy, 63-64, 78; role in informing political decisions, 17, 63-64; role in policy development, 17. *See also* polling

Praxicus Public Strategies, 83

press gallery. *See* parliamentary press gallery

Prime Minister's Office (PMO): blurring between Privy Council Office (PCO) and, 117, 119, 133; market intelligence gathering, 134; message event proposals (MEPs) and, 111; restriction of media access to, 112; size of, 109, 112, 114-15, 117; and the sponsorship scandal, 110; staff of, 110, 114, 133-34

Privy Council Office (PCO): access to public information and, 113; blurring between Prime Minister's Office (PMO) and, 117, 119; central control of, 113-15, 117, 119; message event proposals (MEPs) and, 111; size of, 108-9; staff of, 133

product delivery: 124, 135, 137, 251. *See also* political product
product-oriented party (POP), 7-8, 80-81, 83
professionalism, xiii, 62, 243
public opinion research (POR): centralized control of, 113-15; and citizen efficacy, 233; Conservative Party, 134, 152; democratic implications of, 76, 155, 252; federal government, 20, 30, 103, 109, 139-40, 141(f), 142-47, 151-54; impact of on politics, 77; NDP, 243; policy development and, 65, 103; in political decisions, 98, 244; unions, 165
public relations: political advertising and, 177, 185-86, 188, 242; political marketing and, 4, 8, 9(f), 10; political parties and, 188, 242; public opinion research and, 150; strategic marketing and, 185-86, 242
public sphere: branding and, 213-23; definition of, 213; political advisers and, 133; Tim Hortons and, 215-23

Rae, Bob, 97
Reagan, Ronald, 105, 122n1
recruitment: business groups and, 161; Facebook for, 199(t), 201-6; interest groups and, 157-59, 161-66, 170; the Internet for, 166; labour groups and, 164, 166; market intelligence for, 23; relationship marketing for, 194, 199(t), 201-6
Reform Party of Canada: development of policy, 65; earned media coverage and, 70; Elections Act and, 68; evolution of, 15, 75n3, 212, 243; market intelligence, 63, 80-82, 84, 87; market positioning, 27(t); and member efficacy, 228, 236; negative

advertising, 11; regional advertising, 68
regionalism, 13, 46, 68, 72-73, 221
register of electors, 32
Reid, Scott, 93(t), 97
relationship marketing: benefits of using, 194, 197; business groups, 163; characteristics of, 193; democracy and, 207-8, 245; democratic malaise and, 176; Facebook for, 199-202, 204(t), 205-8; importance of technology in, 194; permanent campaign and, 73, 196; political parties, 193-202, 204(t), 205-8; problems with the development of, 205; web 2.0 and, 195
Republican Party (USA), 72, 81, 87, 123; Canadians' knowledge of, 42(f); techniques used by, 66, 69, 236
Responsive Marketing Group, 83
responsiveness: as external efficacy, 232-33, 254; market orientation and, 6, 55, 89, 135, 137, 226; marketing research and, 243; public opinion research and, 37, 146-47, 153-55
Rogers, Chad, 93(t), 95-96, 98, 104
rules: effects on political marketing tactics, 29, 34, 35(t), 36, 248; the Elections Act and, 31-33, 68; the Federal Accountability Act and, 127; finance rules, 130; history of institutional rules in Canada, 31; inter-election period regulations, 29; public opinion research regulations, 140-42, 150-52

sales-oriented party (SOP): Conservative Party transition from, 83, 243; characteristics of, 7-8, 82, 159; in contrast with other parties, 7, 157, 158(t); interest groups as, 169, 246;

Liberal party as, 137; Reform Party as, 82

satisfaction with democracy, 49. *See also* democratic malaise

segmentation: as an alternative to brokerage politics, 16; in Canadian politics, 13-14; citizen efficacy and, 232-33, 236; concerns about, 17-18, 55, 91; Conservative Party, 85-87, 214, 221, 243-44; democracy and, 226, 250-51, 253, 255; efficiency of, 10, 26, 89; employers organizations and, 162, 165; further potential of, 101; media coverage of, 181(t), 186; in other countries, 87, 249; public opinion research and, 147; regionalization and, 231; the single-member plurality (SMP) system and, 72; as a tool of political marketing, 8-9, 241-42

single member plurality (SMP), 13, 30, 48, 61, 231. *See also* electoral system

sponsorship program, 109, 114

Strategic Counsel, 45, 145-46

strategy: branding strategy, 212-13; brokerage politics as, 24-25; campaigns and, 60(t); Canadian politics and, 26; Conservative Party media strategy, 118; consumers and, 170, 178; development of Conservative Party strategy, 130-31; leader decisions and, 105; market intelligence and, 59, 63, 74, 77-78, 82-83, 224, 242-43; of market-oriented parties, 53, 65, 67, 71, 127; party attachments and, 53; political marketing and, 9(f); polling and, 84-85; of product-oriented parties, 7; public opinion research and, 150, 157; recruitment strategies, 162-64; regional differences and, 101-2;

relationship marketing strategy, 193-95, 197, 201, 204-5, 207-8; segmentation strategy, 226, 231; strategic marketing, 179, 184; strategies for product development, 135-36

Thatcher, Margaret, 66, 122n1, 228, 249

Tim Hortons: branding and, 20, 213-23; democracy and, 246; market intelligence and, 242; market positioning and, xi; political marketing and, 162; as a political model, 95-96; the public sphere and, 213-23

tobacco control: as counter-marketing, 147; government and, 152; Health Canada and, 143; public opinion research and, 143, 146-54; social marketing and, 150-51

trade unions, 160-61, 164-65, 168-69, 171n3, 246

transparency, 70, 112, 115, 170, 251. *See also* accountability

Trudeau, Pierre, 93

turnout: Canada and low turnout, 48; democratic malaise and, 19; direct marketing and, 86; explanation of low turnout, 40-41, 44, 89; generational displacement and, 40; market orientation and, 55-56; mention in the news media, 181(t), 189; negative advertising and, 12; relationship between marketing and, 237-38, 254

voter ID, xii, 68-69

voting: class and vote choice, 23, 46, 53, 56n5; decline of, 19, 50, 55, 237-38; democratic malaise and, 19, 50, 55; economic-based, 52; external efficacy and, 237; gender based, 47;

generational replacement and, 40; old-age groups and, 40; party identification and vote choice, 53; region and vote choice, 45-46; turnout in Canada, 48; unique behavior of, 120; voting intentions and media coverage, 183-84. *See also* turnout

voting behaviour, 60(t). *See also* voting

war room: Conservative Party, 71, 86, 88, 136; direct voter contact program (DVC) and, 86; general, 59; interest groups, 157; Liberal Party, 64, 69, 242

web 2.0: implications for democracy, 207-8; political parties, 204; relationship marketing and, 195; Tim Hortons and, 219; United States and, 94

Wright, John, 93(t)

Printed and bound in Canada by Friesens
Set in Scala and Giovanni by Artegraphica Design Co. Ltd.
Copy editor: Judy Phillips
Proofreader: Lana Okerlund